MW01702864

SMITH'S SEWING SINGLE SHEETS

Keith A. Smith

First Edition May 2001

Published and distributed by keith smith *BOOKS*
1115 East Main Street
Suite 219, Box 8
Rochester, New York 14609–6152 USA
Telephone or Fax: 585 482 2496
Email information and book orders:
keith@keithsmithbooks.com
Website:
http://www.keithsmithbooks.com
Library of Congress Control Number: 2001 126033
ISBN: 0–9637682–8–X

SMITH'S SEWING SINGLE SHEETS

NON–ADHESIVE BINDING VOLUME IV

BOOK NUMBER 202

Keith A. Smith

KEITH

For Adéle

TABLE *of* CONTENTS

TABLE OF CONTENTS

PROLOGUE

At any one time I have a dozen books in some state of progress — that's just the way I work. Three or four books will have chapters written in my computer, waiting for my return. The starts of other books exist as sewn prototypes, or maybe even a single section (or sheet) sewn, the needle still dangling on the thread just as my notes are scribbled on the sheets to remind me of how this one was sewn. The remaining books in progress are sown only in my mind. Finishing a book brings some sense of order to the on–going clutter.

Grade school teachers would chide, "Do one thing at at time, Keith, and do it well." Although I would try, I could not comply. An imaginative mind is a blessing and a curse — all these books swirling in my head.

Last October I started writing Volume IV, *Non–Adhesive Binding.* The summer before I had experienced surgery for the first time and mortality was in my thinking. Instead of eventually writing the next three books, I would present them as three parts of a single book, perhaps a hundred pages each. I would not be able to elaborate any of the approaches, but I would be ahead of the game.

The first part would be single sheet sewings. The second would be — no. I won't tell you what the other two ideas are until I present them as finished books. I have learned never tell anyone what you are going *to do,* just *do it.* If I would say I am going to write a book on this or that, I would start getting emails and phone calls wanting to know when that book will be ready.

Anyhow, my plan of writing this book on non–adhesive binding as three books in one was doomed. I never got beyond single sheet sewings. Actually, I probably only have begun to write on the subject. In 1996 I sewed a few sheets taking notes on it as how to sew sheets of unfolded paper which would open and lie flat. I made six such sketches. When I got around to writing this book in October 2000, I looked at the first sketch. I started writing and sewing what I thought those notes had told me. This led to other single sheet Coptic sewings which I made, wrote up and diagrammed. It started to snowball.

I am nearly finished with the layout, if not the writing of this book and never did look at the other five sketches from 1996. Maybe some were better. I know at least a couple were not Coptic sewings, but other unsupported sewings I had devised for single sheets. I dare not look at them. I want to write about those other two ideas which were supposed to be parts of Volume IV. And my next book will be what was supposed to be the second part of this book. Did I tell you what it is? I am excited to get back to writing *that* book.

Keith Smith
1 February 2001

INTRODUCTION

In *Books without Paste or Glue,* Volume I, *Non–Adhesive Binding,* I showed all the single sheet bindings I knew. There are the four traditional Japanese stab bindings: The *Japanese 4–Hole Binding,* the *Tortoise Shell Binding, Hemp–Leaf Binding* and the *Noble.* The other two single sheet bindings described are the *Single Sheet Pamphlet Stitch* and the *Album Binding.* These six bindings are all that are available when a book requires binding sheets rather than sections.

This is a stabbing.

The Japanese 4–Hole Binding is a stabbing. The book does not open flat. This Chinese book block is tissue paper. Each sheet is folded in half and stab bound as separate folios with the fold on the foredge. This peppers the spine–edge with fragments of the printing as a lovely decorative element. Some chapters are black and a few are printed red. The foredge indicates where to find each.

Stitching vs Sewing

All six are stab bindings; they are not *sewings. Stabbing* is stitching; it is not sewing. The stations are in on the sheet close to the spine–edge. A sewing has stations on the fold. Stitching, or stabbing, does not permit the pages to lie open flat.

Sewing provides a perfect hinge — the fold of the section/signature. Sewing is engineered not to interfere with the action of turning the page to lie open flat.

TO LIE OPEN FLAT: There is a need to be able to bind a stack of individual sheets with no folds and to have the resulting book open flat at any position. That is why this book was written.

To explain traditional sewing of sections, Betsy Palmer Eldridge told me that the pierced hole is not necessarily the sewing station. In sewing onto tapes a hole is pierced on each side of each side of the tape. In this instance, those two holes are not the station. The tape is the station. That thought remained with me, though dormant.

It finally sunk in and gave insight: I knew I could devise sheet bindings which are sewn, not stabbed. True, to attach the sheet with thread, the sheet is stabbed in from the spine–edge in many *positions,* but not as *stations.* The vertical *gap* between the sheets (gutter) *is* the sewing station, not the pierced holes on the sheets. That is the key. The sewing is hinged in the gutter, not at the pierced hole, as in the case of the stab bindings.

Unsupported Bindings Described

Unsupported sheet sewings described are three Coptic sewings:

- *Single Sheet Coptic Sewn Across the Spine,* with three board attachments.
- Single Sheet Coptic Sewn Across the Spine without paired stations.
- *Single Sheet Coptic Sewn Along the Spine.* See pages 97–179.

UNSUPPORTED SEWING OF SHEETS: Keith Smith, Single Sheet Coptic Sewn Along the Spine, November 2000. 20.5 x 16 x 2 cm.
Sheets of alternating color and size of BFK paper constitute the book block in this Coptic sewing. The book opens flat to an page.

Supported Bindings Described

Supported sheet sewings described are one sewn onto tapes and another sewn raised cords:

- *Single Sheets Sewn onto Tapes,* page 189.
- *Loop Pack with Climbing Pack,* long stitch in on the sheet, page 213.

SUPPORTED SEWING OF SHEETS: Keith Smith, Sheets Sewn onto Tapes, January 2001. 17.5 x 12.3 x 3.5 cm.

Separate sheets form the book block. Leather to be used as tapes is stiffened by gluing decorative paper on the back since the back side will show if woven through the board. The paper backing also can be seen on the inside of the open cover at the gutter. After pasting and drying the paper–backed leather, cut it into strips.

Appropriate Sheets

All the supported and unsupported sewings have a book block of a stack of unfolded sheets. The book block can be sheets of a sturdy paper. Thinner paper, the weight of notebook paper should be avoided. It is too delicate and can rip out. I prefer Stonehedge, Canson or some other paper with a little bulk. Book board or 2–ply mat board can be used. Wooden boards–as–pages will open flat with a clapping sound. Glass, Plexiglass™ (perspex) or metal plates can be drilled and sewn and the book will open flat at any position. The book block can also contain sections using the same sewing.

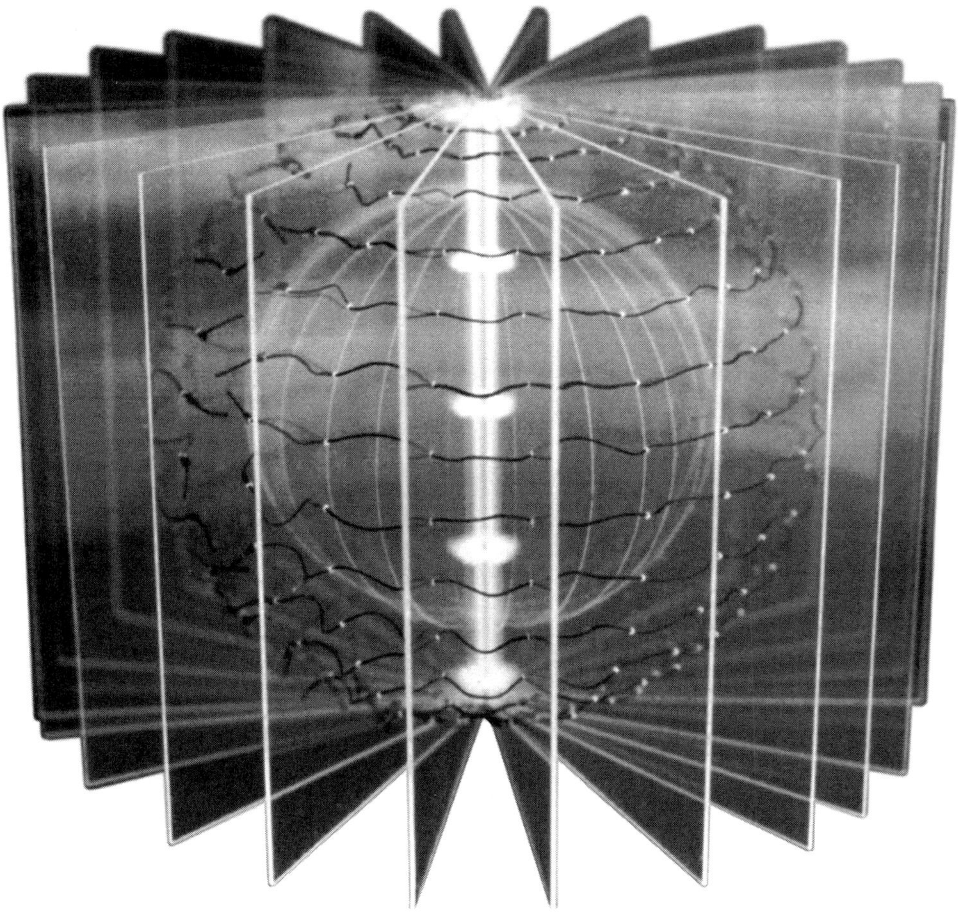

Adéle Outteridge, *Saturn,* one–of–a–kind, 1997. Edition of 5 plus 2 artist's proofs. Perspex (Plexiglass), engraving, thread. Single sheet binding. 19 x 13 x 5 cm. closed.

Adéle Outteridge

In 1997 giving a workshop in Hobart, Tasmania for Penny Carey–Wells, I violated my own rules and told them I was working on a new book. I never speak of a book until it is completed. I said said this next book on binding would have sheets sewn, rather than paper folded into sections. I said they were *single sheet Coptics,* as I had not yet considered supported sewing of sheets.

One person in the class had flown down from Brisbane. I caught her interest with that statement. Her name is Adéle Outteridge. Modestly, all that she said was that she would be interested in seeing what I had come up with.

Later, she would send photos of one of her books which the cover and book block consisted of clear sheets of Plexiglas™ (perspex) with a Coptic sewing. Adéle does not refer to them as *single sheet Coptics,* but uses the term *single sheet bindings.*

Whatever the label, she had come up with the *same* idea halfway around the world. I was so excited I reproduced the pictures of her books in the book I was writing at the time, *Bookbinding for Book Artists,* even though her single sheet binding did not represent what that textbook was describing. I couldn't wait for the public to see a single sheet binding — the first, as mine were only in my head and a half dozen sketches.

GIVING CREDIT: It is important to point out Adéle also devised sewing single sheets which lie flat. I have the advantage of publishing this book promoting my single sheet sewings, but I am obliged to point out her work, as well. Pictures of her books are on pages 19, 20, 267–269, 274, 275 and 277.

When we went back to Australia in 1999, Scott McCarney and I did a couple workshops for Adéle's students in Brisbane. In her studio I got to examine several of her bindings of sheets of perspex when I would get a break from teaching and Scott would take over. I believe her sewings all use the same link stitch; the linking looked identical. I do not know the sewing path she uses, but the results are beautifully formed chains on the spine, identical to a 2–needle Coptic sewing across the spine of sections. It was inappropriate to ask her how she sewed them, so I do not know if her sewing path is superior to those I show in Volume IV, or her sewing ability is above mine, or both.

I was impressed.

Two views of a sample Coptic sewing of various single sheets of paper, metal, cardboard, as well as sections. The Coptic sewings in this manual can be used to sew sections/signatures as well as sheets, or a combination.

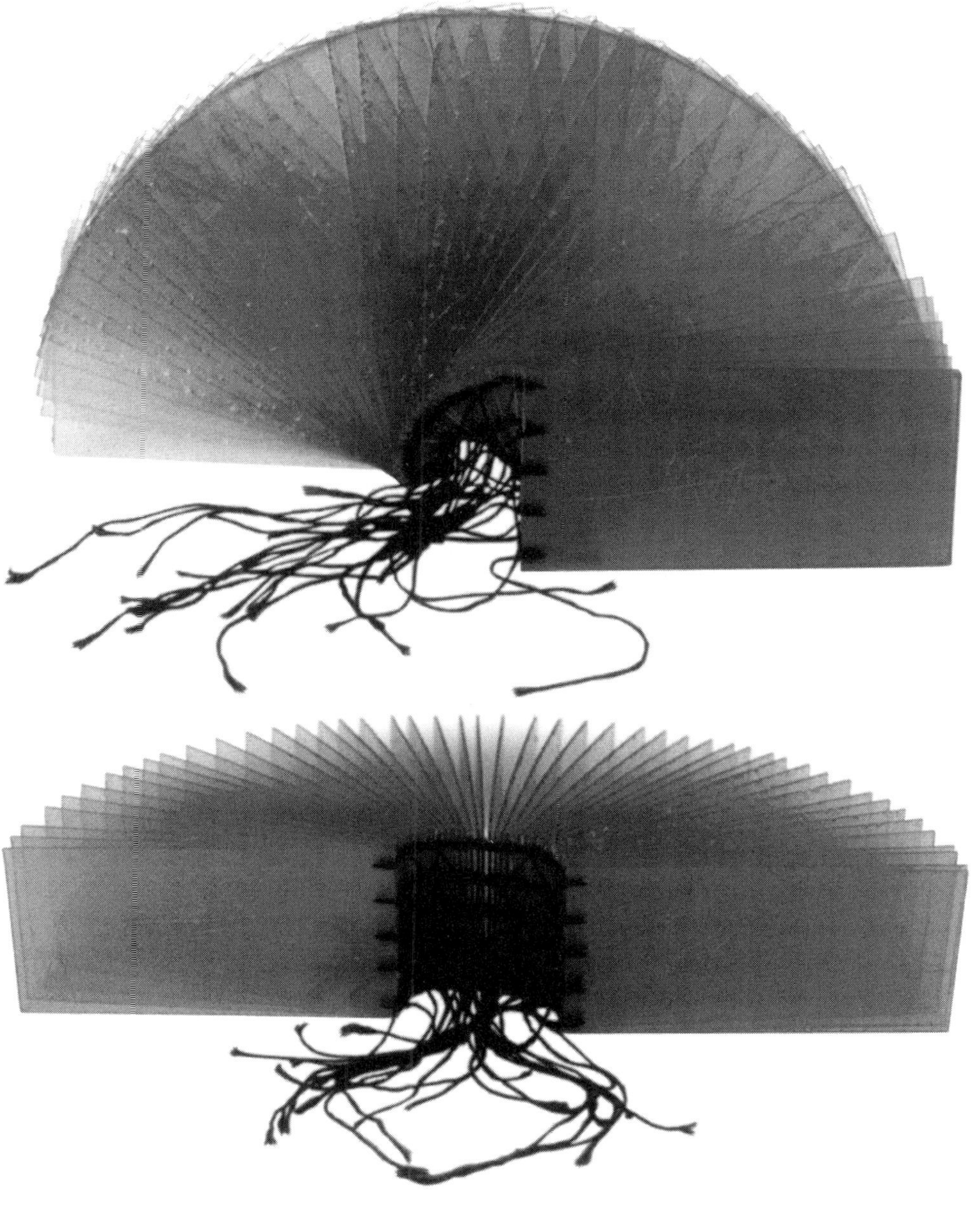

Adéle Outteridge and Wim de Vos. Two views of *Book of Golden Light,* 1994, one–of–a–kind. Polycarbonate, linen thread, engraving. A large range of tones are seen looking through the amber translucent sheets of plastic. Single sheet binding. 6 x 37 x 15 cm.

Adéle Outteridge, *Red Heart Book for Inga,* 1995, one–of–a–kind. Paper, paint, thread. Single sheet binding. 7 x 5 x 3 cm. closed.

PART I

PRELIMINARIES

MATERIALS & TOOLS

As with all the books I have written, there are few tools and no equipment needed for these bindings.[1] Tools and terminology for parts of the book are covered in this chapter. Specialized words are in the Glossary.

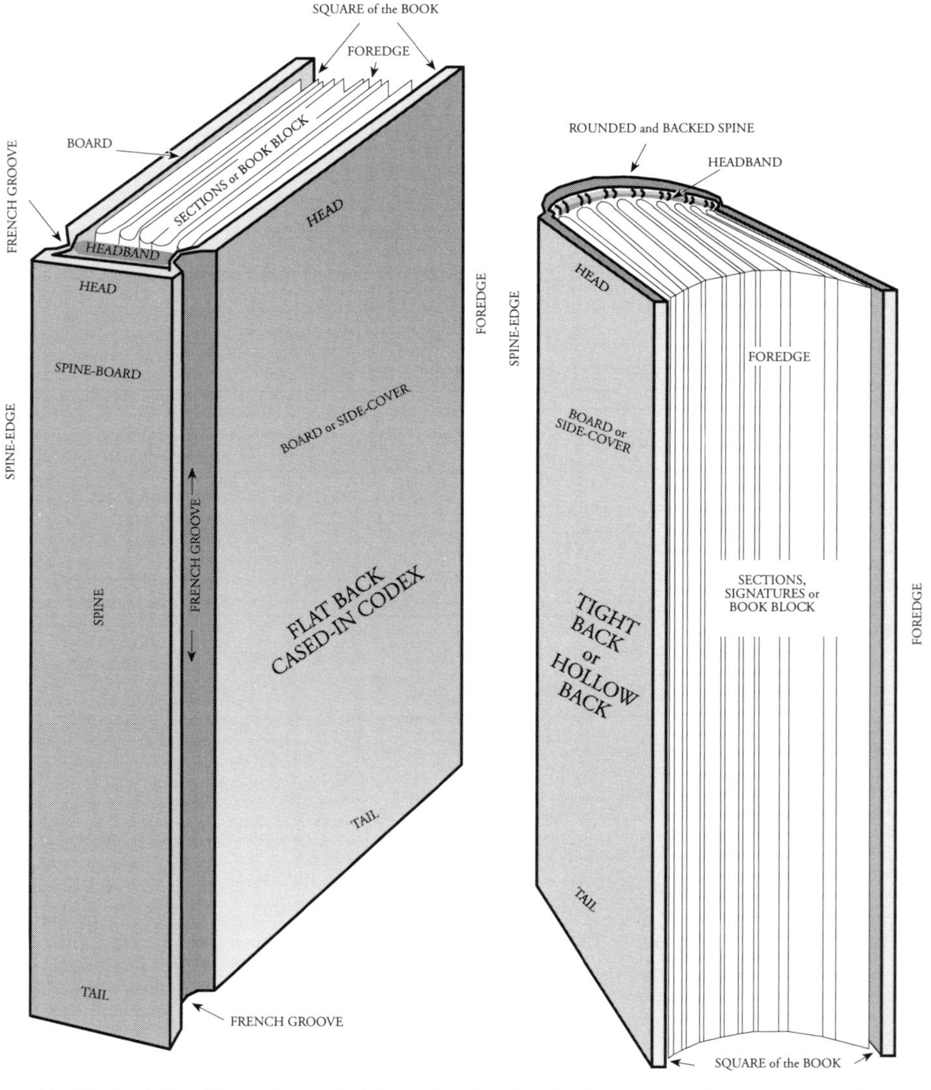

The Flat Back Cased–In Codex on the left has three boards and a flat spine. The drawing on the right is a book which is rounded and backed, either a Tight Back, or Hollow Back, also referred to as a *Spring Back*. These sewn and pasted bindings with covered spines will not be described in this manual.

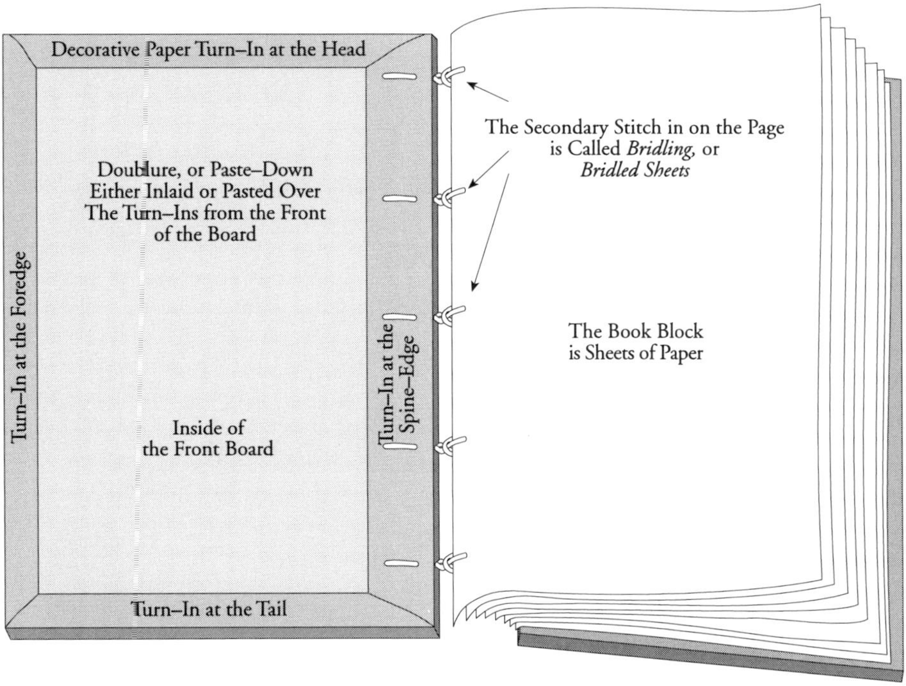

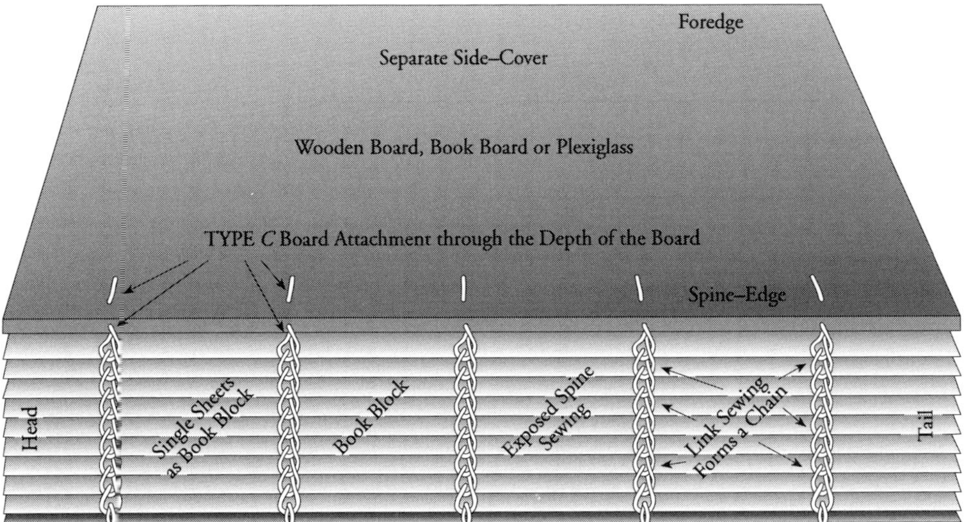

All the bindings in this book have two separate side–covers with no covering over the spine. The exposed spines are sewn, but not pasted. The inside of the board has an island paste–down, usually decorative or laid paper. I will refer to this paste–down as a *doublure.* Doublures are usually inlaid silk, leather or vellum, but they can be paper laid on top of the turn–ins.

TOOLS NEEDED

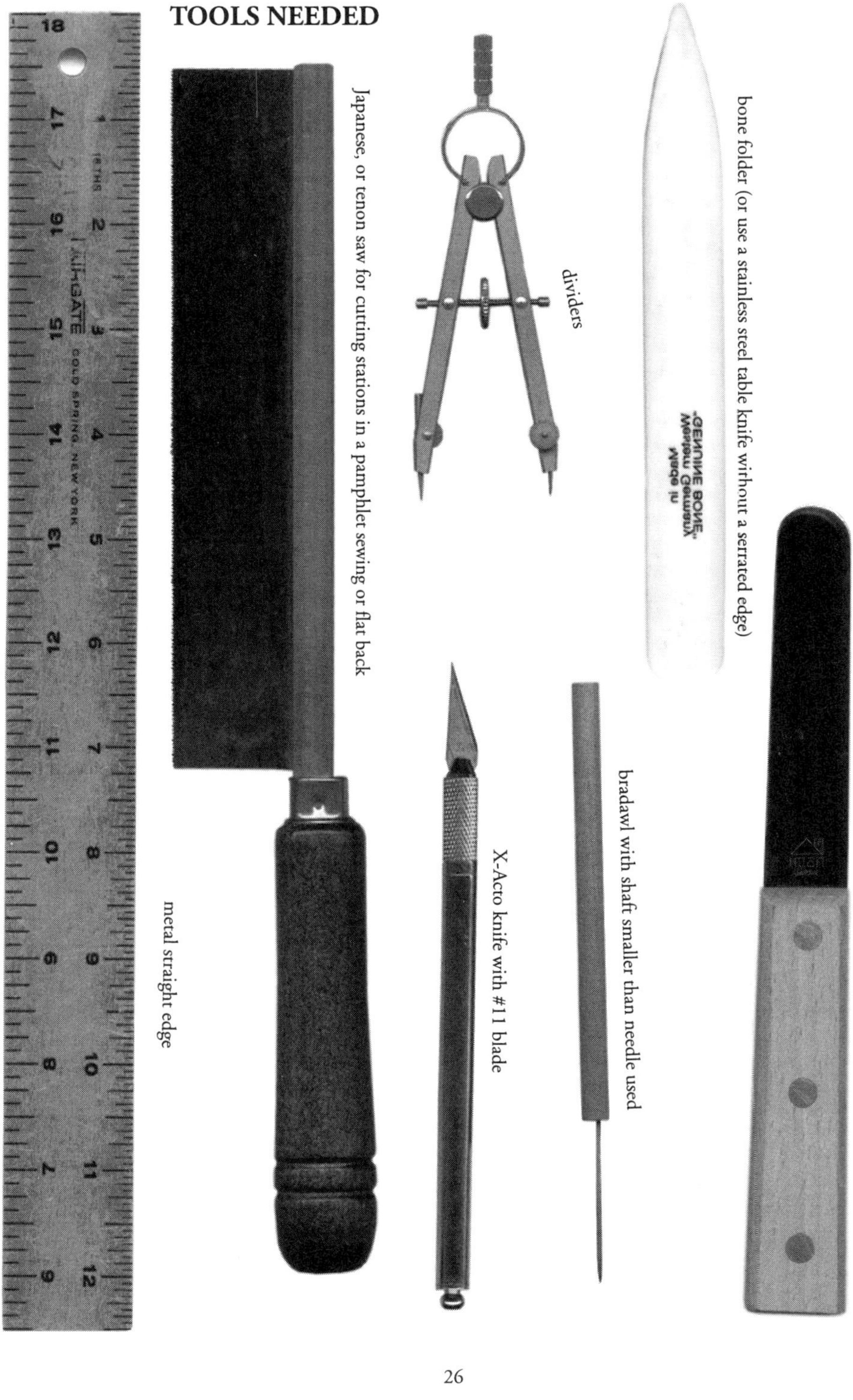

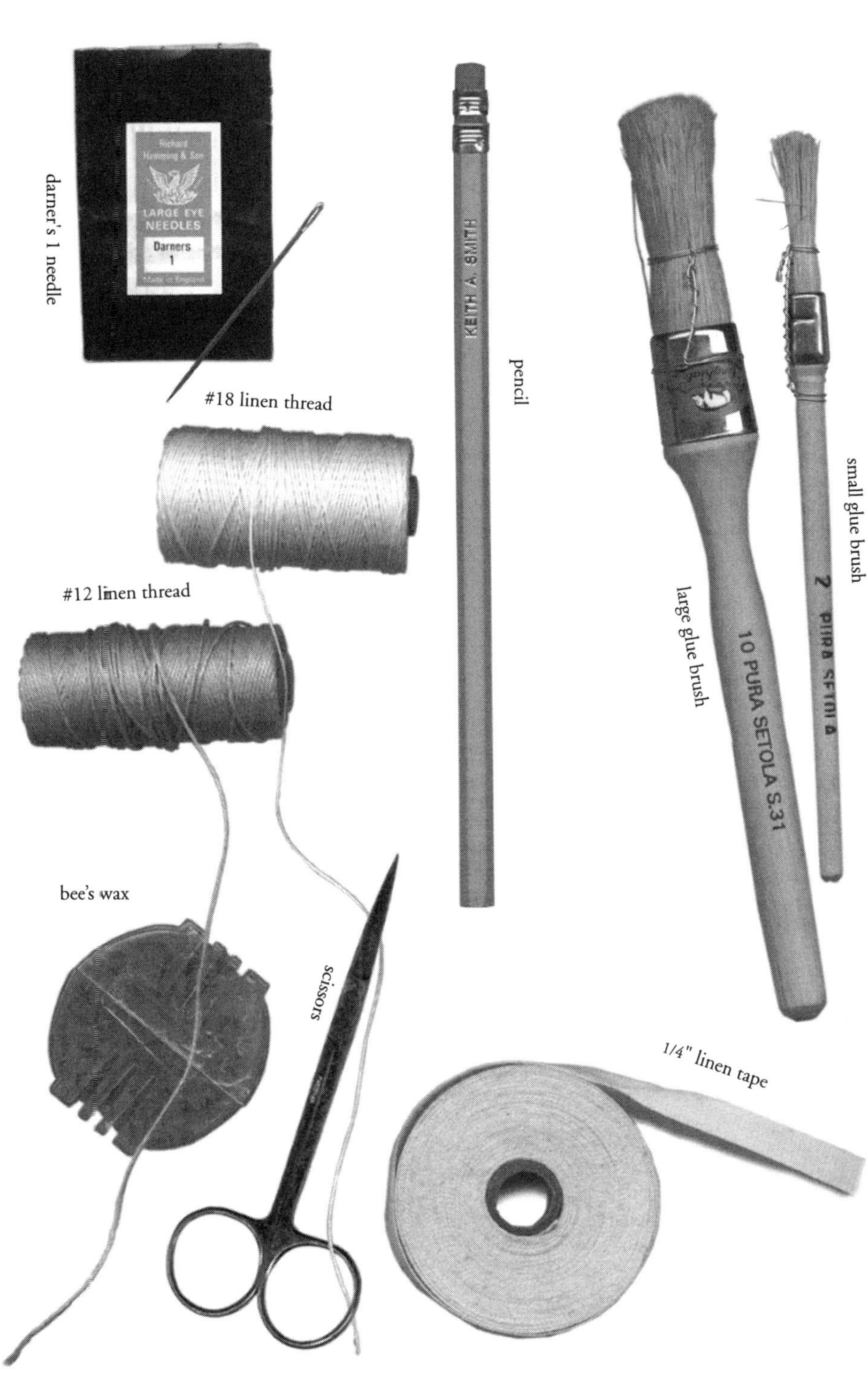
darner's 1 needle
Richard Hemming & Son
LARGE EYE NEEDLES
Darners 1
Made in England
#18 linen thread
#12 linen thread
bee's wax
scissors
KEITH A. SMITH
pencil
large glue brush
10 PURA SETOLA S.31
small glue brush
2 PURA SETOLA
1/4" linen tape

Besides marbled papers, there are many decorative papers from various countries. Above are mostly Italian print and paste papers. On the facing page are Japanese papers.[2]

MAKING A SEWING FRAME

Sewing frames are necessary for sewing recessed cords and make sewing raised cords easier. But when I sewed the prototype raised cord sewings of single sheets for this book I simply taped the cords to the edge of the table. The table must have a right angle; it cannot be beveled.

None of the other sewings in this book would need a sewing frame or a makeshift substitute. Still, I feel I should include directions for making a sewing frame for those who might wish to have one.

EXPENSE of a HAND–MADE FRAME: I have little to no building skills. The frame I created below and on the following page will be well within my reader's ability to construct. Expense of this frame is minimal: the carriage bolts each are about $1.50 now; nuts, 10¢ each; washers, 9¢ each. The wood was salvaged from our basement. Total cost of supplies for a frame is less than $10.00. Plans for an even more simple frame are on page 32.

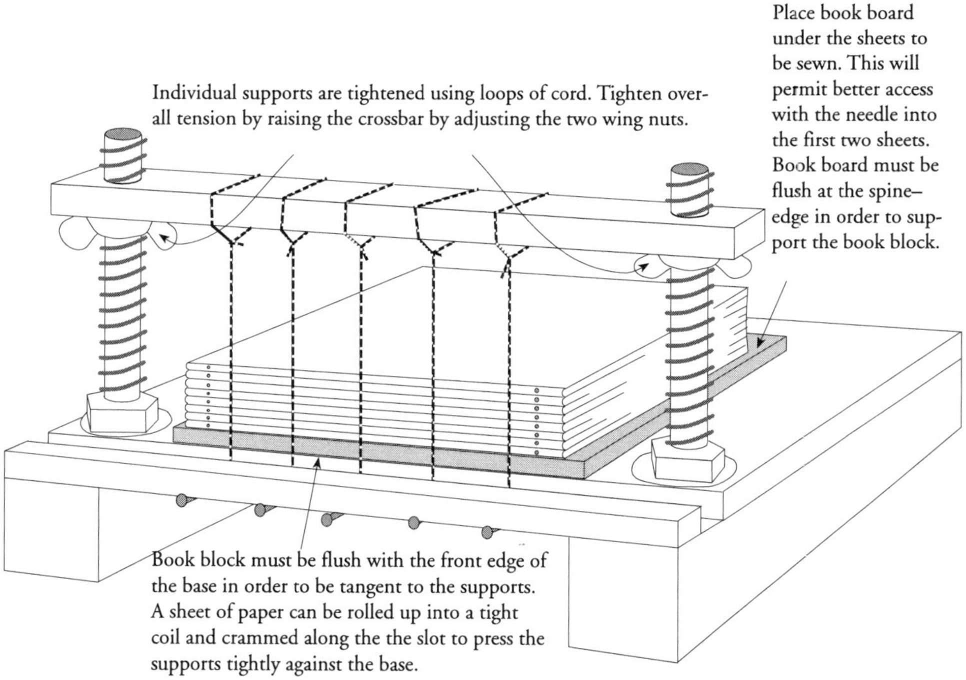

SEWING FRAME *A*

You will not need a sewing frame for any of the sewings in this book; sewing Single Sheets Raised Cords is the exception. But in the text above I explain that you can simply tape the cords to the depth of your table and that will suffice. However, if you wish to have a simple sewing frame, I have included two plans for constructing a frame. I much prefer the frame above and on the facing page, which has an adjustable crossbar to the frame on page 32. Purchase large wing nuts; they are easier on the fingers when tightening.

SUPPLIES to CONSTRUCT SEWING FRAME *A*

2 2x2's 11 1/4" long (feet)

1 3/4" board 10 x 16" (base)

1 3/4" board 16 x 3/4" (lip)

1 3/4" board 16 x 1 1/4" (crossbar)

nails or screws for assembly

2 8" long carriage bolts, 1/4" in diameter, threaded to within 2" of the head

2 washers, 1 on each bolt on top of base before nut tightens bolt to base and foot

4 nuts: 2 nuts above the base, and 2 wing nuts below crossbar

several 3" nails (as substitute keys)

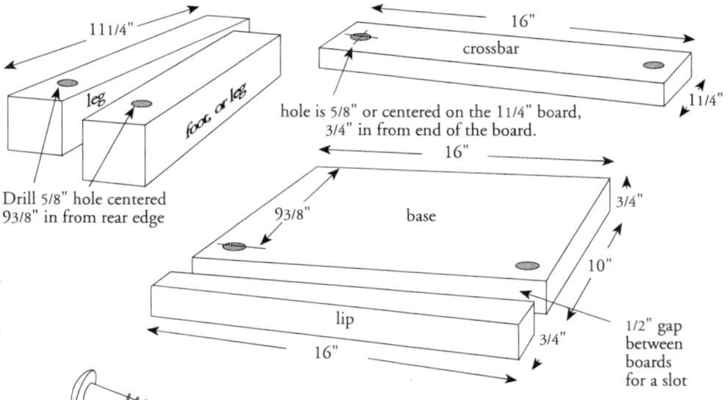

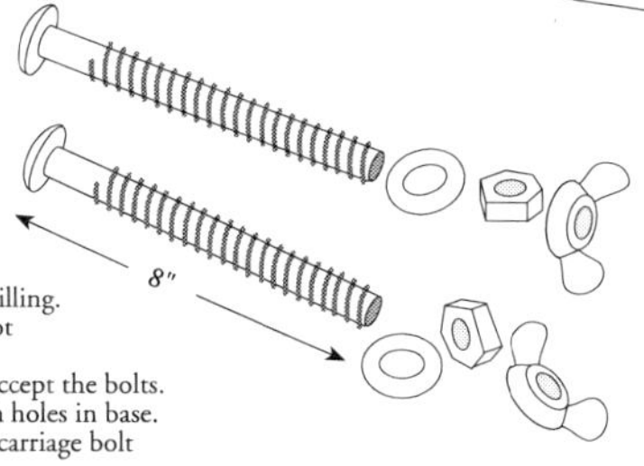

1. Nail or screw base and lip onto feet prior to drilling. Gap of 1/2" between lip and base provides a slot as access to the keys.
2. Drill 5/16" hole though each 2x2 and base to accept the bolts.
3. Drill 5/16" holes through crossbar to align with holes in base.
4. Enlarge holes in bottom of the feet so head of carriage bolt will be flush with the bottom of the feet.

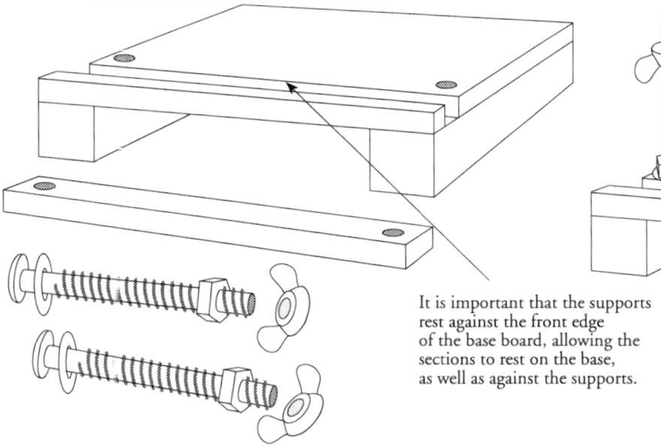

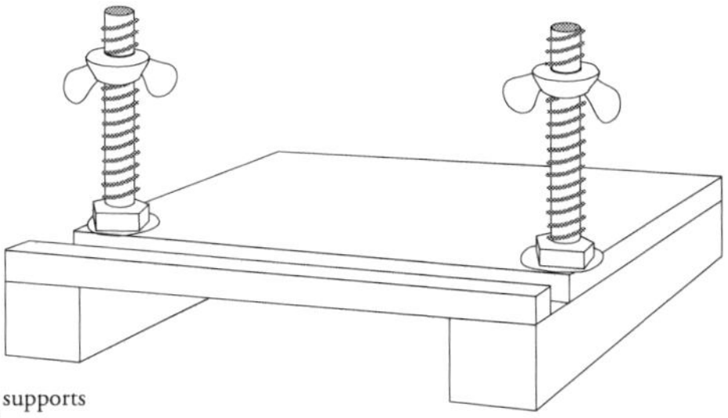

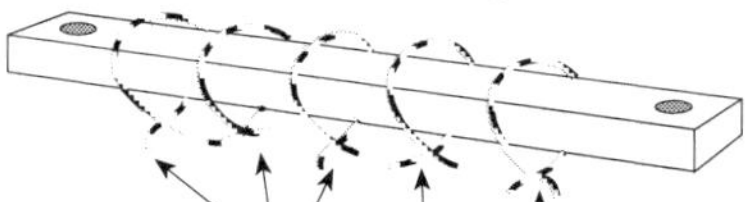

5. Insert bolts into the drilled holes of the feet, up through the base.
6. Add a washer to each bolt. Use one nut to tighten each bolt against washer, base and feet. This is why bolt must be threaded to within 2" of the head.
7. Add a wing nut to the bolt, down about 2" from the top. The bolt permits the crossbar to be adjusted to tighten the supports.
8. Place the crossbar onto the bolts, to rest upon the wing nuts.
9. Tie loops of cord on the crossbar, one each onto which to attach the supports.
10. Glue felt on the bottom of the feet to prevent scratching the surface of your table.

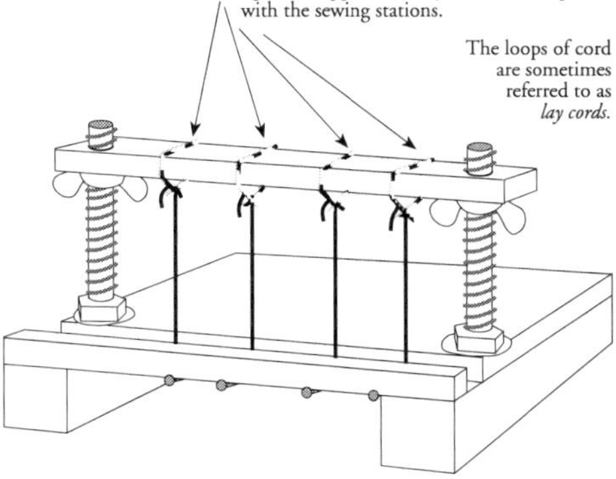

Completed SEWING FRAME *A*
Crossbar can be adjusted to tighten the supports.

SUPPLIES to CONSTRUCT SEWING FRAME *B*

2 2x2's 11 1/4" long (feet)

1 3/4" board 10 x 20" (base)

1 3/4" board 20 x 3/4" (lip)

1 3/4" board 20 x 3/4" (crossbar)

2 2x2's 12" tall (posts)

nails or screws for assembly

several 3" nails (as substitute keys)

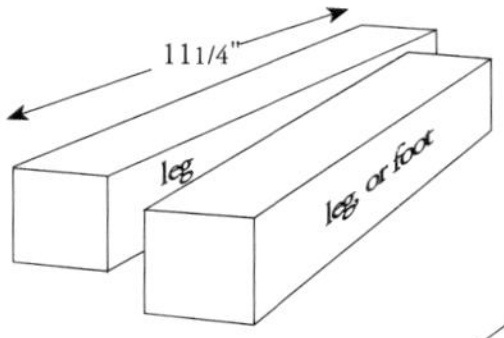

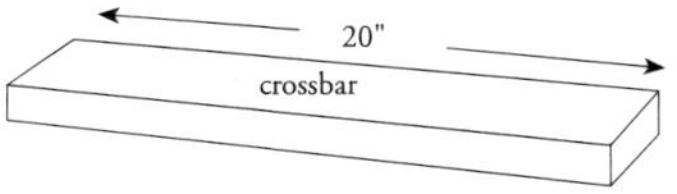

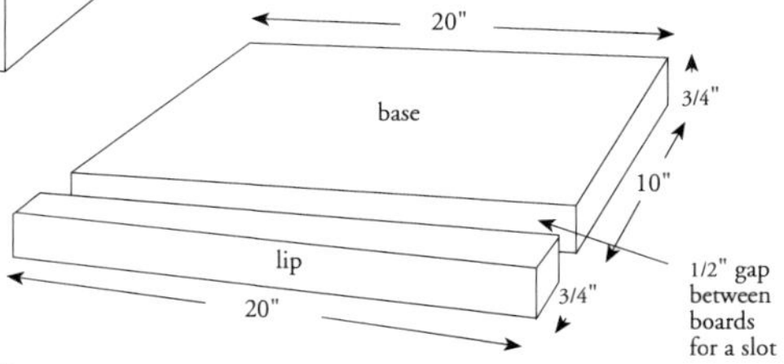

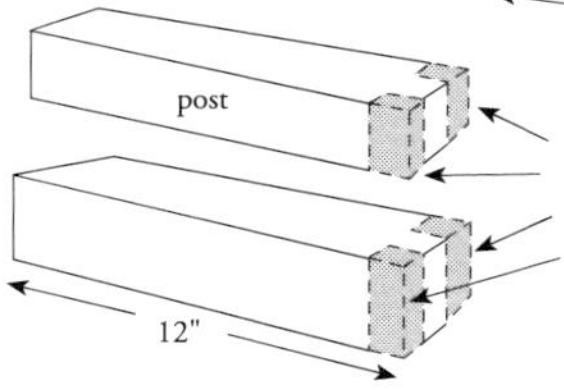

Saw the bottom of the posts to fit into the slot. Cut 3/4" up from the bottom. Cut in on each side to leave a depth of 1/2" for the thickness of the opening of the slot.

1. Nail or screw base and lip onto feet. Gap of 1/2" between lip and base provides a slot as access to the keys.
2. Saw each 2x2 post to fit into slot. Glue posts into position.
3. Nail or screw through lip into posts.
4. Nail or screw crossbar onto posts.

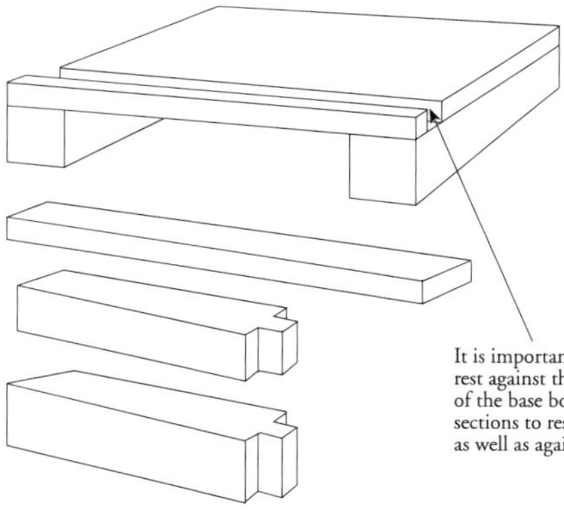

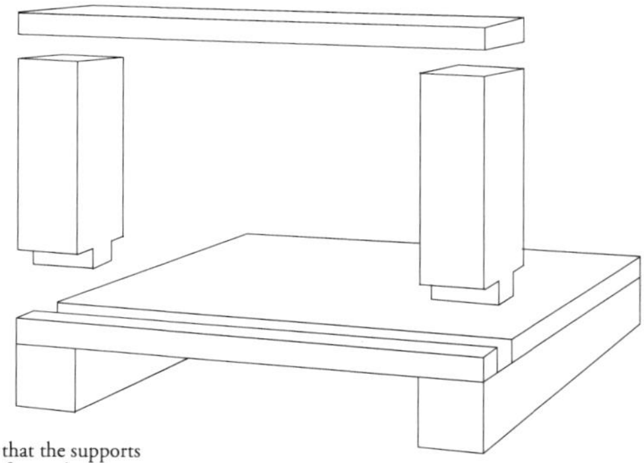

It is important that the supports rest against the front edge of the base board, allowing the sections to rest on the base, as well as against the supports.

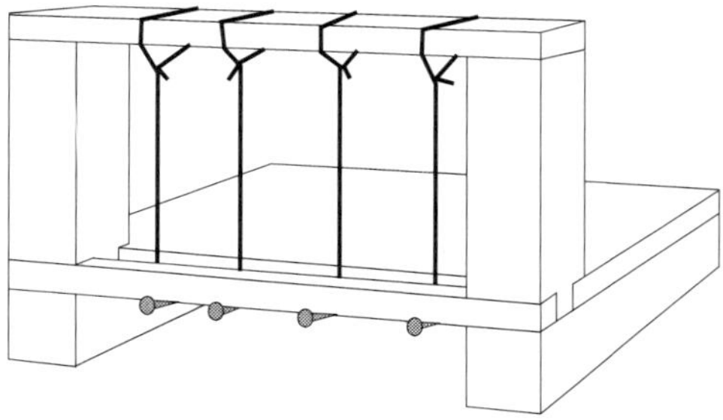

Completed SEWING FRAME *B*
Crossbar is not adustable.
This design does not need to drill any holes.
It is more simple to construct.

HOW TO USE A SEWING FRAME WITHOUT HOOKS

LOOPS of CORD: The commercial sewing frame, keys and hooks are illustrated on the following page. Most commercial frames do not have a slotted crossbar which accepts hooks. Threaded hooks permit individual tightening of each support. Instead, *loops of cord* are tied around the crossbar, one for each support. These loops are often referred to as *lay cords.*

Tie as many loops of cord around the non–slotted crossbar as the number of supports in your sewing. Position of the loops can be adjusted along the bar to line up with the sewing stations, and, they are reusable, replacing the need for hooks.

Set the book block on the sewing frame base and adjust the crossbar so the loops are about 3" above. This will allow enough length of the supports above the book block to attach the boards.

Cut lengths of cord or tapes for each station. Length should be approximately 5" longer than the distance from the loop to the base. Set aside all sheets (or sections) except for the first to be sewn.

For either frame on page 30 or 32, substitute keys are used. I suggest ten penny nails. Tie each support to a nail with a slip knot, as a square knot will be difficult to untie. Leave 2" of the support dangling from the slip knot, so you will have enough length later on to attach to the boards.

Position the first nail under the base, lined up with the first sewing station. Head of the nail extends from the lip. Pull the support up through the slot, and through the loop. Pull tight and pinch the support at the loop to hold the support tight, maintaining pressure as you tie the support to the loop. Tie with an overhand knot, releasing the pinch only after you pull up on the knot. An overhand *K* is half a square knot. *See* overhand *K,* page 59.

Position each successive nail. Pull the support up through the slot and tie to the corresponding loop with an overhand *K.* The partial square knot will suffice to hold the supports taut temporarily, but sufficiently loose to permit upward adjustment of the crossbar. This will tighten each support individually. Use of the inflexible square knot would result in some supports being tight, while others would sag.

Turn the nuts on the carriage bolts to adjust the crossbar slightly higher, tightening each support. Now, tie another overhand *K* on each support at the loop. This results in each support now being held by a square knot. Turn the wing nuts to raise the crossbar once again. This assures the supports will be permanently taut, and, you are ready to sew.

Use of the loops of cord eliminates the need to drill and saw a slot in the crossbar. This approach saves on cord and the expense of hooks. It is even preferred by most binders. Substituting nails saves the expense of keys.

STRINGING A SEWING FRAME WITH HOOKS AND KEYS

Do not use a frame which has a dowel in front of the base rather than a slot to accept keys. Keys save on the length of the supports, and can be more easily adjusted. Keys are more convenient than substituted nails, allowing the support to be looped, instead of tied. Keys are easier to undo after the sewing is completed than the slip knot on the nail.

For sewing supports traditionally 5– to 8–ply linen cord is used, available from any binders' supply. Before measuring the length of the supports, adjust the crossbar fairly close to the top of the book block with the two adjusting rings. This will save on supports. For each support, cut approximately 6" in addition to the distance between the base of the frame and the crossbar.

1. Lay the support over the key from left to right. Allow about 1" of the support to extend on the left. Keep your left thumb on top of the support and the side of the key that is facing you.
2. With your right hand, pull the long end of the support tightly to the back of the key and below the shorter end of the support.
3. Angle up, over the support and the left arm of the key. Pull the support snugly downward, centered on the key.

View of the key (step 3) will be the bottom. Holding the loop securely in position, turn the key upside down. Without releasing pressure on the loop, place the key under the front edge of the base of the sewing frame, close to where the first support will be positioned. Pointed edge of the keys face outward. See illustration below and on the facing page.

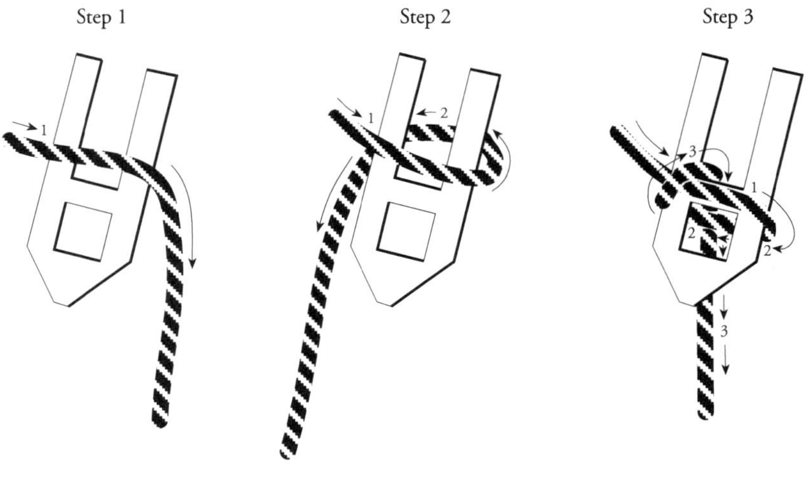

Reach with your free hand and pull the longer end on the support up through the slot in the base of the frame. Pull upwards with pressure, releasing your grasp on the key. Do not release pressure, or the loop will fail to secure the key against the frame. If the key falls off, repeat steps 1 through 3. Keeping constant upward tension, tie or attach the loose end of the support to the lay cord (loop), or onto a hook, if available. Leave sufficient length of supports at each end to attach the book block to the boards with the supports.

SUBSTITUTE FOR SEWING FRAME: Tape the cords to the edge of a table which has a right angle rather than a rounded edge. Leave at least 2" of cord below the first sheet to be sewn. If you do not have such a table, tape the cords to a board which sits on the table. The tape cords will keep the loops of thread on the bottom of the first sheet tight. That said, I strongly suggest you make a sewing frame.

COMMERCIALLY AVAILABLE SEWING FRAME: If you continue to sew on a frame, you will probably want to invest in a good sewing frame. I suggest one with a slotted crossbar and hooks.

Not only is the crossbar adjustable, but individual supports can be tightened easily with the use of threaded hooks. No one considers keys a luxury, but a decided convenience.

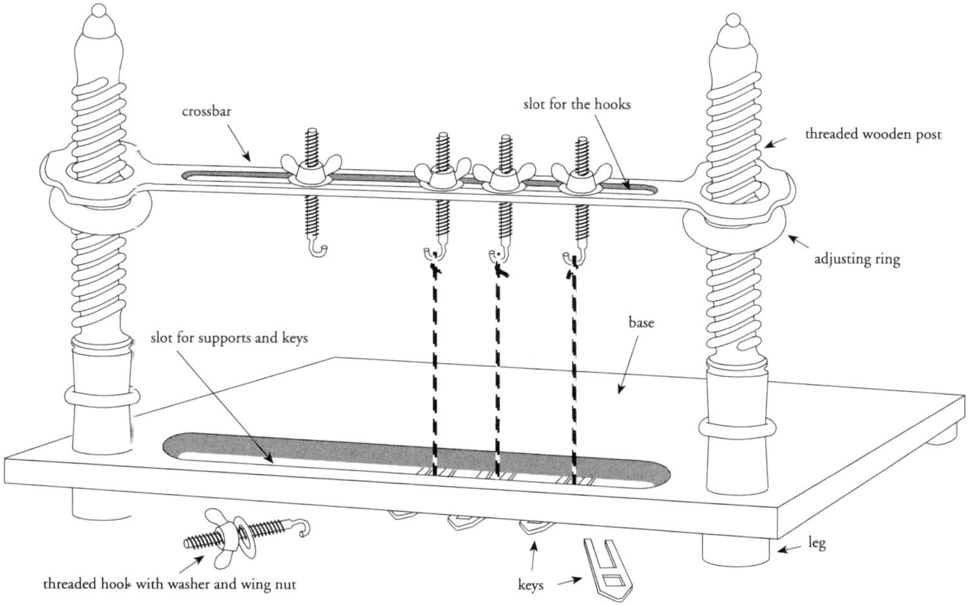

Commercially Available
SEWING FRAME

PAPER TRAITS

This chapter discusses paper, grain, sheets, thread, knots and sewing. These are basic to all sewings. There are many factors to consider in the seemingly simple act of folding paper.

GRAIN OF PAPER: Machine–made paper is easier to fold in one direction than the other. In making paper commercially, water runs across the surface. More of the fibers settle in this direction. That direction is referred to as the *grain* of the paper. It is easier to fold with the grain than against it. You will not be folding paper into sections, since this book describes sewing single sheets.

Direction of the grain is still critical; the book block should be assembled with grain parallel with the spine. This allows the pages to roll open. The paper will naturally curl open. If some of your sheets are grained incorrectly, the pages will bow from head to tail, rather than from foredge to spine–edge.

Book board has a grain also. Again, cut the side–covers so the grain is parallel with the spine.

Hand–made paper and certain commercial papers have multi–directional fibers, so there is no strong direction of grain. These papers can be folded in either direction with no concern for grain.

TESTING FOR GRAIN: Rolling a sheet first in one direction, then the other, is a test for direction of the grain. There will be less resistance rolling the paper when the grain is parallel with the curve of, and potential fold of, the roll.

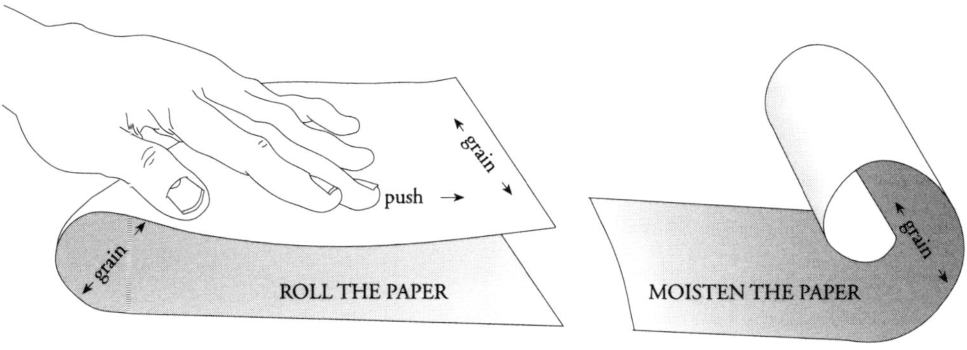

TESTS FOR GRAIN DIRECTION: Roll a sheet of paper without creasing it, first in one direction, then the other. The direction in which the rolling is less resistant, the grain runs parallel with the fold.

If you cannot tell, moisten a scrap piece. It will curl with the grain.

If it is difficult to determine the direction, moisten the edge of the sheet. It will naturally curl with the grain. That is, the curl is determined by the grain, by not bending the grain.

Book board is easy to test. Bending a full sheet, the board will flex more easily in the direction that is parallel with the grain. It is difficult to test a scrap of board. Therefore, before you cut a new board, run several light pencil lines across the board to indicate the direction of the grain. Later on, when you have a small portion of the board, you will know which direction to turn the board so that the pencil line is parallel with the spine of your book.

SPECIFYING THE DIRECTION OF THE GRAIN: Paper is usually grain long. Paper companies generally list the direction of the grain as the second dimension: 32 x 48". Other companies will point out the direction of the grain by underlining that dimension: 48 x 32".The same paper stock can be long or short grain, depending on the size of the sheet the store handles. The diagram to the right shows a full sheet as grain long. The identical paper, if offered in half sheets, would be grain short.

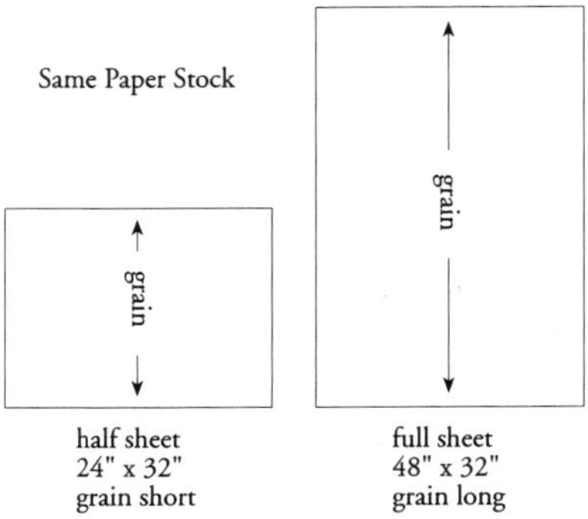

SPECIFYING THE DIMENSIONS OF A FINISHED WORK: The dimensions of a book, pages or a photograph are usually listed with the height first, then the width. If the work has a third dimension, it is listed third. The book you are holding is 9 x 6 x 13/32".

MARKING THE MEASUREMENT: The full sheet of paper will be cut down into sheets which are the desired dimensions of the book you are going to bind. Indicate the measurements on the full sheet. Never use ink or ballpoint. An unsharpened pencil mark can be erased, but is inaccurate because of its width, leaving to chance whether the fold is on the left, right or center of the mark.

A light pencil dot with a sharpened pencil is better. More accuracy is gained by a pin prick or indentation. An ideal tool is the edge of your thumbnail.

TO TEAR PAPER: Torn paper edges are often attractive in a hand–bound book. They are impossible in a commercially–made production book, which makes them all the more desirable in small edition hand–bound and one–of–a–kind books. Sometimes the deckled–edge is incorporated in the binding but the sheet is larger than the page. The other edges must be either machine cut or torn. Tearing paper can imitate the deckled–edge. Instead of placing all deckled–edges at the head and your torn edges at the tail, alternate the deckled–edge with the torn to offer less comparison between the two. Each method of tearing gives a different edge:

- Lay a straight edge where the paper is to be torn. Firmly hold it in place with one hand while you tear against the straight edge.
- For a more exaggerated torn edge, use a wooden ruler which has a metal edge inserted. Since the metal is raised above where the paper is held down to the surface of the table, the tear will peel as it frays. The higher the metal edge is from the surface, the more exaggerated the tear. You can increase the height of the metal by placing masking or duct tape on the bottom of the ruler.
- The most extreme and perhaps the best imitation of the deckled–edge by tearing is accomplished by a different approach. Fold and crease the paper where it is to be torn. Reverse the fold and crease. With a damp sponge, stroke the folded edge. Do not run the sponge on the surface of the paper, only across the edge of the fold. Reverse the fold and stroke it with the sponge. Open the paper and gently pull it in two at the weakened fold. The paper will fray more than tear, leaving an edge of hairy fibers.
- Run a Rapidograph™ filled with water along a ruler for Eastern papers with long fibers. Hold ruler in place. Gently pull. If an area resists, scrape the fiber with an X–Acto blade, but don't cut.

TO CUT PAPER: Cutting and trimming paper by hand should be done with a sharp blade using a metal straight edge as a guide. Slits are made in the same manner. An X–Acto knife with a #11 blade is recommended as it has a narrow point which is easily positioned and is thin so it does not throw a burr on the paper.

Rotary knife

Whenever possible, lay the straight edge on the material to be saved. If the knife wanders, it will veer into the excess which is being trimmed rather than into the good material.

CUTTING WET PAPER: Sometimes moisture expands paper more than allotted for. It may become necessary to trim the pasted paper before it can be applied to the board. The paper can be laid on a self–seal cutting mat, paste side up. A straight edge and X–Acto blade will probably tear as it cuts. Lowering the angle and using a new blade helps. Better is to cut with a rotary-blade knife.

Never cut directly on the table, not only to protect the furniture, but to avoid a ragged cut. Always use a self–sealing cutting mat under the sheet to be cut. Scrap book board is a poor substitute. Your cut will be imperfect if it extends over an area where the book board is incised from a previous cut. Only use #11 blades with a self–sealing mat. Heavy–duty blades will shorten the life span of the mat. A cutting mat may seem expensive, but it is a valuable tool and a pleasure to use, and they last for years even when used daily.

PAPER CUTTERS: An ideal paper cutter has a clamp–bar close to the blade to hold the paper in position so the paper does not creep as the blade slices through. The clamp–bar should come down parallel with the plate, so it must be hinged at both ends. A cutter with a clamp–bar having a single hinge located near the fulcrum of the blade is to be avoided.

The right angle bar may be located along the top or bottom edge. It should be adjustable and all paper cutters should be checked monthly with a large metal right angle to determine if the angle bar needs adjusting. Do not take it for granted that all paper cutters cut at a right angle. Few do. Only those capable of being adjusted and which are serviced regularly will give you an accurate cut. In folding, especially concertinas, it is impossible to achieve acceptable folds if you do not start with a sheet with 90° corners.

Never try to cut several sheets of paper at once. The bottom sheets will be ragged and probably not cut at 90°. The practice abuses the hinge of the blade.

CUTTING BOOK BOARD: Never cut book board or card on a paper cutter; you will destroy the potential for precision cutting of paper. If you do not have a board shear, cut book board by hand using a heavy–duty mat knife and straight edge. Place scrap book board underneath.

SWELL

Sewing paper sheets, more than with sections, the spine tends to be thicker than the foredge. This is *swell* from the thread. In sewing sections, folds absorb much of the thread and lessen the amount of swell. The slightly wedged shape in sewing single sheets is not necessarily undesirable. The best advantage is binding the book blank, then afterwards, tipping in images. After the drawings have been added to the binding, the covers may close parallel.

Sew a test binding and slip the drawings between the sheets. If the foredge bulges slightly, sew the next test with a slightly thicker thread. This will increase the swell at the spine–edge. After the drawings are inserted the closed covers should be parallel.

Swell from the thread from attaching the sheets and linking expands the depth of the spine–edge. In sewing, *do not press down on the spine–edge* of the book block to tighten sewing; you will distort the exposed sewing.

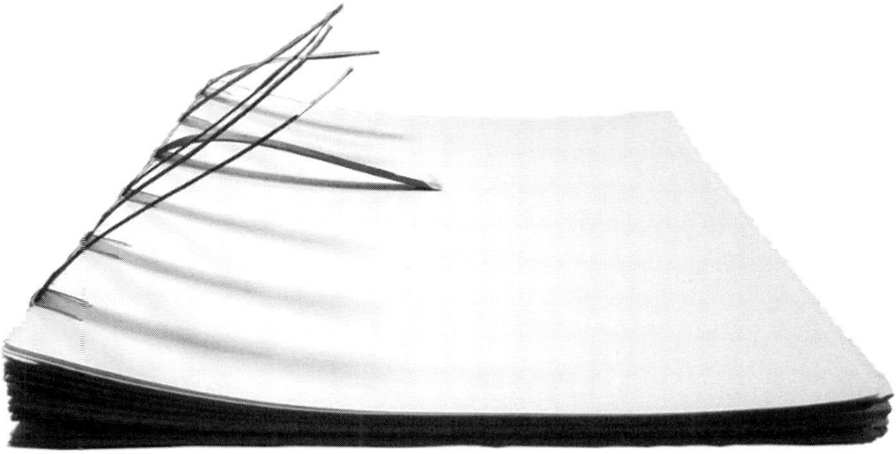

If prints are to be added after the book is bound, swell must be taken into consideration. An ideal binding for a scrap book of photo album is the Single Sheets Sewn Onto Tapes. Notice how the thread swells the spine–edge far more than the foredge in a blank binding of Single Sheets Sewn Onto Tapes. The separate side–covers could be wood, metal or glass with holes drilled to attach the strips of leather which were used as tapes. It has a lovely exposed spine.

The blank binding above now has sheets of paper interleaved between the pages to suggest prints which will later be tipped in. The addition of the inserts brings the book block and foredge up to the level of the spine–edge. When covers are added, they will close parallel.
The completed book is shown on pages 202 and 203.

Book Board As Book Block

Unlike wooden boards, book boards used as sheets for the book block absorb the thread to some degree. The spine–edge is almost identical thickness of the foredge.

Since there is little swell, if you intend to add images to the boards, they should be mounted prior to sewing.

The spine–edge of this Single Sheet Coptic sewn across the spine is approximately the same thickness as the foredge. There is little swell because book board absorbs some of the thickness of the thread. If drawings are to be added, they should be mounted on the boards prior to sewing.

Dimensions of the Boards

Height of the boards for any Coptic sewing should be the same as the sheets, not larger, since they are unsupported sewings. The book block would sag when stood on a book shelf if you made the covers slightly taller.

Height of the boards for supported sewings should leave an overhang at the head and tail the same amount as on the foredge. This is called *the square of the book.* The lip is generally 1 1/2 times the thickness of the cover.

Width of the boards for all single sheet sewings is slightly wider than the sheets, usually 1 1/2 times the thickness of the cover board.

FLUSH SPINE–EDGE: For any single sheet sewing the board is flush with the spine–edge no matter which type of board attachment is used. Board attachment is discussed for unsupported sewings across the spine on page 109 and along the spine on pages 165–168. For supported sewings see page 200 for tapes and pages 206, 207 for attaching cords.

Paper–Covered Boards

Book boards used as separate side–covers are prepared beforehand. If you paste on papers, allow the boards to thoroughly dry before piercing the boards and starting the sewing. *See* Pasting Procedure, page 77 and Covering the Boards, page 83.

Raw book board especially Davey Red™ looks good without being covered with decorative or laid paper.

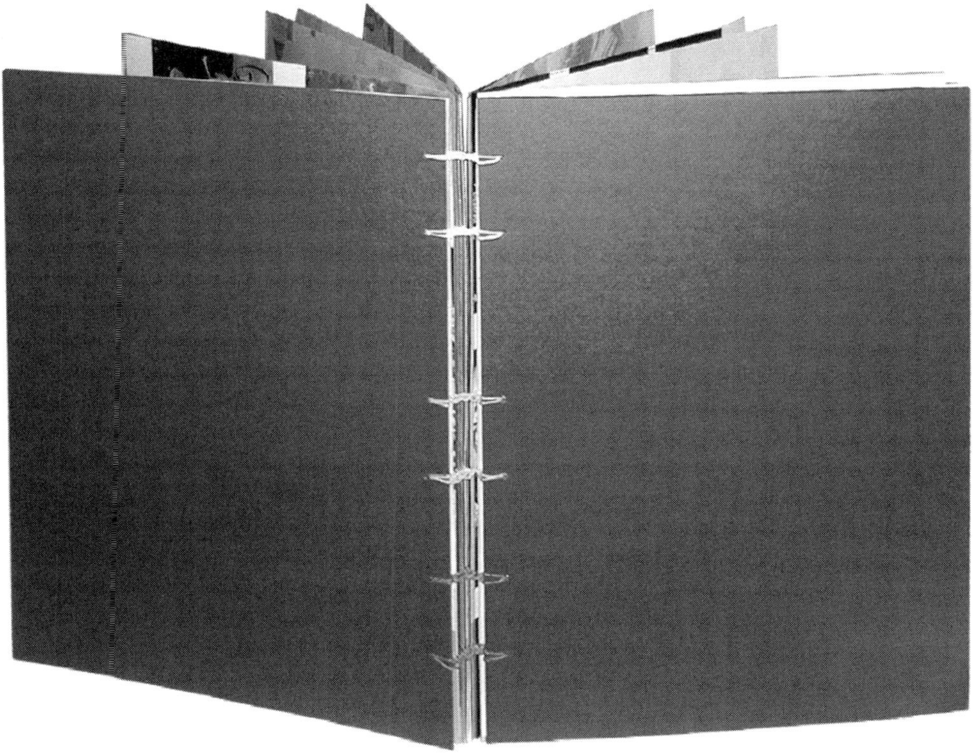

Metal offset plates were pierced and sewn as sheets. Separate side–covers are mat board. Decorative or laid paper is pasted onto the boards and allowed to dry prior to piercing the holes and sewing. Three paired stations were used requiring three threads and six needles, one on each end of the thread. The paired stations at the top were sewn with white thread, the middle with a medium value and the bottom with a dark thread. Other photos of this binding are on pages 134 and 135.

HIDING THE STITCHES

Any of the single sheet sewings can have book board as the pages as well as the covers. Each sheet has the slight intrusion of the threads which attach the boards. These can be hidden so the entire sheet can display a photograph.

All single sheet sewings, Coptics, Onto Tapes, Raised Cords, have a slight intrusion of the threads which attach the sheets. Gary Frost refers to this as *bridled sheets.* These stitches can be hidden on board sheets by grooving the board to recess the thread then pasting paper over both sides of the board sheets.

Thickness of board pages permit grooving the board from the hole to the spine–edge. When it is sewn, the thread will be flush with the board. After it is sewn, a paper image can be glued or laminated to the entire surface of the board and the bulge of the thread will not show.

Use a thin blunt instrument such as a letter opener to indent the board. Or, set on a chisel and strike with a hammer. The groove should be the thickness of the thread, or better, slightly less, not wider, and not deeper.

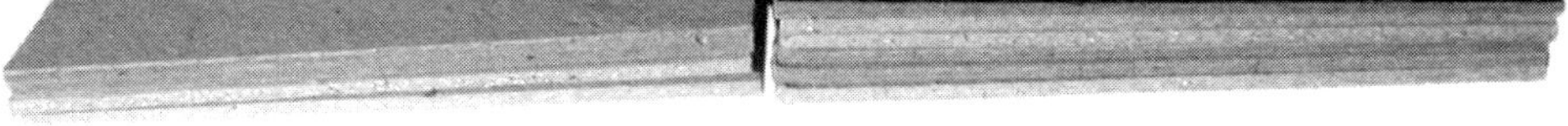

GROOVING THE BOARD: The board can be grooved to recess the thread as shown at the bottom of the facing page. Prints for the 2–page spreads, or print and a blank sheet for the verso, are slipped in between the boards as you sew. This compensates for the thickness of the spine after the prints and blank paper are added. Photographs, prints or drawings are laminated to the boards after the sewing is complete. On the left, the blank paper has not been added. When it is, no threads will show except in the gutter. Laminating the prints is described on the facing page. This makes a fine presentation for photographs using 2–, or 4–ply mat board as the book block. Depth of the book board need not be covered.

Sewing Threads Inlaid

The boards are cut to the size of the photographs or drawings that will be laminated.

FILLER: Cut temporary filler which is the dimensions of the book and the thickness of the prints which will be laminated after the book is bound. You will need as many sheets of filler as there will be prints in the book. These are set in place between the book board as you sew. This will give the proper thickness to the spine in the finished sewing. If you sewed the book without inserting filler, the spine would not permit adding prints later. The book would gape open with a foredge much thicker than the spine–edge.

Sew the boards with the filler using any of the binding descriptions in this manual. Do not pierce or sew the filler. It is only temporarily inserted during the sewing to maintain the proper gap between the board pages.

OPTIONAL STEP: After the book is sewn and prior to laminating the prints, you might take these added steps to insure there will be no bulge of the inlaid thread or indenting from the groove.

- Lightly tap the board in the area of the inlaid thread with a hammer. Do not dent the board.
- Or, wheat paste across the inlaid thread. Place a scrap of wax paper over the paste. Press with a bone folder. Leave the wax paper in place while drying. This is similar to lacing in boards.[3] Add the filler sheets and dry under weight overnight. When the wax paper is removed, the wheat paste will have soaked the thread and filled the cracks and dried mirror smooth.

Laminating the Pictures to the Boards

Avoid moisture of pasting or gluing the print to the board. Use a pressure-sensitive sheet of adherent, such as 3M #568 Cold Mount Adhesive™ which comes in sheets, or Filmoplast® P90 which comes in strips for tipping in. Each uses slight pressure to adhere the print. Both those products are archival and can be purchased from various sources.[4]

Avoid dry mount tissue which requires heat; it is not good for the print and the book would be difficult to get into a heated dry mount press.

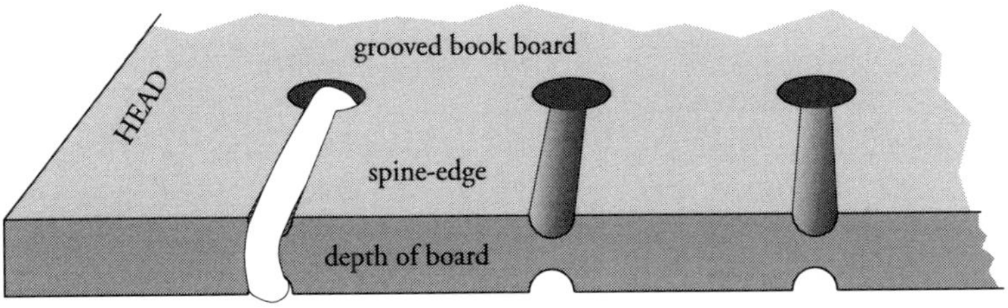

GROOVING THE BOARD: The board can be grooved to inlay the thread prior to sewing. Use a thin blunt instrument such as a letter opener to indent the board. The thread will be inlaid. A paper print can be adhered to the board and no thread will show.

FOLIOS & FOLD–OUTS

MAKING FOLIOS

A sheet of paper is traditionally folded down into a section or signature. This makes a unit of sewing. Sections will not be described in this book; all the bindings use single sheets as the unit of sewing.

A section with the fewest number of pages is a *folio.* A sheet is folded once, in half, with the grain. A folio is 4 pages, whereas a sheet is 2 pages. Sewing would go twice as fast sewing folios rather than sheets. The amount of swell on the spine would also be reduced. *See* swell, page 40. Traditionally, the sewing takes place on the fold, which acts also as a hinge.

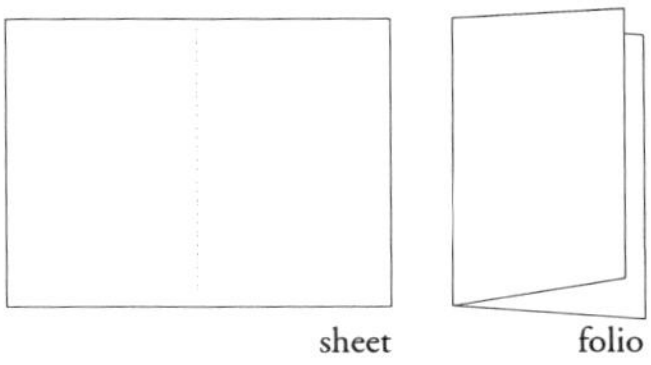

A sheet folded in half is a folio. The fold should be with the grain.

However, folios can be sewn as single sheets when the fold is on the foredge rather than the spine–edge. They are treated as a 2–ply single sheet.

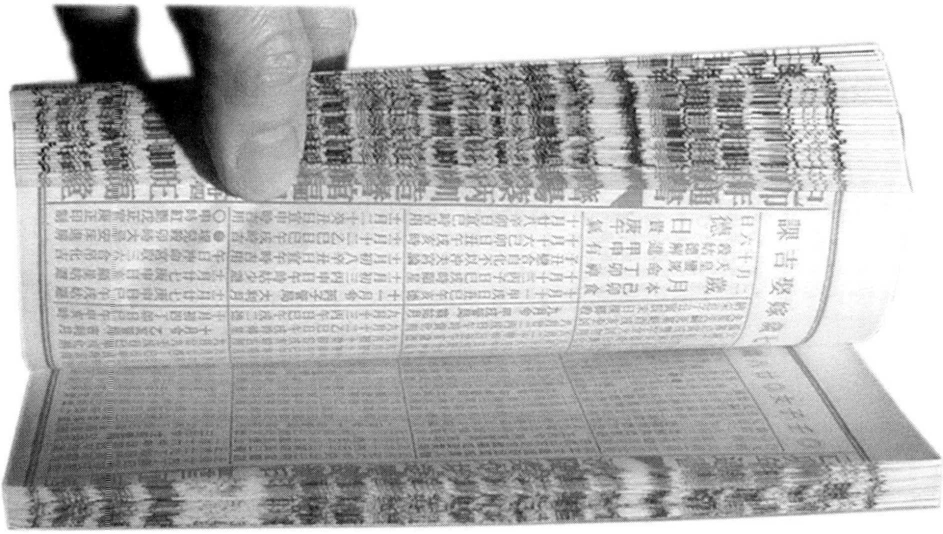

This Chinese book has a stab binding. Tissue–thin paper is printed on one side, folded into folios with the fold on the foredge. The printed border dots the foredge of the closed book.

There are several reasons you might wish to sew folios as single sheets:

- Double–sided printing might be impossible or too costly. The folio would allow printing on both sides of the *page,* even though it is only on one side of the *sheet* before it is folded down.
- You might desire to have text go around the foredge to the verso. You might wish to have a border which extends around the foredge. In both cases the foredge of the closed book is speckled. This makes a nice decoration often used in Japanese stab bindings. See photo on the previous page.
- One half of the folio can be cut as a window protecting the print which is tipped in on the other half of the folio, as shown below.

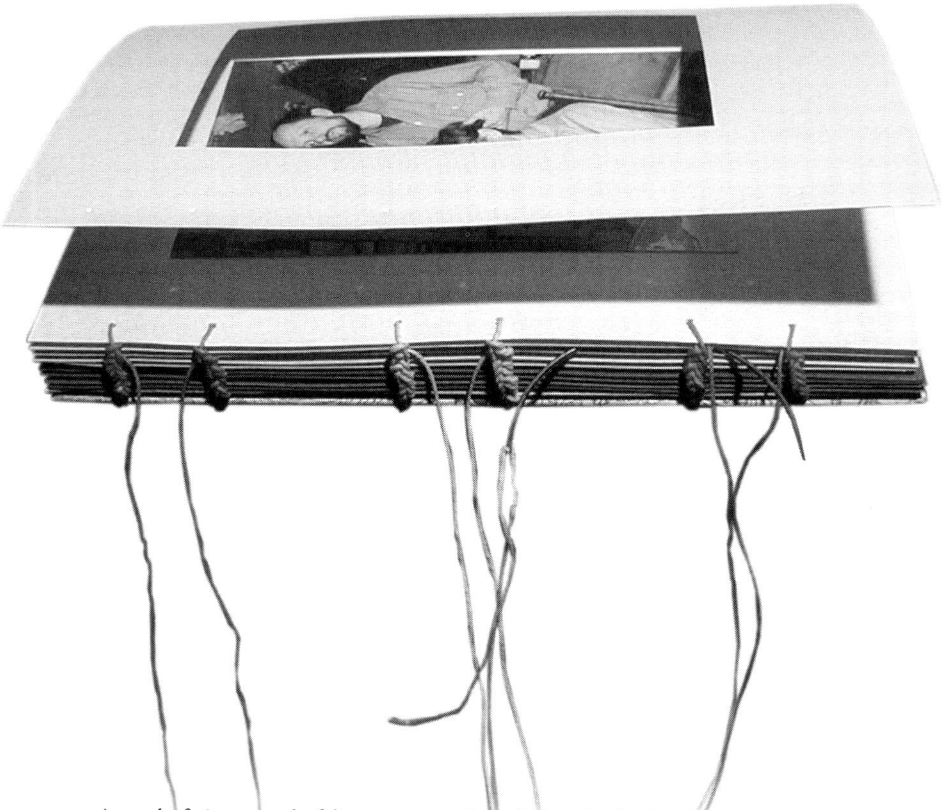

As on the facing page, the folios are sewn with the fold on the foredge. Here, the sewing is in progress. The last folio to be sewn in this photo is cut as a mat to protect the snapshot which is tipped in on the other part of the folio.

On the facing page, one folio has holes punched on one side of the folio. This casts light spots or shadows on the ply of the folio beneath.

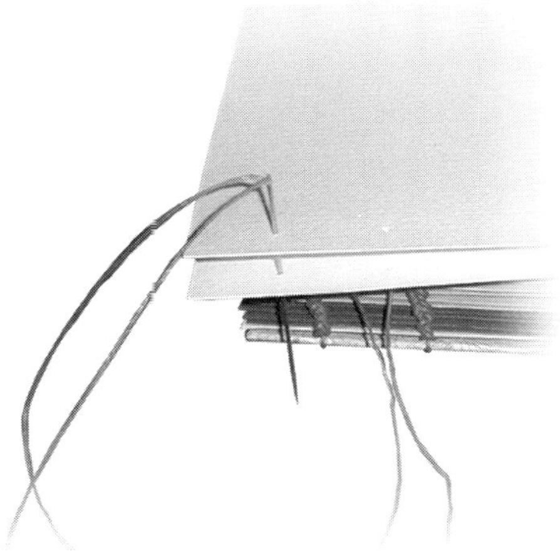

Attaching the folio with the fold on the foredge. In stab bindings, the book would not open flat, but with this approach to Coptic sewings, that problem is resolved.

Individual folios were sewn with the fold on the foredge. The sewing on the two spine–edges without any fold to sew into is a Single Sheet Coptic Sewing. *See* sewing the edges of folios, page 102.

FOLD–OUTS

For the artist making books, the fold–out, or throw–out, offers great potential. Visually, they are exciting. They offer the opportunity for a drawing which is wider or taller than a 2–page spread. They can be a thrown–down, or thrown–up, as well as thrown–out.

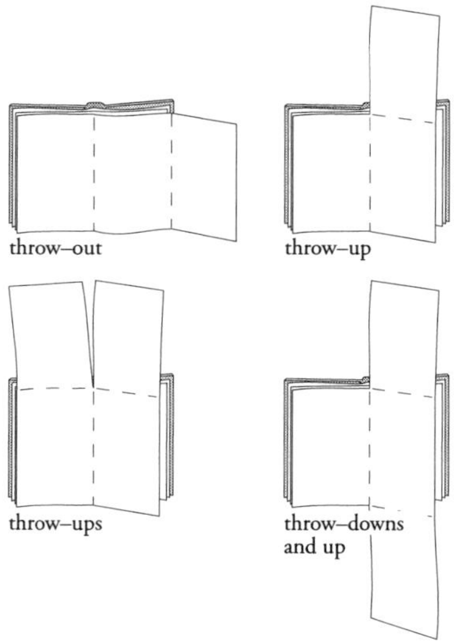

Structurally, they offer protection for prints, with a built–in mat, eliminating the need to insert a tissue over a print. See example 9, page 52.

Design–wise, they free the one–of–a–kind book from the rigidity of dry–mounting photographs onto a heavy page. The result is bulky. The emphasis is on the photograph, not on the composition of the page, the 2–page spread, or the book. This is discussed in *Structure of the Visual Book.*

Even though you are sewing single sheets, you may wish to have an occasional fold–out. You can add a fold–out to be sewn between any two sheets. Or, your entire book may consist of compiled fold–outs.

The most typical fold–out opens to an extra page beyond the foredge of the book. See example 2 on the facing page. Look at old books for examples that can suggest visual possibilities. For instance, an old geography book may have a map of the region as the final page, a right hand fold–out, at the end of a chapter. The first page of the chapter directs the reader to fold out the map, then return to the beginning of the chapter to read. The entire chapter is read with the map to the right of all the opened 2–page spreads.

Each chapter could be so designed. The fold–out may be a picture or text, seen in context with each 2–page spread of that chapter. Or, the fold–out may be part of a drawing. Each 2–page spread of that chapter may contain a partial picture, which is augmented or completed by the throw–out. There are endless possibilities for the fold–out, rather than the obvious — to house a big picture. The fold–out lends itself to the artists' book, to children's books, or even to poetry.

SEWING FOLD–OUTS: During sewing, each fold–out is opened only while it is sewn. It is closed before sewing the next fold–out or sheet. This insures the spine will be swollen to the thickness needed when the book is shelved. If a book of fold–outs were bound with the fold–outs extended, the spine would be a third to a half the required thickness. When the fold–outs would be closed, the foredge would bulge. See examples 3 and 6 below.

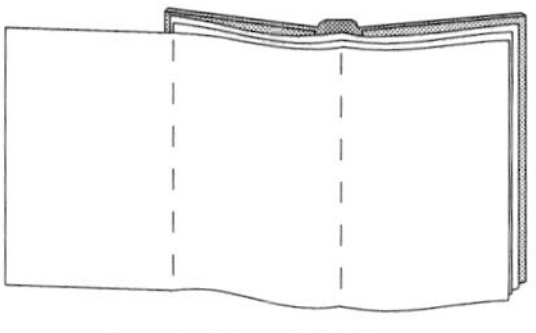

Example 1, left hand fold–out

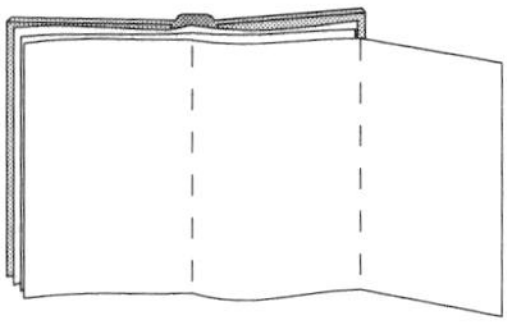

Example 2, right hand fold–out

Example 3

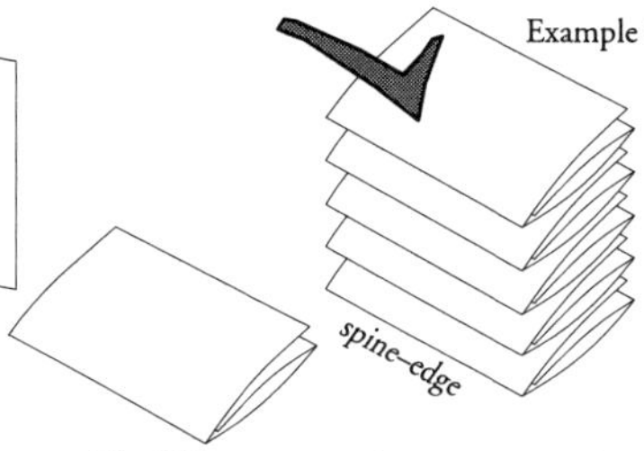

In examples 1 and 2 paper for the single page fold–out is folded into thirds the size of a page. The third which is the fold–out is trimmed slightly less wide to avoid the risk of creasing when folding in with each reading.

Examples 1–2: The fold–out is a single sewing unit. The book block can be sections with one or more fold–outs, or the entire book can be sewn with fold–outs.

Example 3: Close each fold–out after sewing, before sewing the next. This will make the foredge the same thickness as the spine. If sewn open and folded in after the book is bound, the foredge will bulge.

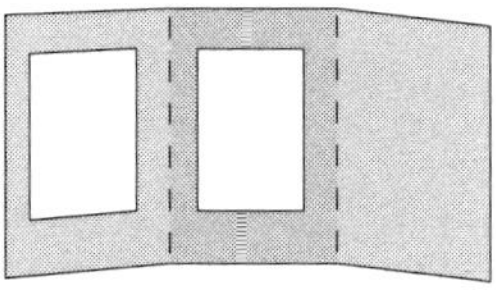

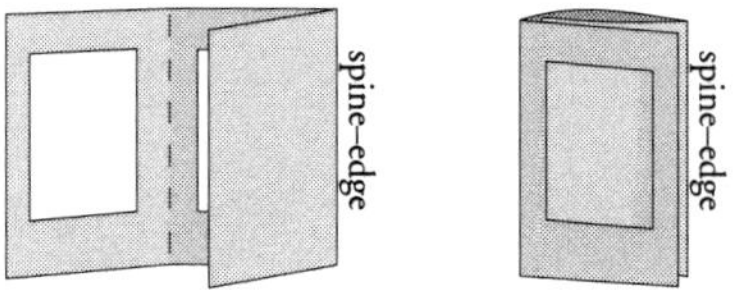

Example 4, variation on the left hand fold–out:
Window openings are cut in the left and center panels. The unit is sewn and closed before the next unit is sewn. Sewing occurs on the fold to the right, between the solid panel and the middle window.

Example 4, variation on the left hand fold–out, continued:
After the binding is completed, prints are tipped in on each side of the third panel. The unit is closed and glued shut with a thin bead of PVA glue. Do not use wheat paste; it will blister the pages.

The result is every recto/verso is a matted print. No tissues are needed to protect the prints.

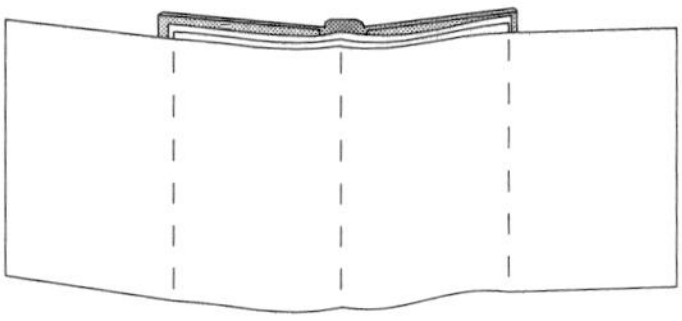

Example 5, gate fold, opened:
The gate fold throws out to the left and the right. The extreme panels, which are the throw–outs, must be trimmed slightly less wide than the middle panels to avoid the risk of creasing when the viewer closes them.

The entire book could be throw–outs, or all sections with one or more throw–outs.

Example 6, gate fold, closed:
While binding, open each gate fold only while it is being sewn. Close each before the next fold–out or section is sewn. This will give the needed depth to the spine.

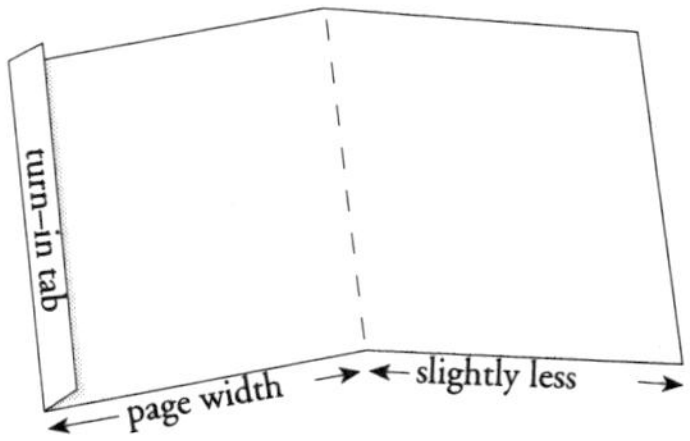

Example 7, fold–out with turn–in tab:
The fold–out with turn–in does not function as a fold–out. After the binding is completed a bead of PVA glue is applied to the turn–in tab. The extended panel is closed over the turn–in tab to be glued shut.

Purposes for this sewing unit is shown in examples 9 and 10.

Example 8, fold–out with turn–in tab, continued:
When sewing, the fold–out is closed over the tab before sewing the next unit. This will keep the foredge the same thickness as the spine. If sewn open and folded in after the book is bound, the foredge will bulge.

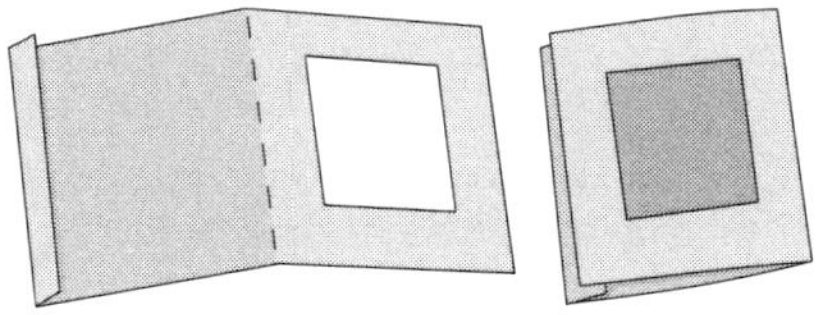

Example 9*A:*

Example 9*B,* fold–out with turn–in tab, continued:
The fold–out with turn–in protects a print on the recto with a printed or blank page on the verso. The tab swells the spine to accommodate the tipped–in print.

Example 9*C,* fold–out with turn–in tab, continued:
After the binding is completed, tip in the print before gluing the turn–in tab and closing the window. It is no longer a fold–out but a 2–ply page with a window protecting the print without the need for inserting tissues over the prints.

Example 10*A,* fold–out with turn–in tab, continued:
The fold–out with turn–in can be a photographic paper which will fold without cracking, such as *A* or *N* Surface paper, ideal for bleeds or printing around the foredge from the recto to the verso expanding design possibilities.

Example 10*B,* fold–out with turn–in tab, continued:
Mounted photos make stiff pages. Graphic design is confined to always having a paper border. The result is the photo is composed, but the page is not. Design of the *book* should take priority. The pictures should be subordinate.[5]

GATE FOLD: The *gate fold* is a fold–out with two facing fold–outs. See example 5, page 51. Each fold–out is hinged on the foredge of an opened folio. When the gate fold is opened, or thrown–out, there are four facing pages, the two at each extreme extend beyond the book block.

The gate fold is the height of a page and four times as wide. After it is folded, open the page flat. Trim the extended pages 1/8" less wide than the book block. When they are folded shut, the turn–ins will not quite meet in the gutter. This will prevent the vertical edge from being creased accidentally when the viewer closes the fold–out. You cannot rely upon each viewer taking care that you would in closing a fold–out. Painfully I have learned from experience. The trimming helps make the closing of fold–outs *fool–proof,* with the accent on the first syllable.

FOLD–OUT WITH TURN–IN: The fold–out with window protects prints, as in example 4, page 51 and example 9, page 52. In both instances, a thinner paper than normally used for the book block can be used since the fold–out will be glued shut along the gutter after the book is bound, creating a 2–ply page. Use a bead of PVA glue on the turn–in after the book is bound and any prints are tipped in. Do not laminate the entire foldout, but keep the glue limited to the small turn–in at the spine–edge.

The small turn–in has two purposes:

- It gives a fold into which to sew and the thread is hidden when the fold–out is closed.
- It is a spacer, adding thickness to the spine, to accommodate the print which later will be tipped in.

The fold–out with turn–in can be photographic paper. A few photo papers, such as *A Surface* and *N Surface,* as well as some photo mural papers, can take a crease without cracking the emulsion. The photographically printed fold–out is also glued shut along the turn–in after the book is bound. The result is a 2–ply page with a photo on each turning page, or, one photo which continues around the foredge, from recto to verso. This gives one solution to graphic design problems of making a one–of–a–kind photo book that is not bulky.

SEWING PREPARATION

Although the type and pattern of stitches vary with different bindings, all codex bindings have certain preparations and procedures in common.

SEWING STATIONS

The holes through which you sew are called *sewing stations* or *stations*.[6] All binding starts with pre–piercing or sawing the sewing stations. Piercing is done with a bradawl, bodkin or a pointed needle.

BRADAWL or *BODKIN:* An inexpensive bradawl is a ceramic tool. It can be made using a 1/4" wooden dowel and inserting a needle in the end, after removing the eye of the needle.

BRADAWL or *BINDER'S AWL:* A binder's awl has a removable point. A variety of points come with the wooden handle. Each point has a shaft, different in diameter. The point is chosen depending upon which size thread is used. The sewing station should be smaller in diameter than the needle used in sewing. The needle should slightly enlarge the station as you sew.

Do not use an awl designed for leather, as shown below. The shaft increases in diameter farther up from the point whereas a bradawl, bodkin and some binder's awls have a shaft constant in diameter.

Never use a leather awl to pierce sewing stations. You cannot control the size of the hole, or sewing station because of the graduated shaft.

BALL POINT NEEDLE: Sewing is with a binder's needle which is also called a ball–point needle, as it has no sharp point. A substitute is to use sand paper on a sharp needle to dull it.

A ball point needle cannot be used for piercing the paper. Pre–piercing the sewing stations, then sewing with a ball point needle permits speedy sewing, without the risk of accidentally scarring the paper, piercing an unwanted hole, or stabbing your finger. That said, I do not sew with a ball-point needle; I use a pointed darner's needle.

MARKING THE STATIONS

Cut all the paper to the same dimensions. This stack of sheets will be the book block. All single sheet sewings have the book block flush with the spine-edge of the boards.

OVERHANG FOR COPTIC SEWINGS: Cut the two cover boards with a slight overhang at the foredge. If the single sheet sewing is a Coptic, do not have an overhang at the head and tail. Sitting on the shelf the book block will sag down since all Coptics are unsupported sewings.

OVERHANG FOR SEWING ONTO TAPES: Cut the boards with a slight overhang at the foredge, head and tail.

STENCIL FOR MARKING THE STATIONS: Take one of the sheets for the book block, or a scrap paper of the same dimensions. Draw a thin pencil line 3/8" to 1/2" in from, and parallel to, the spine–edge. Determine how many pierced sewing stations are needed. This will be described in the introductions to the Coptics and Sewing Onto Tapes.

Mark the stations along the drawn pencil line. Place the stencil on top of three or four or no more than a half dozen of the sheets to be sewn. Jog the stack. Place the spine–edge of this stack about 1/2" to 5/8" off the edge of the table. Pierce the holes with a bradawl or bodkin. Pierce the remainder of the book block in the same manner.

After the boards are covered, place the stencil on the *inside* of the back cover. Pierce the board. Place the stencil on the *outside* of the front cover. Pierce.

THREAD

Archival materials should be used. Linen thread is generally considered to have more strength and longevity than cotton.

Non–traditional sewings might use any unusual linear substance. Plastic fishing line is strong and will last, but risks ripping the paper. After knots are tied, they would have to be fused with a match. Although these substitutes have a nice unusual appearance, they do not function as well as cotton or linen thread.

Binding suppliers sell unbleached and unwaxed linen thread. It is important that the thread be unbleached so that it will not rot. Craft stores often handle spools of pre–waxed linen thread in various colors. No list of suppliers is included in this book. I do not wish to favor some stores over others.

WAXING THE THREAD: Thread should be waxed prior to sewing. Waxed thread is stiffer and will become less tangled as you sew. Stitches will tend to cling in position, remaining tighter during sewing. The main reason for waxing the thread is not for convenience, but archival. After sewing, turning pages will have less friction and the book will wear better.

To wax the thread, run an arm's length of thread across the edge of a cake of beeswax. Speed is more important than pressure. It will create friction, melting the wax onto the thread. Run the length of cut thread two or three times across the wax until it is a little stiff.

THREADING THE NEEDLE: Use as small a needle as you are able to thread. Too large a needle will create larger holes in the paper than the thread can fill.

Sewing is usually done with a single thread, rather than centering the needle on the length of thread and making double threads as the stitches. Cut about an arm's length of thread. Less requires too many knots during the sewing. More is difficult to handle.

It would be awkward and time consuming pulling this entire length through the sewing stations. Thread the needle, pulling a little more than a third of the thread through the needle. This will cut the distance the thread must be pulled through the sewing stations almost in half, without giving a double thread stitch. As more and more thread is used up in the sewing, adjust the needle closer to the loose end of the thread, so that the stitches are not of double thread.

KNOTS

If you are clipping a thread after a knot is tied, clip the loose ends to about 3/4". Do not clip close to the knot to get rid of the loose ends, thinking they are unsightly. The knot might work itself loose and the sewing will come untied. Do not be ashamed of hand–tied knots. They are evidence of the individual and should not be down played. Such irregularities are part of the craft of hand–binding.

There are several knots used in binding: the *overhand K, square knot* or *reef knot;* the *slip knot,* also known as a *running K;* and the *weaver's knot.*

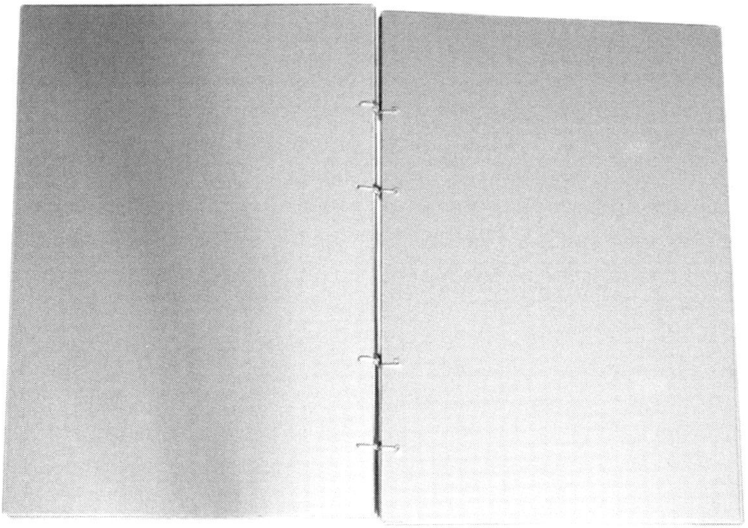

IDEAL PHOTO BOOK: Sheets of mat board sewn as any of the Coptics described in this manual make an ideal presentation for photographs. The thread is recessed in the board as described on page 44. Prints are then adhered to the boards after the book is sewn. The book opens flat to any page. The prints cover the entire page. The thread is seen only on the spine of the closed book, page 133, and in the gutter of the opened two page spread.

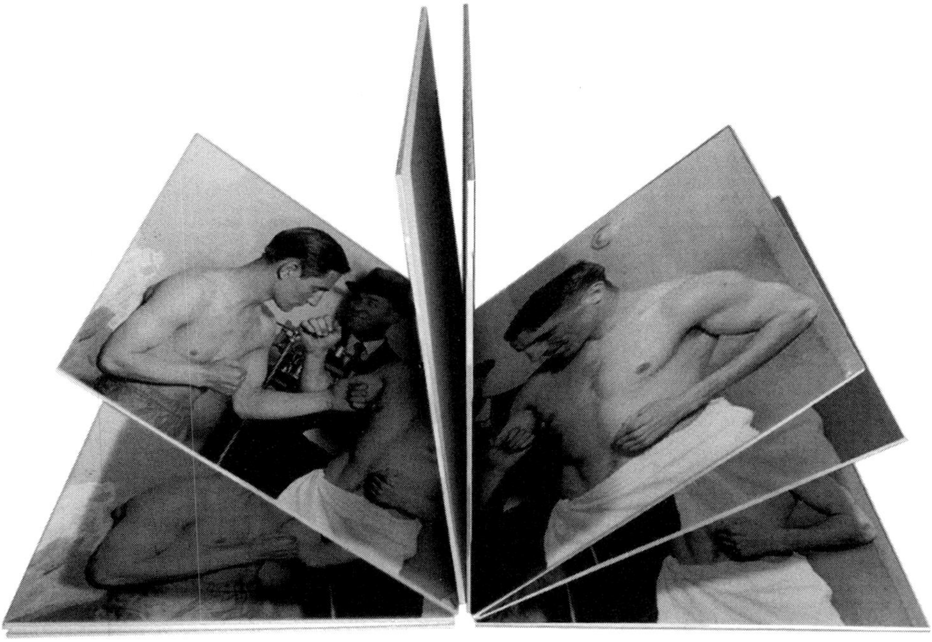

PROCEDURE FOR TYING AN OVERHAND K: Grasp one loose end of the thread with your left hand with an inch of thread extended from your grip. This will be referred to as the left thread. Grasp the other end with your right hand in the same manner. Lay the left thread over the top of the right. Hold this into position with your left thumb and forefinger. Take your right forefinger and push the left thread under and around the right, through the loop. Both loose ends are now pointing upward. Tighten the knot. This configuration is known as the *overhand knot.*

PROCEDURE FOR TYING A SQUARE KNOT: The *square knot* is also known as the *reef* and as the *flat* K.

First, form an overhand *K* by laying the left thread over the top of the right. Take your right forefinger and push the left thread under and around the right thread, through the loop. Tighten.

Second, go through this procedure for a second time, but this time in reverse, or symmetrically:

Lay the right thread over the top of the left. Take your left forefinger and push the right thread under and around the left thread, through the loop. Tighten. When it is tied, this is a single *square knot.* It looks square, also, when it is tightened as shown above.

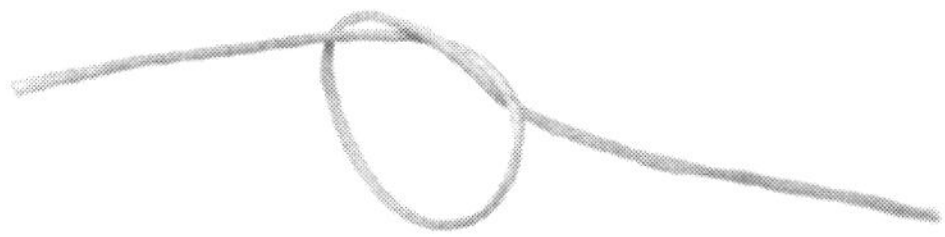

OVERHAND K

loosely tied square knot

tightening the square knot

tightening the square knot

tightened square knot

REEF, SQUARE KNOT, or FLAT *K*
This knot is commonly called a *square knot* in the States. In Australia, it is known as the *reef knot.*

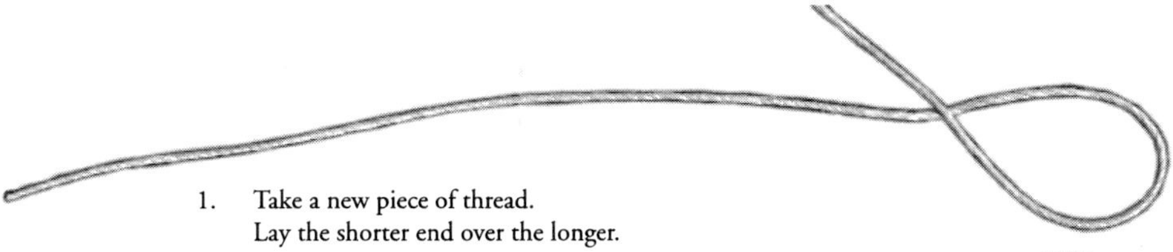

1. Take a new piece of thread.
   Lay the shorter end over the longer.

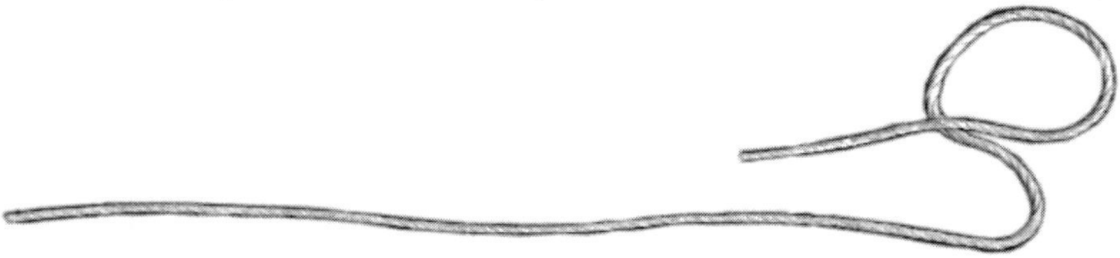

2. Bend the longer thread, close to the loop.

3. Push the longer thread over the loop.

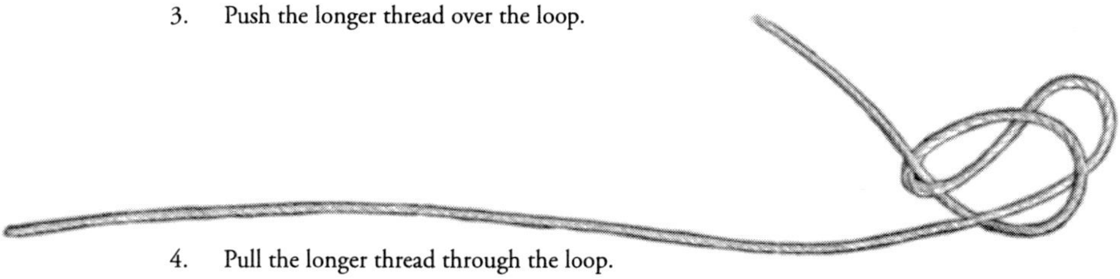

4. Pull the longer thread through the loop.

5. Tighten the knot, not the loop, but not too tight.

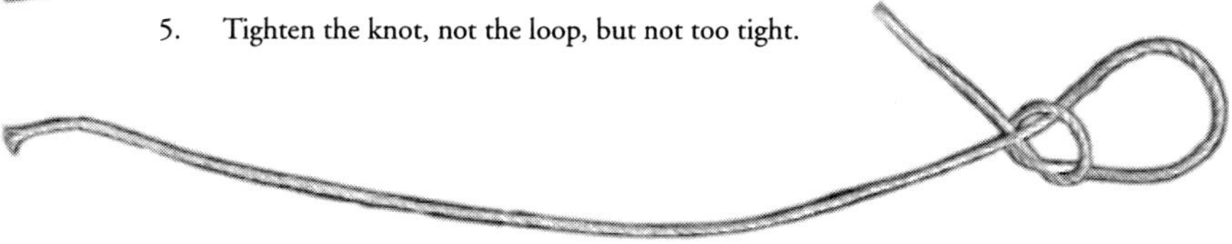

6. Continue to tighten the knot, but not too tight. It will be tightened completely when forming the *weaver's knot.*
   Adjust the size of the loop to about the diameter of a pencil.

SLIP KNOT: Above are the steps in tying a *slip knot.* It is used to form a *weaver's knot,* described on pages 61–64 . Scale: 1:1, #12 thread.

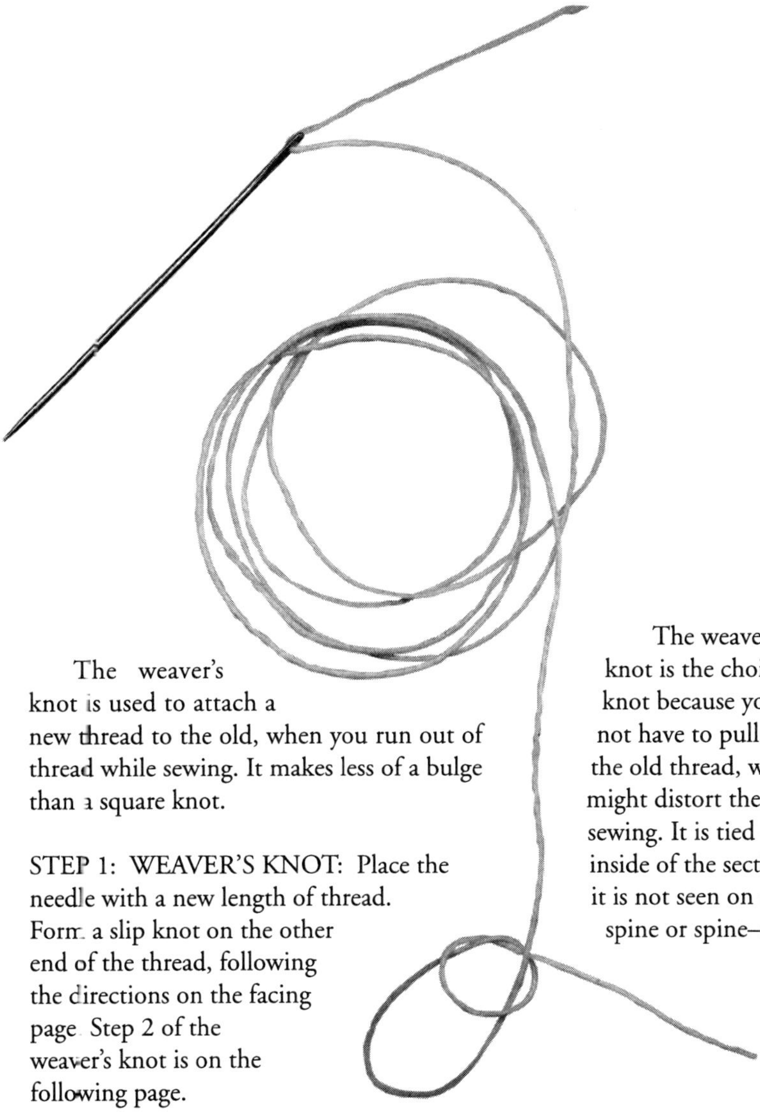

The weaver's knot is used to attach a new thread to the old, when you run out of thread while sewing. It makes less of a bulge than a square knot.

STEP 1: WEAVER'S KNOT: Place the needle with a new length of thread. Form a slip knot on the other end of the thread, following the directions on the facing page. Step 2 of the weaver's knot is on the following page.

The weaver's knot is the choice of knot because you do not have to pull on the old thread, which might distort the sewing. It is tied on the inside of the section, so it is not seen on the spine or spine–cover.

1. To form the weaver's knot, thread the needle. On the other end, form a slip knot, as on page 61.
2. It is important to slip the loop of the new thread over the old thread. Do not slip the old thread though the knot of the slip knot.

   The loop and the knot will be a little smaller than shown in Step 2.
3. Pull the new thread until the knot is very small, but not tight. Adjust the loop until it, too, is small.

   Move the slip knot onto the old thread, illustrated as darker for clarity, to the position you wish to tie the weaver's knot.
4. Tighten the knot by pulling on both ends of the new thread. Pull in opposite directions to tighten. When you have tightened sufficiently, you will feel a slight click when it locks.

   Do not pull on the *old* thread. This will loosen the loop and the new thread will slip off.

   Pull on the old thread only to untie the weaver's knot. To test if the knot is secure, tug on the *new* thread. If it slips off, you did not tighten enough in Step 4.

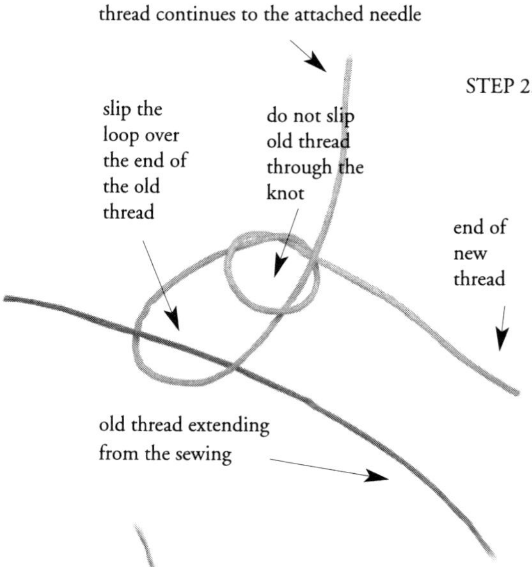

STEP 2.

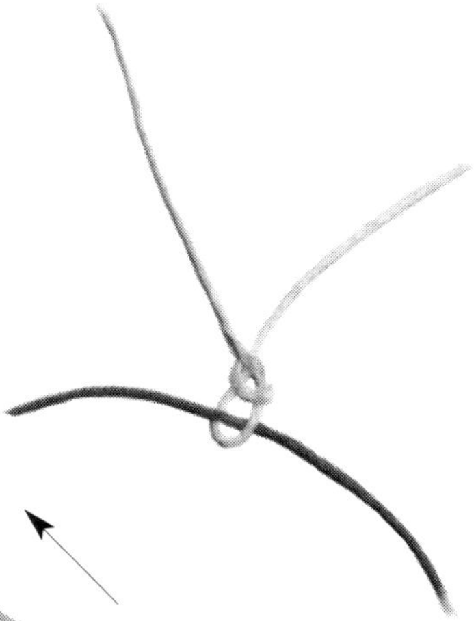

STEP 3.

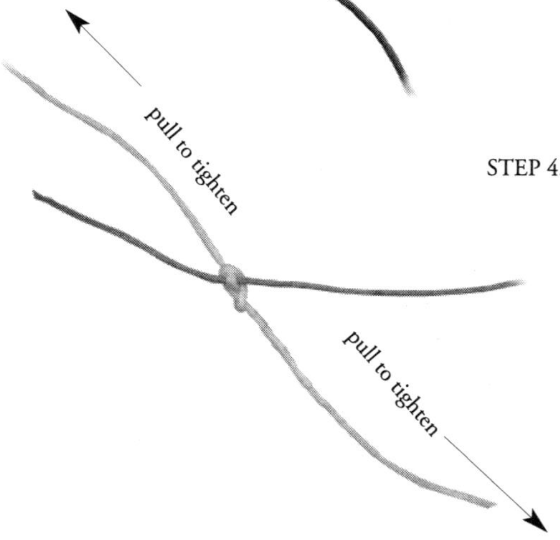

STEP 4.

NOTE: The two views of the weaver's knot shown on this page have not yet been tightened, so that you can see the formation. If you left the knot like this, without tightening it, the new thread would slip through.

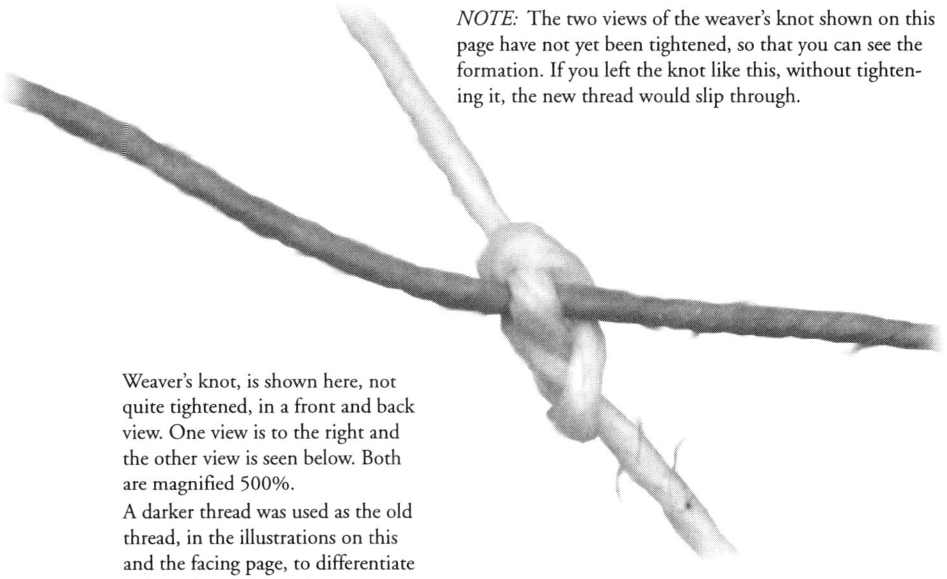

Weaver's knot, is shown here, not quite tightened, in a front and back view. One view is to the right and the other view is seen below. Both are magnified 500%.

A darker thread was used as the old thread, in the illustrations on this and the facing page, to differentiate it from the new thread.

The old thread through the loop of a slip knot, plus the slip knot, once tightened, forms the weaver's knot.

Tightened weaver's knot shown on the following page.

WEAVER'S KNOT, tightened, front and back views. The digital image of the knot was magnified to 500% for easy viewing. The new thread is the lighter color. The darker thread is the old thread.

HALF HITCH: The final knot needed is the half hitch. In completing a sewing, you cannot always tie a square knot, because you have only one loose end of thread. Since all the sewings in this book have exposed spines, the best tie–off is in from the spine–edge at the hole on the sheet. This prevents a lump of a knot and a dangling thread on the spine. Loop around the stitch on the sheet as shown on the facing page. Below is a half hitch inside a *section*.

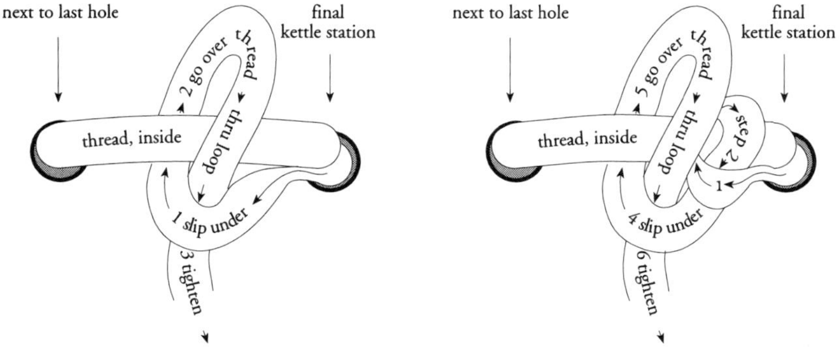

HALF HITCH USED INSIDE A SECTION: At the left are the first steps. These are repeated, as shown on the right. The half hitch is the best way to tie–off when sewing sections when there is only one loose end of thread.

HALF HITCH FOR SINGLE SHEET COPTIC SEWINGS

This half hitch variation is for Single Sheet Coptics and Sewing Single Sheets as Raised Cord. For position of the half hitch for Sewing Single Sheets onto Tapes, see page 66.

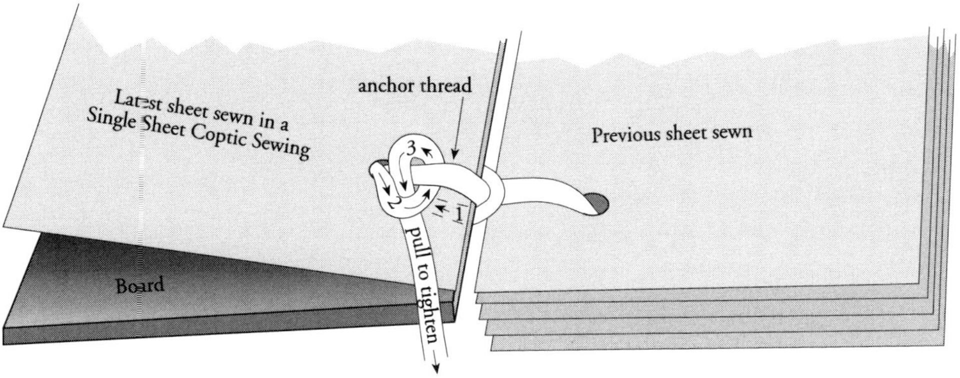

HALF HITCH USED FOR SINGLE SHEET COPTIC SEWINGS: The first step is to proceed between the cover and the final sheet. Go through the hole to the other side of the final sheet. The *connecting thread* on the final sheet, or the sheet where the knot will be tied will be the *anchor thread*.

STEP 2: Slip under the anchor thread and pull until there is a small loop.

STEP 3: Go through the loop and pull to tighten. Pull down and toward the hole so the knot forms at the hole.

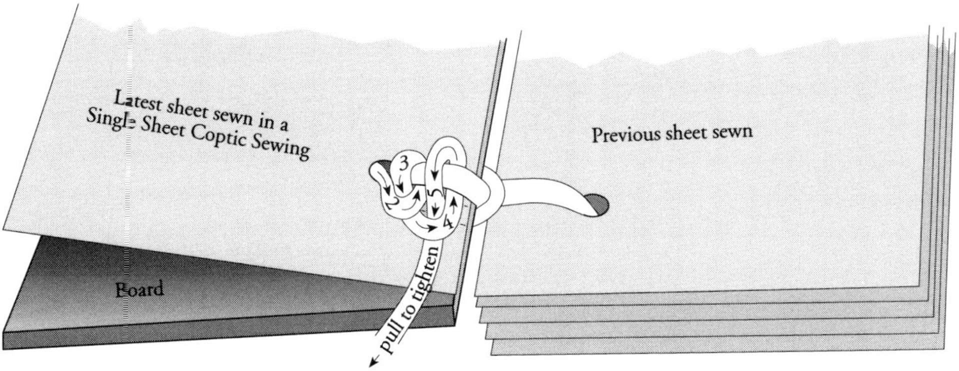

HALF HITCH USED FOR SINGLE SHEET COPTIC SEWINGS continued:

STEP 4: Slip under the anchor thread, again. Pull until there is a small loop.

STEP 5: Go through this loop and pull to tighten in a downward motion and toward the hole so the knot forms at the hole. This knot finishes the sewing.

HALF HITCH FOR SEWING SINGLE SHEETS ONTO TAPES

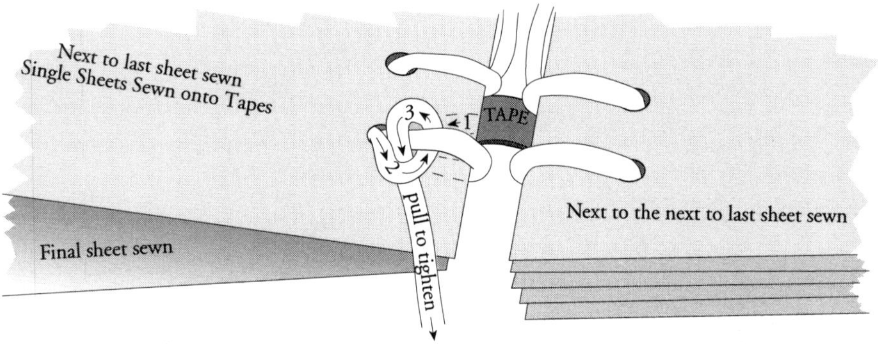

HALF HITCH USED FOR SINGLE SHEETS SEWN ONTO TAPES: The first step is to proceed between the final and next to last sheet. Go through the hole to the other side of the next to last sheet. The thread which connects the final sheet will be the anchor thread.

STEP 2: Slip under the anchor thread and pull until there is a small loop.

STEP 3: Go through the loop and pull to tighten. Pull down and toward the hole so the knot forms at the hole.

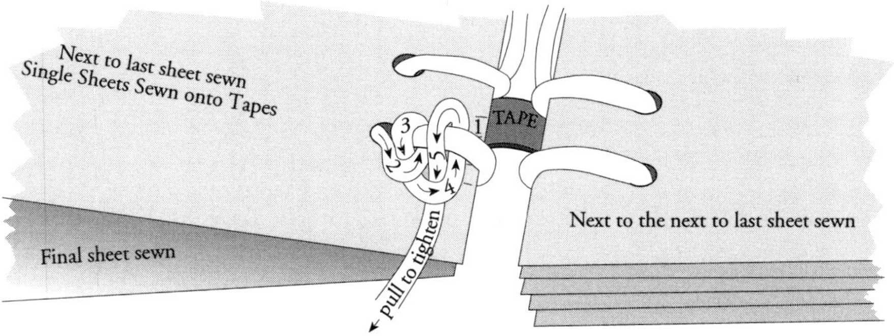

HALF HITCH USED FOR SINGLE SHEETS SEWN ONTO TAPES continued:

STEP 4: Slip under the anchor thread, again. Pull until there is a small loop.

STEP 5: Go through this loop and pull to tighten in a downward motion and toward the hole so the knot forms at the hole. The sewing is completed with this knot.

SEWING ON THE BENCH

Placing the book on a table, or on a sewing frame to sew, is referred to as *sewing on the bench.* This leaves both hands free to sew.

All the instructions and illustrations herein are described for sewing the sheets on the bench. None of the bindings require the use of a sewing frame.

In this manual, for uniformity, all sewings will be described sewing from the head to the tail. The "first" sheet refers to the first to be sewn whether it is the first in the book or the final sheet.

TENSION IN SEWING

Tension must be correct in degree and uniform throughout. Sewing must not be too loose or too tight. Stitches should be uniform in size and shape. To achieve this, it is best to sew the book at one sitting without a break.

Rebecca Goodale, *Four Maine Turtles,* 2000. One–of–a–kind fold book. 30 x 30 x 120 cm. "Silkscreen prints with collage and hand coloring. The accordion is all book board panels bound in red book cloth on the outside. Inside hinges are also red book cloth. Prints mounted on the inside panels. I made this one accordion book with the four turtles listed as threatened and endangered in the State of Maine." — Rebecca Goodale.

PROPORTION ON THE BOARD

Separate boards are used in the bindings described in this book. Width of quarter leather or cloth at the spine–edge can be quite varied.

MEASURING THE WIDTH: You may wish to butt or overlap the decorative paper to the quarter leather or quarter cloth. If you wish the decorative paper to overlap the leather, allow approximately 1/4" of the leather to be covered. Therefore, add 1/4" to the measurement of the paper to obtain the complete width of the quarter leather.

Proportion of a quarter covering to paper depends upon your aesthetics; it's a visual, not a mathematical decision. Some prefer the quarter leather to appear as just a thin strip along the spine–edge and/or foredge. It is important that the leather extend at least 1/2" onto the front of the board so that it is securely attached. Only a fraction of this leather need be seen if you wish to overlap most of it with the decorative paper.

The boards will appear almost completely covered with paper, as in the example on the far left at the bottom of this page. (Actually, there will be more leather on the boards than is seen since the paper overlaps the leather.)

Others take the term *quarter leather* literally and extend it 1/4 the way across the boards. This often appears heavy, depending upon the color and texture of the leather and the colors and design of the paper.

Paper overlaps leather here by 1/2". Otherwise the leather would not be securely attached to the boards.

A narrow strip of leather is elegant.

This is an average proportion of leather to paper for a quarter binding.

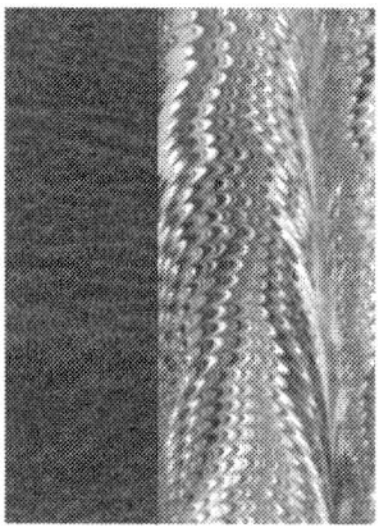

This is a rather wide amount of leather to paper, but some prefer it.

Proportion of quarter cloth or leather to paper on the boards is an aesthetic decision.

ARCHIVAL MATERIALS

All materials should be acid–free. If you take time to hand bind a book there should never be any compromise on materials. One way to insure your materials are safe is to ask your binders supply if they handle only materials which they have tested and declared archival. Most fine suppliers meet this standard. Most marblers use safe pigments with lasting colors and archival paper. Ask before you buy.

BOOK BOARD: Very few book boards are archival. You should ask the supplier. For all bindings in this book I suggest 4–ply rag mat board.

LEATHER: Use a good bookbinding leather. The leather should be 1 millimeter or less in thickness, preferably on the thinner side. Leather is available from binding suppliers that is tanned for bookbinding. Chrome–tanned leather will rot in a relatively short time just sitting on a shelf, without any use. Beware of buying any leather from a craft store, but rather, from a bookbinding supplier.

PVA GLUE: Most PVA glues, poly vinyl acetate, sold in hardware stores and even some sold in art stores are not *pH*–neutral.[7] Archival PVA glues can be purchased at a binders supply.

The term *archival* encompasses other elements besides whether the material is *pH*–neutral. Many conservators do not consider any PVA as "archival" because the process is not reversible. Once applied to paper, it is not easily removed. It is plastic, bonding to the surface.

NO COMMERCIAL PASTE MIXTURE: Never buy commercial wheat paste, even from an art supply store. The majority of it contains additives to keep the bugs away and to stop it from spoiling. You do not wish to purchase a wheat paste mixture that contains additives when it serves no purpose in making paste and renders your work non–archival.

In addition, the commercial mixture will be marked up 10 to 100 times the price of pastry flour.

Do not use wallpaper paste. It is acidic.

Tests for Acidity

You can perform your own tests for acidity on materials with an Abbey *pH* Pen. Touch it to the surface. If the dot turns purple, the paper is neutral or alkaline (*pH* 6.8 or higher).

GLUE & PASTE

GLUE

The only gluing or pasting for bindings described in this book is for attaching decorative papers to the boards. Paste would be better than glue.

For certain jobs, PVA, or poly vinyl acetate, is ideal because it goes on easily, sets almost instantly and dries in five minutes. A good example is in gluing tapes to the board. Hot glue would be difficult. Paste would be impossible, as it does not have the viscosity to stick and requires saturating the surfaces to adhere

One of the drawbacks of PVA is that the brush must be washed at once, or it will be ruined. Hot glue is more forgiving. The brush is left in the glue pot when you are through. The glue pot is turned off. As the temperature lowers in the pot and the cooking smell lessens, the hot glue solidifies and the tip of the brush is laminated in the solid mass. Turning on the pot and heating it up for the next use, the brush is ready to use. Wheat paste causes no problems when accidentally allowed to dry in the brush. Soak it a minute or so and the wheat paste dissolves.

PVA will stain paper if it creeps around to the front surface. It will seep through unsized fabric and leave stains. Wheat paste does not stain fabric or paper. It may on occasion change the tone of black paper if it is spilled on the surface.

PVA is not recommended to attach paper to the boards. Wheat paste is superior because it handles better. See description on the following page.

Hot glue will not be used in any bindings in this manual to eliminate the expense of a glue pot.

CARE OF GLUE BRUSHES: Some place their PVA glue brush in a glass of water when not gluing for a few minutes. The brush is stiff and will not curl and become misshapen like a water color brush. Still, it has to be dried before using PVA again. I think it is better to simply clean it after each use. Even when I am gluing continually, I wash the brush periodically so the glue will not dry at the top of the bristles.

Always wash brushes in cold water. The bristles are attached with adhesive that could melt in hot water. Dry the brush, shape it and store it standing, bristles up, so there is no pressure from the bristles pressed against a surface. The brush would become misshapen.

Plan ahead. Suppliers do not ship PVA in winter, as it must be kept from freezing.

PASTE

Wheat paste is one of many pastes. Some binders make rice paste. Many binders use methyl cellulose and it is considered archival. However, methyl cellulose has no long term record. No one can be certain how it will hold up in time, since it is has only been used for the past few years. Wheat paste is centuries old and can be trusted.

TYPE OF FLOUR: Use only pastry flour. Flour and water form paste. What makes it stick is the gluten in the flour. An all–purpose flour has more gluten than pastry flour, so it has more viscosity. The reason it is not used to make wheat paste s that gluten also attracts bugs while your book sits on the shelf. You want to use a flour with the least amount of gluten yet enough to make the two surfaces adhere, but no more than necessary.

Pastry flour is not the same as cake flour nor bread flour. Pastry flour can be found in some supermarkets; it is available in almost all health food stores.

In Tasmania, Penny Carey–Wells introduced me to tapioca flour. This makes a fine paste, clearer and more gelatin–like than pastry flour.

MAKING PASTE

Wheat paste is one of those elements in a process that is a joy. Preparation of the paste is quick, it is simple to use, it doesn't stain fabric or papers, it does not smell, it cleans up easily and it isn't toxic. You could eat it if you like. In fact, if you added an egg and a teaspoon of vanilla extract to the formula, you would have vanilla pudding.

This formula is from Bernard Middleton:

STOVE–TOP WHEAT PASTE FORMULA

1 part PASTRY FLOUR
4 1/2 parts COLD WATER

Combine flour and water with a whisk. Stir out all lumps. Place over low heat. Stir without interruption until the first bubble appears as it starts to boil. Stir 30 seconds longer, If you cook less, it may not thicken. If you cook more than 30 seconds after it starts to boil, it will be rubbery. Remove from heat. Pour in jar, add lid, refrigerate.

If you start with 1/2 cup white pastry flour, add 2 1/4 cups cold water. This makes quite a bit of paste. You may want to start with half this amount.

STOVE–TOP COOKING PASTE: The recipe on the facing page cooks on the stove. Use low to medium heat, watching carefully, so it does not burn on bottom. If you fail to stir constantly, or have too high heat, it will scorch. The best results, like any cooking, are easier with a good gourmet saucepan which distributes the heat evenly. A good pan can cook the paste in half the time of a beat–up aluminum pan. Start to finish is about two minutes.

MICROWAVE PASTE: When Scott McCarney and I give workshops together, sometimes we find someone who has experimented with microwaving wheat paste. Many more times, people ask us if they can microwave rather than cook wheat paste. So Scott has played around with it. Below is his no-cook for non–cooks formula.

PASTING TIPS

I cook paste. If I am going to paste that day, I can take out the pastry flour, measure, cook and within three minutes be pasting. The paste will be warm, but it will stick. You do not have to wait until the paste is cold to use it.

SURFACE FOR PASTING: It always amazes me when I give a workshop at a book center and their general practice is to paste on scraps of paper. This is because that is the traditional way of doing it.

I find it is difficult to tell if the paper is clean. Some students invariably lay the book right in wet paste. Pasting on papers clutters and makes a disorderly work area. The practice is wasteful.

Pasting is so much easier when done on a glass or formica surface and it does not waste paper. Clean up is easier too.

MICROWAVE WHEAT PASTE

1/4 cup PASTRY FLOUR
1 cup COLD WATER

Thoroughly mix 1/4 cup flour into 1/4 cup cold water. Remove all lumps. Set aside.

Place 3/4 cup water in microwave. Bring to boil. Remove. Slowly pour flour/water mixture into the boiling water, stirring constantly. It should thicken up. Place paste in microwave for approximately 30 seconds if it needs to thicken more.

Pour in jar, add lid, refrigerate.

I paste on my light table. If I want to line up a patterned paper onto the board, I lay the board on the light table after the paper is pasted. The light table is turned on and the pasted paper is held slightly above the board.

Looking through the translucent paper allows the design to be lined up on the board beneath. Hold the paper by opposite corners for better accuracy. Lower the paper into position and tap it down with your fingers. Pick up the board and clip the corners and make the turn–ins on the inside of the board.

I keep a towel on my shoulder as I am pasting. I can dry my hands quickly to handle the decorative paper or answer the phone. I don't have to look for the towel after sponging the glass surface.

Immediately after pasting and covering the board, the glass or formica table top is sponged off and dried with a towel. It is immaculate, dry and ready to paste the next papers. There are no scraps of paste–soaked papers laying around. There is no mess that encourages accidents to happen. It is orderly and makes the job of pasting so much easier.

AMOUNT OF TIME TO PASTE

Pasting times vary with each paper. Newsprint would require 20 seconds of pasting. Typewriter paper would be about 30 seconds. The 80 lb. text weight paper used in printing this manual requires 90 to 120 seconds. Rives BFK heavyweight would require four to five minutes.

In workshops, I invariably find many students are impatient. They will not paste the required time, even though it has been pointed out that each paper has a different thickness and absorbency rate determined by its density.

There is a simple test as to when you have pasted long enough: You start to paste, the paper will start to curl. As you continue to paste, the curling will cease and the paper has relaxed, flat on the surface. It is ready. *Never paste blotters.* Use PVA to attach blotters to the board.

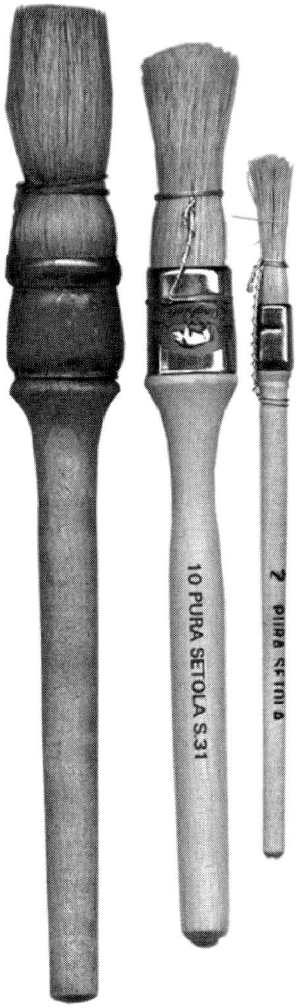

Various size glue brushes. It would be good to have a small and a large brush for pasting.

PASTING PROCEDURE

Apply the paste in very thin coats. The surface of paper being pasted must be kept continuously wet, if not pasted continually. By continually pasting until the paper is saturated with paste, you will insure no area of the paper goes dry. As paste is applied to the surface, it is drawn into the paper like a sponge. This could leave areas of the surface without paste, especially the thinner areas caused by brush strokes.

If the surface of the paper is not saturated when you apply the paper to the board, the pasted paper will continue to absorb the paste. The board will absorb even more of the paste, leaving little to no paste in some areas. Blisters will occur where the paper has not stuck to the board.

PASTING PAPER: Hold down the center of the paper on a clean dry surface with a couple fingers, as you start to paste. Use a brush appropriate to the size of the paper so you do not waste strokes.

Strokes should be from the center, out beyond the paper. Brush in a radiating manner. Lift your fingers to finish pasting the paper. Do not brush from the surface onto the paper, or you may push paste under, to the front side of the paper. As soon as the paper stops curling it will start to relax to a flat sheet.

Do not over–compensate with excessive application of paste. It is not how much you pile up paste but an even and very thin layer of paste on the surface. If the paste was over–cooked and is too thick and rubbery, thin out the paste by misting the jar of paste with water; do not mist directly onto the paper.

PASTING LEATHER: Leather can be glued, rather than pasted, to the boards. That sounds like a travesty to bookbinders in this country, but I found in Australia and New Zealand it is a common practice.

Pasting leather requires several minutes. Test to see when the leather is ready to cover the board by lifting a corner to examine the good surface. If the leather is totally wet it has absorbed enough paste to saturate it. Apply the leather to the board.

If your leather is a light color, mist the good side of the leather prior to pasting to prevent capillary action permitting paste to come through mottled. The disadvantage is you cannot test when enough pasting has been done. You must rely upon experience.

After attaching let leather or cloth dry completely before pasting and adding decorative papers. This can take hours. Place scrap cardboard on each side of the unattached board and dry the leather or cloth under the weight of approximately three books.

COVERING THE BOARDS IN A SINGLE SESSION: Gluing rather than pasting leather permits covering the boards in a single session. The leather does not have to dry for hours before the decorative papers can be pasted and applied to the boards. Gluing the leather also eliminates the need for a press or drying the boards under weight.

WARPAGE FROM GRAIN

It is important to keep the grain of the papers, blotter filler if any, as well as the grain of the board, parallel with the spine. *See* grain of paper, page 37.

WARPAGE FROM TENSION

There must be a counter–balance of tension on each side of a pasted board. Paper, leather and some cloth will pull when they dry. When they are pasted, they expand in one direction, perpendicular to the grain. When they dry, they contract.Warpage from tension is referred to as the *pull factor.*

PERPENDICULAR TO THE GRAIN: Paper expands perpendicular to the grain: When it is pasted to the board with the grain parallel with the spine it will expand side to side, not top to bottom.

The pull factor requires the same weight of paper must be used on each side of the board to counter–balance the pull in order to prevent the board from warping. This is not always true. Handmade paper has no grain and thus, no pull factor. If a handmade paper covers the outside of the board and a commercial paper is used on the inside, the pull from the commercial paper will warp the board. Even if the handmade paper is thick and the commercial paper is thin, the tension is not counter–balanced.

However, if you are using only commercial papers and no paper is extremely low in pull factor, weight of the paper is the main way to determine how much each will pull. A heavier paper usually pulls more than a thinner one.

If one side of the board is covered with a heavier paper, usually it will warp the board in that direction. To prevent this, first paste an additional thin sheet of paper on the other side of the board. This additional sheet is white and pasted down first. The additional sheet of paper is the size of the bare board to be covered, but does not extend around to other side of the board. Then proceed with the instructions for covering boards. The steps in pasting papers are described in the chapter, *Covering the Boards,* page 83.

The two thin sheets should equal and thus counter–balance the pull of the one heavier sheet on the other side of the board.

With experience you will find some heavier papers which have surprisingly little pull.

The other side of the board must be covered with the same paper or a thinner paper which will have the same amount of pull. No amount of time leaving the board in a press will prevent the board from warping later on if you have covered the two sides of the boards with materials which have different pull factors. The cover will come out of the press flat. As soon as the humidity rises, the boards will warp.

WARPAGE FROM DELAYS

If you are covering both sides of the boards in a single session you must work quickly, but not in a rush. You cannot be interrupted by the telephone or doorbell.

FINISH ONE BOARD BEFORE STARTING THE SECOND: Pasting decorative paper onto the boards requires attaching pasted paper to the outside and the inside of one board before attaching pasted paper to the other board.

If you were to attach the front paper to both boards, then paste and attach the paste–down on the inside of both boards. By the time you get around to attaching the paste–downs, moisture from the paper on one side only will cause the board to start warping. If you are using thin book board, this warpage will be an extreme arc.

You will have to add the paste–down on the other side of the board, which will have an extreme arcing curve to it. This will stretch the paste–down over the arc. As the paste–down starts to counter–balance warpage, the board will flatten, distorting the paste–down with wrinkles or blistering.

Covering both sides of the board in a single session requires all the papers to be pre–cut. Papers for both sides of one board must be pasted at the same time. If you pasted paper(s) for one side of the board and attached it, the board would warp while you are pasting the paper for the other side.

Lay out the papers needed to cover both sides of one board on your pasting surface. Be sure you have the board, scissors, bone folder, paste, towel and water mister on hand prior to wetting the paper so you will not have to interrupt pasting. For other factors in warpage, *see* grain of paper, page 37.

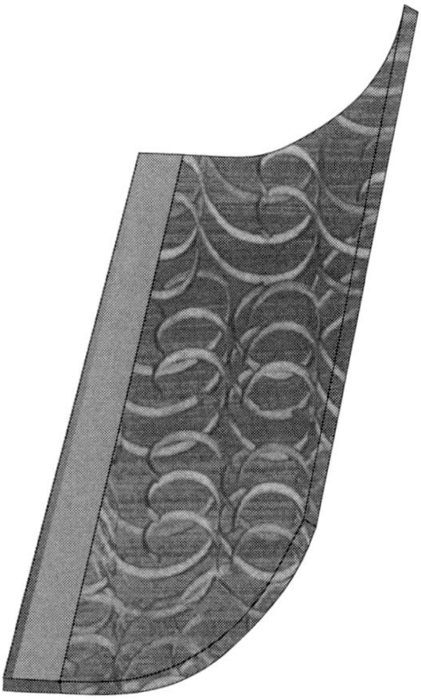

Unless the paste–down is applied immediately to the back side of the book board, the papers and cloth on the front will drastically warp the board. Grain of the paper will distort the boards, making it impossible to add the paste–down.
Boards do not have to be dried under weight to avoid the pull factor, as long as you cover both sides at once.

DOUBLURES vs ENDSHEET PASTE–DOWNS: A doublure, or island paste–down, on the inside of the boards is always used when covering separate board covers. It can involve elaborate layering of papers in a kind of collage. Surface of the papers does not have to be on one level as on the outside of the boards where overlapping papers would be scuffed when placed on or taken off the book shelf.

AIR DRY BOTH SIDES EVENLY: The traditional method to dry the boards after the paper has been pasted on them is to place wax paper on both sides of the boards and dry under weight.

A faster drying method is to stand the boards up to air dry propped up by each other in a *V* shape. This also allows air to get to both sides of the boards so they will dry evenly. Counter–balance of tension will prevent warpage. The boards may warp while drying, but as the papers dry on each side, the board should be pulled back to straight again.

Once dry, if there is a slight amount of warpage, you can carefully bend the board to straight. Be very careful not to crack the board in half. This is also a critical test of whether you waited long enough in pasting. If you did not, the paper will blister, popping from the board as you are straightening it.

BOARDS ARE RARELY PASTED: Rarely is paste applied directly to book board. The leather is glued or pasted and placed onto the board. Paste goes on paper or book cloth and each is applied to the board.

Some Japanese papers have little wet strength. Lace–like papers can fall apart during pasting. The board is brushed with a very thin coating of PVA glue. The dry, delicate paper is laid onto the glued board.

The same approach is used for silk and fine cloth. A thin coat of PVA is applied to the board. This time, wait until the glue is almost dry. It will be tacky. Place the fabric on the board. Cover with a blotter and iron it on a low to medium heat. The results are not always favorable.

REPAIRS

EASY REMOVAL OF SOILED PASTED PAPERS: Restoration work is made easy when the papers are pasted, rather than glued to the boards. If a paper is soiled, the surrounding papers or leather can be covered with wax paper. The soiled paper is then misted with water. When the paper is fairly well soaked, about one minute, it can be peeled off the board. The board will not be scarred and all of the soiled paper will lift in one piece.

MIXING PASTE WITH GLUE: Some form a mixture of half paste, half PVA to paste papers to boards. This does not allow for easy repairs in removing paper. PVA bonds paper to the board. Second, it is easier to handle papers wet with Paste, only. Paper can be slid into position; it is not tacky like PVA. PVA is harder to handle and offers no advantage mixed into the paste.

If for some reason you do mix the two, never dip your brush containing wheat paste into your supply of PVA. The next time you open the PVA, it will have mold growing in it. Obviously, I have done that.

CARE OF PASTE BRUSHES

Pasting can be done with a glue brush. Oil painting brushes are a good substitute if large enough, but an actual glue brush is cheaper than an oil brush.

Unlike gluing, if the brush dries with paste in it, the brush can be soaked in cold water to dissolve the paste. The brush is washed and stood with the bristles up, not to misshapen the bristles.

Do not sit a brush in water for a long period of time. It will misshape the brush.

Do not use hot water to clean any brush. It will dissolve the glue which is holding the bristles in place.

Penny Carey–Wells, *Silence of the Woods,* 1990, Tasmanian Huon pine, paper, metal hinges. 15 x 16 x 3 cm. I had to include this bookwork, not only because it is a non–adhesive binding, but it is also a single sheet binding which opens flat to any page.

COVERING THE BOARDS

MEASURING PAPER FOR SEPARATE SIDE–COVERS

For the Outside of the Boards

For Single Sheets Sewn onto Tapes or a Coptic Sewing, you will have separate side–covers. These are covered with paper on both sides of the boards prior to sewing. This is the formula for measuring papers to cover the boards:

Width of the paper for the outside of the board is the width of the board, plus 1" to 1 1/2". This will give an overhang of up to 3/4" on each side to be turned in. Grain of the paper should be parallel with the spine.

Height of the paper for the outside of the board is the height of the board, plus 1" to 1 1/2" for an overhang of up to 3/4" at the top and the bottom. Overhang of paper is referred to as the *turn–ins.*

The pasted turn–ins will be brought around to the inside of the board. *See* Steps 4–7, pages 84—87.

For the Inside of the Boards

After the outside paper is attached and turned in to the inside, paper is added to the inside of the board. It is referred to as the *paste–down* or *doublure.*

PAPER MEASUREMENT FOR SEPARATE SIDE–COVERS

For any sewing described in this book

The measured and cut paper for the outside of the board has been slipped under the board to check the 3/4" overhang on all four sides prior to pasting.

The measured and cut paper for the inside of the board is called the *paste–down* or *doublure.* It has been cut and laid on the board to check for proper size.

Width and *height* of the doublure, or paste–down paper, for the inside of the board are less than the dimensions of the board. You can allow little or a great deal of the turn–in from the other side to show. Grain of the paper should be parallel with the spine.

FLUSH OUTSIDE PAPERS: If more than one paper is used on the outside of the boards, they must not overlap to avoid snagging when shelved. *See* inlaid papers, page 91.

PASTING THE PAPERS FOR THE BOARDS

All papers must be cut before you begin pasting.

COVER ONE BOARD AT A TIME: Paper for the outside and inside of one board, only will be pasted. This will allow you to cover the outside and immediately cover the inside of one board quickly. If you were to paste paper for the outside of two boards and apply them to the boards, the boards would warp before you could paste and add the paste–downs to the inside of the boards.

Paste the decorative paper for the outside of one board. At the same time, paste the paper for the inside of that one board.

Once the wet paper lays flat on the pasting surface, it is ready to apply to the board. Brush the entire surface of the outside paper once more to remove excessive paste, leaving a thin layer of paste on the paper. Position the pasted paper on the outside of the board. Make sure the overhang top and bottom is nearly equal.

Covering the Board for Separate Side–Covers

1. Lay the board on top of the pasted paper for the outside of the board, leaving an equal amount of overhang on all four sides.
2. Pick up the board and paper. Lightly press across the paper to remove air bubbles. Press along the edges of the pasted paper to show the boundaries of the board.
3. Lay the board on a clean surface with the paper side down.
4. *CUTTING OFF THE PAPERS AT THE CORNERS:* An overhang of the outside paper is about 3/4 to 1" all way around. The excess of paper at the corners must be removed. Do not attempt cutting the corners off prior to pasting. The paper expands once it is wet. Alignment must be exact. You will never position the paper precisely to the board. Cutting the corners off prior to pasting only complicates a simple procedure.
   Since you are covering separate boards rather than boards attached to a book block, cut the corners off the paper at all four corners at a 45° angle. Amount of paper removed must be exact: the cut is out from the board, leaving a paper margin which is 1 1/2 times the thickness of the board.

Position of the cut is critical. If your diagonal cut is too close to the board, the bare board will be exposed at the corner when making the turn–in. If the cut leaves too much paper at the corner, you will have an excess of paper in folding the outside paper around to the inside of the board.

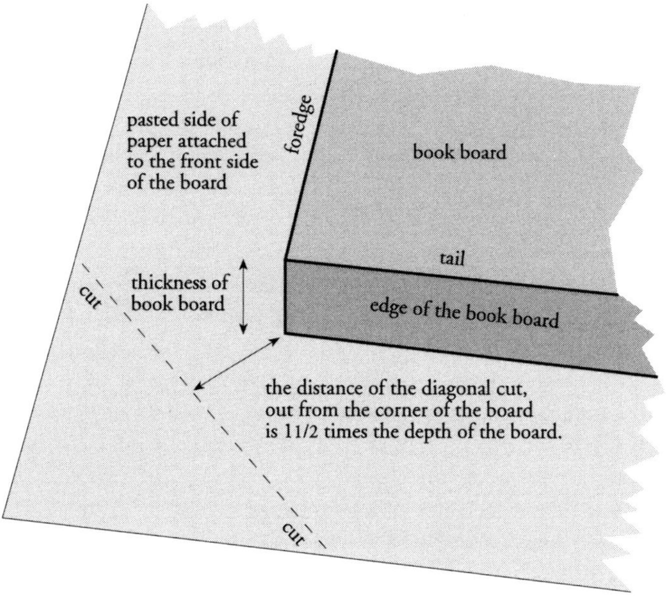

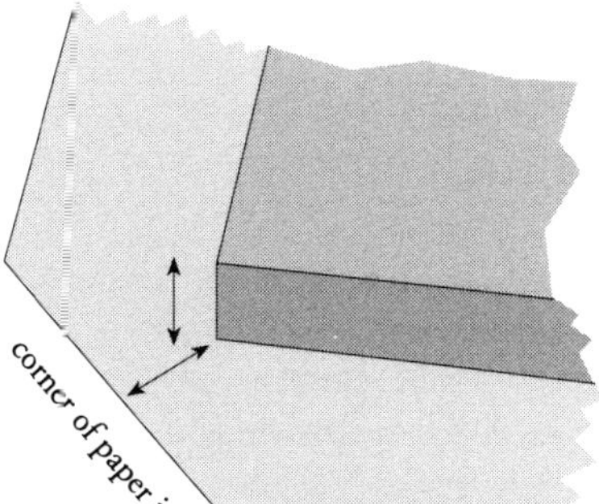

STEP 4: For separate side–covers, cut the corners off the paper at all four corners at a 45° angle. The cut must be out from the edge of the board. Distance out from the board is 1 1/2 times the thickness of the board you are using. Cutting it less the paper will not cover the corner of the board. Leaving more paper on the cut requires folding over too much paper.

5. *Making the Turn–ins:* Fold the paper around the tail, tight against the edge of the board, onto the inside surface of the book board. Push with your thumb on the paper in the direction towards the head. This will tighten the paper on the edge of the board as well as on the inside.
   Do the same at the head. Fold the paper around the head, tight against the edge of the board, onto the inside of the board. Push with your thumb towards the tail.
   The turn–in at the head and the tail can be done at the same time, holding the board cupped in your hands, making the turn–in at the tail with one thumb, while simultaneously using the other thumb at the head. This will assure the position of the paper does not slip on the outside of the board and will tighten the paper to the board.
6. Place the board on the table with the inside of the board facing up. Place the bone folder flat against the edge of the board at the tail, close to the foredge. Take the bone folder tightly around the corner onto the foredge,with the bone folder flat against the edge of the board. This creases the paper at the corner. Do the same at the head.
7. Turn–in the paper along the foredge. Press it tightly over the edge of the board onto the inside of the board. Press in a stroking manner toward the spine–edge to tighten the paper. Check the outside of the board to see if the paper pulled away from its position at the leather or cloth.
   If the board is for a separate side–cover, do the same for turning–in the paper along the spine–edge.
   Tap the foredge of the board lightly on the table. Or, use a bone folder to tap the foredge at the head and the tail. This will crease and flatten the folded paper at the corners. Lay the bone folder over the seam at the corners on the inside of the board. Press downward to crease and flatten the folded over paper.
   If it is an attached cover, do not close the board unless you place a scrap sheet of wax paper on top of the book block.
   TURN–IN: The amount of turn–in on the inside of the board is equal along the head and tail because you centered the paper top to bottom when applying it. However, you may find the turn–in along the foredge is larger than planned. Wet paper expands in one direction, perpendicular to the grain. With certain papers, the expansion is excessive. You may wish to trim the turn–in along the foredge while it is on the book and still wet to keep an equal amount on all three sides. *See* cutting wet paper, page 40.
   When the island paste–down, or doubler, is added, the shape of the bulge from the turn–ins will show if it is not inlaid. You can prevent the bulge from being seen by pasting down a center island filler flush with and butted to, the turn–ins. This would be added just prior to adding the paste–down.

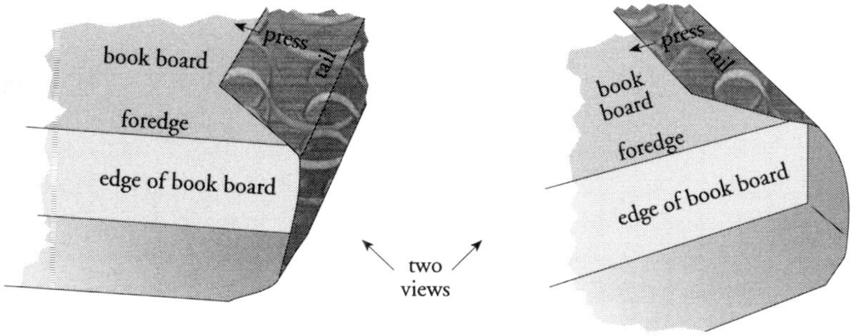

STEP 5: Turn–in at the head and the tail

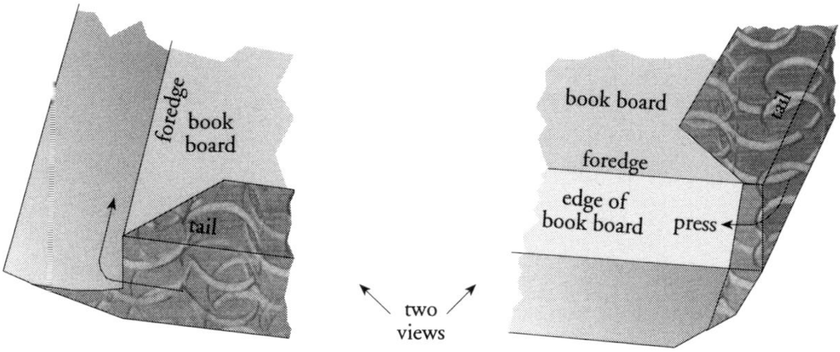

STEP 6: Crease paper with bone folder along the edge of the board, from the tail, around the corner, onto the foredge. Do the same at the head.

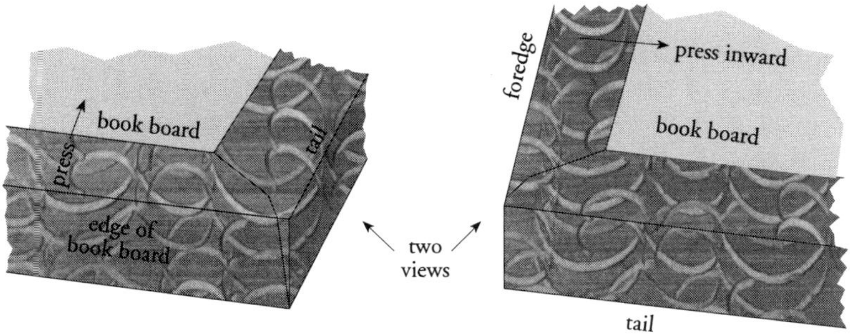

STEP 7: Turn–in at the foredge

8. *ADDING THE DOUBLER:* Lightly coat the doubler, or paste–down, with a fresh thin layer of wheat paste. Place it in position on the inside of the board. Lightly press down brushing across the surface. Lay a sheet of clean white paper on top. Now you can press hard with your finger around the perimeter of the paste–down without fear of wrinkling it. Better, put a sheet of wax paper on each side and place it in a press for thirty seconds only, just to nip it. Remove it from the press to air dry on both sides of the board.

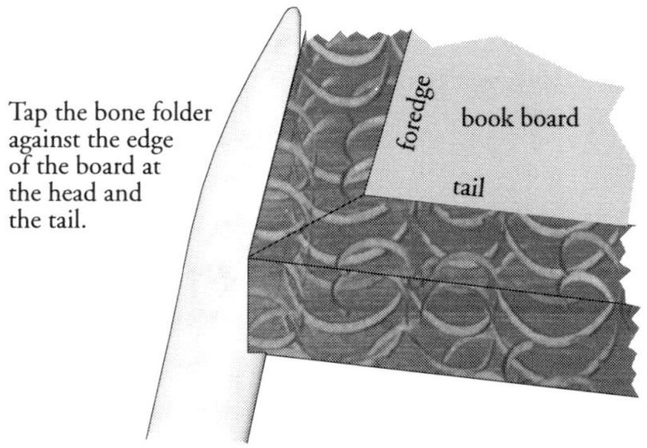

STEP 6: Tapping the edge of the board to crease the folded paper

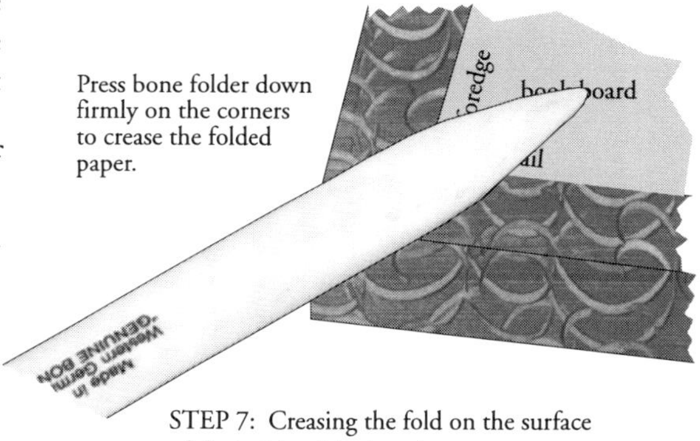

STEP 7: Creasing the fold on the surface of the inside of the board

Wash and dry the pasting surface in preparation for pasting the papers for the remaining board. Paste and cover the second board.

DRYING THE BOARDS: Since the pull factor has been considered, tension on one side of the board will equal the other. There is no need to place the boards under weight to dry.

Air must get to both sides of the board to prevent warpage. The boards can be stood leaning against each other. I dry my boards on the carpet, turning them over every ten minutes or so.

Allow the boards to dry totally before attaching them to a supported sewing. If they are for an unsupported sewing such as a Coptic, they must be dry before the sewing begins, since one board is attached in the first few steps.

Barbara W. Bansley, *Chevrolet,* 1997. Two views of a pop–up book. One–of–a–kind. Paper, book board, water colors and wire. 54.5 x 54.5 x 24.5 cm.
"…43rd Anniversary gift to my husband. Dating in high school we used to drive over to Midway Airport and sit by a wire fence and watch the planes coming in and going out. Hence you see a '46 Chevrolet, chicken wire fence with planes overhead."
—Barbara W. Bansley.

INLAID PAPERS

COLLAGE: Several papers can create a collage for the boards. If they are to be pasted to the outside of the boards, they must not overlap. Otherwise, when the book is placed on and removed from the shelf, edges will tend to catch and peel back or tear. The papers must be inlaid, all on the same surface, all the same thickness. The collage is not fixed prior to pasting. The pasted pieces are slid and butted together on the board.

IMPROMPTU: The design is almost always pre–planned, but can be improvised, contingent pasted pieces, placed side by side until the board is covered.

EVEN OVERHANG ON SEPARATE BOARD SIDE–COVERS: If you are improvising the design on the outside of the board, the touching papers must overhang all four sides to be used as the turn–ins.

EVEN OVERHANG ON ATTACHED BOARDS: Improvising a design on the outside of the board of a cased–in book, the touching papers must overhang at the head, tail and foredge to be used as the turn–ins.

PASTING INLAYS: Paste all papers for the outside and inside of one board only.

1. If you have applied quarter leather or cloth along the spine–edge, butt the paper(s) against the material, centered top to bottom. There must be an even overhang at the head, foredge and tail. See illustration 2 on page 92. After all papers are attached to the outside of the board, you may trim any excessive overhang, but the final trim occurs after the turn–ins are made.
2. Cut the corners. *See* cutting off the paper at the corners, page 84. Make the turn–ins. Make sure the turn–ins butt against each other or overlap so the corner of the board is not seen between the joins. Now use a small straight edge and trim the turn–ins so they are precisely even at the head, foredge and tail. See illustration 2 on page 92.
3. Add the doublure as described on page 88. See figure 3 on page 94. Stand the separate side–cover to dry. If a cased–in book, place a sheet of wax paper inside and close the cover.
4. This board is complete. Cover the remaining board in the same manner.

PRE–CONCEIVED DESIGN

A line drawing can be ruled off. Each shape is assigned a tone, color and/or pattern of paper. Notes can be made on the line drawing.

STRAIGHT CUTS: Use a straight edge and X–Acto knife with a #11 blade to cut the pieces. After cutting, arrange the design to check for fit. Make sure you allow for the turn–ins on the head, tail and foredge.

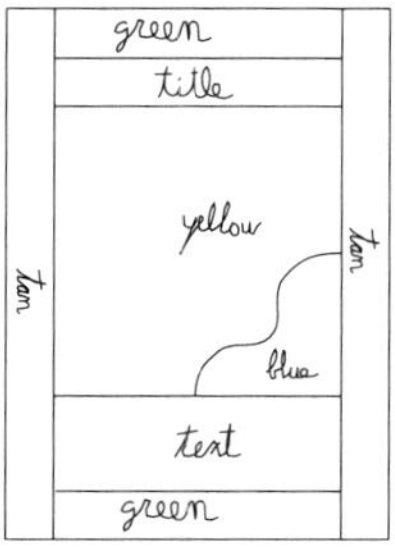

1. line drawing for the board

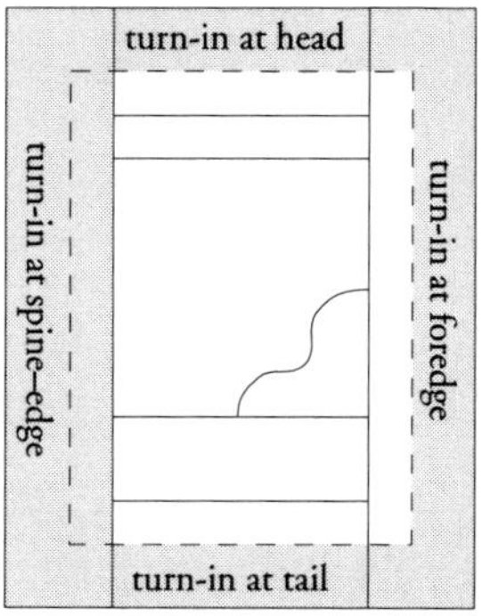

2. drawing with turn–ins

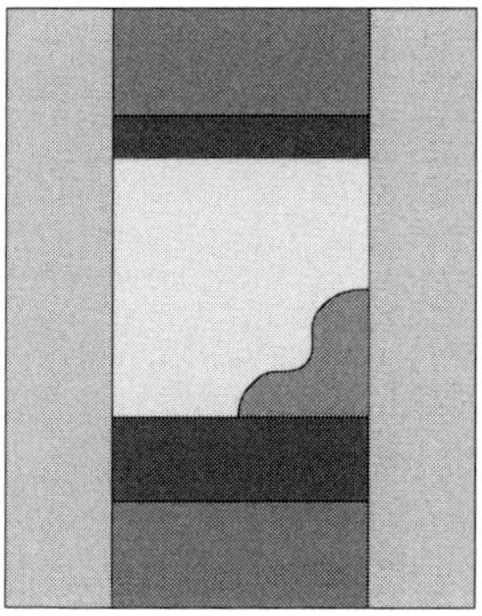

3. assembled pieces of cut papers

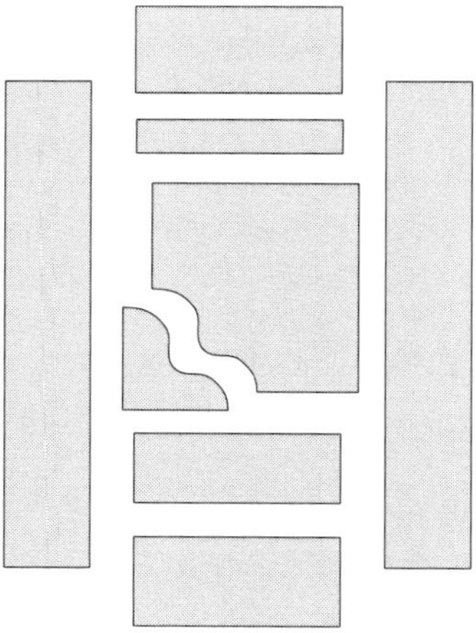

4. pieces flipped over and separated to be pasted

5. separate side–cover completed

1 The design is planned.
2. Space is considered for the turn–ins.
3. The papers are cut and pushed adjacent to see if they fit.
4. All the pieces are flipped over in order, ready to paste. Keep a distance between each piece for pasting. Apply to the front board keeping an even amount of overhang for the turn–ins.
5. Make the turn–ins. Apply the doublure. Cover the back board. Stand to dry so air can get to both sides of the boards.

INLAY CUTS: If curves are involved, pieces cannot be cut individually because the seams would not consistently butt.

1. Lay the adjacent curved pieces on top of each other making sure the bottom piece is large enough for the shape.
2. Cut curve of both papers, the concave and the convex , in a single action.

TOOLS: A thin bladed knife is needed. I use an X-Acto™ knife with #11 blades. Use a new blade for every inlay cut. The once-used blades can be used later for less critical cutting.

A self–seal cutting mat is an ideal surface to cut the inlays. Using book board is perilous. When the blade crosses a previous cut, the diverging blade will cause a disaster.

CUTTING PROCEDURE: Keep the blade perpendicular to the cutting surface, or the bottom paper will be a different size.

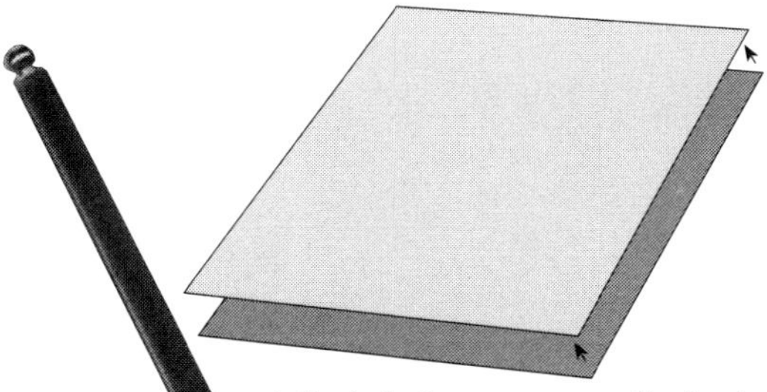

1. Stack the 2 papers on top of each other, lined up with the straight edges they share in common.

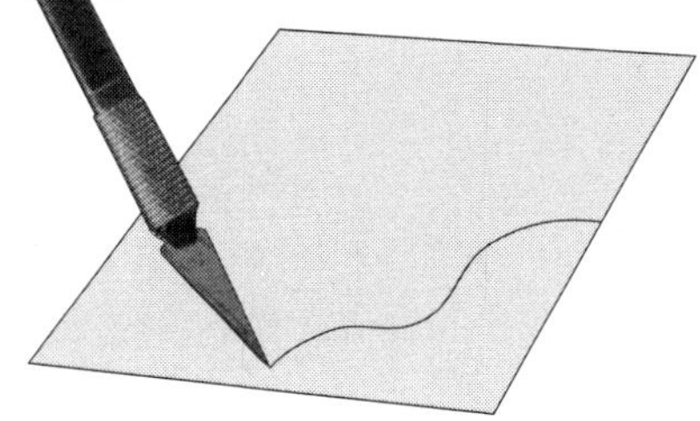

2. Make a single cut through both papers with a new blade. Keep knife perpendicular to self-seal cutting mat.

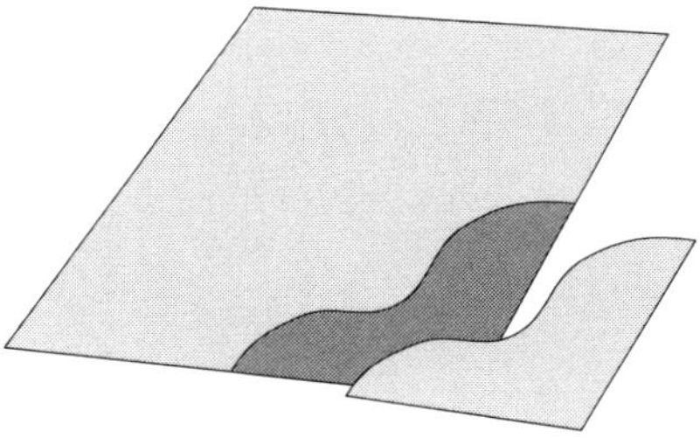

3. Use the larger piece of the lighter color with the smaller piece of the darker. The back cover could use the leftovers, with the design in reverse colors.

Angle of the blade is important to prevent rough edges. I hold mine rather steep for better results. The angle is no more than that shown above. Start at the head, beyond the papers, cut through to beyond the tail, making the curve as well as insuring severing both sheets.

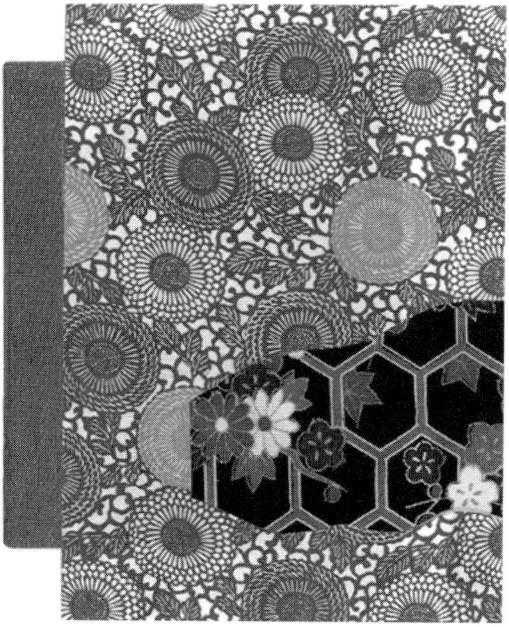

1. Inlaid papers pasted to outside of board.

2. Turn–ins made on inside of board. The separate side–covers have quarter cloth at the spine–edge. The raw board is seen on this side.

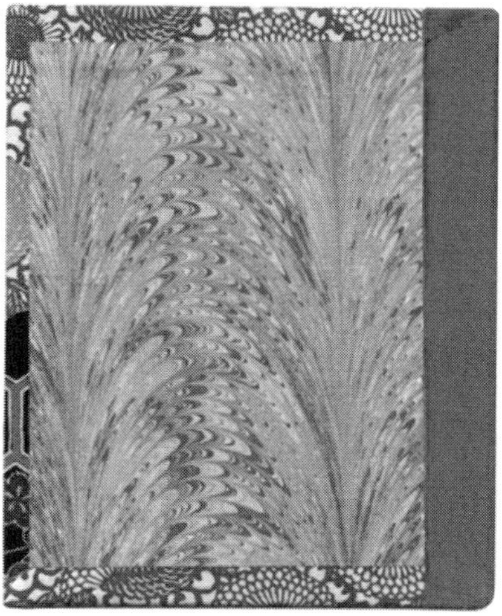

3. The doublure is added on the inside, covering the raw board. It butts against the satin book cloth at the spine–edge and overlaps or butts to the turn–ins at the head, tail and foredge.

4. This front separate side–cover is completed. It has quarter cloth along the spine–edge. Cover the back board. For how to cut inlays of paper, see page 91.

EVEN OVERHANG: If your pre–conceived design is for the outside of the board, place the pasted papers on the board, butting them. After all are in place, check to see that the overhang at the head, foredge and tail are even. If not, there are two approaches to trimming:

- Trim any pieces that need it with scissors before making the turn–ins. Cut the corners. *See* cutting off the paper at the corners, page 84.
  Make the turn–ins carefully to maintain all the seams butted on the edge and the inside of the board.
- Sometimes I wait until the turn–ins of all the pieces are completed before trimming the overhang. I can make a more even turn–in by trimming the wet paper on the inside of the board with a rotary knife and straight edge than I can by trimming the dangling papers with scissors before making the turn–ins. Of course, I run the risk of ripping the wet paper.

SETTING UP DESIGN FOR PASTING: Whether individually cut pieces, or inlay cuts, all the items making up the design are collected and arranged on the table, face down. They should be spread out with an inch of space between each piece. This is so they can be individually pasted without permitting the brush to accidentally slide under a piece which has not yet been pasted. See Step 4, on page 92.

Try to paste all items of the design at once, including paper(s) for the other side of the same board. This is so you can apply all the papers to both sides of the board at once.

If the design is too complicated, paste as much as you can handle and apply them to the board. Weight the board and allow to dry before proceeding with that side of the board and the other side.

PASTE NOT GLUE: Wheat paste lends itself to inlaying because the pasted paper can be slid into place, butting up precisely to the tangent paper. PVA would not permit this, as it is so tacky it will not slide once it touches the surface of the board.

PART II

SINGLE SHEET UNSUPPORTED SEWINGS

INTRODUCTION
SEWING SINGLE SHEETS AS COPTICS

Of the unsupported single sheet sewing prototypes I have devised, I will describe only three Coptic sewings:

- *Single Sheet Coptic Sewn* Across *the Spine.* You can use the more simple TYPE *A* or TYPE *B* board attachment, pages 112 and 116, and the cover will be flush with the book block at the spine–edge. You do not have to use the more elaborate TYPE *C* board attachment, page 119, which goes through the depth of the board. Unlike sewing sections, all three types of board attachment will position the board flush with the spine–edge of the book block. *See* piercing the boards, page 110.
- Single Sheet Coptic Sewn Across the Spine *without paired stations.* The sewing climbs up the spine at a single station. Separate sewings are made across the spine for each station. This sewing can be repeated at all the stations. Or this sewing might be used at one station, while the remainder of the book is sewn with some other across the spine sewing.
- *Single Sheet Coptic Sewn* Along *the Spine.* Sewing along the spine, the board is attached in a different manner, but the boards are flush with the spine-edge of the book block. See pages 165–168.

Any Coptic, including the *single sheet sewings* I, as well as Adéle Outteridge, have devised, allow the book to open flat at any page to which it is turned. These Coptics, along with the various supported single sheet sewings in Part III of this book, are the only single sheet bindings that permit the book to open flat. The Coptic sample above uses book board as the pages as well as the covers.

LINK SEWINGS: Single sheets are attached differently than sections. Gary Frost refers to the stitches that attach single sheets as *bridling,* or sewing *bridle sheets.* See illustration on page 107.

In a Coptic sewing, whether sheets, sections or a combination are used as the book block, once the unit is attached, the thread proceeds to the spine, drops and links. The row of links form a chain. See illustrations on pages 130–133. The links expand as the book is open and contract as it is shut. It is a sophisticated book action.

Coptic stitch is a misnomer. A *link stitch* is used in Coptic sewings. *Chain stitch* is also an incorrect. Chain stitch is an embroidery term, not a bookbinding term. In any Coptic sewing, the links form a chain, but the repetitive stitch is a link stitch.

All Coptics, sheets or sections, are Coptic sewings. *Coptic stitch* is incorrect terminology, and again I thank you, Betsy Palmer Eldridge, for setting me straight on that.

PREPARATION FOR SEWING: Refer to pages 40–45 for information on swell, dimensions of the boards, hiding the stitches, sewing threads inlaid and laminating pictures to the boards.

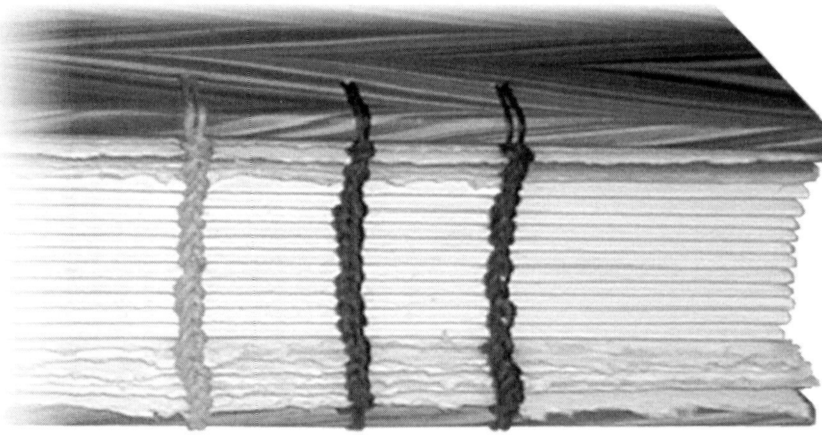

Detail, Single Sheet Coptic Sewing described on page 137. Sections comprise the bulk of this book block with a few sheets stacked at the beginning and at the end of the book. The sections were attached in the traditional manner. The linking for both the sheets and sections drops on the spine to the outside, links under and climbs. If the next sewing unit is a section, the needle climbs and enters in the traditional manner as described in *Exposed Spine Sewings.* If it is a sheet, climb and attach as described on page 137.

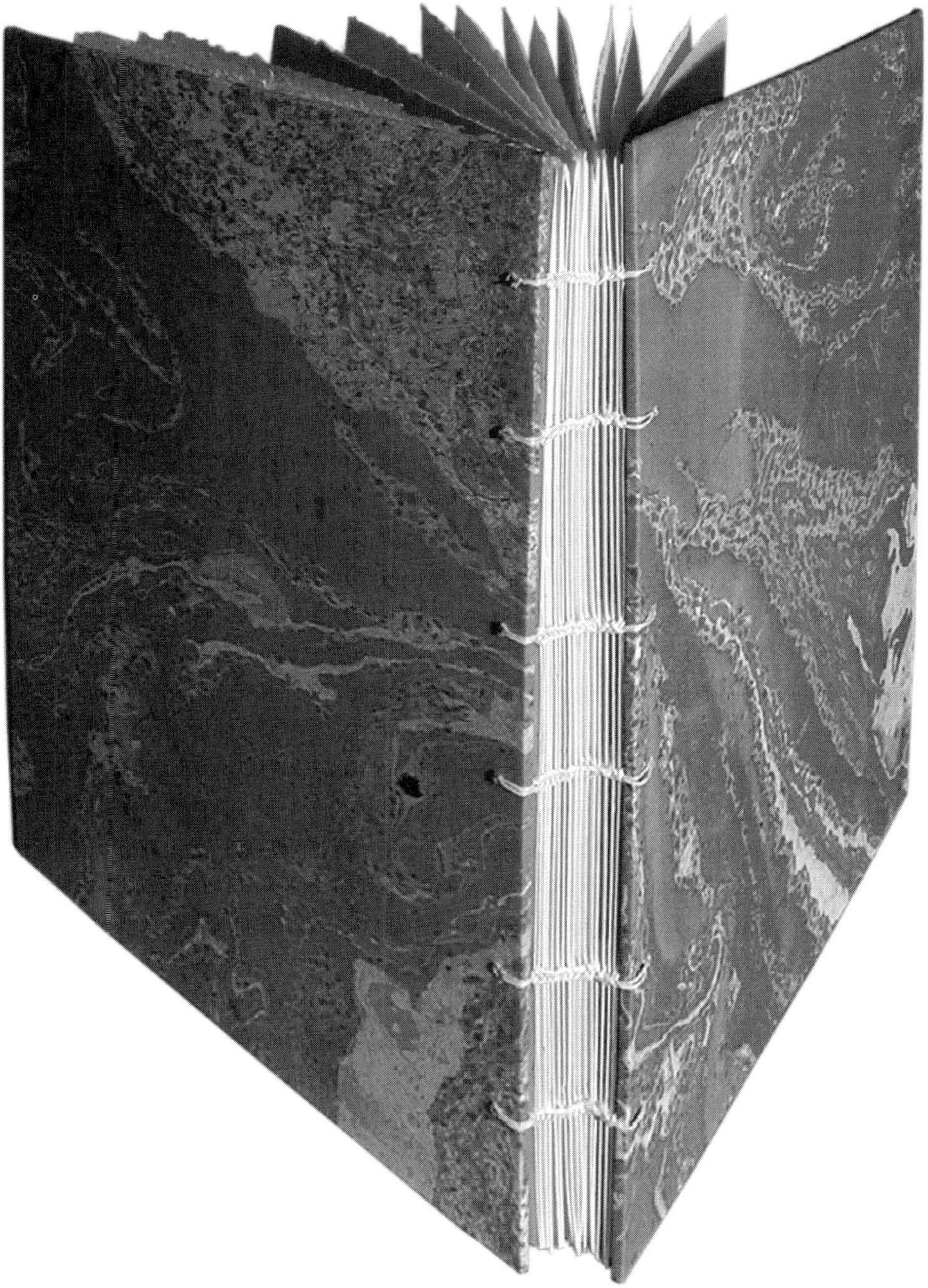

Keith Smith, Single Sheet Coptic Sewn Across the Spine, 1997. The book block is cover weight paper sheets. 29 x 21 x 2.5 cm.

SHAPING THE CHAIN ON THE SPINE

The sewing (chain) on the spine must be corrected to a vertical after each sheet is attached and prior to linking. Tightening and adjusting the sewing is critical. Align the new sheet to the book block. Adjust the sewing. Pull the thread taut by pulling outward, but not so hard as to rip the sheet. Then pull the thread slightly to the outside to align the sewing with the holes. Adjusting tension after linking requires extremely little pressure, but more care than when sewing sections to form the 45° angle chevron shape of the links.

SHAPING THE CHAIN: This early prototype was sewn with disregard of aligning the sewing when each sheet is attached. The sewing is not perpendicular, but crooked.

SEWING EDGES OF FOLIOS WITH THE FOLD ON THE FOREDGE

Often books are designed to be folios, but the fold is desired on the foredge, not the spine–edge. There are several reasons this is desirable:

- Text may be imaged on very thin paper. If printed on both sides, there would be too much show–through. Printing on one side and folding it in half, text can appear on the recto and verso in the book.
- It may be too costly to print both sides.
- Pictures may be possible or practical to image on both sides of a sheet. They can be printed side by side, folded in half. One will appear on the recto and one on the verso of the completed book. Block printing, etching and photographic silver prints are examples. Some photo paper accepts a crease without cracking. *See* fold–outs, page 47.
- Design possibilities are possible to create patterns on the foredge when ink images go into the fold.

In the past, having a book of folios with the fold on the foredge was restricted to a stab binding. The book would not open flat. With the Single Sheet Coptic, the fold of the folio can be on the foredge.

The amount of swell can be controlled by either sewing the spine–edges of the folio as a unit, or separately:

- Each of the two spine–edges of the folio can be sewn at once, as a unit.
- Each spine–edge of the folio can be sewn separately. This is done when a small gap is desired between the two spine–edges of that folio. For instance, I may cut shapes out of half the folio. The gap would place a little distance between the top cutting and the bottom backing for more dramatic lighting. A small amount of space is desired.

  If the top half of the folio is cut as a mat, it will stand slightly above the image on the bottom part of the folio if each spine–edge of the folio is sewn separately.

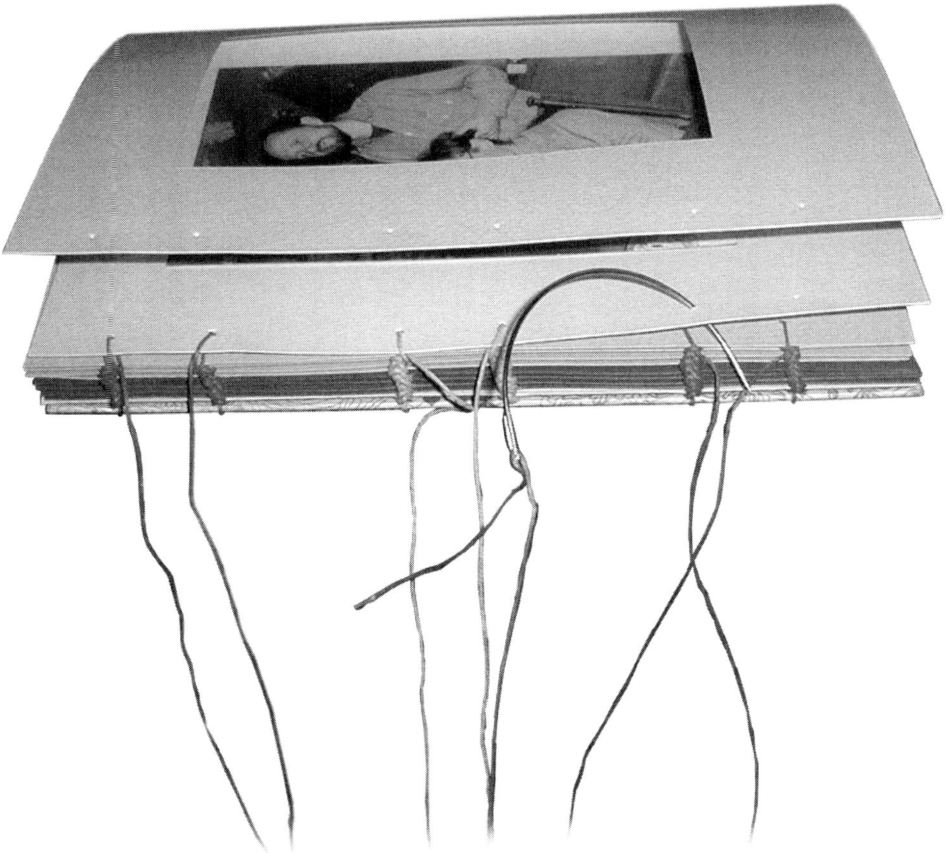

The two spine–edges of a folio can be sewn at once, or as in this photo, sewn separately. Here the bottom half of the folio, which contains a photo, is being attached.

CURVED NEEDLES NECESSARY: Sewing each spine–edge of the folio *separately* requires curved needles. Otherwise it is impossible to link under, since you cannot open the folio after it is attached. Sewing both spine–edges of the folio at once does not require curved needles.

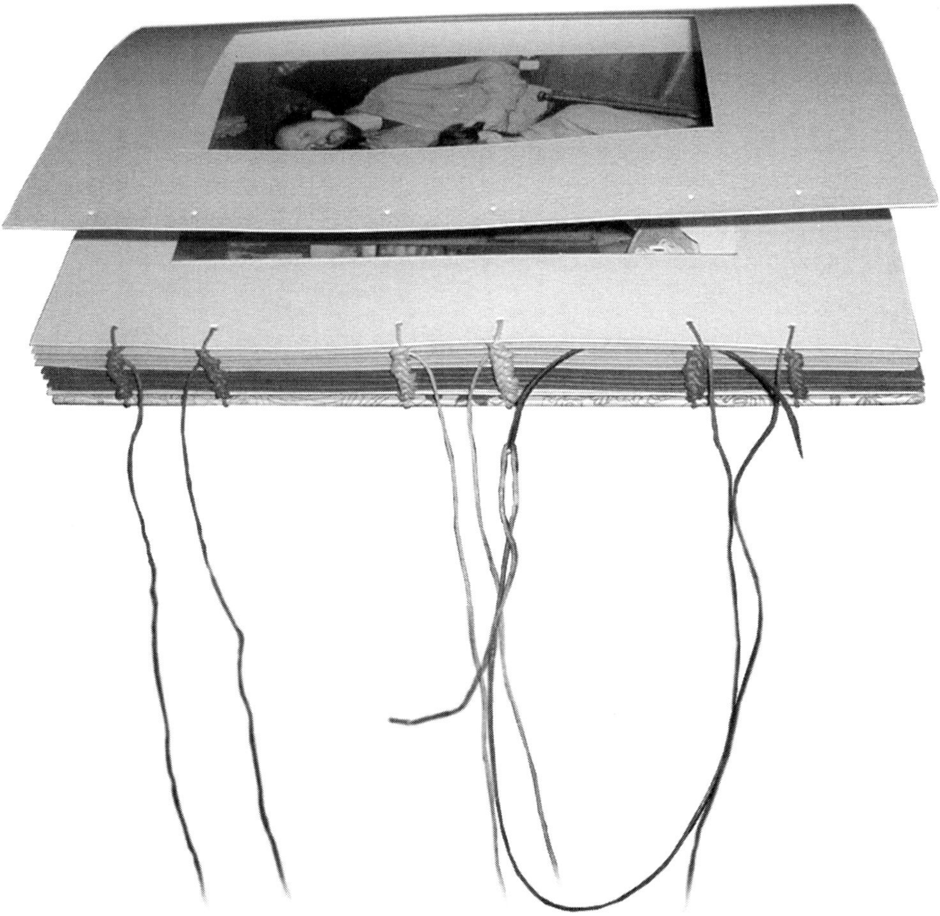

On the previous page the bottom half of the folio was being attached. Here, it is being linked, prior to attaching and linking the top half of the folio. Linking requires a curved needle. Sewing both spine–edges of the folio at once does not require curved needles.

Sewing each spine–edge of the folio *separately* creates swell—there is space between the half of the folio which contains the photo and the top half which is the window mat.

If both edges of the folio are sewn at once, the sewing will swell the folio just enough to accommodate the tipped in photo.

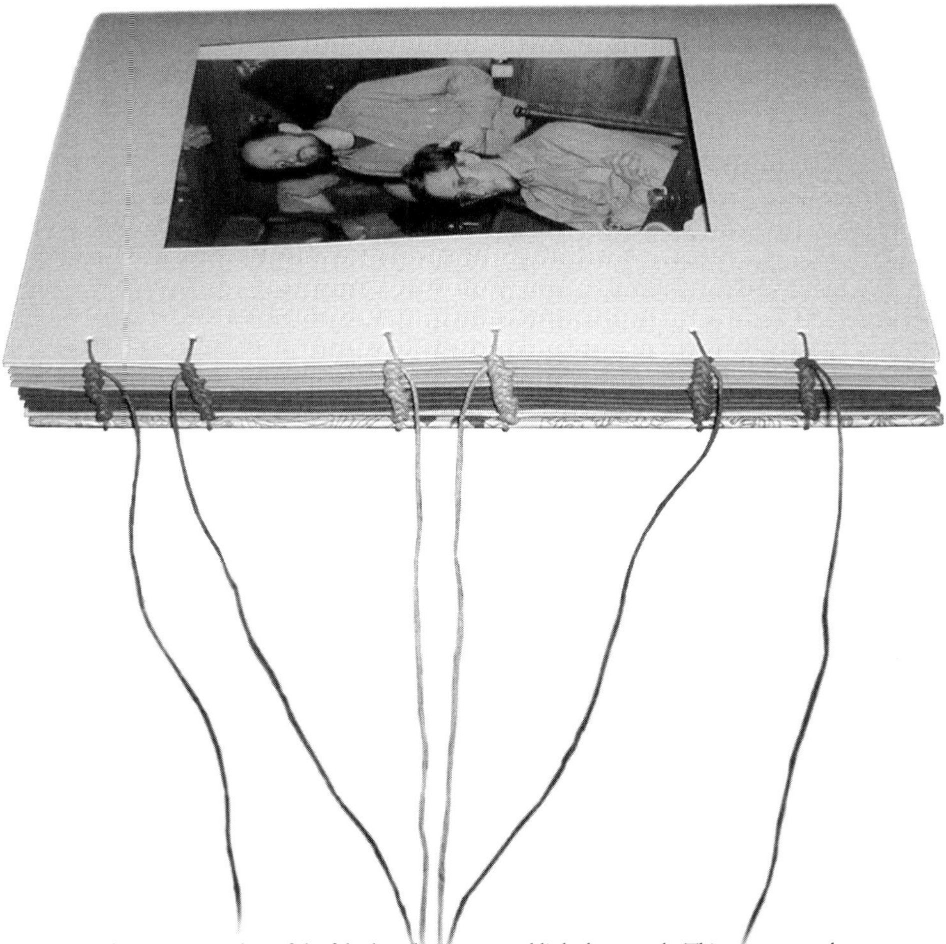

The two spine–edges of the folio have been sewn and linked separately. This exaggerates the amount of swell. The top half of the folio is cut as a mat and stands slightly above the image on the bottom part because of the swell in sewing each spine–edge of the folio separately. More photos of this binding appear on the next two pages.

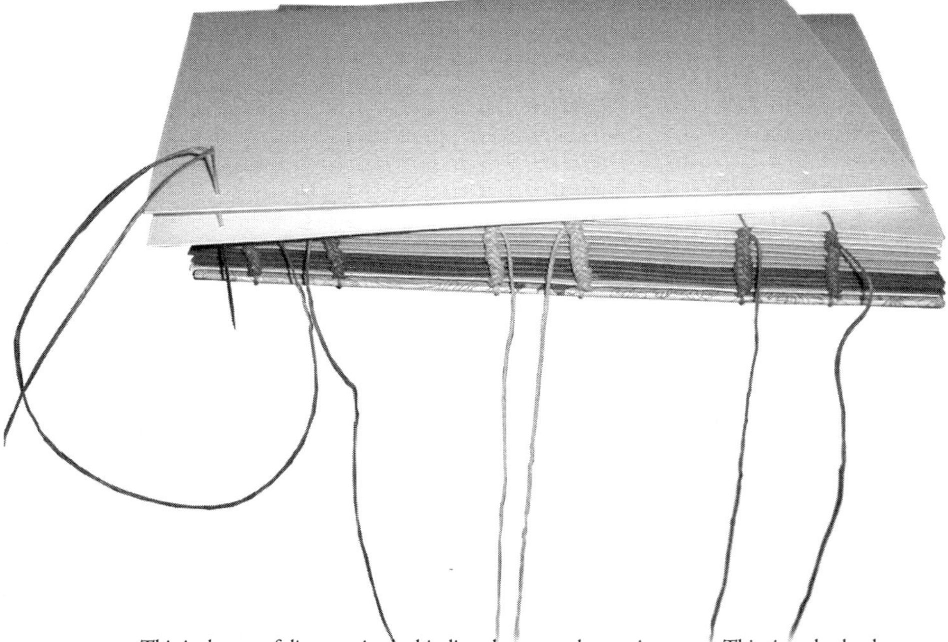

This is the next folio sewn in the binding shown on the previous page. This time, both edges of the folio are sewn at once. The two layers of the folio will lie tightly together, since there is no swell between.

The completed binding has sections, folios sewn on the edges, as well as sheets of paper, metal offset plates and cardboard. One third the way down can be seen the edge of the cardboard page which is shown on the facing page.

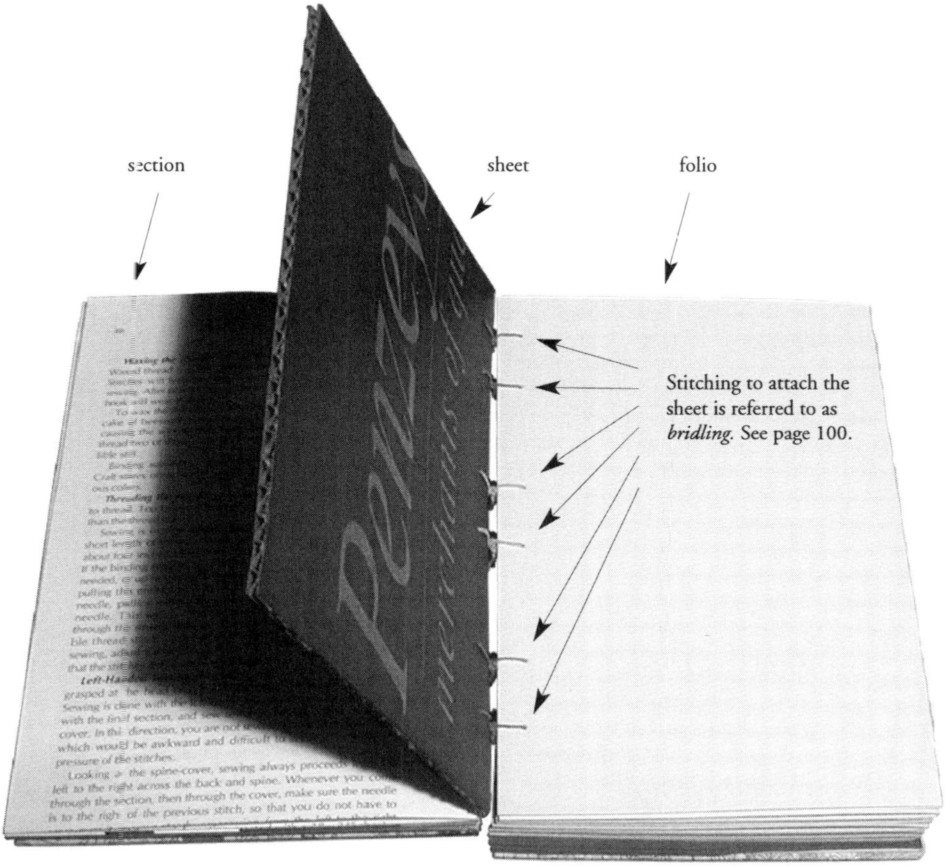

Cropped sections from *Books without Paste or Glue,* cardboard from our Penzeys spice mail order shipping carton and folios with their folds on the foredge are seen in this Coptic sewing. The book opens flat at any open spread.

BOARD ATTACHMENT FOR SINGLE SHEET COPTICS SEWN ACROSS THE SPINE

NUMBER AND POSITION OF HOLES: Traditionally sewings *across the spine* are sewn at paired stations requiring an even number of holes pierced. A needle is placed on each end of the thread. One needle starts at one of the paired stations, the other needle at the other. Since there is a needle at each end of the thread, sewing across the spine is referred to as a *2–needle sewing.*

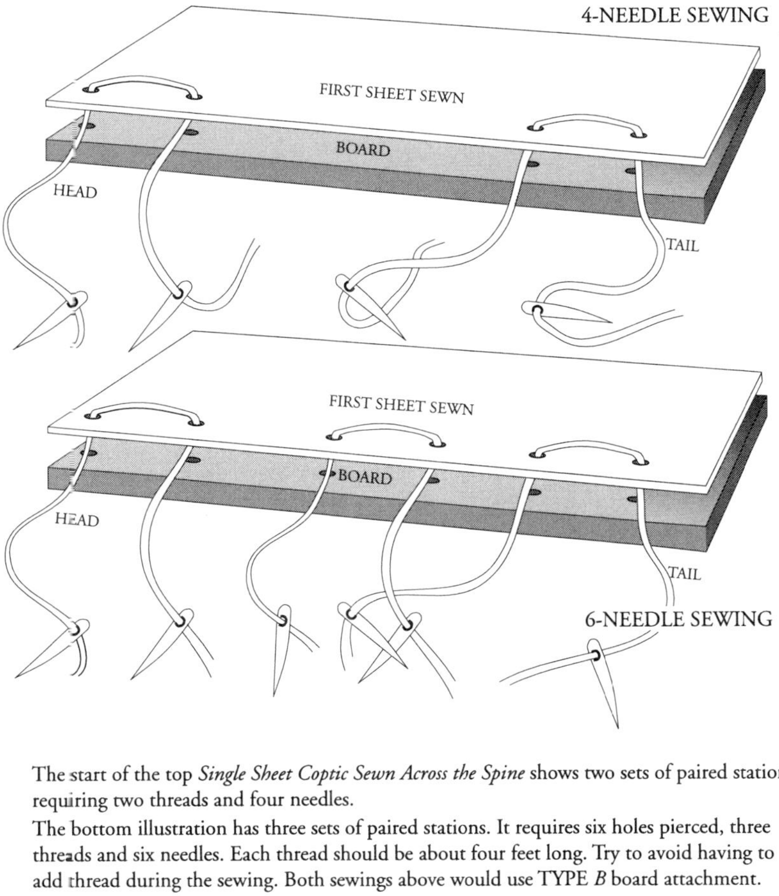

The start of the top *Single Sheet Coptic Sewn Across the Spine* shows two sets of paired stations requiring two threads and four needles.
The bottom illustration has three sets of paired stations. It requires six holes pierced, three threads and six needles. Each thread should be about four feet long. Try to avoid having to add thread during the sewing. Both sewings above would use TYPE *B* board attachment.

Traditional Coptic sewn across the spine must have a minimum of four pierced holes, which makes two sets of paired stations. This requires two threads and four needles. Each set of paired stations is sewn separately, but both sets of paired stations are sewn at once — all the stations on one sheet are sewn with the four needles before the next sheet is sewn.

If the sheets are over 10" tall, three sets of paired stations would be advised. This would require six pierced holes, three threads and six needles. If the book is over 12" tall, probably four sets of paired stations should be used, requiring four threads and eight needles.

The holes should be close to the spine–edge not to interfere with the page. If they are pierced 1/4" in from the spine–edge that will be far enough away from the edge so they do not rip out.

Corners of the sheets need to be secured at the head and tail. In positioning the paired holes for the sewing, pierce one hole no farther away from the head or tail than 1". Do not pierce any hole closer than 3/8" from the end.

PIERCING THE BOARDS: Mark the position of the holes on the board to align with the holes in the book block. Holes on the board should be the same distance in from the spine–edge as the sheets to be sewn. An extra sheet can be used as a template to mark the board positions. If the board has already been covered with decorative paper but not pierced, lay the paper template on the board to eliminate pencil marks on the decorative paper. Line up the spine–edge of the template with the board. Pierce through the template and the board at once.

Pierce the holes with a bradawl or bodkin so the holes in the boards are only slightly larger than the diameter of the needles.

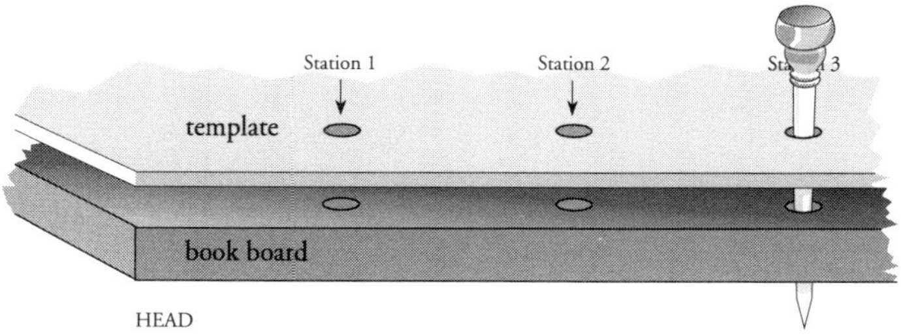

A hole is pierced for each sewing station approximately 1/4 " in from the spine–edge. Mark a paper template. Place the template on top the book board, aligned ready to pierce. (Illustration shows the template floating above to describe alignment.) Extend the board with template slightly off the edge of the table for support close to where you will be piercing. Hold template in place and pierce the holes on the board side–cover with a bodkin or bradawl, not a leather awl. See example on page 26.

SEWING POSITION: Coptics sewn across the spine should be sewn *on the bench,* that is, with the book sitting on the table with the spine facing you. See page 67.

TO ADD MORE THREAD: It is best to use enough thread so you will not run out. If you must add thread, tie a weaver's knot positioned exactly at the hole *after* the needle attaches the sheet. That way you wont have to pull the weaver's knot through the hole. If it is tied exactly at the hole, the clipped ends of thread will not extend beyond the spine–edge and be visible when the book is closed. The knot will only show on the inside of the book. The weaver's knot is described on page 61.

TYPE OF BOARD FOR COVERS: Separate board side–covers are used with all the sewings described in this manual. All have the sewing exposed on the spine. The side–covers are usually book board, although wood or glass can be drilled and attached as covers. The first board is attached to the first section or, in this case, first sheet, as the sewing begins. The other board is attached with the final sheet or section.

In sewing single sheets, attaching the boards is similar to attaching sections in traditional Coptic sewings. Seven methods of board attachment are shown in *Exposed Spine Sewings,* Volume III, *Non–Adhesive Binding.* You could modify any of those. In this manual I will show only three of those attachments adjusted to attach single sheets instead of sections to the board.

IDEAL ATTACHMENT: In traditional Coptic sewings the best hinging action is by attaching through the depth of the board. In this manual this will be referred to as TYPE *C.* However, it cannot be used with thin or medium thickness book board. Even heavy book board may flay open when pierced. TYPE *C* attachment is best with drilled wooden boards or drilled plexiglass side–covers. *See* TYPE *C* board attachment, page 119.

In traditional Coptic sewings attaching the board through the top rather than the depth of the board has another drawback. The spine–edge of the book block cannot sit flush with the boards. That is not a problem with any of the board attachments described in this manual. TYPE *A* or TYPE *B* board attachments permit the boards to be flush with the spine–edge of the book block. TYPE *A* is described on the following page. TYPE *B* is on page 116.

COVERING THE BOARDS: Separate side–covers are covered prior to sewing. *See* glue & paste, page 73; covering the boards, page 83; and inlaid papers, page 91.

BOOK BLOCK: The beauty of these sewings is that the book block can be all sheets, all sections with a single sheet or any combination of sheets and sections. The book block can be paper sheets or paper sheets and sections. The book block could be sheets of paper with some sheets of metal, glass or book board. Any combination will still permit the book to open flat to any page.

TYPE *A* BOARD ATTACHMENT
BOARDS–AS–SHEETS and *PAPER SHEETS TO BOARD COVER*

TYPE *A* is recommended for attaching paper sheets to board side–covers. It is also fine for using boards–as–sheets — when the cover *and* the pages of the book block are all book boards. See examples on pages 127 and 132–135.

The cover will have a single stitch in view on the outside of the covers. TYPE *B* will have two stitches at each hole extending around the spine–edge of the board.

1. Start the sewing on the inside of the board. Take one needle through a hole to the outside of the board. Take the other needle through the paired hole. Even the thread on the dangling needles. Do this at all the paired stations.

2a. Set on the first sheet to be sewn. Come around the spine–edge of the board to the top of the sheet. Go through the hole of the sheet only.

2b. Do the same as Step *2a* at the remaining paired station. Each sewing will have at least two sets of paired stations. Repeat Steps 2 *a* and *b* at all the remaining paired stations before beginning Step 3.

NOTE: With Step *2a,* be sure the thread extends to the right of the stitch connecting the board with the sheet. With Step *2b,* the thread extends to the left. Both threads will be *on the inside of the paired stations.* In attaching each additional sheet, all threads will dangle on the inside. Linking will be on the outside. This will become evident in the description of the Coptic sewing which follows. It is referred to as *drop in, link out.*

3a. Proceed around the board. Go through the hole on the board only from the outside to the inside of the board. This second time through the hole in the board locks the board to the first sheet. The thread will dangle on the inside of the paired stations.

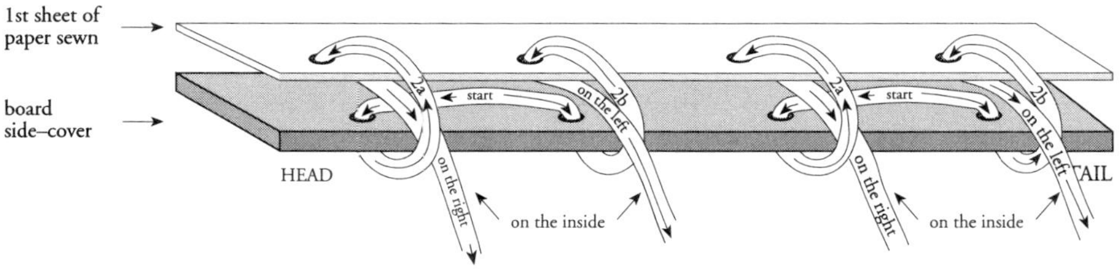

TYPE *A* BOARD ATTACHMENT Steps 1 and 2:
Start on the inside of the board. Take one needle through the hole to the outside of the board. Take the other needle through the paired hole. Even the thread on the dangling needles. Come over the board to the top of the first sheet to be sewn. Go through the hole of the sheet, only. Align the sheet with the spine–edge of the board. Pull the thread taut to tighten the sheet to the board. Do the same at all the paired stations. Make sure the threads dangle between, or on the *inside* of the paired stations.

Align the sheet with the spine–edge of the board. Pull the thread taut to tighten the sheet to the board. Adjust the stitches around the board so they are perpendicular to the holes.

3*b*. Do the same as Step 3*a*. The thread will dangle on the inside of the paired stations.

Repeat Step 3 at all the paired stations. All threads will dangle on the inside of 2*a* and 2*b*.

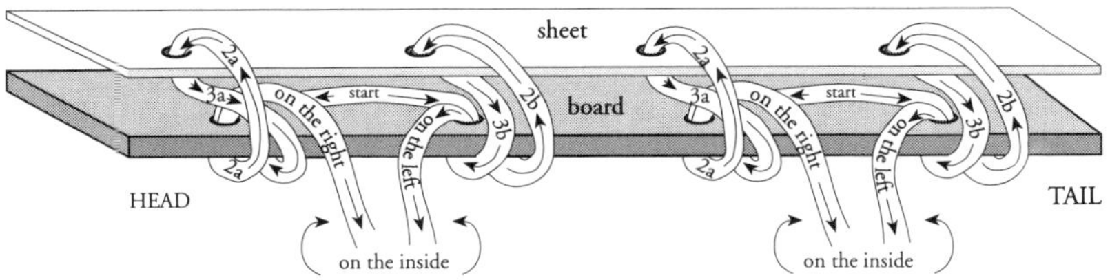

TYPE *A* BOARD ATTACHMENT Step 3:
Proceed around the board *on the inside of the paired stations*. That is, 3*a* will be to the right of 2 *A*, but 3*b* will be to the left of 2*b*. Go through the board from the outside to the inside. Keep the threads on the inside of the paired stations. Align the spine–edge of the first sheet with the board. Pull threads taut. You would now add the second sheet before dropping to link under between the board and the first sheet.

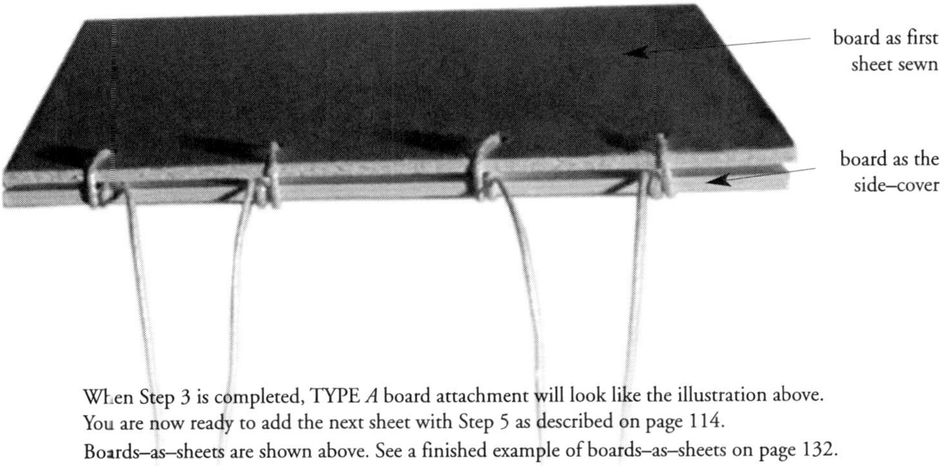

When Step 3 is completed, TYPE *A* board attachment will look like the illustration above. You are now ready to add the next sheet with Step 5 as described on page 114.
Boards–as–sheets are shown above. See a finished example of boards–as–sheets on page 132.

Attaching the Second Sheet

4a. Set on the second sheet to be sewn. Take dangling *a* thread up over the second sheet and go through the hole of the second sheet, only. Let the thread dangle on the inside of the paired stations.

4b. Take dangling *b* thread above the second sheet. Go through the hole of the sheet, only. Let the thread dangle on the inside of the paired stations.

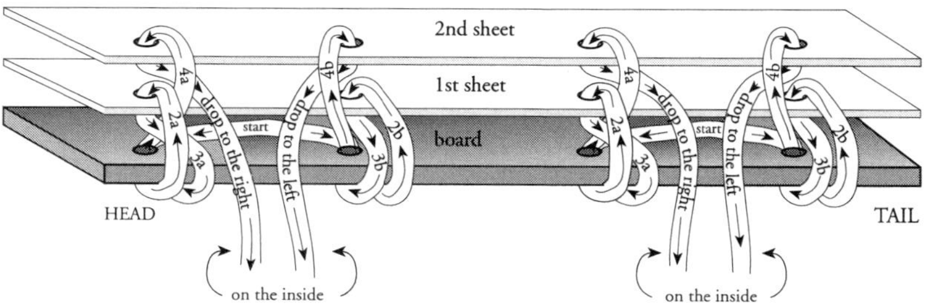

TYPE *A* BOARD ATTACHMENT Step 4:
Set on the second sheet. Take the dangling threads up over and go through the second sheet. Bring the threads out on the inside of the paired stations.

Linking the Second Sheet

5a. Pick up the dangling *a* thread and take it at a 45° angle to the left. Link under between the board and the first sheet from the outside to the inside. That is, take the needle to the inside on the *left* of the threads attaching the board to the first sheet. Go around the connecting threads and exit between the paired stations.

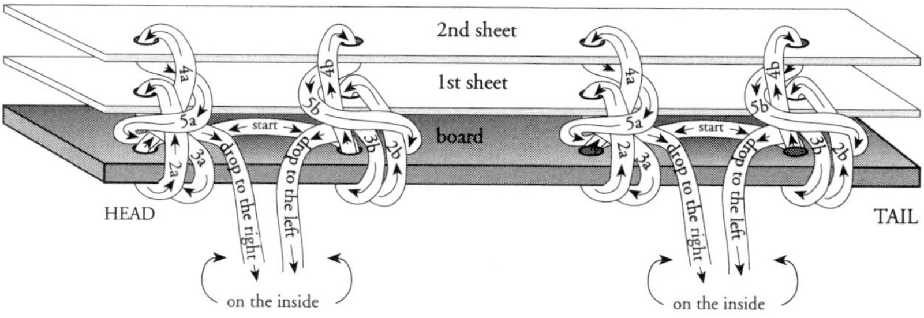

TYPE *A* BOARD ATTACHMENT Step 5:
Take the dangling thread and drop to the outside of the paired station. Link under between the board and the first sheet. The threads will dangle between the paired stations.

5*b*. Pick up the dangling *b* thread and take it at a 45° angle to the right. Link under between the board and the first sheet from the outside to the inside. That is, take the needle to the inside on the *right* of the threads attaching the board to the first sheet. Go around the connecting threads and exit between the paired stations.
Link all remaining stations. Adjust the tension of all the links so they are uniform. This is a critical step so the resulting chain will have equal lengths. I get at eye level and carefully pull on each thread. Each should be at a 45° angle. Do not pull so hard that the link becomes a vertical.

Sewing the Remaining Sheets

The complete description for sewing a Single Sheet Coptic across the spine using TYPE *A* board attachment is described beginning on page 127.

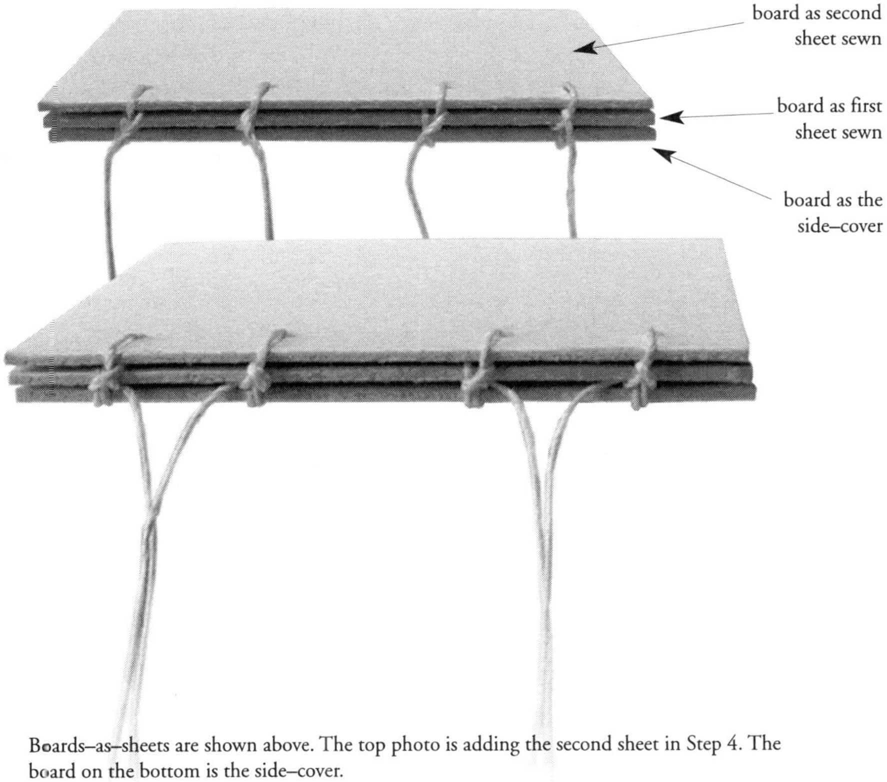

Boards–as–sheets are shown above. The top photo is adding the second sheet in Step 4. The board on the bottom is the side–cover.
TYPE *A* board attachment will look like the illustration in the bottom when the linking is completed in Step5.

TYPE *B* BOARD ATTACHMENT
BOARDS–AS–SHEETS and *PAPER SHEETS TO BOARD COVER*

TYPE *B* is another way of attaching paper sheets to board side–covers. It is also fine for boards–as–sheets — when the cover *and* the pages of the book block are all book boards. See examples on pages 101 and 141–143.

In TYPE *A,* the sewing begins and ends on the boards. Here, the sewing starts and ends on the sheets, as shown on page 101. The advantage is the first sheet is linked between the board and the first sheet to lock the board in place. Every sheet will be linked. Visually, TYPE *B* will have two stitches at each hole on the outside of the board extending around the spine–edge.

1. Start the sewing on the top of the first sheet. This side of the sheet will not be adjacent to the cover. Take one needle through a hole to the other side of the sheet. Take the other needle through the paired hole. Even the thread on the dangling needles. Do this at all the paired stations as illustrated on page 109.

2*a.* Set the board under the first sheet. Come around the spine–edge of the board and bring the needle up through the board from the outside to the inside. The needle will go through the board and the sheet.

3*a.* Continue with the needle up through the sheet to the top. Align the sheet with the spine–edge of the board. Pull the threads taut and adjust the stitches around the board so they are perpendicular to the holes.

2*b* and 3*b.* Do the same as Step 2*a* and 2*b* at the remaining paired station. Each sewing will have at least two sets of paired stations. Repeat Steps 2*a,* 3*a* and 2*b,* 3*b* at all the remaining paired stations before beginning Step 4.

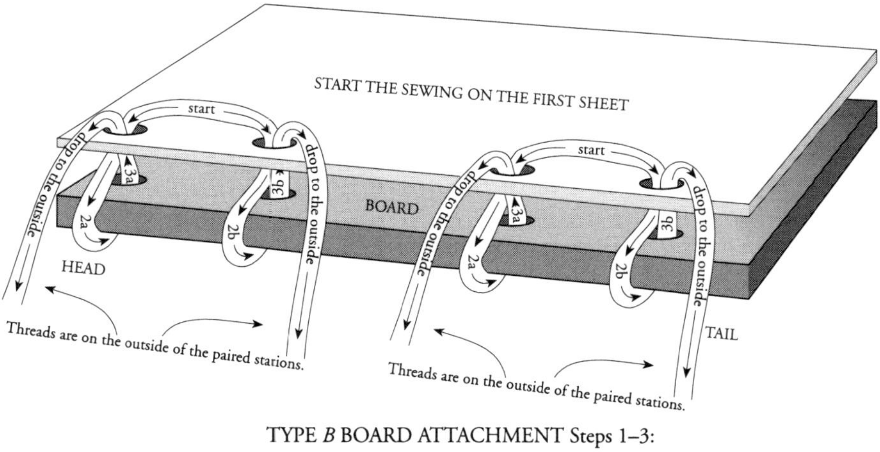

TYPE *B* BOARD ATTACHMENT Steps 1–3:

1. Start the sewing on the top of the first sheet.
2. Come around the spine–edge of the board and bring the needle up through the board from the outside to the inside.
3. Continue with the needle up through the sheet to the top. Align the sheet with the spine-edge of the board. Pull the threads taut and adjust the stitches perpendicular to the holes.

The dangling threads should be on the *outside* of the paired stations. In attaching all remaining sheets, the threads will dangle on the *inside*. Linking will be on the outside. This will become evident in the description of the Coptic sewing which follows. It is referred to as *drop in, link out.*

4a. Drop to the left on the outside of the paired stations. Link under between the board and the first sheet from the outside to the inside. That is, take the needle to the inside on the *left* of the threads attaching the board to the first sheet. Go around the connecting threads and exit between the paired stations.

4b. Drop to the right of the paired stations. Link under between the board and the first sheet from the outside to the inside. That is, take the needle to the inside on the *right*. Go around the connecting threads, Exit between the paired stations.

Link all remaining stations. Adjust the tension of all the links so they are uniform. This is a critical step so the resulting chain will have equal lengths. Do this at eye level. Carefully pull on each thread. Each should be at a 45° angle. Do not pull so hard that the link becomes a vertical.

5a. Set on the second sheet to be sewn. Climb on the inside of the paired stations. Go through the hole in the new sheet from the top to the under side of the sheet. Exit between the paired stations without linking under the starting stitch. The thread will dangle between the paired stations.

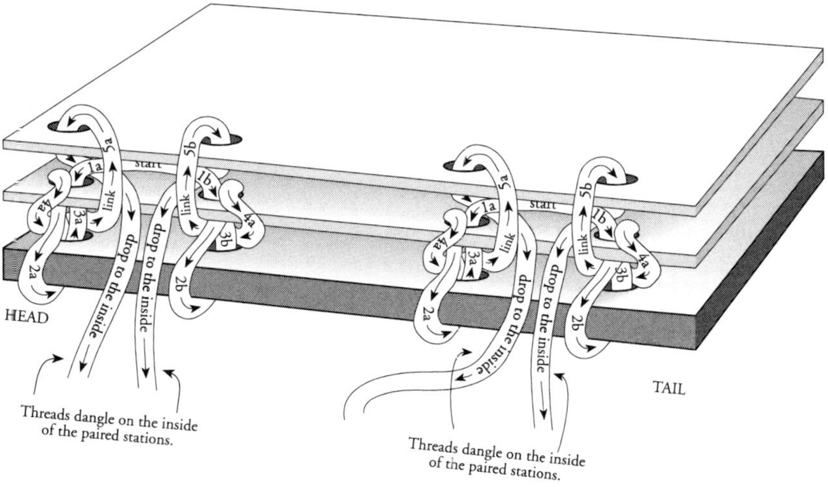

TYPE *B* BOARD ATTACHMENT Steps 4–5:

4. Link under between the board and the first sheet from the outside to the inside.

5. Set on the second sheet. Climb and enter the hole in the new sheet from the top to the under side exiting between the paired stations without linking under the starting stitch.

5*b*. Climb on the inside of the paired stations. Go through the hole in the new sheet from the top to the under side. Bring the needle out between the paired stations. The thread will dangle between the paired stations.

Repeat Steps 5*a* and 5*b* at all the remaining paired stations. Adjust the sheets so both are flush with the board at the spine–edge. Pull the threads taut. Adjust all stitches on the spine–edge so they are perpendicular to the edges of the sheets.

Sewing the Remaining Sheets

The complete description for sewing a Single Sheet Coptic across the spine using TYPE *B* board attachment is described beginning on page 137.

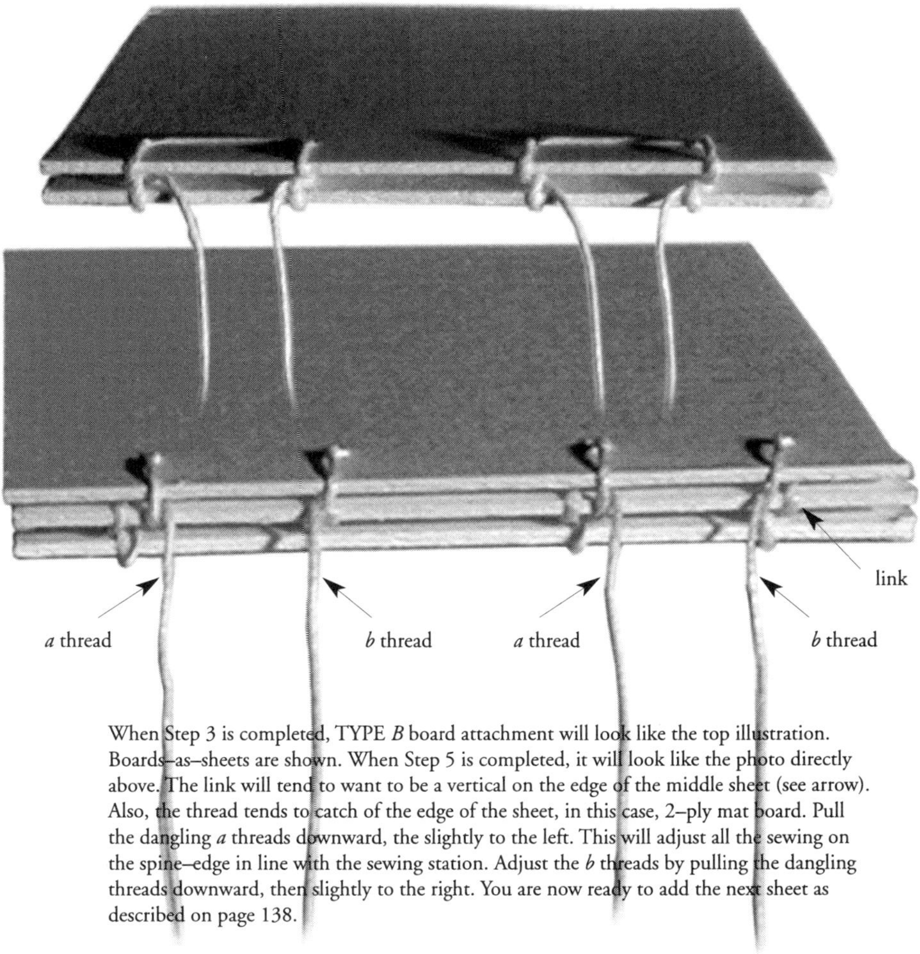

When Step 3 is completed, TYPE *B* board attachment will look like the top illustration. Boards–as–sheets are shown. When Step 5 is completed, it will look like the photo directly above. The link will tend to want to be a vertical on the edge of the middle sheet (see arrow). Also, the thread tends to catch of the edge of the sheet, in this case, 2–ply mat board. Pull the dangling *a* threads downward, the slightly to the left. This will adjust all the sewing on the spine–edge in line with the sewing station. Adjust the *b* threads by pulling the dangling threads downward, then slightly to the right. You are now ready to add the next sheet as described on page 138.

TYPE *C* BOARD ATTACHMENT
For *ATTACHING WOODEN BOARDS* and *GLASS SIDE–COVERS*

The ideal hinge is on the depth of the board, as in TYPE *C*. This is because the hinging action takes place on the depth of the board. It can be used on good quality thick book board, if it does not flay open when pierced. TYPE *C* attachment is best with drilled wooden boards or drilled glass side–covers.

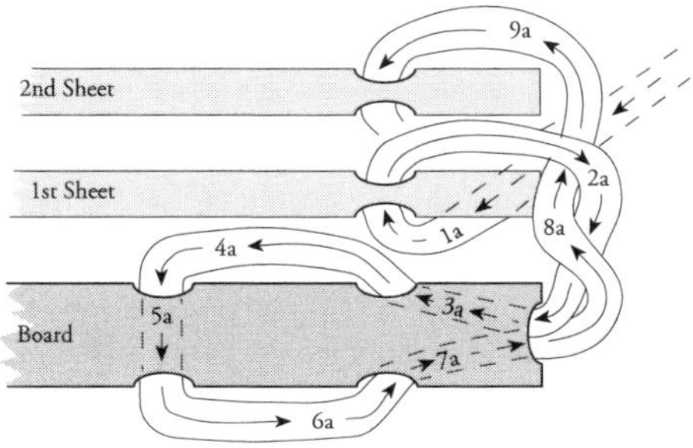

TYPE *C* board attachment, cross section

Attaching Wooden Boards

Wooden boards are quite attractive in an exposed spine sewing.[8]

SUPPLY: It is difficult to find a binder's supply which keeps wooden planks on hand. I have found it easier and cheaper to go to a fine cabinet maker who sells exotic hardwoods. You can choose a grain you like and have it planed to probably 3/16" to 1/4" depending on the dimensions of the board.

QUARTER–CUT VS GRAIN: Boards can be cut with the grain, or quarter–cut. Hardwood floors are a good example of with the grain — Flowing grain pattern is evident. Quarter–cut appears dotted, as it has been cut against, or perpendicular to the grain.

The advantage of with the grain is its beauty, but it tends to warp far easier than quarter–cut.

The advantage of quarter–cut is that it tends not to warp, but it is apt to crack and break in two, since the stress in hinging is parallel with the grain — movement is on the fault line, so to speak, of the grain.

Drilling the Holes

An easy method of drilling in wood is to use a Dremel® Moto-Tool. It is a handy tool for delicate needs of grinding, sanding, drilling, polishing and buffing.

The hole created through the board as a sewing station can be sized to fit your needle. You can curve the pathway.

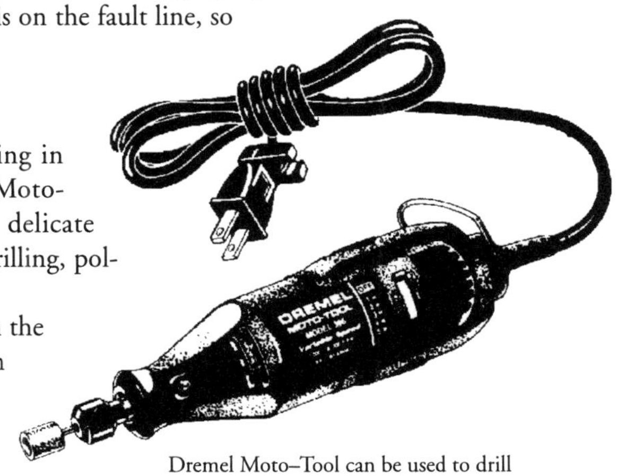

Dremel Moto–Tool can be used to drill proper size holes in wooden boards.

Recessing the support in the board is easy. The shank diamond wheel points come in a variety of sizes and shapes. Shaping a groove or beveling an edge of the board is accomplished almost without effort. Picking up the book you feel the difference. With this tool you can even cut out the depth of your paper or leather, so that when it is applied, it is flush with the wooden board.

STRESS ON WOODEN BOARDS: Board is brittle. The stress on the wood is markedly at the spine–edge of the board, in the area closest to the book block inside of the board. That area of the board is diagrammed on the right in a darkened value. Hinging action of the board places stress at this point.

To lessen the stress, the thread that goes through the depth, (3*a*) to the inside of the board should be slightly slack, as suggested in the illustration at the bottom of the page.

Step 7*a* enters the board from the outside and exits on the depth of the spine–edge. With step 7*a*, the thread should be slightly more taut in order to carry the stress.

All of this is an attempt to put more of the hinging action on the exiting thread (8*a*) and less on the entering thread (2*a*).

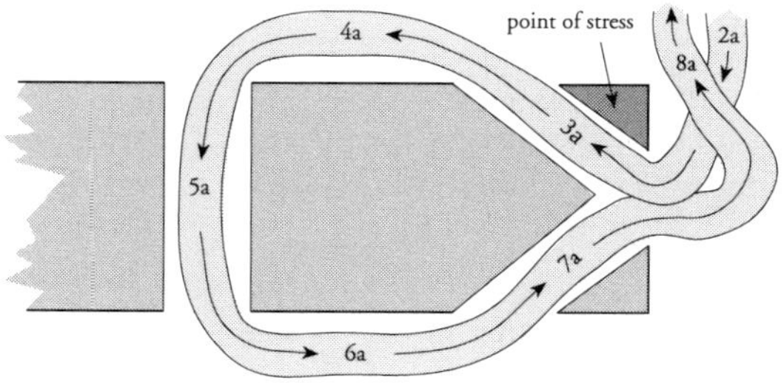

Loosen the tension of thread 3a to lessen the stress on the board as it hinges open and closed.

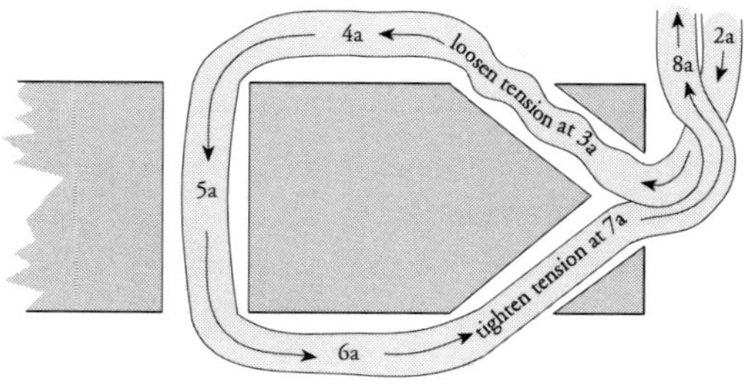

Book Board Preparation

Book board is far easier to pierce the holes for sewing. Book board is pierced with a bradawl. See page 26. It is critical that an awl not be used since it has a graduated shaft.

Mark the stations to be pierced on the top as well as on the depth of the board. The holes on the depth of the board are centered.

1. Place the board with the spine–edge sightly extended over the edge of the table. Pierce straight down to pierce all the holes on the top of the board.
2. Set the bradawl on the pencil dot on the depth of the board. Adjust the angle of the bradawl to somewhere between 30° and 45° and push upward, coming out on the front side of the board. Pierce all the remaining holes on the depth of the board at the exact same angle, so all the holes resulting on the top of the board will be the same distance in from the spine–edge.

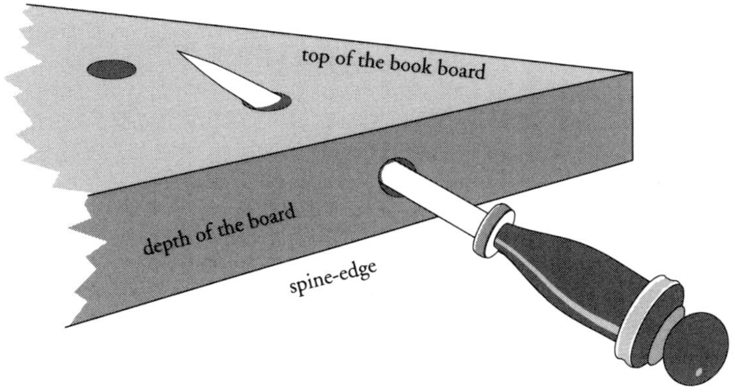

PIERCING THE BOARD, Step 2:
Set the bradawl at a 30° to 45° angle on the pencil mark on the depth of the board. Push upward, coming out on the front side of the board. Pierce all the remaining holes on the depth of the board at the exact same angle, so all the holes resulting on the top of the board will be the same distance in from the spine–edge. For Step 3, turn the board over. Set the point of the bradawl at the hole on the depth of the board. Use the same angle to pierce.

3. Turn the board over. Set the bradawl on the same hole on the depth of the board at the same 30° to 45° angle as before. Push upward, coming out on the back side of the board. Pierce all the remaining holes on the depth of the board at the exact angle, so the resulting holes on the bottom of the board will be the same distance in from the spine–edge.

Sewing Procedure

1. Start the sewing on the inside or bottom of the first sheet to be sewn. Take the *a* needle up through the left paired station and the *b* needle up through the right. Pull the threads so there is an even amount dangling from the paired stations.

2*a*. Drop and set the needle in the hole on the depth of the board.

3*a*. Enter the depth of the board, holding the needle pointing upwards so that you come through to the inside of the board. Do not go through the hole of the sheet.

4*a*. Proceed in on the board to the next hole.

5*a*. Take the needle down through the hole to the outside of the board.

6*a*. Proceed towards the foredge to the next hole on the board.

7*a*. Take the needle out through the hole through the depth of the board.

2*b*–7*b*. Do the same at the other paired station as you did with Steps 2*a*–7*a*.

8*a*. Set on the second sheet to be sewn. Take the needle through the left hole of the paired station from the top of the sheet to the inside. Bring the needle out to the spine between the paired stations. Let the thread dangle.

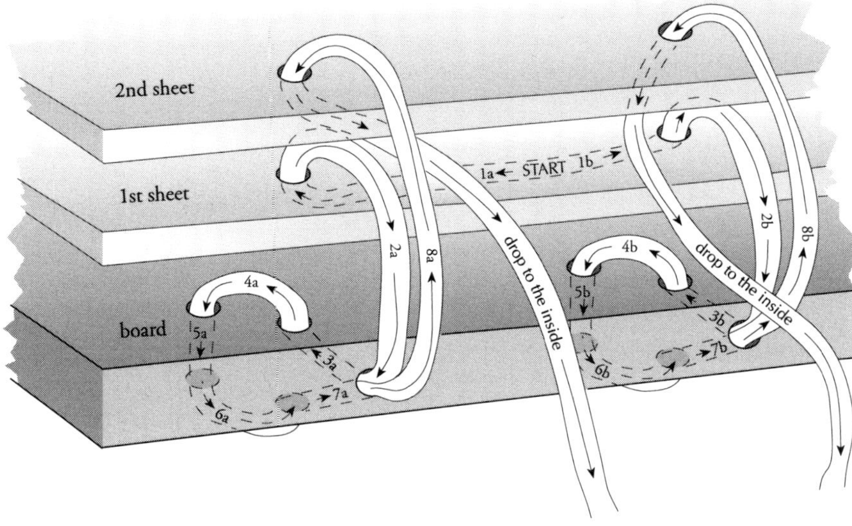

TYPE *C* BOARD ATTACHMENT Steps 1–8:
1. Start the sewing on the inside of the first sheet. Take the *a* needle up through the left paired station and the *b* needle up through the right. Pull the threads taught and even
2*a*.–8*a* Drop and set the needle in the hole on the depth of the board. Enter the depth of the board, holding the needle pointing upwards so that you come through to the inside of the board. Enter the next hole on the board. Exit at the outside. Enter the remaining hole exiting on the depth of the board. Set on the second sheet and enter from the top.
2*b*.–8*b* Do the same at the paired station.

NOTE: Thread 2*a* can be parallel to thread 2*a*. as illustrated on the previous page. Or, you can link around thread 2*a* with thread 8*a* as diagrammed in the cross section view on page 120.

8*b*. Take the needle through the right hole of the paired station from the top of the sheet to the inside. Bring the needle out to the spine between the paired stations. Let the thread dangle.
Repeat Steps 8 *a* and *b* at all the remaining paired stations before linking with Step 9.

9*a* and 9*b*. Take the *a* thread and drop to the outside (to the left). Link under between the board and the first sheet. That is, go around the two threads connecting the board with the sheet. Exit to the outside between the paired stations. Link the *b* thread in the same manner.

NOTE: Linking is done easily by sitting the book on the table with the spine-edge facing you. Open to the position you are linking, which will be two sheets down in these Coptic sewings. Form the link and close the book. Adjust the tension of the link at eye level to maintain a 45° angle on the thread. Do not pull so hard the link becomes a vertical thread.
Repeat Step 9 at all remaining paired stations on this sheet.

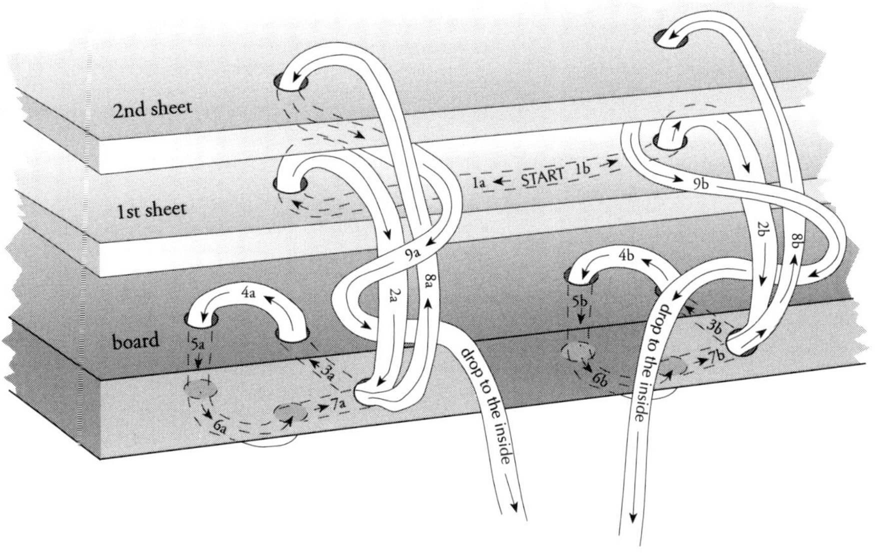

TYPE *C* BOARD ATTACHMENT Step 9:
Linking is by dropping to the outside of the paired stations. For this first link, link under between the board and the first sheet. Exit to the inside of the paired stations.
NOTE: The illustration shows loose threads to follow the path easily. You want to have your sewing taut. See photo on the following page.

Sewing the Remaining Sheets

The complete description for sewing a Single Sheet Coptic across the spine using TYPE *C* board attachment is described beginning on page 145.

Enlarged detail of the linking shown below exaggerated by drawing into the photo.

When Step 9 is completed, TYPE *C* board attachment will look like the illustration above. In this example, paper is used as sheets. Thick book board is used as the cover. Paper used as sheets should be slightly heavy, so the sewing will not rip out. I prefer Stonehedge which I can image on my inkjet printer. Something like Canson is all right, but is not a smooth surface unlike Stonehedge.

You are now ready to add the next sheet as described on page 145. See finished example on pages 145 and 150.

Sewing Preparation

Whether you use TYPE *A, B* or *C* board attachment there is this final note of caution. Preparation is more than cutting the sheets and covers, pasting paper on the cover boards and piercing the boards. I must also advise you of what to look out for when sewing this unusual Coptic. Thus, I wish to state beforehand the need to adjust the sewing as you go:

In sewing sheets instead of sections, the thread tends to snag on the spine-edge of the sheet when linking. Care must be taken to adjust the thread in forming the link.

A stray thread can be adjusted as you go. After linking pull the thread taut and slightly to the side. This will align all the sewing to the sewing stations. If you notice a stray thread several links previous, push the stray thread close to the chain with a small bone folder or your fingernail.

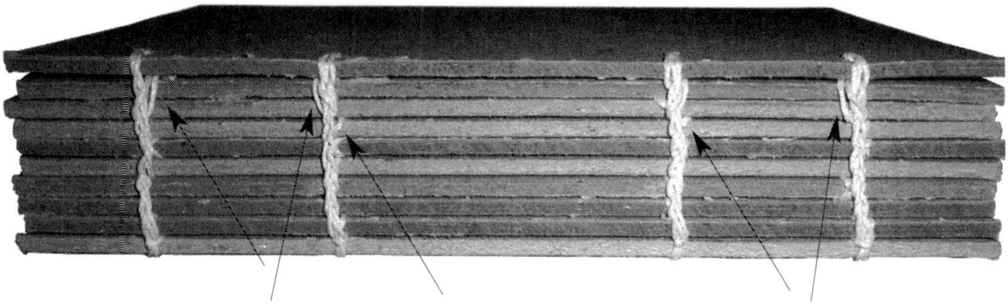

Heavy book board was used as the covers and the book block in this Coptic Sewing of sheets sewn across the spine. This was one of the first prototypes I sewed and it has several mistakes. After sewing this example of boards–as–sheets, I became aware that the thread tends to snag on the edge of the board when linking (arrows above). Care must be taken to adjust the thread in forming each link. Push the stray thread close to the chain with a small bone folder or your fingernail. It must be corrected before you proceed with the sewing.

SINGLE SHEET COPTIC SEWN *ACROSS* THE SPINE

USING TYPE *A* BOARD ATTACHMENT

Coptics sewn across the spine will be shown first, and on page 161 is a Coptic sewn along the spine. I prefer sewing *across the spine:*

- There is a full chain formed by the link stitches at the head and the tail. Sewing *along the spine* requires a kettle stitch at the head and tail in order to climb to the next unit to be sewn. The kettle looks like a partially formed chain and is not as attractive.
- Each sewing of paired stations across the spine is independent. If a thread breaks, only that sewing is affected. Sewing along the spine, if a thread breaks the entire sewing is compromised.
- With separate sewings across the spine, each thread can be a different color.
- Sewing along the spine, the final sheet or section must be sewn along with the separate side cover. This is difficult. Adding the second board is easy sewing across the spine.
- The only disadvantage of sewing across the spine is that instead of one needle, a minimum of four and as many as 16, needles might be used. This can cause tangles and takes patience.

Cover and book blank block of this Single Sheet Coptic are 2–ply mat board.

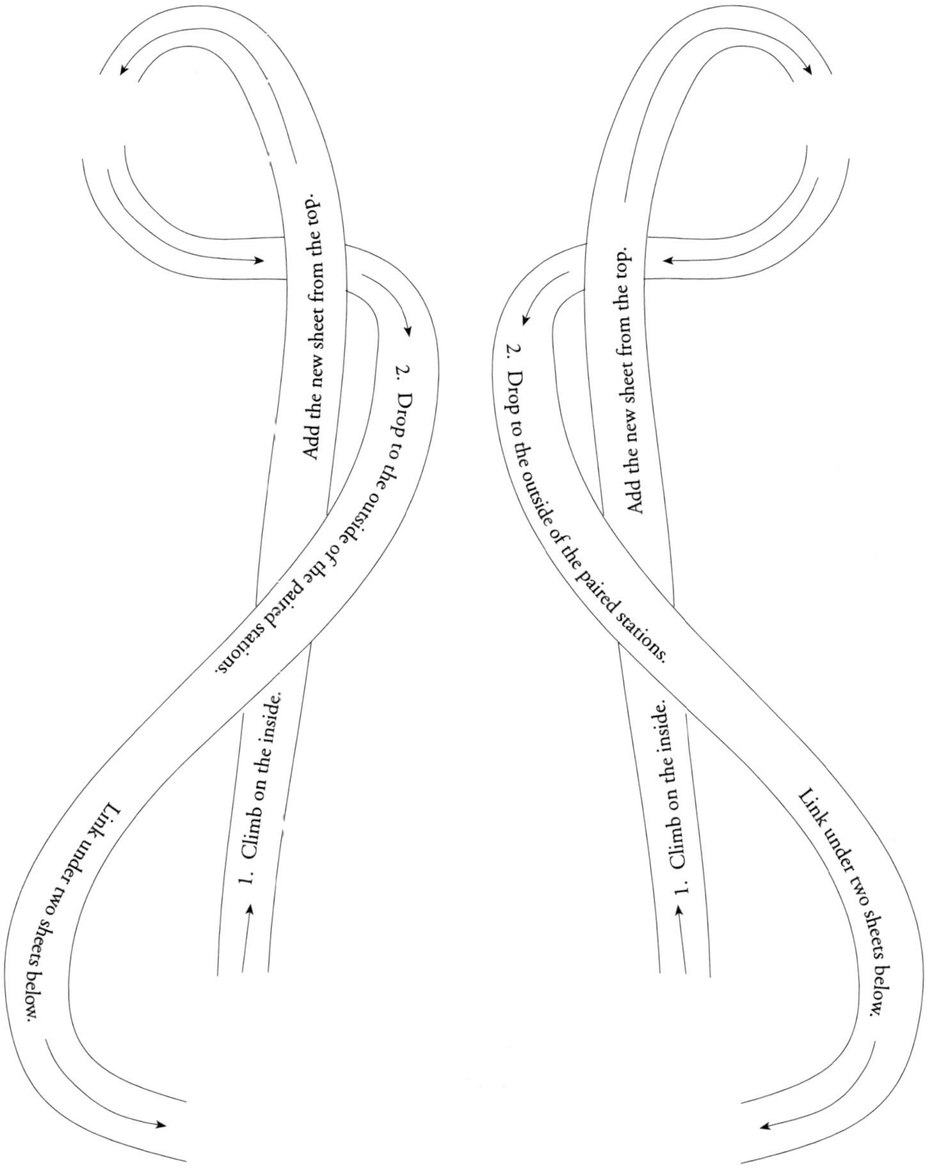

SEWING PATH: After the board is attached add a new sheet. The sewing path is this:

1. Climb on the inside. Add the new sheet and go through the hole from the top.
2. Drop on the outside. Link under at two sheets down.

Sewing Path

The diagrams on pages 131, 139 and 147 seemed complicated, but they aren't. Don't be intimidated! After the board is attached add a new sheet. The sewing path is this:

1. Climb on the inside of the paired stations. Attach the new sheet from the top
2. Drop on the outside. Link under at two sheets down, between the second and third sheets below.

The rest is repetition. After linking, repeat climbing and attaching, then dropping and linking for each additional sheet, except the final sheet to be sewn. I think it helps to take your two index fingers and form the sewing path in the air in front of you. It is symmetrical movement. Doing it with your fingers will set the pattern in your head preparing you to sew. I devise all my sewings in the air in front of me, but do not always use my index fingers to see the path. I see them in my imagination.

SEWING DESCRIPTION

Attaching the Board and Sewing the First Two Sheets

Steps 1–5 are attaching the board and sewing the first two sheets. It is described and illustrated starting on page 112. Continue with Step 6 on this page.

6*a*. Set on the (third) next sheet to be sewn. Take the *a* thread up over the new sheet. Attach the new sheet from the top to the inside. Bring the thread out on the spine–edge between the paired stations.

6*b*. Take the *b* thread up over the new sheet. Enter from the top to the inside. Bring the thread out between the paired stations. Repeat Steps 6*a* and 6*b* at all remaining paired stations on this sheet.

7*a*. Count down two sheets including the new one. Place a book mark between the second and third sheet down. Take the *a* thread and drop to the outside of the paired stations (a 45° angle to the left). Open the book block at the book mark. Link under from the outside to the inside. That is, take the thread to the inside. Go around the threads connecting the sheets at this station. Exit to the outside between the paired stations.

7*b*. Take the *b* thread. Drop to the outside (a 45° angle to the right). Open the book to the book mark. Link under from the outside to the inside. Repeat Steps 7*a* and 7*b* at all remaining paired stations on this sheet.

Sewing the Remaining Sheets Except the Final

Repeat Steps 6*a,* 6*b* and 7*a,* 7*b* to attach and link each additional sheet as shown on the facing page, and diagrammed on the page 131. After attaching the sheet and prior to linking, tightening and adjusting the sewing is critical.

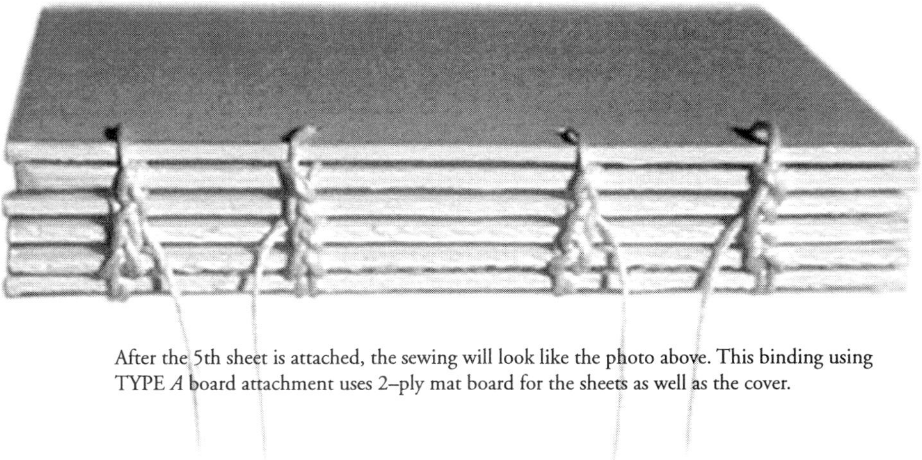

After the 5th sheet is attached, the sewing will look like the photo above. This binding using TYPE *A* board attachment uses 2–ply mat board for the sheets as well as the cover.

Pull the thread taut by pulling outward, then to the outside to align the sewing with the holes. Adjusting tension after linking requires care.

Sewing the Final Sheet and the Board

The example diagrammed on the facing page has only six sheets in the book block. This is a small book for illustration purposes. Step 10 attaches the next to last sheet. Step 11 drops and links under.

12*a*.Set on the final sheet to be sewn. Climb with the *a* thread up *under* the final sheet. Attach the new sheet from the bottom up through to the top.

13*a*.Set on the cover. Take the needle through the hole in the cover from the bottom to the top. Pull the thread through. Align the final sheet and cover with the book block.

12*b*.Climb with the *b* thread up *under* the final sheet. Attach the new sheet from the bottom up through to the top.

13*b*.Take the needle through the hole in the cover from the bottom to the top. Pull the thread through. Align the final sheet and cover with the book block. Repeat Steps 12*a* and 12*b* at all the remaining paired stations.

14*a*.Drop to the outside. Link under from the outside to the inside between the next to last and second from last sheet.

14*b*.Drop to the outside. Link under from the outside to the inside between the next to last and second from last sheet. Repeat Steps 14*a* and 14*b* at all remaining paired stations.

15*a* and 16*a*. Climb and attach the cover again. This time attach from the top to the inside of the cover. Exit on the inside of the paired stations.

15*b* and 16*b*. Climb and attach the cover from the top to the inside. Exit on the inside of the paired stations. Repeat Steps 15*a* and 15*b* at the remaining stations. Pull the threads taut to align the sewing with the holes.

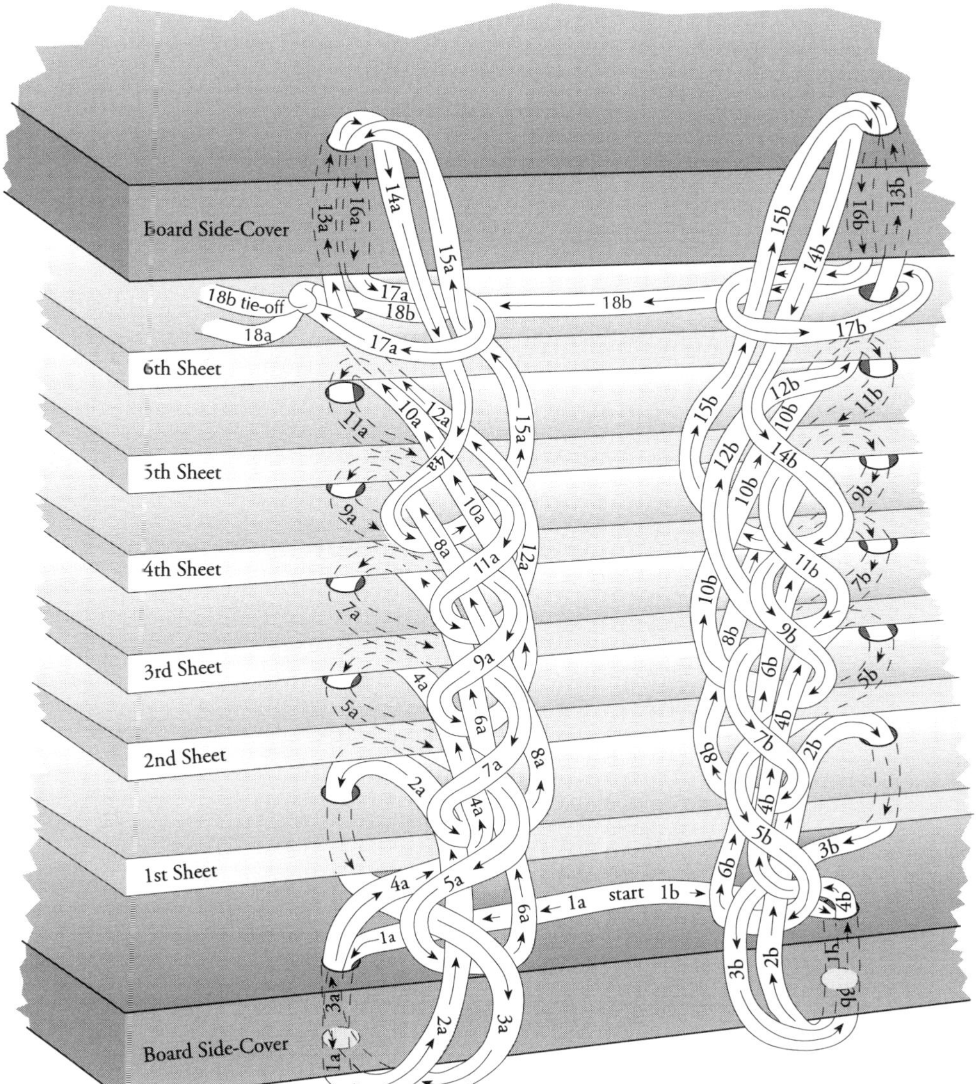

Diagram for sewing the Single Sheet Coptic across the spine using TYPE *A* board attachment.

17*a* and 17*b*. Link around the threads connecting the final sheet and the cover from the inside to the outside of the paired stations. Leave the threads temporarily inside between the final sheet and the cover. removing the needles so they do not indent the sheet.

Tying Off

18*a*. Take the *b* thread along the inside of the cover to the paired hole. Tie the *b* thread with the *a* thread using a square knot. *See* square knot, page 59. Repeat Step 18 at the remaining stations.

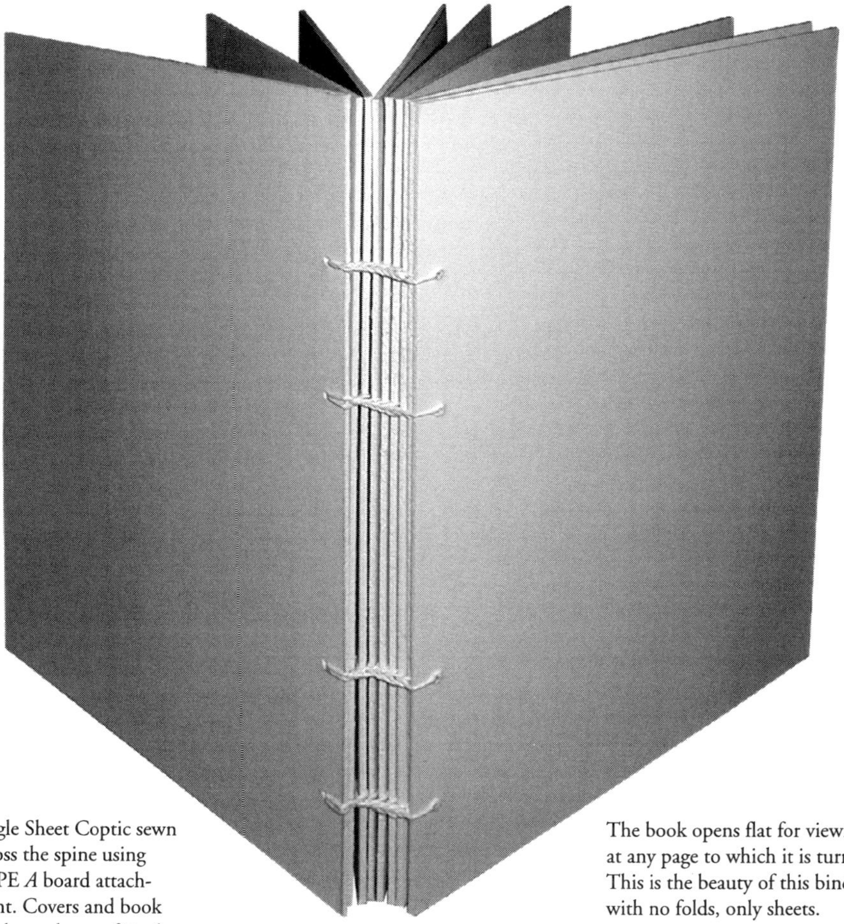

Single Sheet Coptic sewn across the spine using TYPE *A* board attachment. Covers and book block are sheets of 2–ply mat board.

The book opens flat for viewing at any page to which it is turned. This is the beauty of this binding with no folds, only sheets.

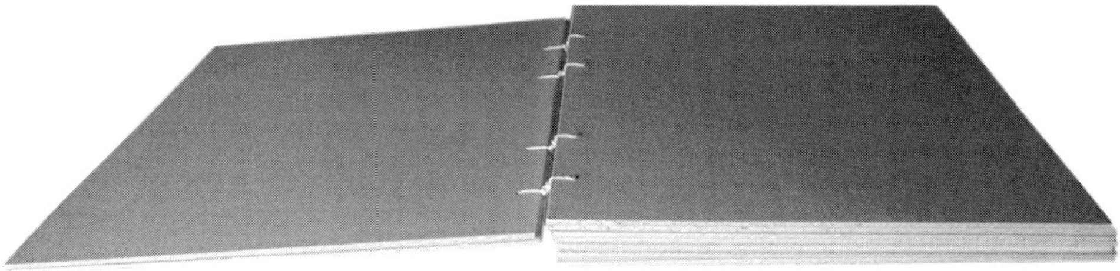

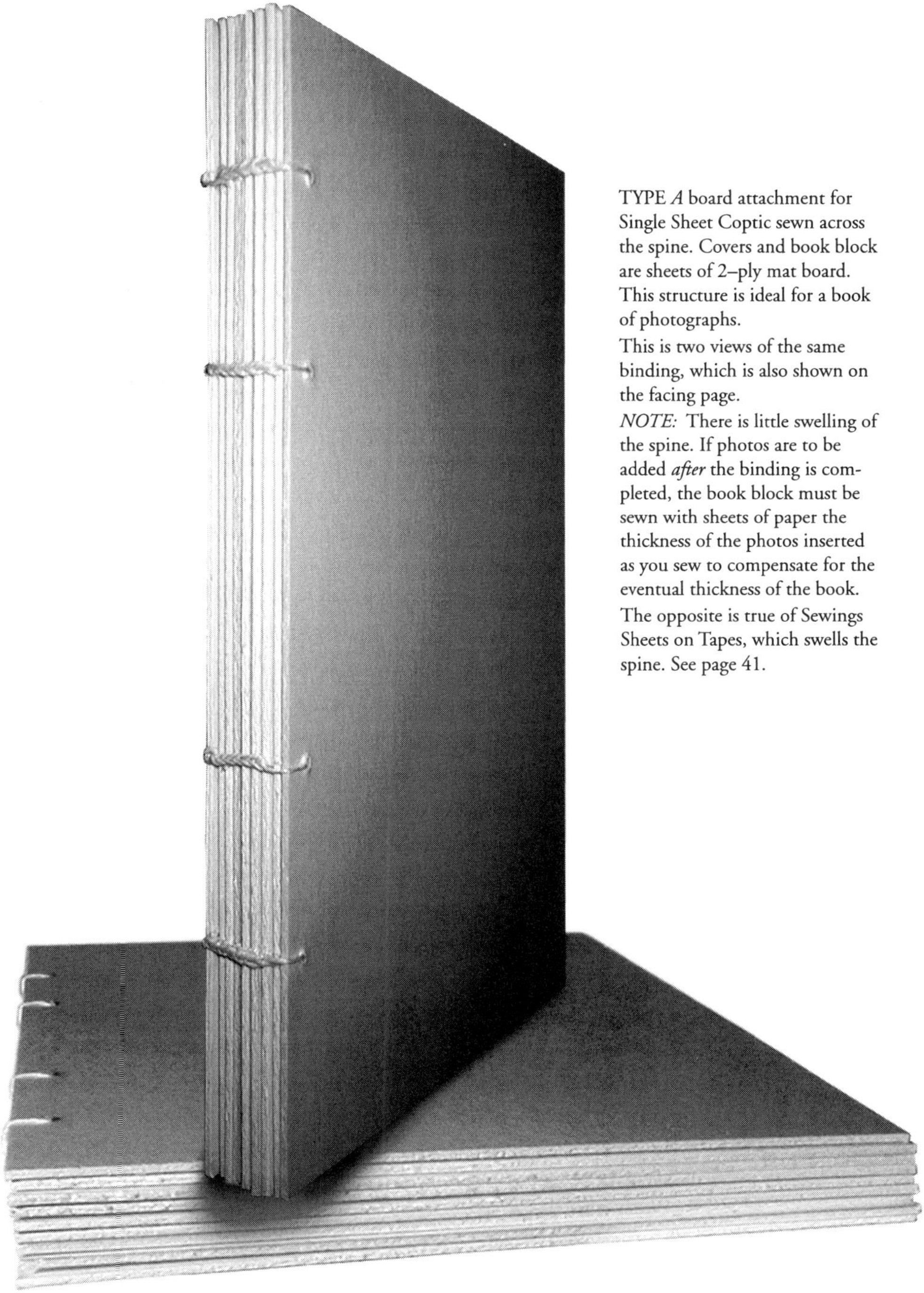

TYPE *A* board attachment for Single Sheet Coptic sewn across the spine. Covers and book block are sheets of 2–ply mat board. This structure is ideal for a book of photographs.

This is two views of the same binding, which is also shown on the facing page.

NOTE: There is little swelling of the spine. If photos are to be added *after* the binding is completed, the book block must be sewn with sheets of paper the thickness of the photos inserted as you sew to compensate for the eventual thickness of the book.

The opposite is true of Sewings Sheets on Tapes, which swells the spine. See page 41.

Metal offset plates donated by Philip Zimmermann sewn as a Single Sheet Coptic. The entire book block is chopped down plates. The book block could have been augmented by paper sheets, or even paper folded into sections, with only a few offset plates as pages. The book will open flat to any page. Another photo of this sample binding is on the facing page.

TYPE *A* board attachment for Single Sheet Coptic sewn across the spine. Here, metal offset plates have been pierced and sewn as sheets. The separate side–covers are mat board.

SINGLE SHEET COPTIC SEWN *ACROSS* THE SPINE
USING TYPE *B* BOARD ATTACHMENT

The only difference between this Coptic and the previous is the board attachment. There is only one thread at each hole connecting the book block and the cover board. The sewing begins on the sheet instead of the board.

TYPE *B* board attachment for Single Sheet Coptic sewn across the spine. Folios are sewn here, but the fold is on the foredge. Both spine–edges of the folio could be sewn at once. However, each spine–edge of the folios have been sewn separately. Attaching each edge and linking separately doubles the thickness of the spine. This exaggerates the cast shadows of cut shapes on the first part of the folio, looking through to the inside of the remainder of that folio. Other views of this binding are on pages 18, 106 and 141.

SEWING DESCRIPTION

Attaching the Board and Sewing the First Two Sheets

Steps 1–5 are attaching the board and sewing the first two sheets. It is described and illustrated starting on page 116. Continue with Step 6 on this page.

6*a*. Drop to the outside. Again, link under between the board and the sheet from the outside to the inside of the paired stations.

7*a*. Set on the (third) next sheet to be sewn. Climb on the inside. Take the *a* thread up over the new sheet. Attach the sheet from the top to the inside. Bring the thread out on the spine–edge between the paired stations.

6*b*. Drop to the outside. Link under between the board and the sheet from the outside to the inside of the paired stations.

7*b*. Climb on the inside. Take the *b* thread up over the new sheet. Attach the sheet from the top to the inside. Bring the thread out on the spine–edge between the paired stations.
Repeat Steps 7*a* and 7*b* at all remaining paired stations on this sheet.

8*a*. Count down two sheets including the new one. Place a book mark between the second and third sheet down. Take the *a* thread and drop to the outside of the paired stations (a 45° angle to the left). Open the book block at the book mark. Link under from the outside to the inside. That is, take the thread to the inside. Go around the threads connecting the sheets at this station. Exit to the outside between the paired stations.

8*b*. Take the *b* thread. Drop to the outside (a 45° angle to the right). Open the book to the book mark. Link under from the outside to the inside.
Repeat Steps 8*a* and 8*b* at all remaining paired stations on this sheet.

Sewing the Remaining Sheets Except the Final

Repeat Steps 7*a*, 7*b* and 8*a*, 8*b* to attach and link each additional sheet as shown on page 139, as well as diagrammed on the facing page. After attaching the sheet and prior to linking, tightening and adjusting the sewing is critical.

Pull the thread taut by pulling outward, then to the outside to align the sewing with the holes. Adjusting tension is critical.

Sewing the Final Sheet and the Board

The example diagrammed on the facing page has only six sheets in the book block. For such a small book, Step 11 attaches the next to last sheet. Step 12 drops and links under.

13*a*. Set on the final sheet to be sewn. Climb with the *a* thread up over the final sheet. Attach the new sheet from the top.

14*a*. Go through the sheet coming out on the inside of the paired stations.

13*b*. Climb with the *b* thread up over the final sheet. Attach from the top.

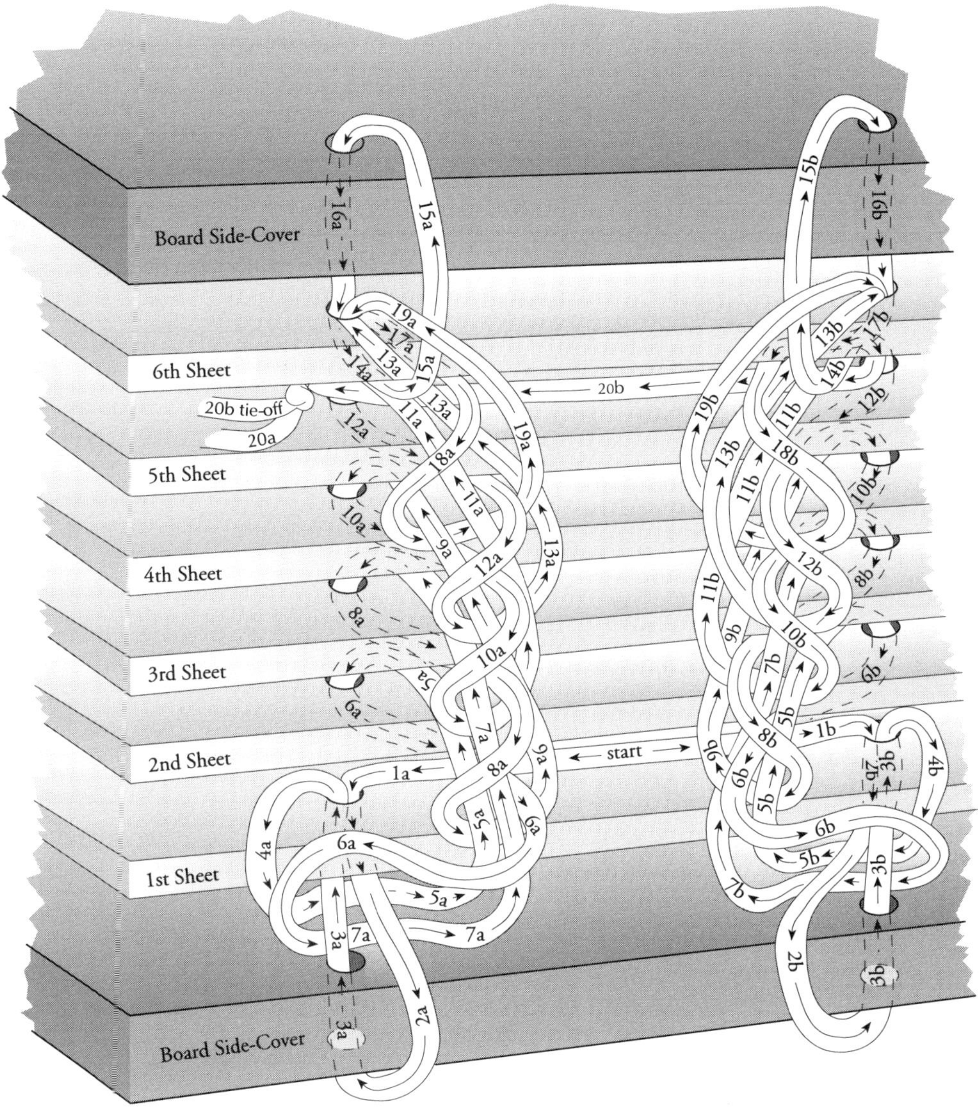

Diagram for sewing the Single Sheet Coptic across the spine using TYPE *B* board attachment.

14*b*. Go through the sheet coming out on the inside of the paired stations. Repeat Steps 13*a*, 13*b* and 14*a*, 14*b* at all remaining paired stations on this sheet.

15*a*. Set on the cover. Climb and attach the board from the top.

16*a*. Take the needle through the cover hole from the top to the bottom.
17*a*. Pull the thread through to the inside of the paired stations.
15*b*. Climb and attach the board from the top.
16*b*. Take the needle through the hole in the cover from the top to the bottom of the board.
17*b*. Pull the thread through. Come out on the inside of the paired stations. Repeat Steps 15*a*, 15*b* through 17*a*, 17*b* at all remaining paired stations on this sheet. Align the final sheet and cover with the book block.

NOTE: The sewing (chain) on the spine must be corrected to a vertical after each sheet is attached, prior to linking. Tightening and adjusting the sewing is critical. To adjust the sewing, pull the thread taut by pulling outward, but not so hard as to rip the sheet. Then pull the thread slightly to the outside to align the sewing with the holes.

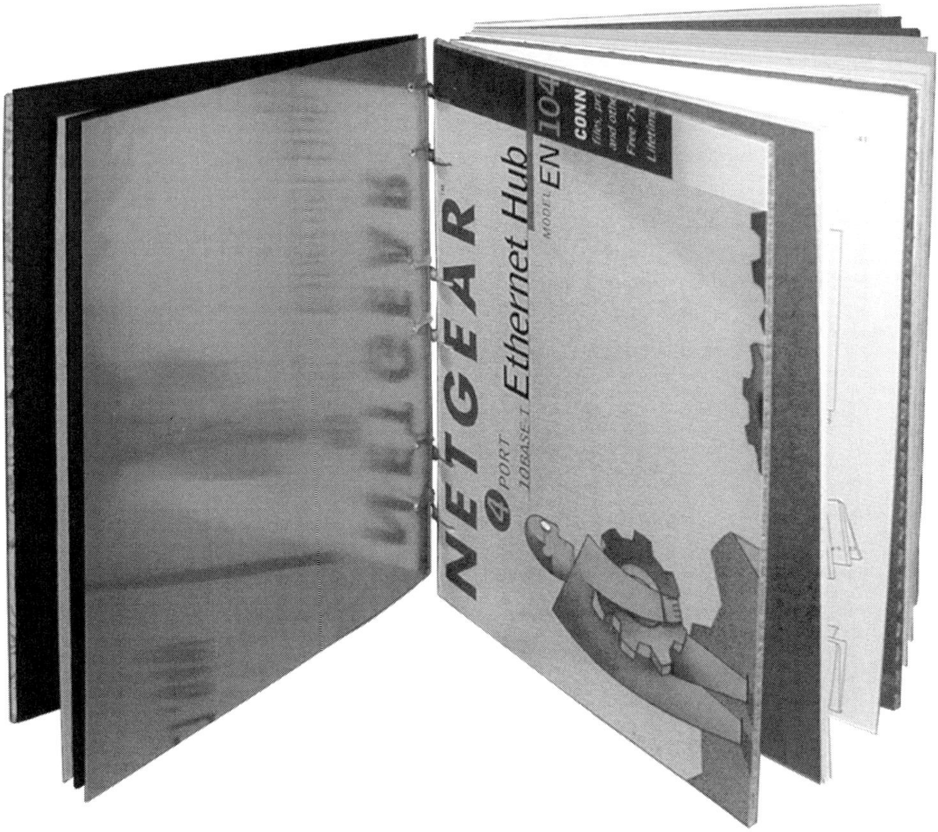

Sample of the Single Sheet Coptic across the spine using TYPE *B* board attachment. On the left is an aluminum plate. On the right is part of a shipping box for my latest computer toy.

Adjusting tension after linking requires extremely little pressure to form the 45° angle links.

18*a*. Drop to the outside. Link down two sheet from the outside to the inside.

18*b*. Drop to the outside. Link under two sheets down from the outside to the inside.

Repeat Steps 18*a* and 18*b* at all remaining paired stations

Optional Link

As the first part of Step 19, you can first link around the two threads attaching the board and the final sheet *prior to attaching* the final sheet. This link is optional. It is *not* shown in the diagram on the previous page. This will lock the board in place.

19*a*. Open the cover. Climb on the inside of the paired stations with the *a* thread and attach the top sheet from the top through to the bottom unless you are going to add the optional link first, as described above. Remove the needle so it does not indent the sheet. Leave the thread inside temporarily.

19*b*. Climb with the *b* thread on the inside and attach the top sheet from the top through to the bottom. Remove the needle and leave the thread inside.

Repeat Steps 19*a* and 19*b* at all remaining paired stations.

Step 19 will place two stitches on the final sheet. The first was Step 13.

20*b*. Bring the *b* thread to *a* station. Tie–off the *a* and *b* threads with a square knot. *See* square knot, page 59. Repeat the tie–off at all the paired stations.

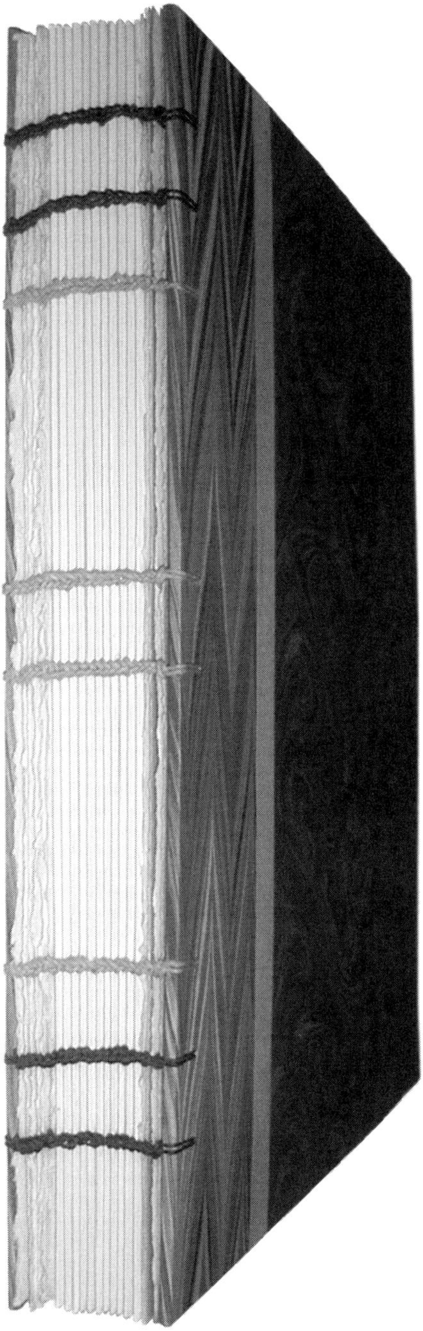

Single Sheet Coptic across the spine using TYPE *B* board attachment. The center of the book block is sections with single sheets sewn as the first few pages and the final dozen pages.

Single Sheet Coptic Sewn Across the Spine.
This binding of sheets of cardboard uses
TYPE *B* board attachment

Additional views of the sheets of cardboard bound with the Single Sheet Coptic Sewing.

SINGLE SHEET COPTIC SEWN *ACROSS* THE SPINE

USING TYPE *C* BOARD ATTACHMENT

TYPE *C* board attachment is ideal when using wooden boards or glass as the side–covers. It can also be used on thick book board, as long as the board does not flay open when pierced through the depth of the board.

SEWING DESCRIPTION

Attaching the Board and Sewing the First Two Sheets

Steps 1–9 are attaching the board and sewing the first two sheets. It is described and illustrated starting on page 122. Continue with Step 10 below.

10*a*, 10*b*. Set on the (third) next sheet to be sewn. Climb on the inside. Take the *a* thread up over the new sheet. Attach the sheet from the top to the inside. Bring the thread out on the spine–edge between the paired stations. Repeat this at all the remaining paired stations for the third sheet.

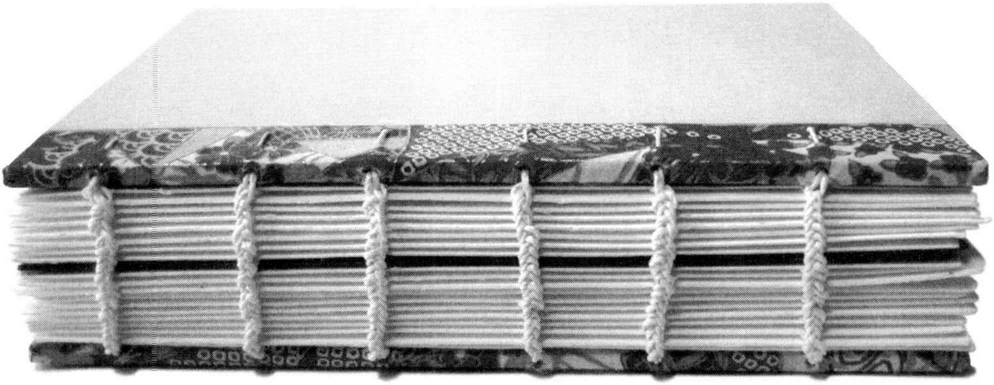

This sample of the Single Sheet Coptic Sewn Across the Spine uses TYPE *C* board attachment. Other photos of this binding are on pages 124 and 150.

11*a,* 11*b.* Count down two sheets including the new one. Place a book mark between the second and third sheet down. Drop down on the outside of the paired stations. Open the book at the book mark. Link under from the outside to the inside of the paired stations.
Repeat Steps 11*a* and 11*b* at all remaining paired stations on this sheet.

Sewing the Remaining Sheets Except the Final

Repeat Steps 10*a,* 10*b* and 11*a,* 11*b* to attach and link each additional sheet as shown on page 145, as well as diagrammed on the facing page. After linking, adjust the sewing by pulling the threads taut, then to the outside to align the sewing with the holes.

Sewing the Final Sheet and the Board

The example diagrammed on the facing page has only six sheets in the book block. For such a small book, Step 14 attaches the next to last sheet. Step 15 drops and links under.

16*a,* 16*b.* Set on the final sheet to be sewn. Climb on the inside of the paired stations. Attach the final sheet rom the top to the bottom. Pull the thread to the out on the spine on the inside of the paired stations.

17*a.*Set on the cover. Climb on the inside of the paired stations. With the *a* thread, set the needle point in the hole on the depth of the board.

18*a.*Take the needle through to the top of the board. Pull the thread through. Grasp the cover with one hand and hold it vertically just above the final sheet. Hold it in this manner until Steps 17*a*–20*a* and 17*b*–20*b* are completed.

19*a.*Proceed to the remaining hole on the top of the cover at this station.

20*a.*Take the needle through the hole to the inside of the board. Pull the thread through beyond the foredge.

17*b,* 18*b.* Take the *b* thread up and go through the hole on the depth of the board to the top of the board.

19*b.*Proceed to the remaining hole at this station.

20*b.*Take the *b* needle through the hole to the inside of the board. Pull the thread through beyond the foredge.
Repeat Steps Steps 17*a*–20*a* and 17*b*–20*b* at all remaining stations. Turn the book 180°.

21*a.*Take the needle to the remaining hole on the board at this station.

22*a.*Go through the board, exiting on the depth of the board. Pull the thread through to dangle down the spine.

21*b,* 22*b.* On the inside, take the *b* needle through the remaining hole at this station, exiting on the depth of the board.
Repeat Steps 21*a,* 21*b* and 22*a,* 22*b* at all remaining paired stations. Turn the book 180° so the spine is facing you.

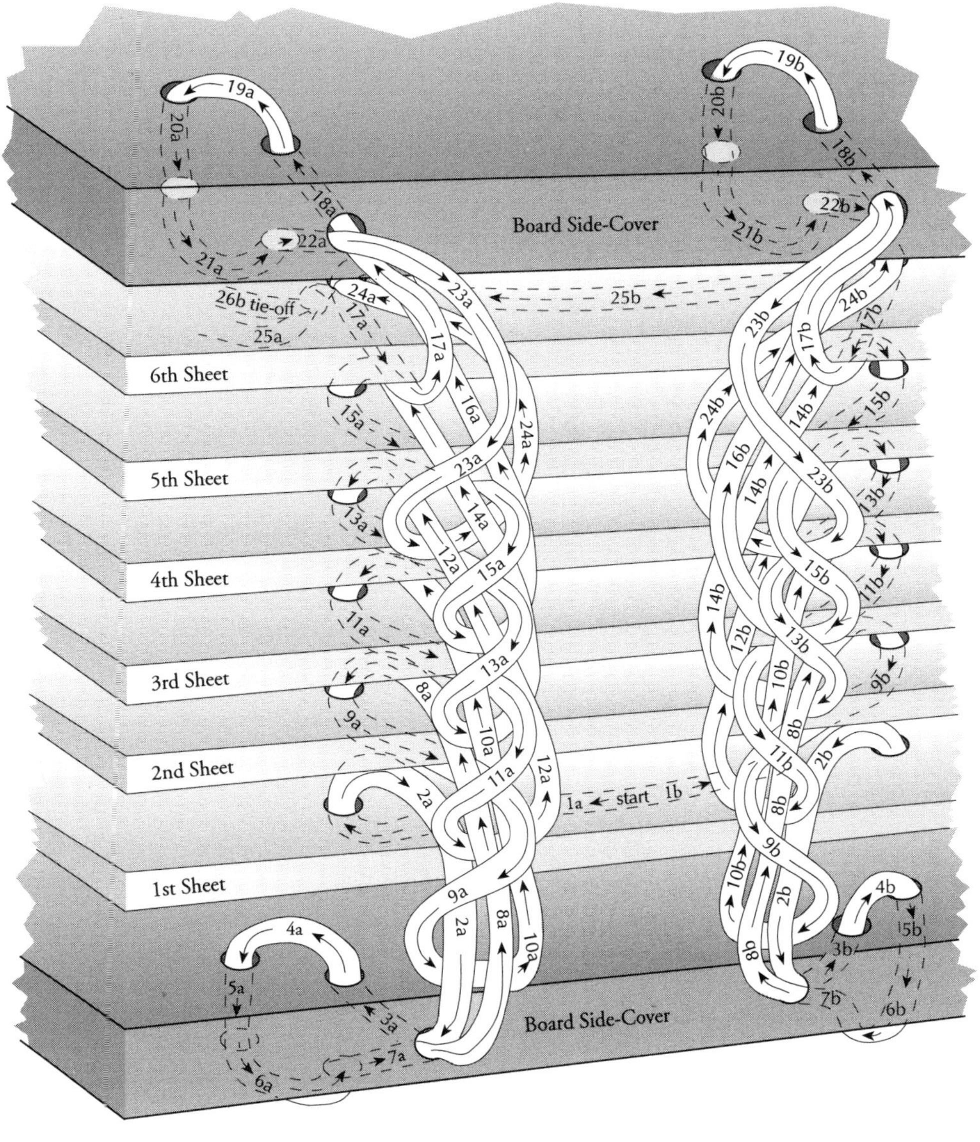

Single Sheet Coptic Sewn Across the Spine. This diagram shows TYPE *C* board attachment. The optional linking of the final sheet is not diagrammed here but on page 149.

Adjust the cover so that it aligns with the book block and the edge of the cover is flush with the spine. Pull all the threads taut. The final sheet now will be linked. Place a book mark between the second and third to last final sheet.

23*a*. Take the *a* thread and drop to the outside. Open the book block at the book mark. Link under from the outside to the inside. Exit to the spine on the inside of the paired stations.

23*b*. Take the *b* thread. Drop to the outside. Open the book to the book mark. Link under from the outside to the inside.

Repeat Steps 23*a* and 23*b* at all remaining paired stations.

NOTE: If you wish to have an optional link which would occur between the last and next to last sheet, follow *Optional Link,* Steps 24–27 at the bottom of this page, *rather than* Steps 24–26 immediately below.

Tying Off Without the Optional Link

24*a*. Without the optional link, take the *a* thread and again attach the final sheet from the top to the bottom. Remove the needle. Let the *a* thread rest inside between the final and next to last sheet.

24*b*. Take the *b* thread and again attach the final sheet from the top to the bottom. Remove the needle. Let the *b* thread rest inside between the final and next to last sheet.

Repeat Steps 24*a* and 24*b* at all remaining paired stations.

25*b*. Take the *b* thread over to the *a* thread.

25*a,* 26*b.* Tie–off with a square knot, page 59 at the *a* station.

Optional Link

Open the cover to a vertical. Hold it with one hand.

24*a*. Climb on the inside of the paired stations. Link from the *inside* to the *outside* between the board and the final sheet. That is, take the needle inside between the final sheet and the board on the inside of the paired stations. Go around the threads connecting the board and final sheet. Take the thread to the outside of the paired stations.

24*b*. Climb on the inside. Link from the *inside* to the *outside* between the board and the final sheet. Take the thread to the outside.

Repeat Steps 24*a* and 24*b* at all remaining paired stations

25*a*. Drop to the outside. Link under from the outside to the inside two sheets down, between the second from last and third from last sheets.

25*b*. Drop to the outside. Link under from the outside to the inside between the second from last and third from last sheets.

Repeat Steps 25*a* and 25*b* at all remaining paired stations.

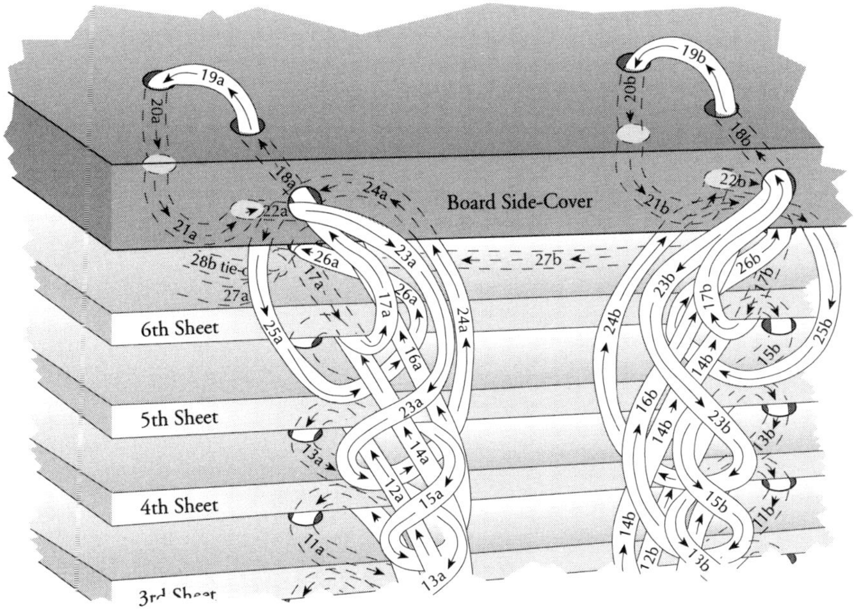

OPTIONAL LINK: Steps 24, 25 link around the board and the final sheet on the inside, so the thread can drop on the outside to make a link under between the second to last and third to last sheet, which is Steps 25, 26. The thread then goes through the hole in the final sheet to tie–off the same as without the optional link.

Tying Off After the Optional Link

26*a*. Take the *a* thread and again attach the final sheet from the top to the bottom. Remove the needle. Let the *a* thread rest inside between the final and next to last sheet.

26*b*. Take the *b* thread and again attach the final sheet from the top to the bottom. Remove the needle. Let the *b* thread rest inside between the final and next to last sheet.

Repeat Steps 26*a* and 26*b* at all remaining paired stations.

27*b*. Take the *b* thread over to the *a* thread.

27*a*, 28*b*. Tie–off with a square knot at the *a* station. See page 59.

Single Sheet Coptic Sewn Across the Spine with TYPE *C* board attachment through the depth of the book board cover. The book block is sheets of cream colored Stonehedge paper with one sheet of purple to demonstrate there are no folds, only sheets.

Single Sheet Coptic Sewn Across the Spine. The bulk of the pages in this book are sewn as sections. Only the first few pages and the final dozen pages are sewn as sheets with no folds. The sections use the same link pattern of dropping to the outside to link under. Obviously, the sections are attached in the traditional manner, whereas the single sheets rely upon the secondary stitching of bridled sheets.

This book represents why I devised these sewings. — I wanted to be able to have pages in a book to be the maximum size sheet I could run through my inkjet printer. The digital images are the largest I can make with my current computer setup.

The inside of the front board is seen. All the decorative papers are inlaid, although I often paste down the strips on top of the doublure. On the outside of the board it is imperative that all papers be inlaid to present scuffing.

SINGLE SHEET COPTIC SEWN *ACROSS* THE SPINE
WITHOUT PAIRED STATIONS

Sewing across the spine is traditionally at paired stations; there always must be an even number of stations. Structurally this is fine, but for purposes of design, paired stations may not be always desirable. I devised this sewing across the spine with one thread, one needle at one set of stations. In this manner you can have an even or odd number of stations. There might be three or five separate sewings. You might use the previous sewing with paired stations at the head and tail, which would be four stations. A fifth station in the center of the spine would use this sewing. This would require three sewings, instead of five separate sewings if you sewed each station with this particular sewing.

This new sewing is of minor use, but then *design* is always considering the minute details; *structure* is a consideration of major factors.

BOARD ATTACHMENT: This sewing requires a unique board attachment. It is described as the first steps of the sewing.

Sewing Preparation

APPROPRIATE PAPER: The book block should be 80 lb. cover weight or fairly stiff. The sewing would rip out of delicate or thin paper sheets.

NUMBER AND POSITION OF HOLES: The holes should be close to the spine–edge not to interfere with the imagery on the page. If the sheets are pierced 1/4" in from the spine–edge that will be far enough away so they do not rip out. There can be an even or odd number of sewing stations. Pierce as many holes for the sewing stations as you like, but there should be no more than 1 1/2" between the holes. Cover the boards prior to sewing.

Single Sheet Coptic Sewn Across the Spine without paired stations. This first prototype has only three separate sewings requiring three threads and three needles. It is laterally wobbly and should have had five sewings across the spine. It is also bowed because of loose tension in the middle sewing.

Corners of the sheets need to be secured at the head and the tail. Pierce the first hole no farther away from the tail than 1/2", and no closer than 3/8". Do the same for the final hole at the head.

Pierce the sheets and the boards with the same number of stations and the same distance in from the spine–edge for the boards as well as the sheets.

NUMBER OF NEEDLES: Thread a needle for each of the stations, as they are separate, independent sewings.

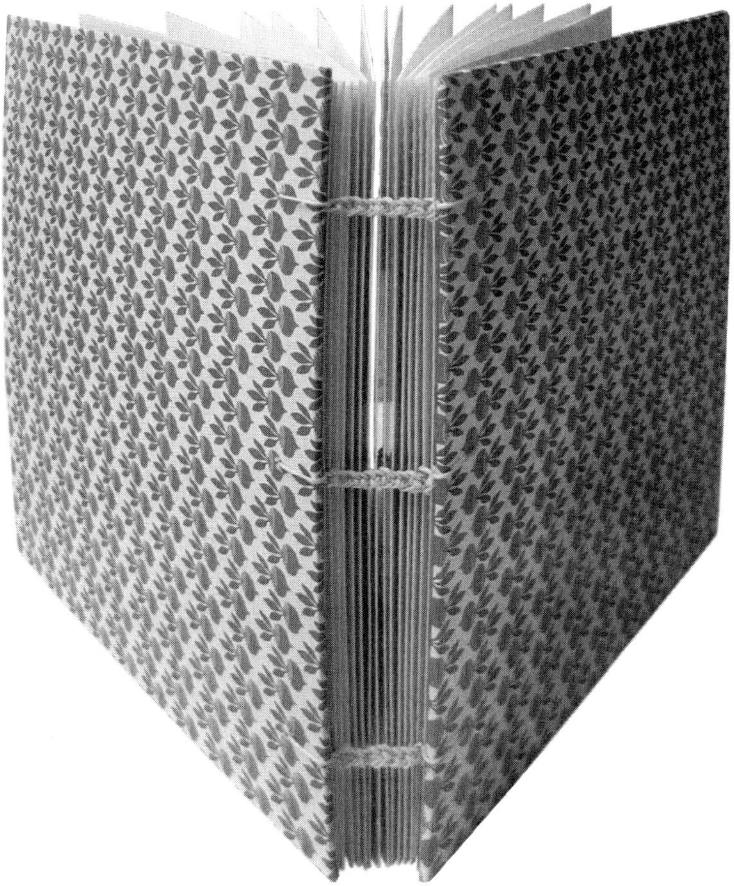

Single Sheet Coptic Sewn Across the Spine without paired stations. Each station has a separate sewing across the spine. Each sewing on the spine could be a different color.

Starting the Sewing

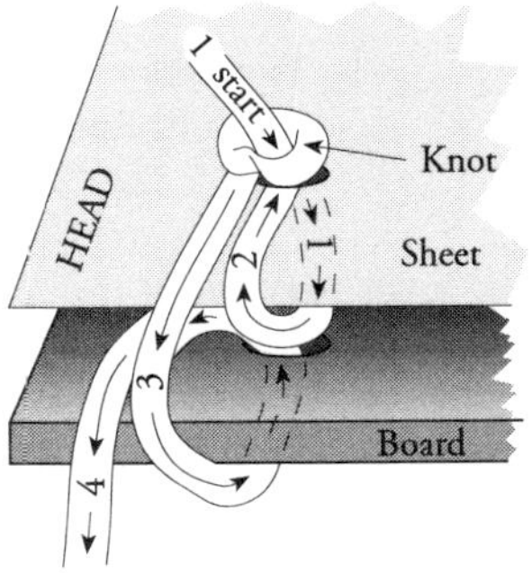

STEP 1: Enter the hole in the sheet from the top through to the underneath.
STEP 2: Come around the spine–edge. Tie a square knot.
STEP 3: Set the board. Proceed to the spine–edge left of the station. Go around the spine–edge. Enter the board, only, from the outside of the board to the inside.
STEP 4: Exit to the spine on the left of the station.

1. Go through the hole in the first sheet from the top through to the underneath. Leave 3" of thread on top.
2. Come around the spine–edge of the sheet. Tie a square knot exactly at the station. Clip the shorter thread fairly close to the knot. Do this with each thread at each of the remaining stations. Each step is repeated at all the stations before proceeding to the next step. This keeps the sewing even.
3. Set the board under the sheet. Proceed from the station on the sheet to the spine–edge to the left of the station. Go around the spine–edge of the sheet and the board. Go through the board, only, from the outside of the board to the inside.
4. Exit to the spine on the left of the station. Pull the threads taut and align the board with the sheet. Do this at each of the remaining stations.
5. Link under both threads on the sheet from the left to the right.
6. Set on the next sheet. I prefer holding it slightly above the previously sewn sheet to attach the next sheet.

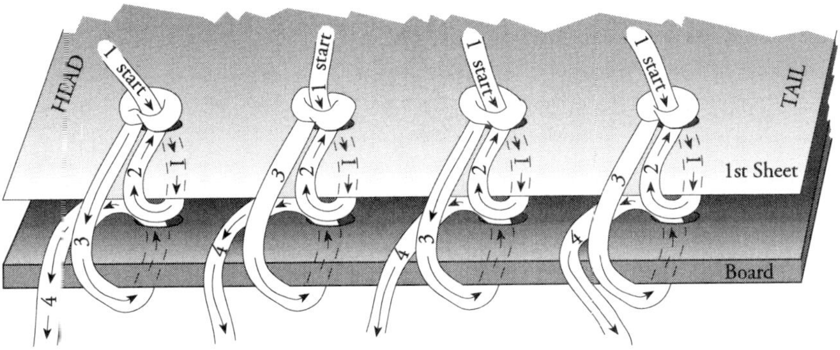

Complete Step 1 at the first station, then repeat Step 1 at all the remaining stations before beginning Step 2. Then do Step 2 at all stations prior to starting Step 3. This will help keep the tension in the sewing uniform.

Climb on the right. Enter the new sheet from the top. Exit to the left. Allow the thread to dangle on the spine. After attaching all the threads, position the new sheet on the book block. Pull all the threads snug, but not tight; you will rip the paper. This forms an almost vertical thread on the spine, slightly to the right of the station.

7. Link the stitch on the top sheet counter–clockwise. Pull to the left until almost taut. Then pull out from the spine. This will tighten the sewing and align the vertical thread on the spine exactly at the station so the forming chain on the spine will not go askew. Again, do not pull tight, just taut.

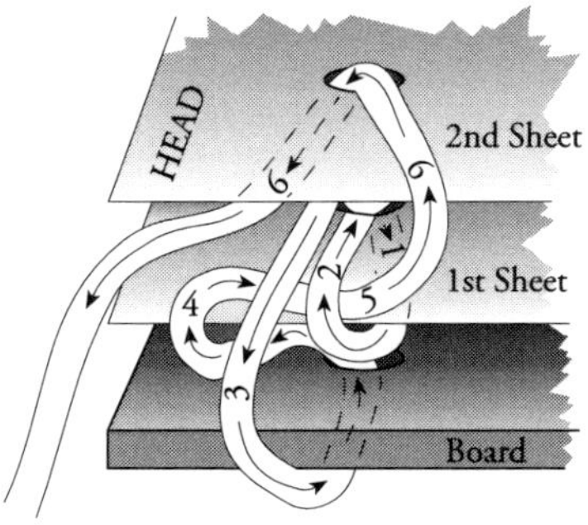

STEP 5: Link under both threads on the sheet from the left to the right.
STEP 6: Set on the next sheet. Climb and enter the hole in the new sheet from the top. Exit to the left.

Forming the First Link on the Spine

8. Drop to the left, down two positions/sheets. Link under.

NOTE: For this sheet, you will link under between the board and the first sheet. Sewing the next sheet, you will link under between the first and second sheet. Always open the book to the position you are linking. It is easy to pass the needle to the inside on the left and exit on the spine. The thread goes around the connecting thread at this station.

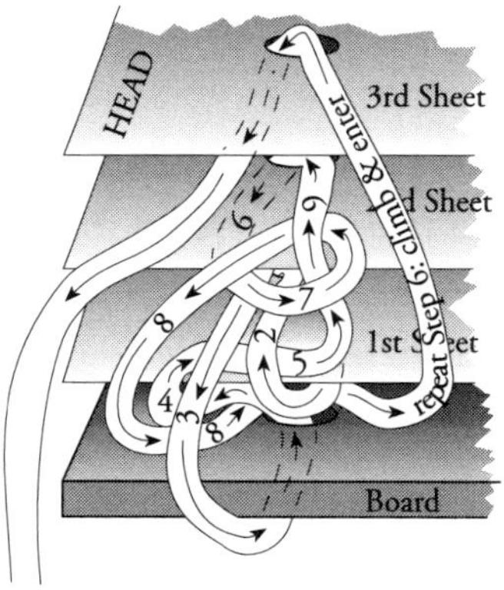

STEP 7: Link the stitch on the top sheet from the right. Pull to the left until almost taut. Then pull out from the spine to align the sewing.
STEP 8: Drop to the left, down two positions/sheets. Link under.

Complete Steps 1–8 for all the stations on the first sheet. After linking all the stations for this sheet, close the book. At eye level with the spine gently tug to tighten each thread just enough so it is not loose. If you pull too hard, you will have two vertical threads on the spine, rather than a teardrop shape. The teardrop linking forms a chain on the spine. Each teardrop needs to be precisely the same size. Adjusting tension is critical.

Sewing the Remaining Sheets

Repeat Steps 6–8 to sew each new sheet except the final sheet.

Sewing the Final Sheet and the Board

Set on the final sheet to be sewn. The description will start as Step 9:

9. Climb on the right. Enter the final sheet from the top, exiting to the left. Attach all the threads at each station. Pull all the threads snug.
10. Link the stitch on the top sheet counter–clockwise. Pull to the left until almost taut. Then pull out from the spine to tighten the sewing.
11. Set on the board, or hold slightly above the book block while attaching the board. Enter the board from the top to the inside. Exit to the spine on the left of the station.
12. Link the stitch on the board counter–clockwise. Pull to the left until almost taut. Then pull out from the spine to tighten the sewing.

Forming the Next to Last Link on the Spine

13. Drop to the left, down three positions, that is, the board plus two sheets. Simply open the board with two sheets. Link under.
14. Close the two sheets but leave the cover open. Climb on the right side of the station. Link under between the board and the final sheet. Simply go around the thread that connects the board to the book block from the right, exiting to the spine on the left. Adjust the tension of the threads.

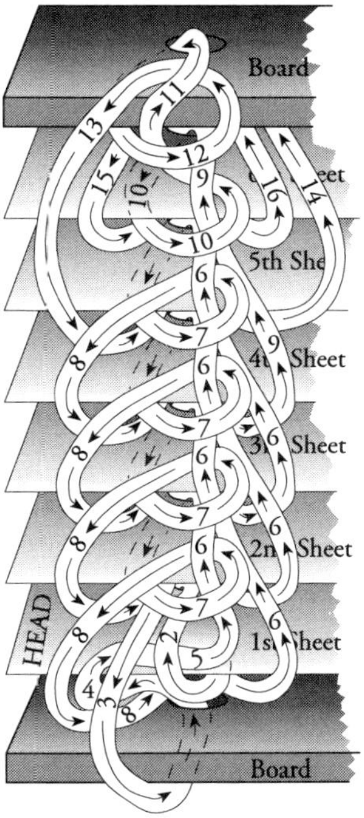

STEP 9: Climb and enter the hole in the final sheet. Exit left.
STEP 10: Link the top stitch on the sheet.
STEP 11: Set on the board. Enter from the top. Exit on the left of the station.
STEP 12: Link the stitch on the board counter–clockwise.
STEP 13: Drop to the left, down three positions, the board with two sheets. Link under.
STEP 14: Close the two sheets but leave the cover open. Climb on the right. Link under between the board and the final sheet. Exit on the left.
STEP 15: Drop to the left, two positions, the board plus the final sheet. Open the board with the final sheet. Link under.
STEP 16: Close the final sheet but leave the cover open. Climb on the right side of the station. Take the thread to the inside on the right of the station so that it is between the board and the final sheet. Adjust the tension of the threads on the spine.

Forming the Last Link on the Spine

15. Drop to the left, down two positions, that is, the board plus the final sheet. Open the board with the final sheet. Link under.
16. Close the final sheet but leave the cover open. Climb on the right side of the station. Take the thread to the inside on the right of the station so that it is between the board and the final sheet. Adjust the tension of the threads on the spine.

Tie–off

17. Take the thread through the station on the final sheet. The thread will be between the final and next to last sheet.
18. Tie–off with a half hitch by linking under the thread on the final sheet and forming a half hitch. *See* half hitch, page 65.

NOTE: If the shape of the chain looks good with Step 13, omit Steps 14 and 15 and tie–off as described in Steps 16–18.

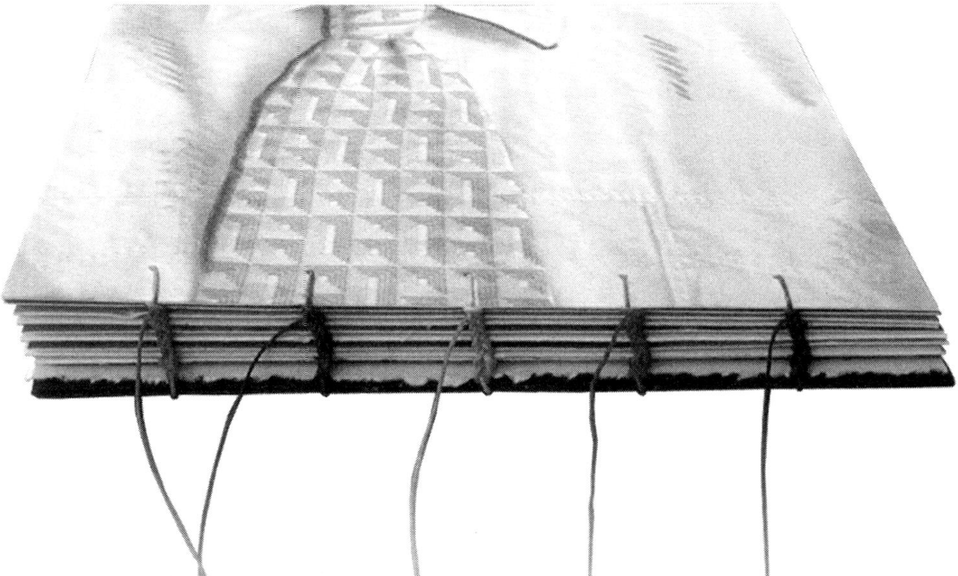

Single Sheet Coptic Sewn Across the Spine without paired stations. The sewing is incredibly simple: Attach the sheet exiting to the left. Link under the stitch on the top sheet to the right. Drop to the left two positions and link under. Add next sheet and repeat.

NOTE: This sewing has a tendency to twist to the left. It must be straightened after each sheet is added. If you have problems with the book block slanting to the left, sew every other station as a mirror image: Attach the sheet exiting to the *right.* Link under the stitch on the top sheet to the *left.* Drop to the *right* two positions and link under. Add next sheet and repeat.

Keith Smith, *A Little Valentine to Scott,* Book 201, one–of–a–kind, 2001. A large inkjet print of Scott was randomly cut in different directions into the same size units. These were colored with crayons and bound. My work today was a valentine and another illustration for this book. Effort must achieve layered results for an economy of time. 17 x 15.5 x 3 cm.

This second example of a Single Sheet Coptic Sewn Across the Spine *Without Paired Stations* has a different color thread at each station to illustrate that there are five separate sewings across the spine. Each step must be repeated at each station before beginning the next step or the sewing will not be consistent. The tension will vary.

SINGLE SHEET COPTIC SEWN *ALONG* THE SPINE

As I finish writing the descriptions and importing the photo illustrations for Coptics sewn across the spine, I go to the cabinet to get some cover weight paper to start sewing prototypes for Coptics sewn along the spine. There I find a half dozen prototypes with notations of Coptics sewn along the spine that I had devised in 1997. What luck in timing. I do not have to re–invent them.

These sketches range from simple to one which is sewn with two threads and four needles along, not across the spine. Sewing alternates with the threads which could be of contrasting colors. The colors would be layered parallel with and on the spine. The chain formed by the linking would drop down past the other color. It reminds me of dovetails.

A rather nice looking one which is not too complicated seems to be ideal to include in this book. Probably that will be the only one of these sewings I describe, depending upon how lengthy the book becomes. But, someday, I may describe some of these other sewings.

I have sewn up an example and have taken notes to compare it with the 1997 notations. I was able to simplify the steps slightly. Then I bound a finished example you see below, checking my notes for any errors in sewing.

This is a sturdy sewing with no side to side flex of the spine.

Single Sheet Coptic sewn along the spine. By far the sturdiest Coptic I have sewn. There is no side to side flex. It is as sturdy as a sewn and pasted binding. Note that there are no kettle stitches at the head and tail. The sewing climbs with the link stitch.
This is not difficult to sew, but if you have never sewn a Coptic, this should not be your first attempt. There are many steps and you might become confused.

Swell

Notice how much thicker the spine–edge is than the foredge in the illustrations below. The exaggerated swell comes from multiple linking. Unlike the Single Sheet Coptics sewn across the spine, this sewing not only has the links which form the chains, but also the connecting stitches at the spine–edge are linked on both sides of each sheet. This makes for a sturdy sewing, but one which is more limited to tipping in images after the binding is completed. It is a good structure for a photo album, with lovely exposed chains on the spine formed by the linking.

Three views of the sample Single Sheet Coptic sewn along the spine shows a large amount of swell on the spine is from multiple linking from the sewing. This binding is better for tipping in images after the binding is completed. It is excellent as a photo album.

Sewing Preparation

NUMBER AND POSITION OF HOLES: The holes should be close to the spine–edge not to interfere with the imagery on the page. If the sheets are pierced 1/4" in from the spine–edge that will be far enough away so they do not rip out. Since the sewing is done along, rather than across the spine there can be an even or odd number of sewing stations. Pierce as many holes for the sewing stations as you like, but there should be no more than 1 1/2" between the holes.

The book block in the sample Single Sheet Coptic sewn along the spine alternates light and dark sheets to emphasize there are no folds. To further exaggerate, the lighter sheets are smaller with torn edges.

Corners of the sheets need to be secured at the head and the tail. In positioning the holes for the sewing, pierce the first hole no farther away from the tail than 1/2", and no closer than 3/8". Do the same for the final hole at the head. The boards are the same height, but slightly wider for a lip at the foredge. The boards but flush on the spine–edge.

TO ADD MORE THREAD: When you are running out of thread in this particular binding, the knot must be tied at a specific place to hide the clipped threads. Form the diagonal stitch on the inside and link, as shown in Steps 8 and 9 on page 166, as well as on the facing page. Proceed to the hole at that station.

Go through the hole in the previous sheet to the other side.

1. Tie a weaver's knot positioned exactly at the hole, so the clipped ends of thread will not extend beyond the spine–edge and be visible when the book is closed. *See* weaver's knot, page 61.
2. Proceed to the spine–edge of the sheet. Come up on the sheet.
3. Link under the two connecting threads from forward of the sewing. Continue the sewing.

ADDING THREAD WITH THE WEAVER'S KNOT

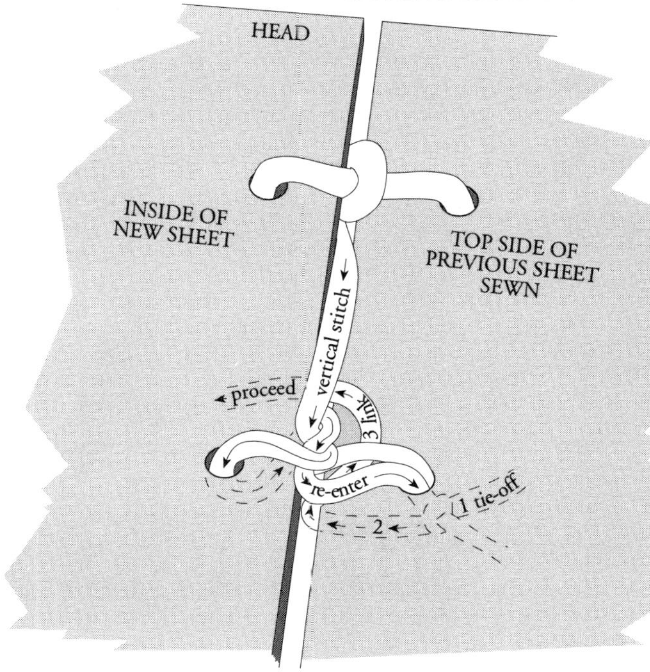

After forming the vertical stitch, instead of dropping backward, linking the stitch on the previous sheet and exiting, first re–enter the hole on the previous sheet. This will make a *second* stitch at this hole. On the other side of the sheet, tie a weaver's knot and come up to the top of the sheet through the seam or gutter. Then, proceed as usual: Link under (both stitches) from behind, and exit backward. Close the new sheet and proceed with the sewing.

Adding more thread with the weaver's knot takes place at the hole, on the inside of the sheet so the clipped ends of thread do not hang out on the spine.

STARTING THE SEWING

On traditional Coptic sewings, linking drops down two (sections) positions to link under. With this sewing, linking will be 3–down. Linking will start with the third sheet. The shape of the chains on the spine formed by the links looks better 3–down, since sheets do not have the thickness of sections. Strange, because in the Single Sheet Coptics Sewn *Across* the Spine, I found no fault with the 2–down linking.

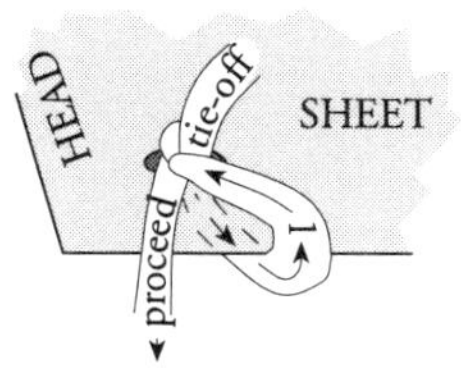

STEP 1: Starting the sewing.

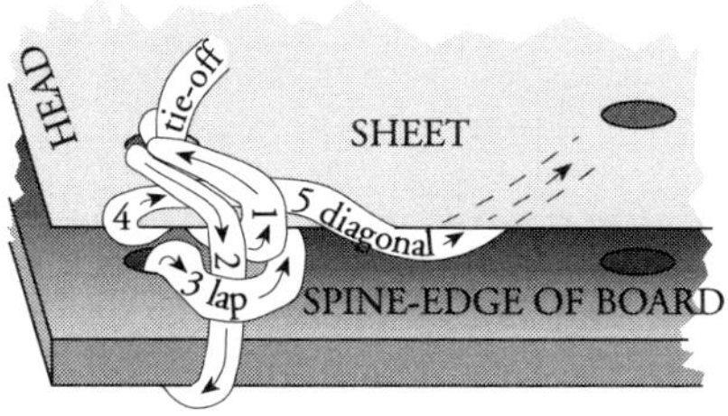

STEP 2: Attaching the board.

1. Start at the head with the first sheet to be sewn. Go down through the hole and leave a small amount of thread on top. Proceed to the spine–edge. Come around the spine–edge to the top and tie a square knot at the hole.
2. Set on the board below the sheet. Proceed to the spine–edge of the sheet. Go around the spine–edge of the board and enter the board, only, from the outside to the inside. Exit backward of the station at the head.
3. Lap the connecting thread between the board and the sheet. Open the sheet. Link under the short stitch on the board heading toward the head. Exit to the outside, back of the station.
4. Close the sheet. Link under the two stitches on the top of the sheet heading towards the tail.

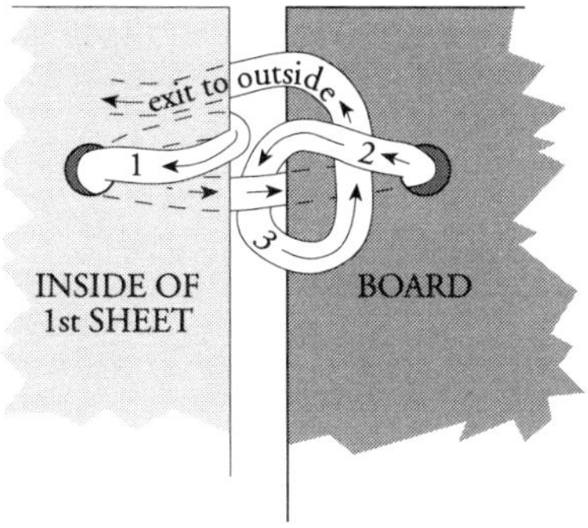

STEP 3: With the book opened, link the stitch on the board from behind the station towards the head. Exit to the outside.

Attaching the Sheet at the Second Station

5. Proceed to the next station. Enter the sheet from the inside to the out. This can be done without opening the sheet, but just lifting it slightly. Pull on the thread so the thread on the spine is pulled inside all the way back to the previous station. There will be a slight amount of thread showing on the spine. Don't pull so hard as to kink the sheet.
6. With the sheet closed over the board, take the thread around the tail to the inside of the sheet. The thread will extend beyond the foredge, between the sheet and the board.

FORMING THE DIAGONAL STITCH
SEWING THE FIRST SHEET AND BOARD

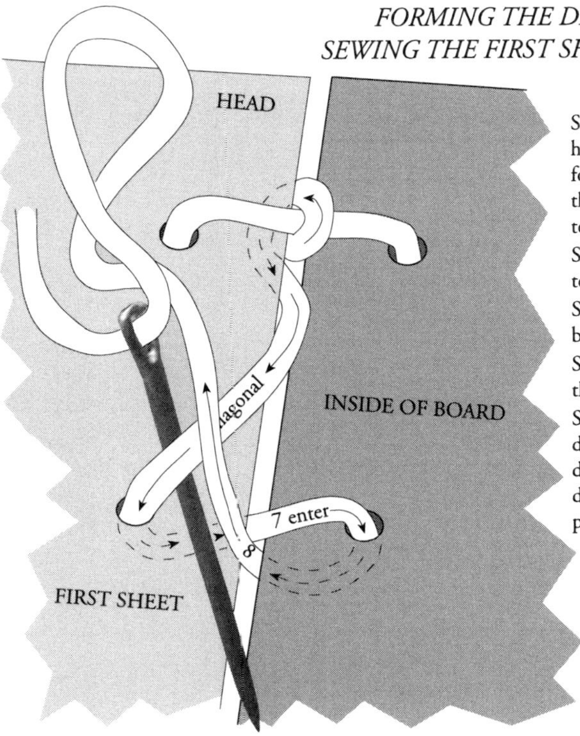

STEP 5: Enter the next hole on the inside. This forms a diagonal stitch. In this example the sewing is towards the tail.
STEP 6: Take the thread to the inside.
STEP 7: Attach the board.
STEP 8: Come up through the gutter.
STEP 9: Link under the diagonal stitch in the direction you are sewing, described on the facing page.

STEP 9 continued: Pull the thread towards the gutter to bring the diagonal thread to a vertical which rests in the gutter between the two sheets. Tension is important. If the diagonal thread is too tight, it cannot be pulled to a vertical. If it is too loose, the resulting vertical thread will not be taut.
STEP 10: Link under the short stitch on the board from behind, heading towards the head.
STEP 11: Exit back of the station between the vertical thread and the sheet.

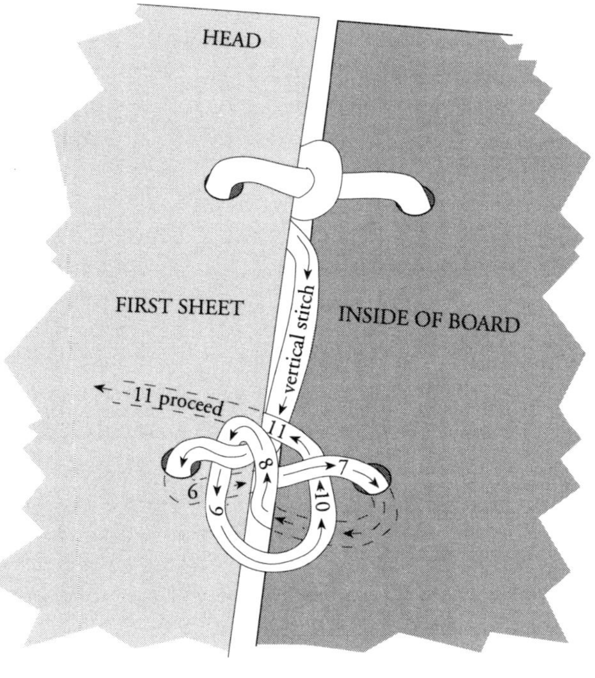

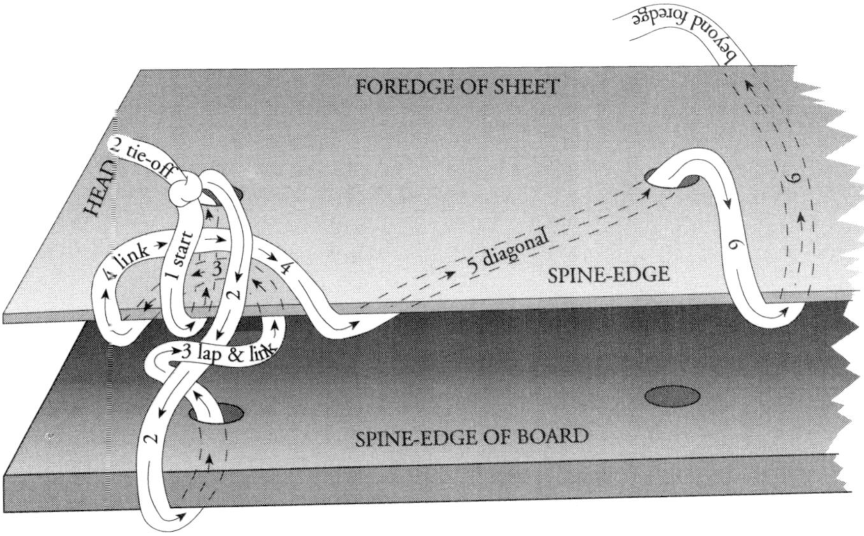

The sewing starts at the head on the sheet and attaches the board.

Turn the book 90° clockwise. With the sheet on top the board, pull on the thread at the foredge to form the stitch at this station. It should be at a right angle to the spine–edge. See illustration on the following page.

7. Open the sheet with the gutter vertical, head at the top. Take the thread through the board from the inside to the outside. Pull the thread taut.
8. Pull the thread up through the gutter/seam from the forward side (tail.) Pull the thread up against the horizontal thread which connects the sheet with the board. See illustration on the top of the facing page.
9. Link the diagonal thread from the back of this station heading in the direction you are sewing (towards the tail). Pull towards the right to change the diagonal thread to a vertical. It will rest in the gutter. If the thread does not become a vertical, loosen the link. Pull on the diagonal thread slightly to give a little slack. Adjust the link so the thread lies in the gutter. It is important that the link brings the thread to a vertical, that the thread is positioned in the gutter and that it is taut. See illustration on the facing page.
10. With one hand, keep tension on the thread so the link does not loosen. With the other hand, link the short stitch on the board at this station from forward of the stitch, heading in the opposite direction you are sewing.
11. Exit through the gutter back of this station. The needle exits between the vertical stitch and the sheet to center between the sheet and the board the thread which is parallel to the spine.

ATTACHING THE BOARD

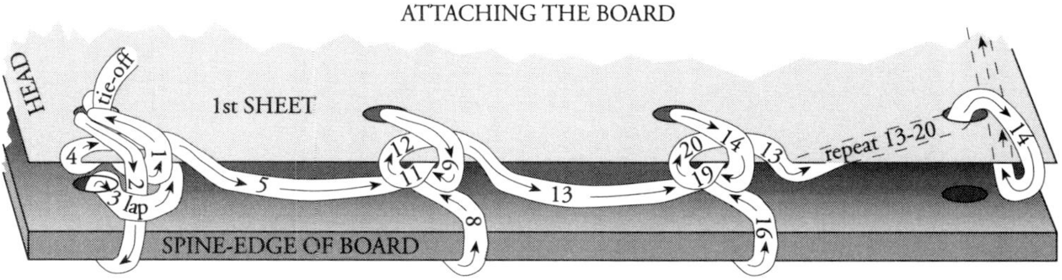

After the first two stations, repeat Steps 13–20 at all the remaining stations on the first sheet.

12. Close the sheet. Turn the book 90° counter–clockwise so the spine is facing you. Align the sewing at this station by tugging on the thread sideways in the direction you are sewing. The stitch on the sheet should be directly above the stitch on the board. This is done each time to keep the chain from forming askew on the spine. Link under the top stitch from behind the station.

Attaching the Sheet at the Third Station

13. Proceed to the next station. Enter the hole in the sheet from the inside to the out. This can be done without opening the sheet, by just lifting it slightly. Pull on the thread so the thread on the spine is pulled inside all the way back to the previous station. There will be a slight amount of thread showing on the spine. Don't pull so hard as to kink the sheet.
14. With the sheet closed over the board, take the thread around the tail to the inside of the sheet. The thread will extend beyond the foredge, between the sheet and the board. Turn the book 90° clockwise. With the sheet on top the board, pull on the thread at the foredge to form the stitch at this station. It should be at a right angle to the spine–edge.
15. Open the sheet with the gutter vertical and head at the top. Take the thread through the board from the inside to the outside.
16. Pull the thread up through the gutter from the forward side (tail). Pull against the thread connecting the sheet with the board.
17. Link the diagonal thread from the back of this station heading in the direction you are sewing (towards the tail). Pull towards the right to change the diagonal thread to a vertical. It will rest in the gutter. If the thread does not become a vertical, loosen the link. Pull on the diagonal thread slightly to give a little slack. Adjust the link so the thread lies in the gutter. It is important that the link brings the thread to a vertical, that the thread is positioned in the gutter and that it is taut. See illustration on page 166.

18. With one hand, keep tension on the thread so the link does not loosen. With the other hand, link the short stitch on the board at this station forward of the stitch, heading the opposite direction you are sewing.
19. Exit through the gutter back of this station. The needle exits above the vertical stitch, next to the sheet.
20. Close the sheet. Turn the book 90° counter–clockwise so the spine is facing you. Align the sewing at this station by tugging on the thread sideways in the direction you are sewing.
    Link under the top stitch from behind the station.

Sewing the Remaining Stations on This Sheet

Repeat Steps 13–20 at the remaining stations on this sheet, including the final.

SEWING THE SECOND SHEET

NOTE: Please do not assume the second sheet is sewn the same as the first. It is not. The first three sheets are all sewn differently, the pattern is set with the third sheet. After that, it is repetitious.

21. Set on the second sheet. Enter this sheet at the station at the tail from the top to the bottom. Exit backward (to the right of the connecting stitch).

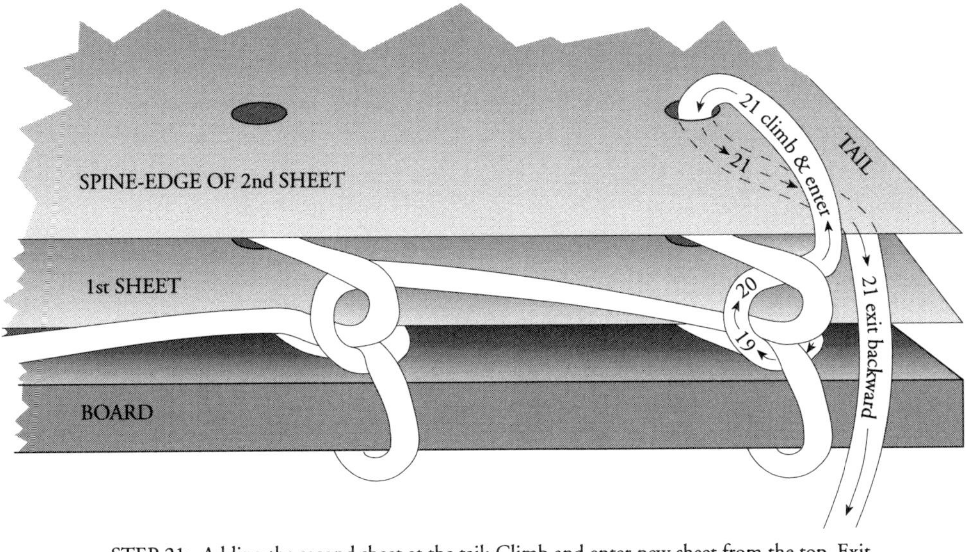

STEP 21: Adding the second sheet at the tail: Climb and enter new sheet from the top. Exit backward, which for the second sheet, is towards the tail.

STEP 22: Lap the connecting stitch and enter forward.
STEP 23: (not shown): Link the short stitch inside in the opposite direction you are sewing this sheet.
STEP 24: Exit back of the station.
STEP 25: Link the short stitch on top. Proceed to next station. Enter the hole from the inside to the outside.
STEP 26: Take the thread around the spine–edge to the inside.

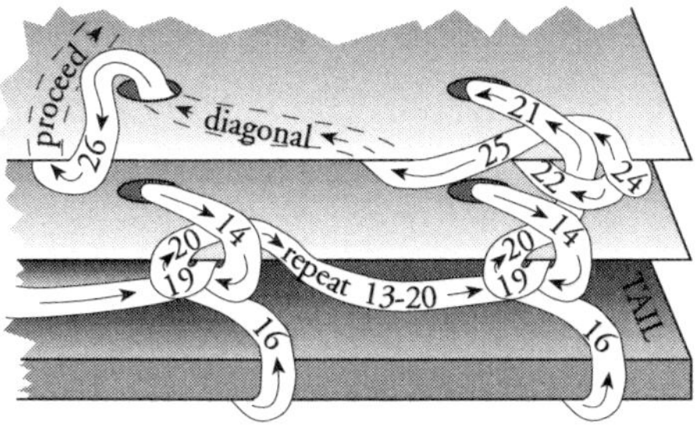

22. Lap the connecting stitch and enter forward (to the left) between the new and the previous sheet.
    Pull the thread taut beyond the foredge, between the top and next to top sheet. Turn the book 90° clockwise, with the head pointing up.
23. With one hand, keep tension on the thread while you open the top sheet. With the other hand, link the short stitch on the previous sheet at this station from forward of the stitch, heading in the opposite direction you are sewing.
24. Exit through the gutter back of this station. Close the sheet. Turn the book 90° counter–clockwise so the spine faces you.

Attaching the Sheet at the Remaining Stations for The Second Sheet

25. Link the short stitch on the top of the second sheet from back of the station. Proceed to the next station. Enter the hole in the sheet from the inside to the outside. Turn the book 90° clockwise.
26. With the sheets closed, take the thread around the head to the inside of the top sheet. The thread will extend beyond the foredge between the top and the previous sheet. Pull on the thread at the foredge to form the stitch at this station at a right angle to the spine–edge. Keep tension on the thread. Open the top sheet.

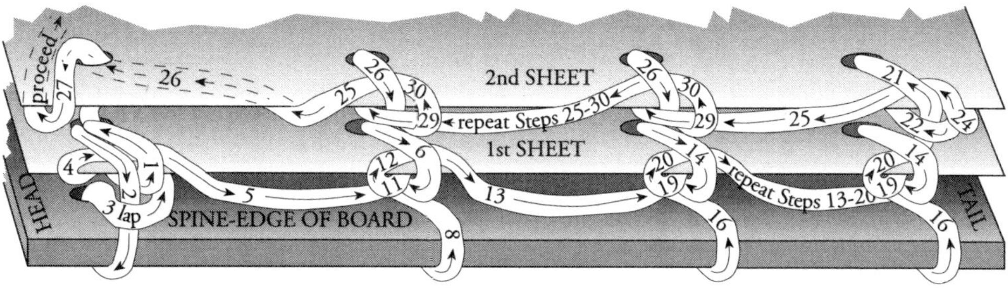

Repeat Steps 25–30 at all remaining stations to attach the second sheet. Steps 27–29 are done with the top page opened. These steps are illustrated on the facing page.

FORMING THE DIAGONAL STITCH SEWING SHEET TO SHEET

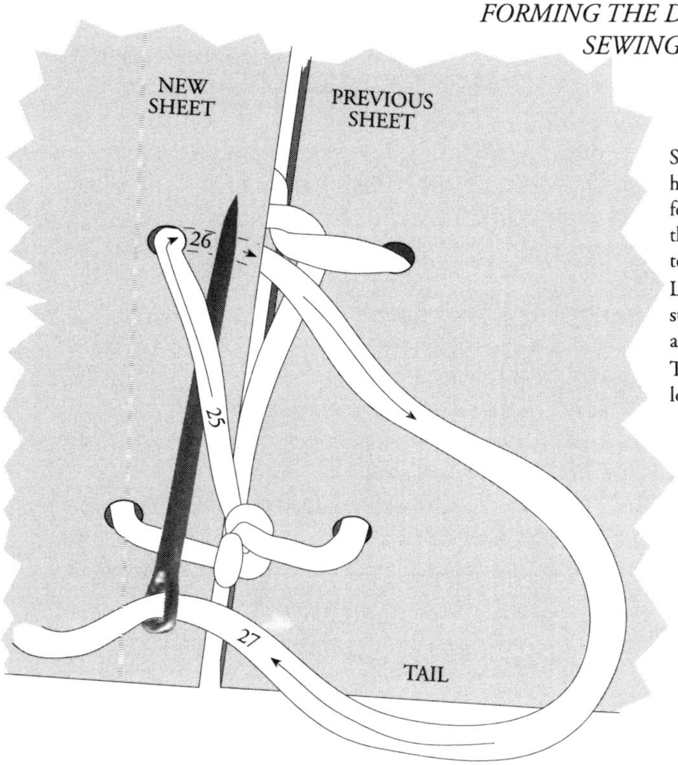

STEP 27: Enter the next hole on the inside. This forms a diagonal stitch. In this example the sewing is towards the head.
Link under the diagonal stitch in the direction you are sewing.
This is described on the following page.

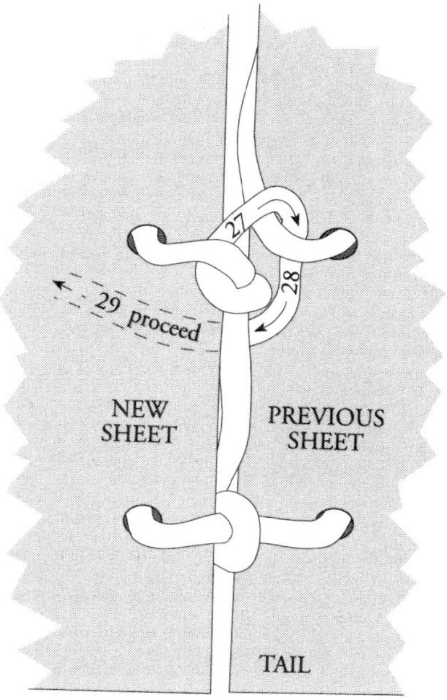

STEP 27 (continued): Pull the thread towards the gutter to bring the diagonal thread to a vertical which rests in the gutter between the two sheets.
Tension is important. If the diagonal thread is too tight, it cannot be pulled to a vertical. If it is too loose, the resulting vertical thread will not be taut.
STEP 28: Link the short stitch on the previous sheet at this station. Link from forward of the stitch, heading in the opposite direction you are sewing.
STEP 29: Exit through the gutter back of this station.
STEP 30: Close the sheet and align the sewing by tugging on the thread in the direction you are sewing.

27. Link the diagonal thread from the back of this station heading in the direction you are sewing (towards the head). Pull towards the right to change the diagonal thread to a vertical. It will rest in the gutter. See illustration on the previous page.
28. Keep tension on the thread while you link the short stitch on the previous sheet at this station. Link from forward of the stitch, heading in the opposite direction you are sewing.
29. Exit through the gutter back of this station. The needle exits above the top vertical stitch.
30. Close the sheet. Turn the book 90° counter–clockwise so the spine faces you. Align the sewing at this station by tugging on the thread in the direction you are sewing.

    Repeat Steps 25–30 at all the remaining stations on this sheet.

NOTE: For sewing the final station of the second sheet at the head in Step 28, link under both stitches on the first sheet.

Whenever there is a knot tied, such as adding thread during the sewing, there will be two stitches instead of one around the spine–edge at that station. When linking, link under both threads. *See* to add more thread, page 164.

SEWING THE THIRD SHEET WITH 3–DOWN LINKING

Set on the next sheet.

31. Enter the hole in the new sheet at the station at the head from the top to the bottom. Exit backward (to the left of the connecting stitch).
32. Lap the connecting stitch and enter forward (to the right) between the new and the previous sheet.

    Pull the thread taut beyond the foredge, between the top and next to top sheet. Turn the book 90° clockwise.
33. With one hand, keep tension on the thread while you open the top sheet. With the other hand, link the short stitch on the previous sheet at this station from forward of the stitch, heading in the opposite direction you are sewing.
34. Exit through the gutter back of this station. Close the sheet. Turn the book 90° counter–clockwise so the spine faces you.
35. Link the stitch on the top sheet from behind the station.

Dropping Forward to Link

36 Drop forward three sheets, that is, between the board and the first sheet. Open the book. Link, taking the needle to the inside between the vertical stitch and the board.

37. Exit back of the station. Climb and link the stitch on the top sheet from back of the station.

38. Proceed to the next station. Enter the hole in the sheet from the inside to the out. Turn the book 90° clockwise.
39. With the sheets closed, take the thread around tail to the inside of the top sheet. Pull on the thread at the foredge to form the stitch at this station at a right angle to the spine–edge. Keep tension on the thread. Open the top sheet.
40. On the inside, link the diagonal thread from the back of this station heading in the direction you are sewing. Pull towards the right to change the diagonal thread to a vertical. It will rest in the gutter.
41. Keep tension on the thread. With the top sheet open, link the short stitch on the previous sheet at this station. Link from forward of the stitch, heading in the opposite direction you are sewing.
42. Exit through the gutter back of this station. The needle exits between the two vertical stitches.
Close the sheet. Turn the book 90° counter–clockwise so the spine faces you.
43. Link the stitch on the top sheet from behind the station. Align the sewing at this station by tugging on the thread in the direction you are sewing.

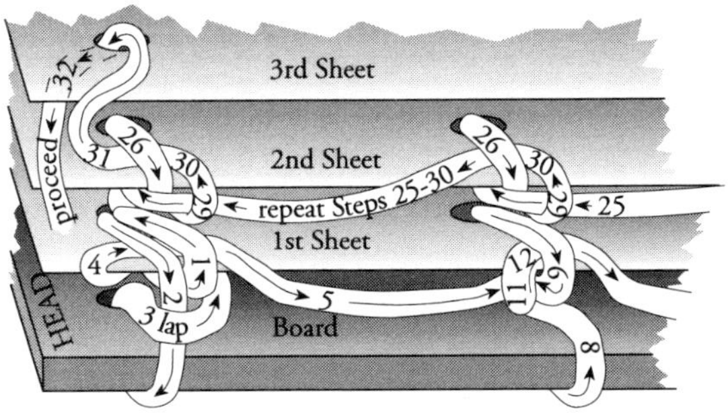

Repeat Steps 25–30 to finish sewing the second sheet.
STEP 31: Set on the third sheet. Climb, enter and exit backward, which for the third sheet is towards the head.

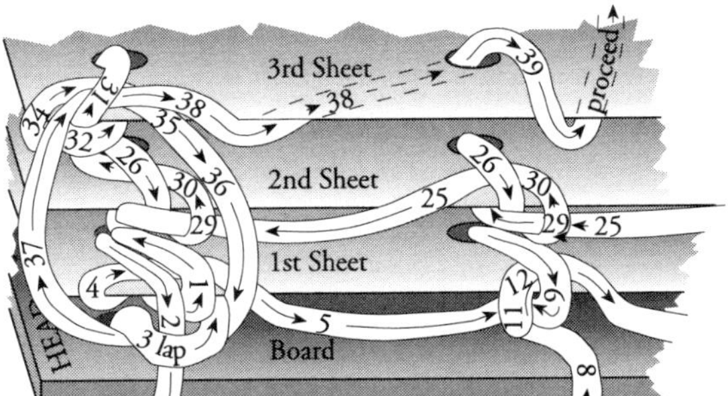

STEP 32: Exit backward (towards head) to the outside. Link the connecting threads and enter.
STEP 33: (not shown) Link the short stitch on the inside heading towards the head.
STEP 34: Exit backward.
STEP 35: Link the stitch on the top sheet.
STEPS 36–37: Make the first link on the spine which forms the chain by dropping forward. Open the book between first sheet and the board. Link under. Exit. Climb on the back side of the station. Link the small stitch on the top of the third sheet.

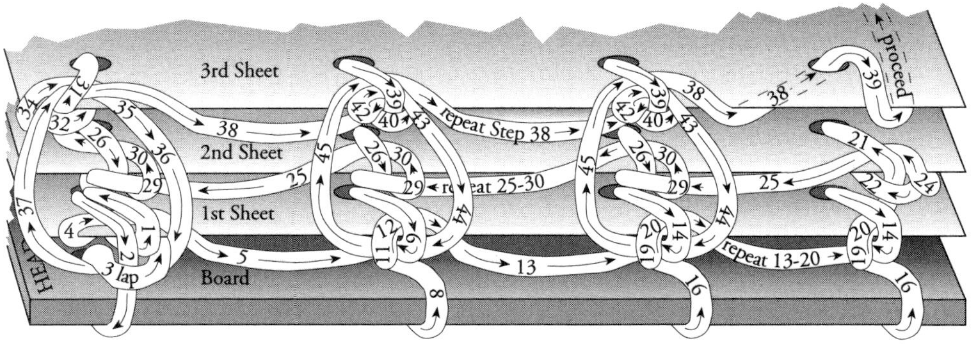

STEP 35: Link under the stitch on the top sheet.

STEP 36: Drop forward, down 3 sheets and link under. For sewing the third sheet, link under between the board and the first sheet. For sewing the fourth sheet, link under between the first and second sheet.

STEP 37: Climb on the back side. Link under the the stitch on the top sheet.

STEP 38: Proceed to the next station. Enter the sheet from the inside to the out.

STEP 39: Take the thread around tail to the inside. Open the top sheet.

STEP 40: Link the diagonal thread from back of the station. Pull to form a vertical stitch.

STEP 41: Link the short stitch on the previous sheet. Link from forward of the stitch, heading in the opposite direction you are sewing.

STEP 42: Exit backward through the gutter. Close the sheet.

STEP 43: Link the stitch on the top sheet from behind the station.

STEP 44: Drop forward, three sheets and link under. For sewing the third sheet, link under between the board and the first sheet. The needle should go between the vertical stitch and the board.

STEP 45: Exit back of the station. Climb and link the stitch on the top sheet from back of the station. Proceed to the next station. To sew the remaining stations on this sheet, repeat Steps 38–45.

Dropping Forward to Link

44. Drop forward three sheets and link under For sewing the third sheet, link under between the board and the first sheet. The needle should go between the vertical stitch and the board.
45. Exit back of the station. Climb and link the stitch on the top sheet from back of the station.

Sewing the Remaining Stations for This Sheet

Repeat Steps 38–45 to complete the sewing at this station and all remaining stations on this sheet, including the final station at the tail.

SEWING THE NEXT EVEN–NUMBERED SHEET

46. Set on the next sheet to be sewn. Enter at the station at the tail from the top to the bottom. Exit backward (to the right of the connecting stitch).
47. Lap the connecting stitch and enter forward (to the left) between the new and the previous sheet.
    Pull the thread taut beyond the foredge, between the top and next to top sheet. Turn the book 90° clockwise.
48. With one hand, keep tension on the thread while you open the top sheet. With the other hand, link the short stitch on the previous sheet at this station forward of the stitch, heading in the opposite direction you are sewing.
49. Exit through the gutter back of this station. Close the sheet. Turn the book 90° counter–clockwise so the spine faces you.
50. Link the stitch on the top sheet from behind the station.

Dropping Forward to Link

51. Drop forward towards the head three sheets and link under. (For sewing the fourth sheet, link under between the first and second sheets).
52. Exit back of the station. You will have to watch not to pierce the thread in the gutter that runs parallel to the gutter at the station at the tail. In exiting all other stations, watch when exiting not to pierce the parallel thread. It does not matter if you exit above or below the parallel thread, as long as you do not distort it.
    Climb and link the stitch on the top sheet from back of the station.
53. Proceed to the next station. Enter the sheet from the inside to the out. Turn the book 90° clockwise.
54. With the sheets closed, take the thread around head to the inside of the top sheet. Pull on the thread at the foredge to form the stitch at this station at a right angle to the spine–edge. Keep tension on the thread. Open the top sheet.
55. Link the diagonal thread from the back of this station heading in the direction you are sewing. Pull towards the right to change the diagonal thread to a vertical to rest in the gutter.
56. Keep tension on the thread while you link the short stitch on the previous sheet at this station. Link from forward of the stitch, heading in the opposite direction you are sewing.
57. Exit through the gutter back of this station. The needle usually exits between the two vertical stitches, but it does not matter if you exit above or below the parallel thread, as long as you do not distort it.
    Close the sheet. Turn the book 90° counter–clockwise so the spine faces you. Align the sewing at this station by tugging on the thread in the direction you are sewing.

58. Link the stitch on the top sheet from behind the station, heading towards the head.
59. Drop forward towards the head three sheets and link under.

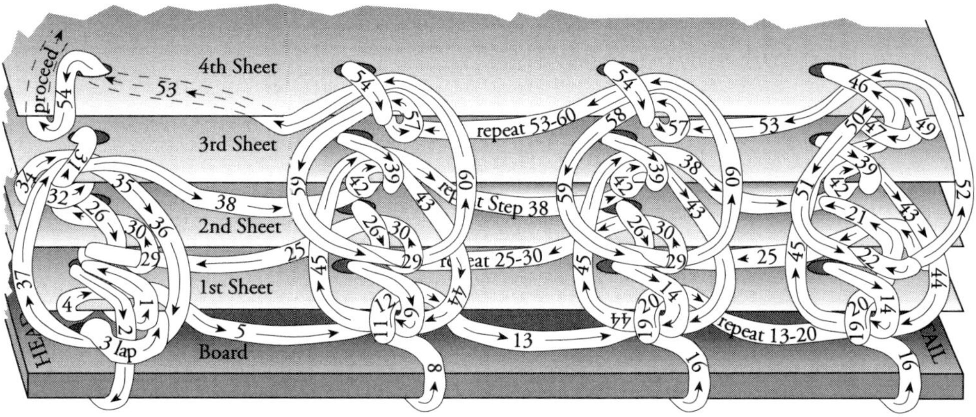

STEP 46: Set on the next sheet. Enter at the station at the tail from the top to the bottom. Exit backward.

STEP 47: Lap the connecting stitch. Enter forward between the new and the previous sheet. Pull the thread taut beyond the foredge, between the top and next to top sheet. Turn the book 90° clockwise.

STEP 48: Open the top sheet. Link the short stitch on the previous sheet at this station forward of the stitch, heading in the opposite direction you are sewing.

STEP 49: Exit back of this station. Close the sheet. Turn the book 90° counter–clockwise.

STEP 50: Link the stitch on the top sheet from behind the station.

STEP 51: Drop forward, (towards the head) three sheets and link under.

STEP 52: Exit back of the station. It does not matter if you exit above or below the parallel thread, as long as you do not distort it. Climb and link the stitch on the top sheet from back of the station.

STEP 53: Proceed to the next station. Enter the sheet from the inside to the out.

STEP 54: Take the thread around head to the inside of the top sheet. Open the top sheet.

STEP 55: Link the diagonal thread from the back of this station. Pull towards the right to change the diagonal thread to a vertical.

STEP 56: Link the short stitch on the previous sheet from forward of the stitch, heading in the opposite direction you are sewing.

STEP 57: Exit through the gutter back of this station. It does not matter if you exit above or below the parallel thread, as long as you do not distort it. Close the sheet. Align the sewing at this station by tugging on the thread in the direction you are sewing.

STEP 58: Link the stitch on the top sheet from behind the station, heading towards the head.

STEP 59: Drop forward towards the head, three sheets and link under.

STEP 60: Exit back of the station. Watch when exiting not to pierce the parallel thread. Climb and link the stitch on the top sheet from back of the station.

60. Exit back of the station. Watch when exiting not to pierce the parallel thread. It does not matter if you exit above or below the parallel thread, as long as you do not distort it.
    Climb and link the stitch on the top sheet from back of the station.

Sewing the Remaining Stations for This Sheet

Repeat Steps 53–60 to complete the sewing at this station and all remaining stations on this sheet. Set on the next sheet to be sewn.

SEWING THE REMAINING SHEETS

For all odd numbered sheets, repeat Steps 31–45. For all even numbered sheets, repeat Steps 46–60, including the final sheet to be sewn.

Final Sheet

Unlike other Coptics, the cover is not sewn with the last sheet, but separately. Sew the final sheet, whether odd or even numbered, the same as any previous sheet, attaching and dropping down three sheets to link under at each station. After linking the final station of the last sheet, exit on the back side. Set on the board, listed as Step 61 in the following description.

ADDING THE COVER

61. Set on the board. Climb and enter the board *from the top* through to the inside. This will be either at the head or tail, depending on whether the final sheet is odd or even numbered. In the illustration, the sewing of the board begins at the head.
    Exit to the spine, back of the station. Pull the thread taut.
62. Lap the thread that connects the board heading in the direction you are sewing. Open the cover. Enter forward to the inside between the board and the final sheet.
    Pull the thread in the direction of the foredge until it is taut. Turn the book 90° clockwise.
63. Link the short stitch on the final sheet at this station from forward of the stitch, heading in the opposite direction you are sewing.
64. Exit through the gutter back of this station. Close the cover. Turn the book 90° counter–clockwise so the spine faces you.
65. Link the stitch on the top of the board from behind the station. Pull until it is taut. The thread will slide off the top of the board to the spine.

The First Drop Forward to Link

66. Drop forward three positions, the cover is counted as one, plus two sheets. (Simply open the cover with two sheets.) Link under.

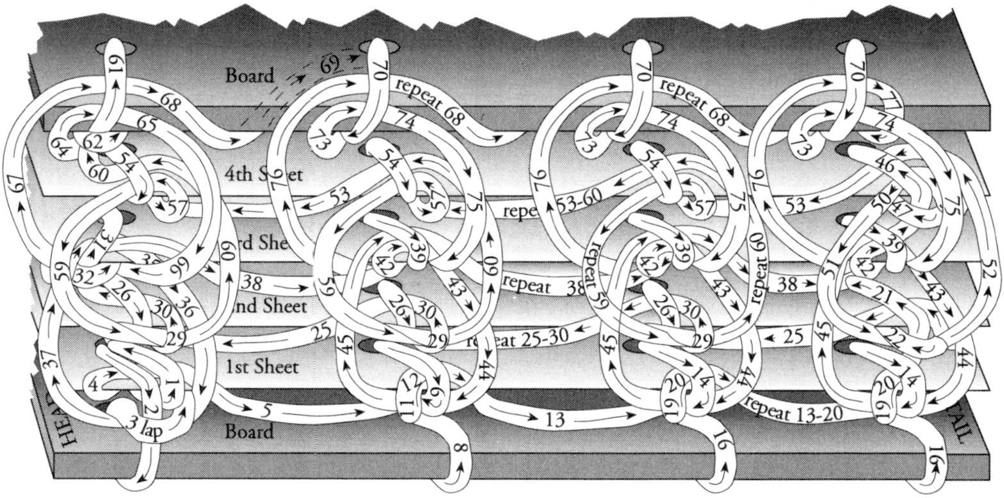

STEP 61: Set on the board. Climb. Enter the board from the top. In the illustration, the sewing begins at the head. Exit to the spine, back of the station. Pull the thread taut.

STEP 62: Lap the thread that connects the board heading forward. Open the cover. Enter forward to the inside between the board and the final sheet. Pull the thread in the direction of the foredge, until it is taut.

STEP 63: Link the short stitch on the final sheet at this station from forward of the stitch.

STEP 64: Exit through the gutter back of this station. Close the cover.

STEP 65: Link the stitch on the top of the board from behind the station. Pull thread taut. It will slide off the top of the board to the spine.

STEP 66: Drop forward, three positions, which is the cover plus two sheets. Link under. Exit back of the station between two threads which are parallel to the spine.

STEP 67: Climb on the back side.

STEP 68: Link under the stitch on the top of the board from behind the station.

STEP 69: Proceed to the next station. Enter the board from the inside to the top.

STEP 70: Open the board. Come around the spine–edge taking the needle to the inside.

STEP 71: Link the diagonal thread from behind. Tug on it so the thread lies in the gutter.

STEP 72: Link the stitch on the final sheet from forward, heading in the opposite direction.

STEP 73: Exit behind the station between the board and the thread in the gutter.

STEP 74: Close the cover. Link the stitch on the board from back of the station.

STEP 75: Drop forward three positions, which is the cover plus two sheets. Link under. Exit back of the station between two threads which are parallel to the spine.

STEP 76: Climb on the back side.

STEP 77: Link the stitch on top of the board from behind.

Repeat Steps 68–77 at all the remaining stations on the board, including the final station.

STEP 78: Open the board. Take the needle inside on the forward side of the station. Hold the final sheet up from the book block. Take the needle through the last station on the final sheet. The thread will be between the final and next to last sheet.

Link under the thread on the final sheet, tying off with a half hitch. The next to last sheet will have two stitches on one side and the tie–off knot on the other at this final station.

Exit back of the station. The needle exits between two threads which are parallel to the spine.

67. Climb on the back side.
68. Link under the stitch on the top of the board from behind the station.
69. Proceed to the next station. Slip the needle under the board. Enter the hole in the board from the inside to the outside, to the top.
70. Open the board. Come around the spine–edge of the board taking the needle to the inside.
71. Link the diagonal thread from behind the station heading in the direction you are sewing. Tug on it so the thread lies in the gutter.
72. Link the stitch on the final sheet from forward, heading in the opposite direction you are sewing.
73. Exit behind the station between the board and the thread in the gutter.
74. Close the cover. On the outside of the book, link the stitch on the board from back of the station.
75. Drop forward three positions, the cover is counted as one, plus two sheets. (Simply open the cover with two sheets.) Link under.
    Exit back of the station. The needle exits between two threads which are parallel to the spine.
76. Climb on the back side.
77. Link the stitch on top of the board from behind.

Sewing the Remaining Stations on the Board

Repeat Steps 68–77 at all the remaining stations on the board, including the final station.

Tie–Off

78. Open the board. Take the needle inside on the forward side of the station. Hold the final sheet up from the book block. Take the needle through the last station on the final sheet. The thread will be between the final and next to last sheet.
    Link under the thread on the final sheet, tying off with a half hitch. *See* half hitch for Single Sheet Coptic Sewings, page 65. The next to last sheet will have two stitches on one side and the tie–off knot on the other at this final station.

PART III

SINGLE SHEET SUPPORTED SEWINGS

INTRODUCTION
SHEETS SEWN ONTO TAPES

At coffee break I told Scott I was devising a sewing onto tapes method in my head using single sheets instead of sections. "Why would you want to sew it onto tapes?" he asked. I think he was thinking that sewing onto tapes is only a functional structure with the spine covered with leather or cloth.

I told him that it would be an exposed spine sewing. I wouldn't use the common 1/4" linen sewing tape. Leather "tape" supports would be used. These would be attached to separate board side–covers. It would be elegant. It *was* elegant in my mind's eye. I only half listened to him as I revised the sewing path of this yet unsewn prototype. Scott is used to me being withdrawn, drawn by a dream of a drawing.

After coffee I went up to my studio and sewed my first attempt using scrap paper and a single sheet as page. I took notes on the sheet of the pathway. With the second attempt the thread went from station to station at the holes instead of parallel and adjacent to the spine–edge of the sheet. After the third start I took good paper–backed leather supports and sewed the first prototype. I giggled, and must admit, I was quite pleased with myself.

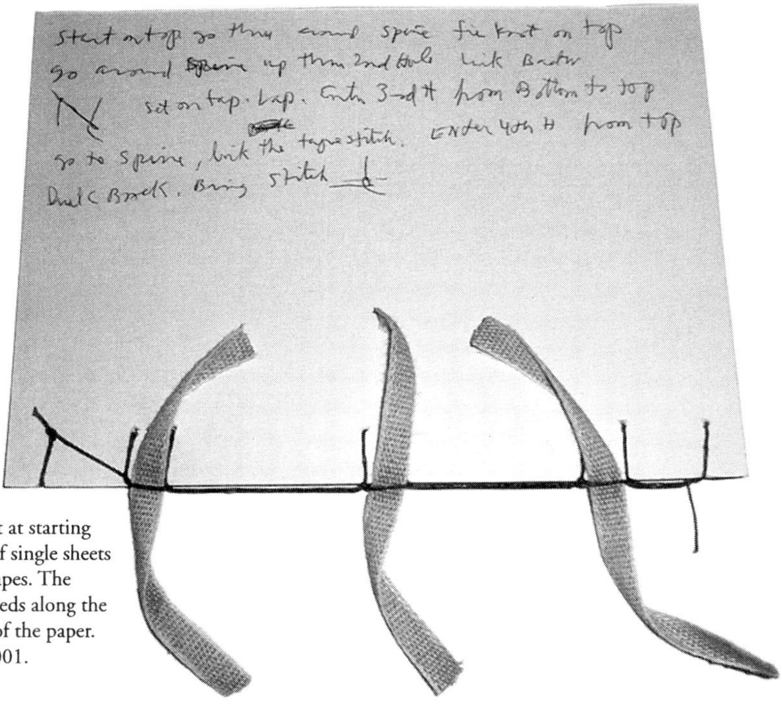

First attempt at starting the sewing of single sheets sewn onto tapes. The thread proceeds along the spine–edge of the paper. 7 January 2001.

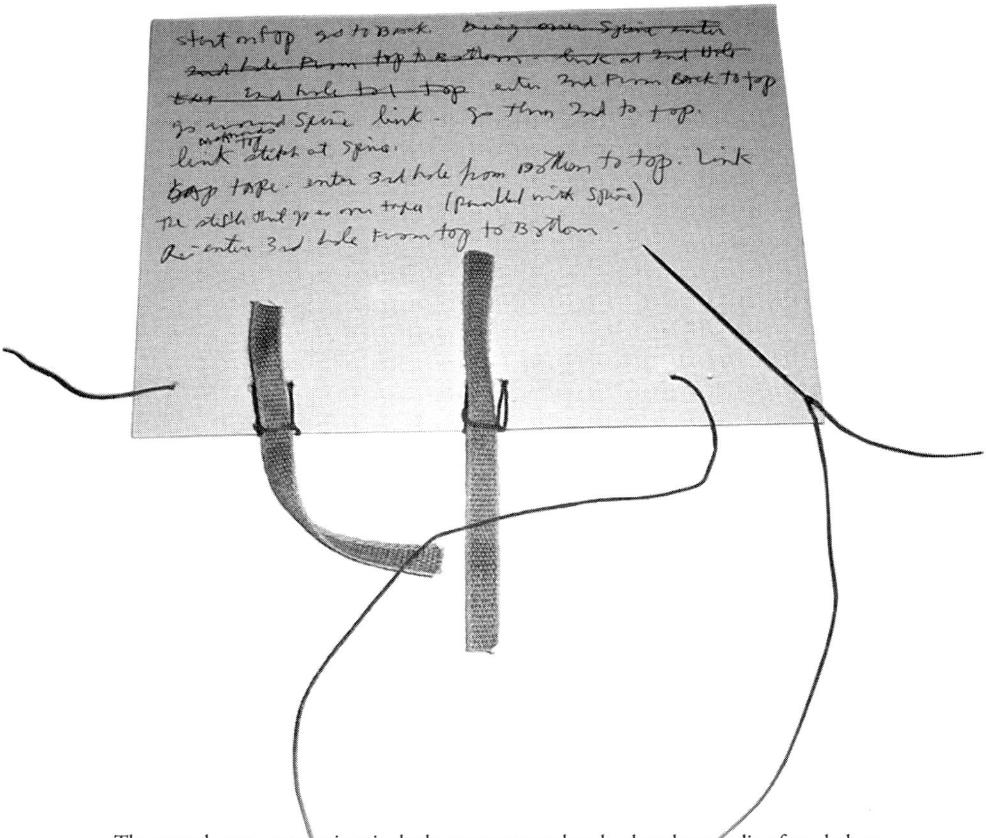

The second attempt at sewing single sheets onto tapes has the thread proceeding from hole to hole on the reverse side of the paper. I decided to go back to the thread along the spine–edge of the sheet. It was fewer steps and would decorate the spine of the closed book. 7 January 2001.

Evolving the Stations for This Sewing

In the first and second attempts, shown above, I pierced a single hole at the head and the tail for the kettle stitch. This was done without thinking, but simply habit of how sections are sewn onto tapes.

There was no need to have a kettle stitch to climb to the next sheet. And, with any exposed spine sewing I create, I prefer eliminating the kettle as a means of climbing if at all possible. It is functional, and when the spine is covered, it is ideal. But it severely limits decorating the spine with the sewing when there is an exposed spine.

With the third attempt I punched six holes in each sheet instead of eight — one on each side of the three tapes I would be using.

Stations vs Holes

A sewing station and a pierced hole are not synonymous.

In any binding that requires sewing onto tapes, the *tape* is the station. However, unlike sewing raised cords, sewing onto tapes requires a hole pierced on each side, and tangent to, the tape support. Those two holes are not stations, the tape between the two is the station. If you use four tapes there will be eight holes pierced but only four sewing stations, which are the tapes.

To honor this terminology, the description of sewing onto tapes which follows will not refer to *the station,* but to *the holes* which will be numbered from the head to the tail. Pointing out which hole to proceed to will cause less confusion.

Number of Tapes Needed

Determine the dimensions of the book block and the width of the strips of leather to be used as tape supports. The number of supports needed can then be determined. The supports should ideally be no further than 4" apart. If only a couple supports are used, the book may flex when opened, although I have made many concertina bindings using only two supports on books that are up to 14" high. I think the concertina pleat helps stabilize the book block. Also, in the sewing you are about to do, the book block is separate sheets of paper which really need to be supported by several tapes to prevent flex.

The following is the traditional approach to the number of tapes to use when sewing onto tapes: a minimum of three tapes are needed for any binding. Use four tapes if the book is 8 to 10" high and five tapes for a book 11 to 15" tall.

Uses for This Binding

This sewing of sheets has threads on each side of the sheet which swell the spine–edge. That means the binding is more appropriate for housing items that are tipped in. It would make an ideal photo album. Stiff paper could be used for the book block. The leather supports, exposed spine sewing and separate boards will give an elegant presentation.

If the book block is 2–ply mat board, a photographic sequence could be ideally housed.

A pop–up book would contain the folded papers which would be activated as the pages are turned. These paper pop–ups would swell the foredge so the covers might be nearly parallel.

Covering the Boards

Separate side–covers are added after sewing onto tapes. *See* glue & paste, page 73; covering the boards, page 83; and inlaid papers, page 91.

MAKING LEATHER SUPPORTS

Leather can be cut into strips and used as tapes for Sewing onto Tapes. However, the leather is limp. When the thread laps the leather it can pinch it making it narrower at that point.

With several sheets or sections sewn, the leather begins to distort horizontally. The thread acts like a belt pinching in on the strip of leather so it begins to look like a washboard.

To eliminate the problem the leather needs to be stiffer, yet must remain pliable since it will make a concave arc when the book is opened. The solution is to glue or paste a sheet of paper on the side of the leather which will not be seen. Rather than try to fit the paper to the shape of the tape which will be used, apply a large piece of paper to a large piece of leather.

SIZE OF THE LEATHER AND PAPER: If the strips of leather need to be 8" long, take a scrap of leather which is about 9" x 4". Cut a piece of laid or decorative paper which is slightly larger, about 10 x 5".

If you are using PVA glue, you will want to glue the paper not the leather.

If you are wheat pasting, paste the leather, not the paper. The leather would absorb all the paste from the paper and the two would not bond. For pasting leather, *see* pasting leather, page 77. It is far quicker to use PVA.

Leather can be pasted and the paper applied, but you will have to wait overnight for it to dry. Here, the paper was glued with PVA, then placed under weight five minutes. It is now ready to be cut into strips to be used as tapes.

CUTTING THE LEATHER INTO STRIPS: After the paper–backed leather is dry it is ready to be cut into strips to be used as tapes in sewing. Place the paper side up on a self–seal cutting mat.

MARKING THE PAPER: With a sharp pencil, draw a line down the longer dimension very close to the edge. Out from the top of this line measure the width you wish to have the tape. Place a small pencil dot. Continue on across and place another dot the same distance out. Keep marking for as many tapes as needed.

At the bottom of the pencil line measure across marking the widths of the tapes. Do not draw any more pencil lines as they might show in the binding. Instead, align your metal straight edge with the first point at the top and the bottom. Cut the paper/leather with a thin bladed knife such as an X–Acto knife with #11 blade.

Move the straight edge over to the next pair of dots and continue cutting the remaining strips of leather.

SEWING PREPARATION: Refer to pages 40–45 for information on *Swell, Dimensions of the Boards, Hiding the Stitches, Sewing Threads Inlaid* and *Laminating Pictures to the Boards.*

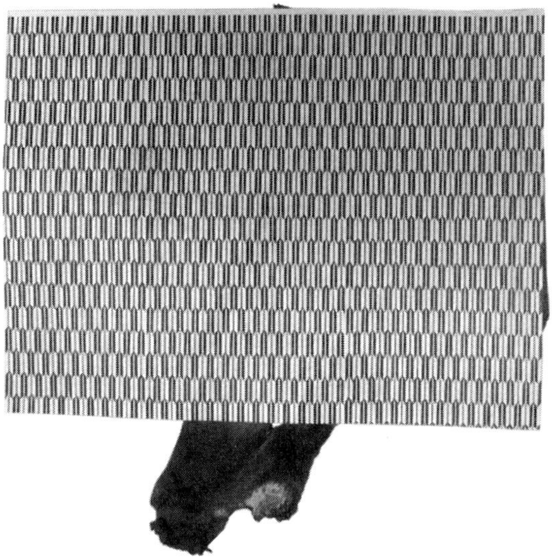

Cut the strips on the leather side for economy of the leather. Cut on the paper side to align the pattern for the back side of the tapes.

Use a straight edge and X–Acto knife to cut the paper–backed leather into strips for sewing onto tapes.

SINGLE SHEETS SEWN ONTO TAPES

Holes

POSITION OF THE HOLES: Using a scrap sheet which is the same dimensions as your book block. Place the tapes on this sheet at, and perpendicular to, the spine–edge. Arrange the amount of space between by your eye. Refine this measurement with a ruler.

MARKING THE HOLES: With a sharp pencil, place a dot on each side of each tape. With a ruler, draw a line in from, and perpendicular to, the spine–edge at each one of the dots. These are the six vertical lines below.

Measure in from the spine edge about 1/4" to 1/2" at the head. Make the same measurement at the tail. With a ruler, draw a line connecting these dots. It will be parallel to, and close to, the spine–edge. This will be your *stencil.*

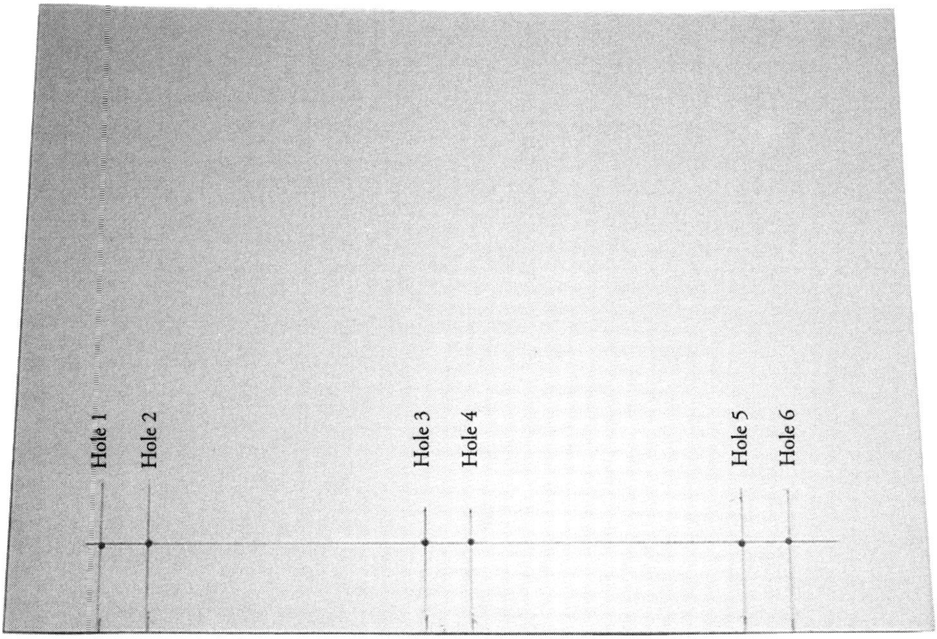

Making a stencil for punching the holes. Use a scrap sheet of paper to determine how many tapes will be used, their width and position. Above, there will be three tapes requiring six holes to be punched on each sheet. The tapes are evenly spaced apart. The top tape is closer to the head than the bottom tape is to the tail. This suggests a base.
Use the stencil to pierce no more than 4 or 5 sheets at a time.

PIERCING THE HOLES: Place the stencil on top of four or five sheets of the book block. Jog it. Carefully place it on the table with the spine–edge slightly out from the edge of the table. With a bradawl, pierce through the sheets using the stencil as a guide.

Continue in this manner to pierce the remaining sheets of the book block.

Separate Side–Covers

Cut the boards with an overhang at the head, tail and foredge. The boards will be flush with the spine–edge of the book block. Cover the boards and allow them to dry. *See* covering the boards, page 83.

Place the spine–edge of the board about 1/2" to 5/8" off the edge of the table. Place the stencil on top of the *inside* of the back board with the head to the left. Center it. Pierce the holes with a bradawl or bodkin.

Place the stencil on the *outside* of the front cover, head to the left. Center the stencil and pierce the board.

SEWING PROCEDURE

This method will use three tapes with six holes, numbered from the head to the tail.

1. Start the sewing at the head with the first sheet to be sewn. Go down through hole 1 to the underneath side of the sheet. Leave a small amount of thread on top. Proceed to the spine-edge. Come around the spine–edge to the top and tie a square knot at hole 1.
2. Link under the stitch at the spine–edge from forward of the hole toward the head.
3. Set on the tape. Position the tape so that below the sheet is the amount of tape you wish to have attached to the back cover. *Lap* (cross over) the tape.
4. Enter hole 2 from *below* the sheet to the top. Pull the thread through by pulling toward the foredge leaving a small loop of thread on the spine.

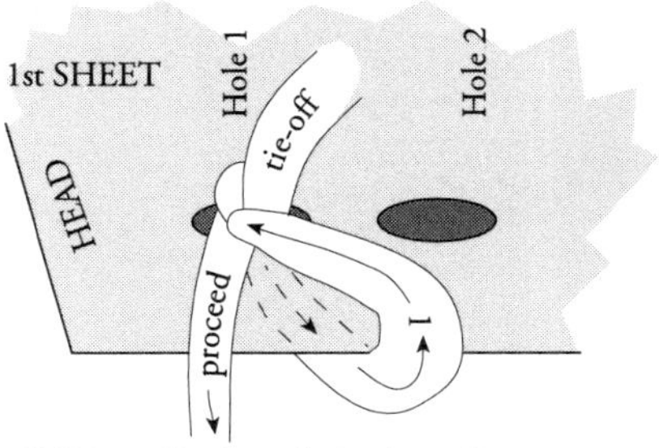

STEP 1: Go through the sheet, Come around to the top and tie a square knot at hole 1.

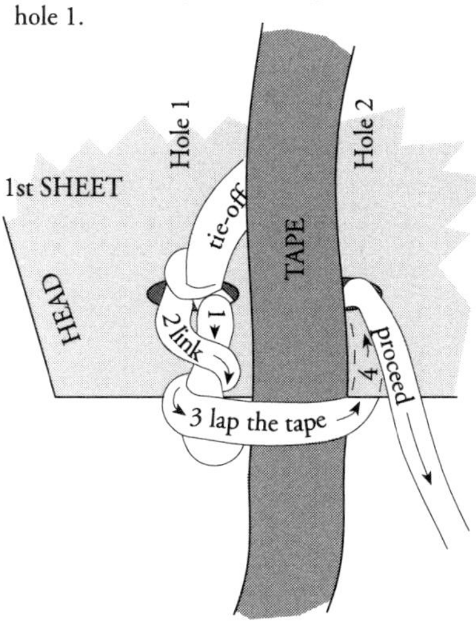

STEP 2: Link the stitch at the spine–edge.
STEP 3: Lap the tape.
STEP 4: Enter hole 2 from bottom to top.

5. Proceed to the spine–edge. Drop the needle through the loop to link the horizontal stitch which is across the tape. In the remainder of the description the horizontal thread that laps the tape will be referred to as the *tape stitch.* Pull the thread taut, but be careful not to rip the paper at hole 2.

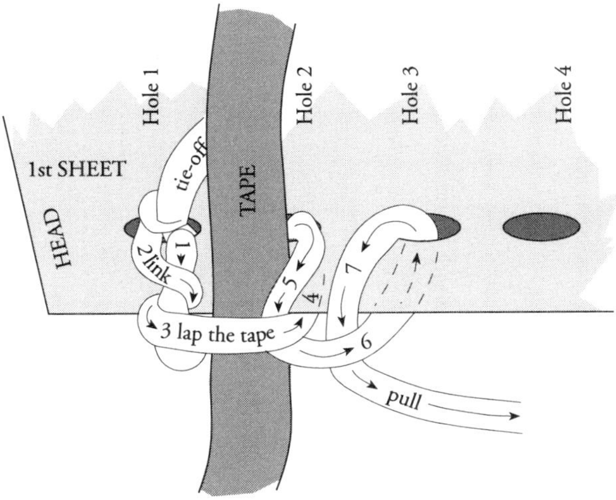

STEP 5: Proceed to the spine–edge. Pull the thread taut. Link under the horizontal stitch which is across the tape from the top to the bottom. Don't tighten Step 3 until you link with Step 5. That way you can drop the needle through the loop of thread which crosses the tape to form the link.
STEP 6: Proceed to hole 3. Enter hole 3 from underneath to the top. Do not pull the thread tight. Leave a small loop of thread as shown above.
STEP 7: Proceed to the spine–edge. Link the diagonal thread (this loop). Pull parallel to and along the spine–edge.

6. Proceed to hole 3. Enter hole 3 from underneath the sheet to the top. Pull the thread through. Do not pull this diagonal thread tight, or you cannot adjust it parallel to the spine–edge without loosening the tension. Instead leave a small loop of thread on the spine as shown above and in the photo on page 193. (In the photo, the sewing is proceeding towards the head.)

7. Proceed to the spine–edge. Be careful not to rip the paper. Link the diagonal thread (the loop on the spine–edge) by simply dropping the needle through the loop. Pull out and in the direction of the sewing until it becomes parallel to and along the spine–edge. If the resulting horizontal thread (Step 6) does not reach along the spine–edge to the position of hole 3, tug on the loop to adjust. If the horizontal thread is baggy, pull the thread at hole 3 toward the foredge to adjust.

NOTE: I do not raise the sheet from the table top in sewing. In Step 6, I slide the needle under and bring it up through the hole. In Step 7, I pull until a small loop of thread remains on the spine. This is approximately the right amount of tension. Link under the loop and adjust the diagonal thread so that it becomes snug, parallel to, and rests on the spine–edge of the sheet. This will make a right angle with the thread that extends from hole 3 to the spine–edge.

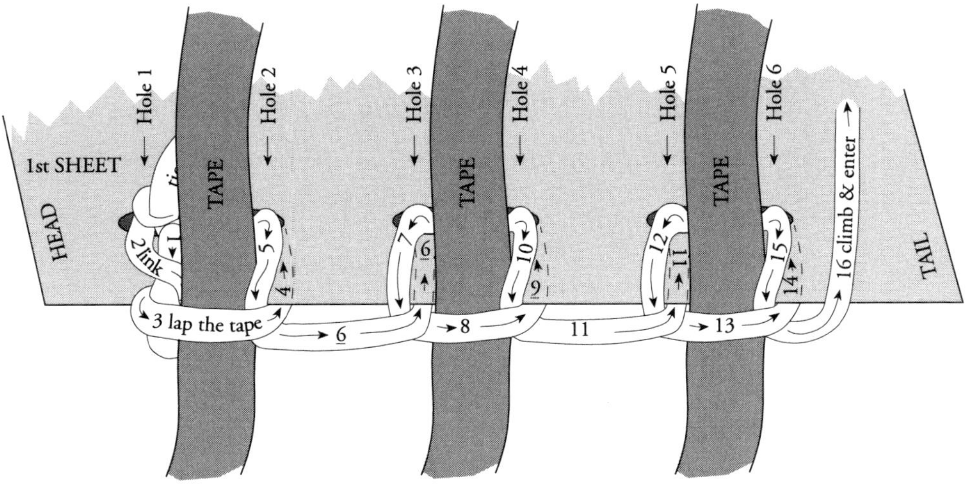

Sewing the first sheet.

8. Set on the second tape between holes 3 and 4. Lap the tape.
9. Enter hole 4 from below the sheet to the top. Pull the thread through until taut by pulling toward the foredge.
10. Proceed to the spine–edge. Be careful not to rip the paper. Pull the thread taut, but be careful not to rip the paper at hole 4. Link under the tape stitch from the top to the bottom.
11. Proceed to hole 5. Enter hole 5 from underneath the sheet to the top. Pull the thread through but not tightly. Leave a small loop of thread on the spine.
12. Proceed to the spine–edge. Link the diagonal thread (the loop on the spine–edge). Pull out and in the direction of the sewing until it becomes parallel to and along the spine–edge. Adjust the tension, if necessary.
13. Set on the third tape between holes 5 and 6. Lap the tape.
14. Enter hole 6 from below the sheet to the top. Pull the thread through until taut by pulling toward the foredge.
15. Proceed to the spine edge on the tail side of the tape. Link under the tape stitch from above to below. Tighten the thread that extends to the spine–edge from hole 6 by pulling out and slightly toward the tail.

Sewing the Second Sheet

16. Set on the next sheet. Climb and enter the new sheet from the *top* to the bottom of that sheet.
17. Exit backward, so the thread is on the right of the climbing thread. Be careful not to rip the paper at hole 6.

18. Lap the climbing thread and the tape, heading toward the head.
19. Enter hole 5 from the underneath up to the top of the sheet.
20. Proceed to the spine–edge. Link under the tape stitch from the top to the bottom.
21. Proceed to hole 4. Enter hole 4 from underneath the sheet to the top. Pull the thread through. Do not pull the diagonal thread tight, but leave a small loop of thread on the spine as shown in the illustration below.

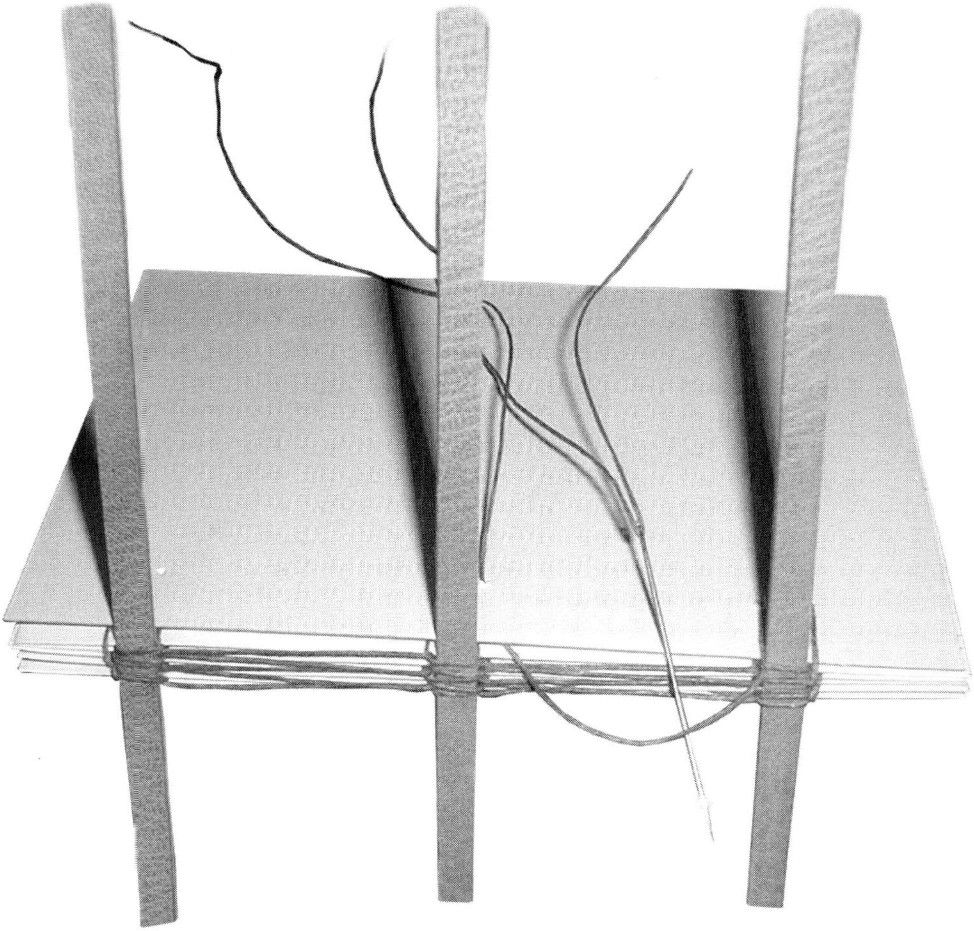

PULLING THE DIAGONAL THREAD TO HORIZONTAL: In the illustration above the sewing of the sixth sheet is progressing toward the head. The loop of thread on the spine–edge is Step 21. The needle going down through the loop to link is Step 22. It will pull the loop to a horizontal lining up on the spine–edge.

If the sewing were heading toward the tail the loop would happen with Steps 6 and 11. The needle going through the loop to link would be Steps 7 and 12.

22. Proceed to the spine–edge. Link the diagonal thread (the loop on the spine–edge). Pull out and in the direction of the sewing until it becomes parallel to and along the spine–edge.
23. Lap the second tape.
24. Enter hole 3 from below the sheet to the top. Pull the thread through until taut.
25. Proceed to the spine–edge. Pull the thread taut, but don't rip the paper at hole 3. Link under the tape stitch from the top to the bottom.
26. Proceed to hole 2. Enter hole 2 from underneath the sheet to the top. Pull the thread through leaving a small loop of thread on the spine.
27. Proceed to the spine–edge. Link the diagonal thread, which is the loop on the spine–edge. Pull toward the head until the loop thread is horizontal and along the spine–edge of the sheet.
28. Lap the first tape.
29. Enter hole 1 from below the sheet to the top. Pull the thread through.
30. Proceed to spine edge on the left side of the tape with the thread tangent to the tape.
31. There are two horizontal threads across the first tape. Link under both tape stitches from above to below on the left side of the tape. Tighten the thread that extends to the spine–edge from hole 1. Pull down and toward the head.

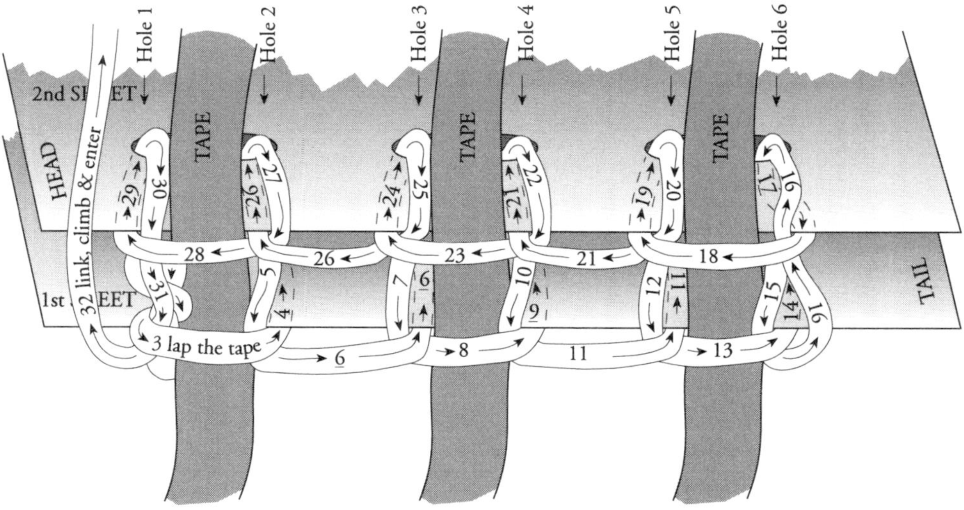

Sewing the second sheet.

Sewing the Third Sheet

32. Set on the next sheet to be sewn. Climb and enter the new sheet from the *top* to the bottom of the sheet.
33. Exit on the left side of the climbing thread.
34. Lap thread which is Step 32 and lap the tape.
35. Enter hole 2 from the bottom to the top of the sheet. Tighten by pulling the thread toward the foredge.
36. Proceed to the spine with the thread against the forward side of, and tangent to, the tape. Pull the thread taut, but be careful not to rip the paper at hole 2. Link the tape stitch from above to below.
37. Proceed to hole 3. Enter hole 3 from the bottom to the top. Pull the thread through leaving a small loop on the spine.

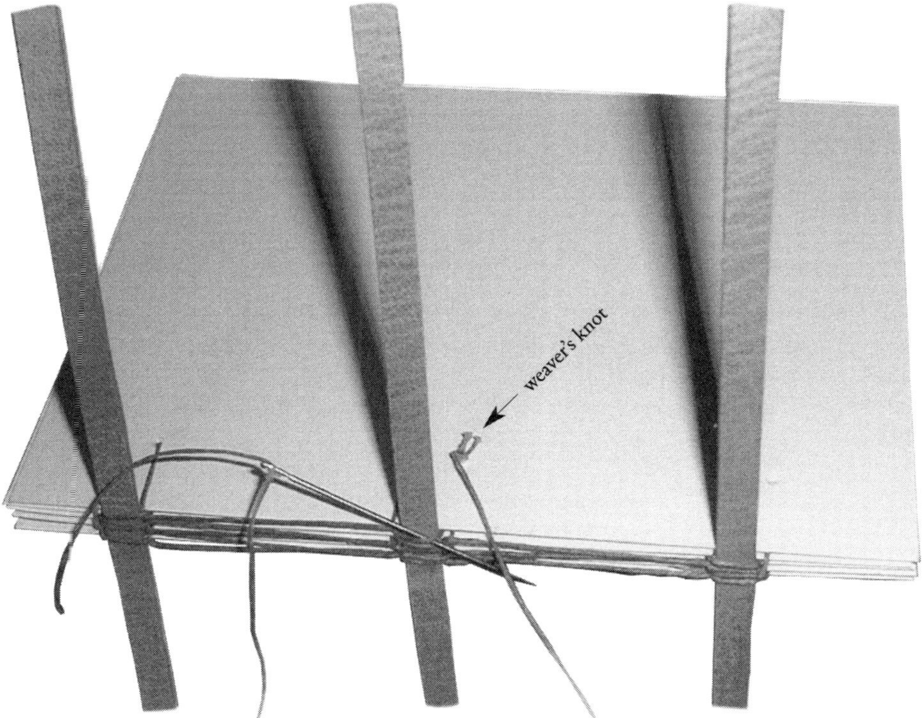

ADDING THREAD WITH THE WEAVER"S KNOT: If you run out of thread you will need to add thread with a weaver's knot. When sewing toward the tail, as above, tie the knot after exiting to the top at hole 4. If you are sewing toward the head, tie the knot after exiting hole 3.
Above, the needle proceeds to the spine–edge and has linked under the top tape stitch.

38. Proceed to the spine–edge. Link the diagonal thread (drop the needle through the loop on the spine–edge). Pull out and in the direction of the sewing until it becomes parallel to and along the spine–edge.
39. Lap the second tape.
40. Enter hole 4 from below the sheet to the top. Pull the thread through until taut by pulling toward the foredge.
41. Proceed to the spine with the thread against the forward side of, and tangent to, the tape. Pull the thread taut. Link the tape stitch from above to below.
42. Proceed to hole 5. Enter from the bottom to the top. Pull the thread through leaving a small loop on the spine.
43. Proceed to the spine–edge. Link the diagonal thread and adjust the tension until it becomes parallel to and along the spine–edge.
44. Lap the third tape.
45. Enter hole 6 from below the sheet to the top. Pull the thread through until taut.

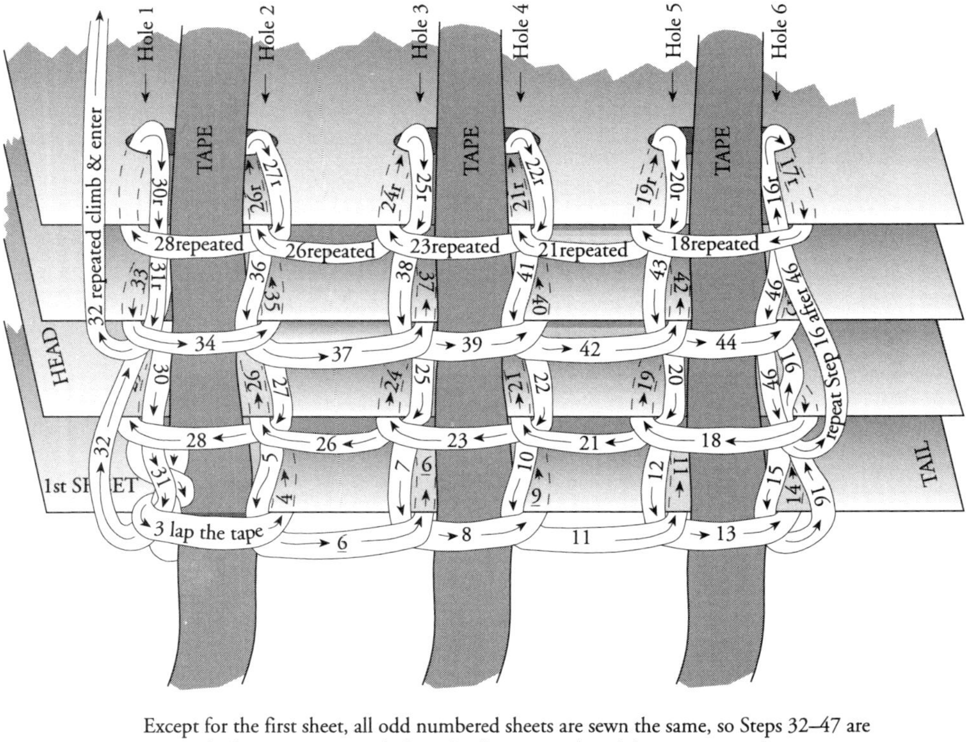

Except for the first sheet, all odd numbered sheets are sewn the same, so Steps 32–47 are repeated when sewing towards the tail. All even numbered sheets are sewn the same, repeating Steps 16–30.

46. Proceed to the spine–edge. Link the top two tape stitches in a downward motion. Be careful not to loosen the tension of the tape stitches. You can tighten only the top tape stitch after linking. Tighten the thread from hole 6 by pulling down then slightly toward the tail. Do not distort the tape stitch from the horizontal.

Sewing the Next Even Numbered Sheet

Repeat Steps 16–30. Then link the top two tape stitches from above to below on the left side of the tape. Tighten the thread that extends to the spine–edge from hole 1. Pull down and toward the head.

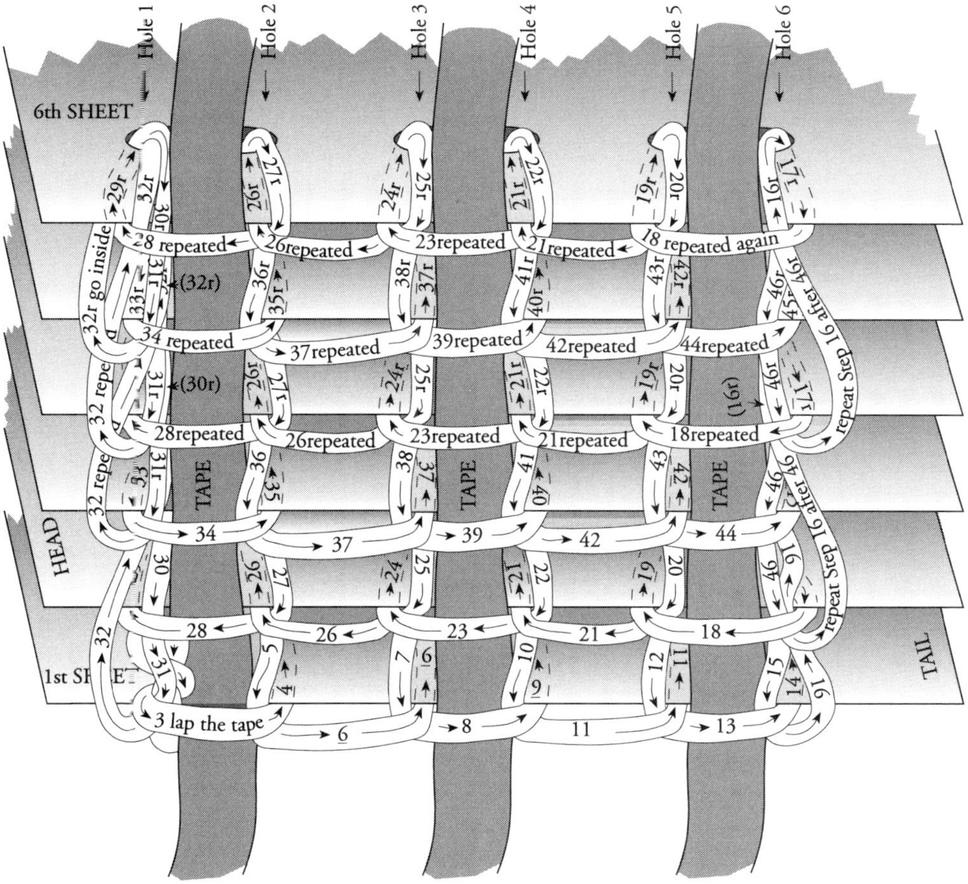

At the end of the last sheet, after dropping to link the last two stitches that lap the tape, climb and enter between the final and next to last sheet to tie–off.

Sewing the Next Odd Numbered Sheet

Repeat Steps 32–46.

Tying Off the Sewing

After sewing all the sheets you will end at either hole 1 or 6. Link the top two tape stitches as usual. The following steps are how to tie–off. They are numbered starting with Step 1:

1. Take the needle to the inside between the final and next to last sheet.
2. Open the top sheet. Take the needle through the hole of the next to last sheet coming out between the next to last and the second from last sheet.
3. Tie–off with a half hitch by slipping the needle under the stitch on the next to last sheet and going through the loop. Do this twice. For a diagram of forming this knot *see* half hitch for Sewing Single Sheets Onto Tapes, page 66.

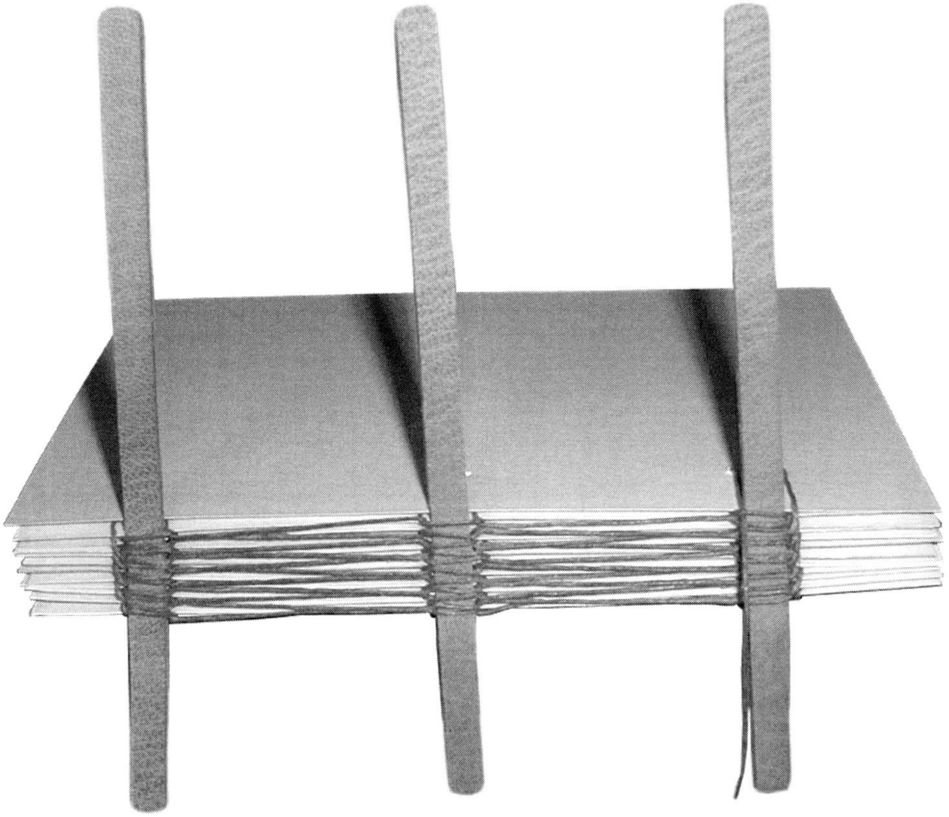

Sewing Single Sheets onto Tapes, in progress. Paper was glued to the back of the leather with PVA. After it was dry, the paper–backed leather was cut into strips.

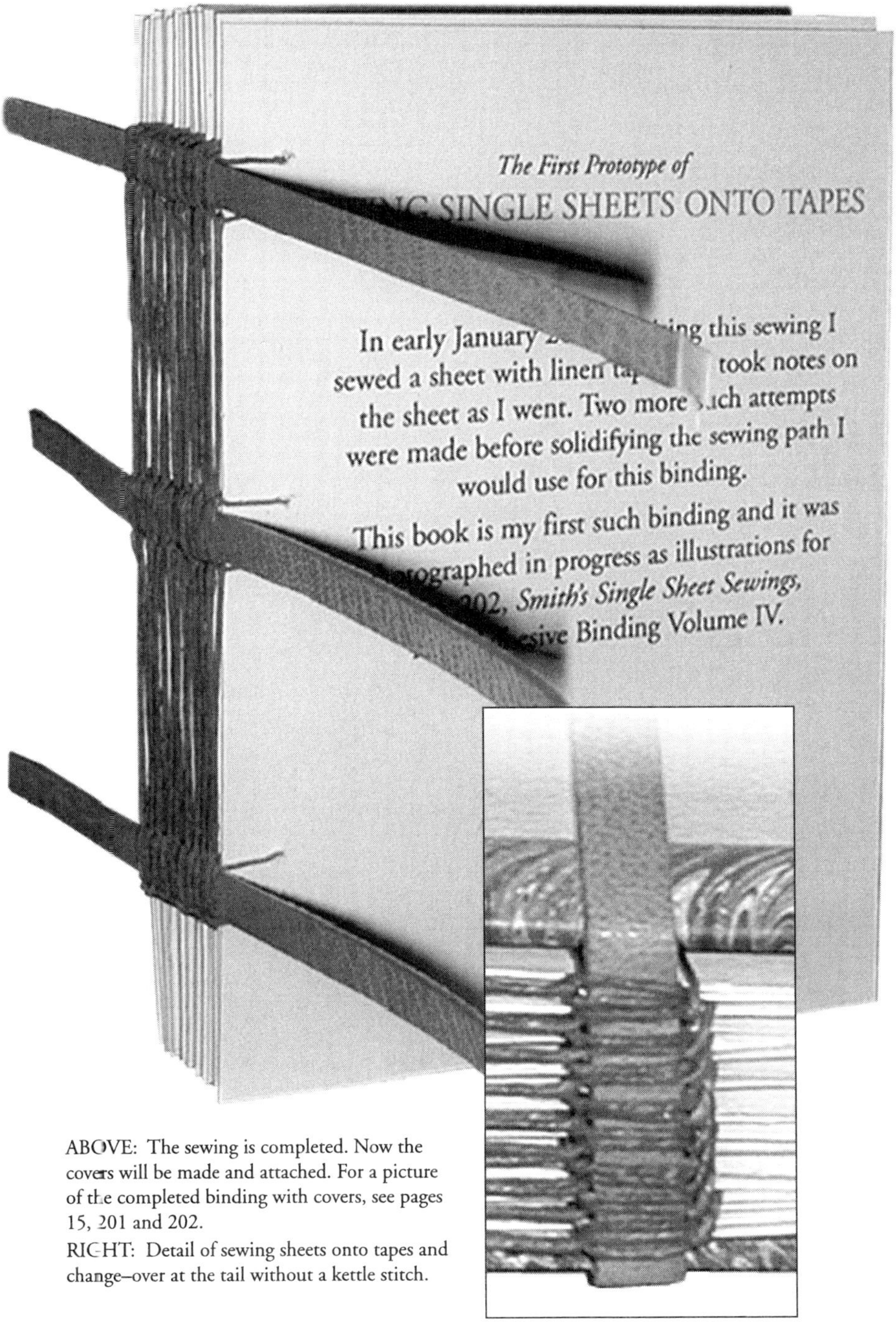

ABOVE: The sewing is completed. Now the covers will be made and attached. For a picture of the completed binding with covers, see pages 15, 201 and 202.

RIGHT: Detail of sewing sheets onto tapes and change–over at the tail without a kettle stitch.

ATTACHING SEPARATE SIDE-COVERS by SEWING on the TAPE SUPPORTS

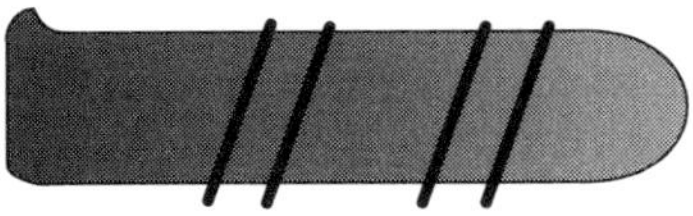

DIAGONAL outside view

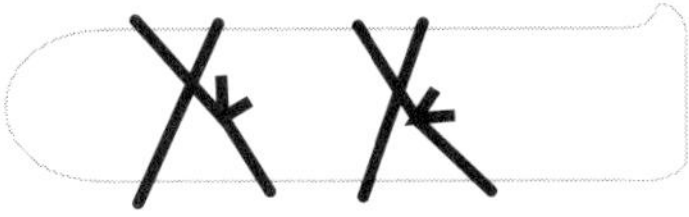

inside cover tie-off

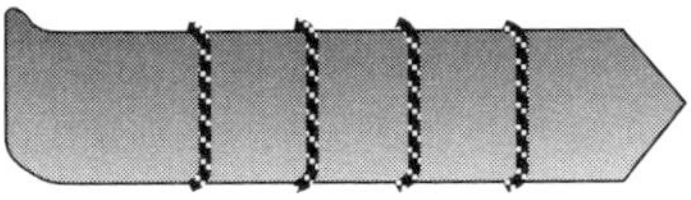

VERTICAL outside view

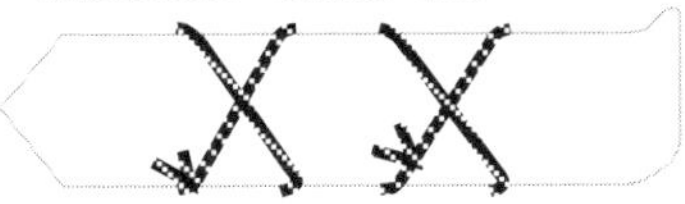

inside cover tie-off

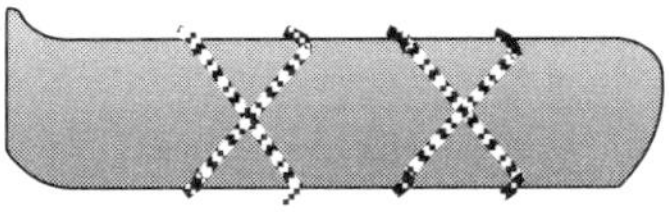

"X" outside view

inside cover tie-off

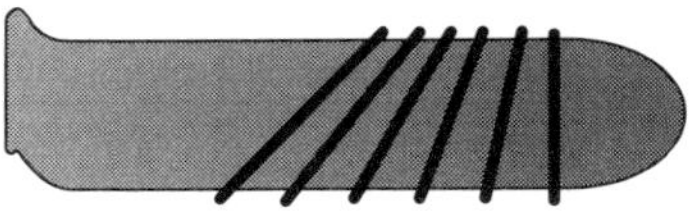

FALLING DOMINO outside view

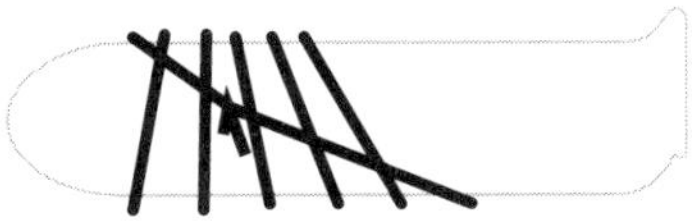

inside cover tie-off

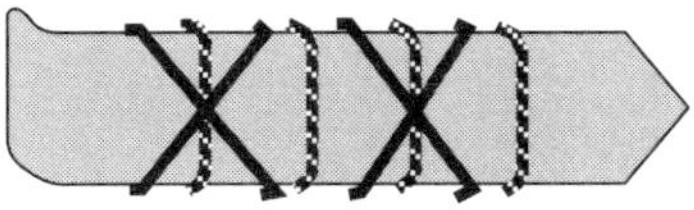

"X" and VERTICAL in 2 COLORS

inside cover tie-off

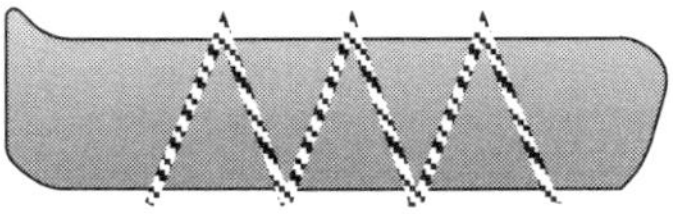

ZIG - ZAGS outside view

inside cover tie-off

BOARDS FOR SEWING ONTO TAPES

After the sewing is completed cut two boards for the covers. Boards are flush on the spine–edge and overhang at the head, tail and foredge.

Cover the boards and allow to dry. Separate side–covers can be attached by gluing with PVA and/or sewn on. The tapes can be woven through the boards. *See* glue & paste, page 73; covering the boards, page 83; and inlaid papers, page 91.

Tapes are structural. Paper–backed leather supports are meant to be seen. They can be woven through slots in the board. Ends of the leather are glue and/or sewn to the boards.

After covering the boards, tapes can be glued across the *outside* the board. Never attach tapes to the inside. Placing the book on the shelf could pull the boards loose. These tapes were glued and sewn to the boards. Patterns for sewn attachment are on the facing page.

In the Single Sheets Sewn Onto Tapes described, the long stitch from tape to tape is designed along the spine. It could be hidden if the sewing path had the long stitch from hole to hole, but I enjoy the pattern of thread exposed on the outside of the book.

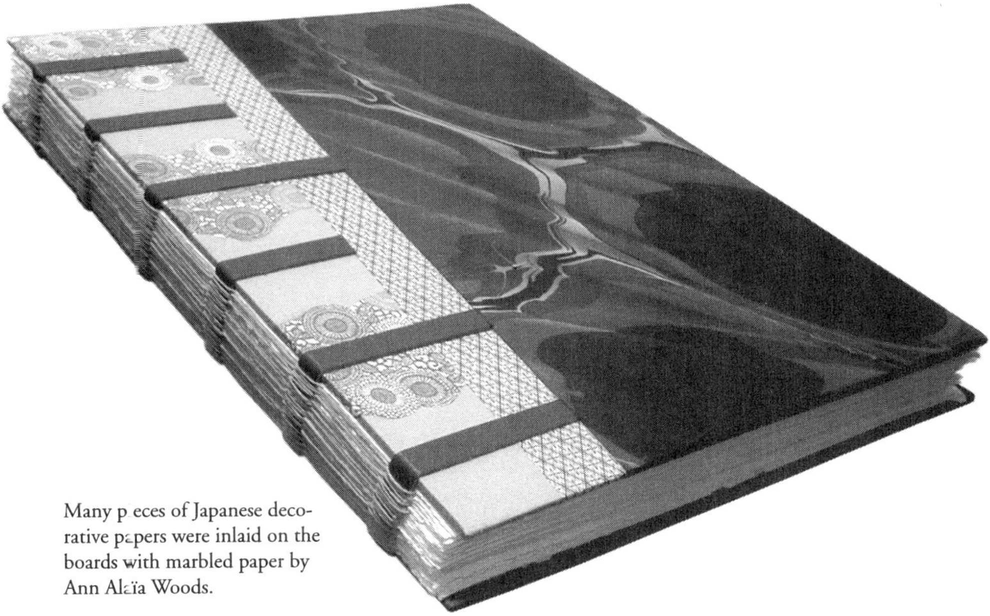

Many pieces of Japanese decorative papers were inlaid on the boards with marbled paper by Ann Alaïa Woods.

This oversize Single Sheets Sewn Onto Tapes has Stonehedge paper as the book block. It is shown in–progress on page 41. Since the spine swells greatly with this sewing, it is ideal for use an album. January 2001. 37.5 x 29.5 x 4 cm.

INTRODUCTION
SINGLE SHEETS
SEWN RAISED CORDS

As long as I am devising sewing onto tapes for sheets, I figure I might as well see what I can do with cord supports. Of course I cannot sew sheets onto recessed cords, so they must be raised. What one would do with this binding, I do not know, but then I have not given it any thought. Besides, if I show it, there will be those who find a perfect use for it.

So last evening I sewed a sheet with 3 cords and took notes as I went. The first cord was wrapped twice. I thought, the cord will be hidden by the thread since I am sewing sheets. This will make a lovely packing. The next cord I went under the sheet, looped the cord, proceeded up and entered on top to the bottom. I then looped the cord from the opposite side, went up and re–entered the top. The thread formed an *X* on the spine! It was similar to the 1–Section *X* Sewing described in *Exposed Spine Sewings,* Volume III *Non–Adhesive Binding* which I learned from Betsy Palmer Eldridge. I learned so much from her and again I thank Betsy for all she has taught me.

Sewing those two stations on a single sheet last evening I knew I had two fine new bindings. What luck. In five minutes it all came so easily. It's nice when that happens. I knew also I could not have written Volume IV without having written Volume III. I learn so much by writing a book.

I always thought one wrote a book because the writer had so much knowledge. Not me. I know little about the subject matter when I begin writing a book and learn as I go along. I knew nothing about binding single sheets, except Japanese Stab Bindings and the Album Binding, and those were *not* the approach I wanted. I had a need to be able to use single sheets in binding, but I wanted a structure that would open flat at any page.

Last night, sewing the second station on that single sheet–as–sketch, I realized the *X* sewing would not show up since the depth of the sheet is only a fraction of that of a section. But after I complete sewing and describing this first raised cord sewing, I will cut a stack of book boards and sew them with nice *X's* on the spine!

I can't wait. ks 24 January 2001

CORDS

THICKNESS: Binder suppliers sell various diameter of linen cord for supports. Thickness is based on the number of plies. Generally a 5–ply cord will do unless you are sewing an oversized book. You can substitute for the traditional cord. In sewing small books I often take 3 strands of #18 linen thread and twill it. If I am going to have the cord attachment to the board visible, the cord is untwisted at the ends after the sewing is completed. Each ply is attached to the board separately. See example at the bottom of the facing page.

LENGTH: Make each cord at least 4" longer that the thickness of the book block. This will give 2" of thread at each end to attach the boards.

NOTE: In measuring the thickness of the book block double the depth of the stack of sheets you will sew. This will allow for the swell which will occur with the sewing. Better too much than too little amount of cord to attach to the boards.

Attaching Frayed Cords

The traditional multi–ply linen cord is heavy duty in thickness and not always needed. It is meant to be laced through the boards. This means the board and backbone are covered after the boards are attached. This eliminates the possibility of an exposed spine as it is next to impossible to cover separate side covers after boards have been laced in.

The following is one solution: Sew the single sheets on raised cords using traditional heavy 5–ply cord. After the separate side–covers are covered, drill holes through the board first with a bradawl, then widen the holes with a leather awl.

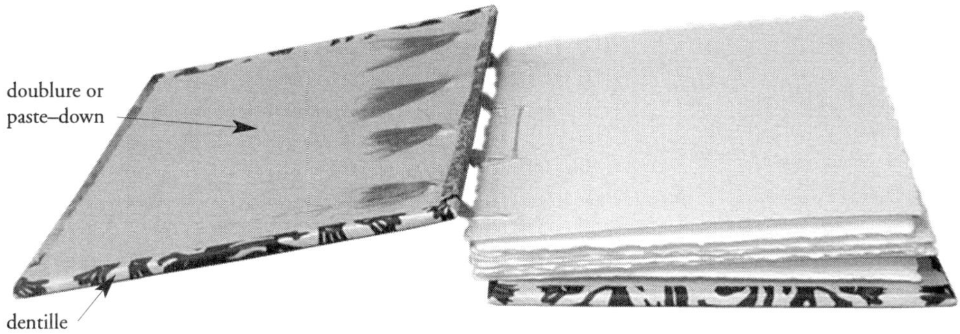

Single sheets were sewn on raised cords using traditional heavy 5–ply cord. The exposed spine is not pasted; it is a non–adhesive binding. Separate side–covers were covered, pasting on decorative papers. Holes were drilled through the board first with a bradawl, then widened with a leather awl.

Ends of the cord were untwisted then frayed. They were temporarily re–twisted and pulled through the holes in the board, then frayed again and glued to the board. A new paste–down or doublure could be applied to the inside of the board to cover the ends of the cords.

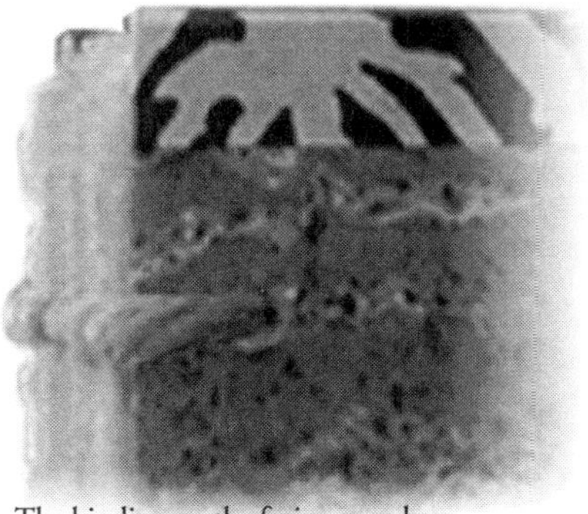

The binding on the facing page has 5–ply cord is pulled through the board.

Cut the cords to 2" long. Untwist each cord. Fray the cords by running a bradawl through them many times. This will untwist most of the individual strands as well as eliminate some of the strands. A short–toothed wire dog brush is quicker than a bradawl.

Temporarily re–twist the frayed cord, moistening it to form a tip. Cut the straggly end off so you can thread the end through the hole in the board.

Pull the cord through the hole to the inside of the board. The support always comes around the board and enters from the outside to the inside.Pull all the cords toward the foredge so the board is tight against the spine. Fray the cords again into a fan shape so the strands are spread out flat.

Place a scrap piece of wax paper under all the cords. Glue the cords with PVA making sure to maintain the fan shape of the cords so they do not bunch up. Remove the wax paper pulling toward the foredge. Lightly tap down the frayed cords with your fingertip.

Place a clean sheet of wax paper over the first page. Close the book and press with the palm of your hand. Open the cover. The wax paper will be on top of the cover and cords. Place the board only, on the table. The remainder of the book is off the table with the spine pressed against the depth of the table top. Lightly tap each cord with a hammer. This will flatten the cord and the edge of the holes. Be careful not to dent the board. Close the board and attach the other board in the same manner. Allow the glue to dry 15 minutes before removing the wax paper.

You may consider the book on the facing page unfinished. If so, another doublure can be pasted to the inside of the board over the cords.

Attaching Individual Plies of Cords

To alleviate pulling a heavy cord through the boards, plies of cord can be taken through holes on the board individually. In the example of a raised cord sewing on the right, two 6–ply cords are attached using 12 holes. Plies can be tied inside, or frayed and glued as described on the previous page.

The 6 plies of the cord are pulled through holes on the board individually, requiring much smaller holes in the board.

3–Ply Thread Substitute for Cords

Coptic sewings allow for easy thread attachment to the boards. In *Exposed Spine Sewings,* Volume III of *Non–Adhesive Binding,* I made several raised cord sewings on 3–ply thread which I twisted together. After the sewing is completed it is simple to take the three threads though a single hole, or to take the threads through three holes individually and tie them on the inside of the board. Three separate colors of thread can be used. If the threads are taken through a single hole, you can leave them twisted, or braid them and take the flat braid through a tiny slot in the board.

PREPARATION FOR SEWING RAISED CORDS

Stations

Unlike Sewing Sheets Onto Tapes, in any raised cord sewing, the *holes* and the *stations* are synonymous. I will refer to the holes as *stations.*

Choose any number of sewing stations, odd or even. Place one close to the head and another close to the tail—within an inch or 2.5 cm. The remaining number of stations should be no more than 2" or 5 cm. apart.

Pierce all the sheets and the two separate side–covers.

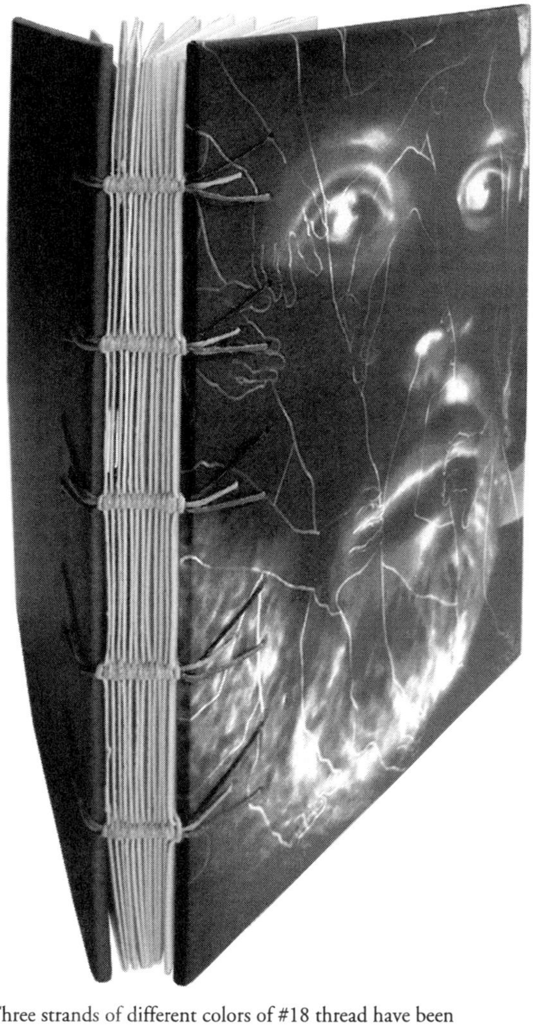

Three strands of different colors of #18 thread have been twisted together to create a 3–ply "cord". After the sewing was completed, the dangling ends of cord were untwisted. Each of the three threads were separately attached to the board. Stands of thread twisted to be used as a cord require a sewing frame to keep the twists tight.

Holes for each should be set in from the spine–edge at least 3/8" or 1 cm. so they do not rip out. The distance the hole is in on the sheet does not affect the page opening flat, as the hinge is at the cord support, not at the hole.

MARKING THE STATIONS: Using a scrap sheet which is the same dimensions as your book block, place the cords on this sheet at, and perpendicular to, the spine–edge. Arrange the amount of space between by your eye. Refine this measurement with a ruler. With a sharp pencil, place a dot at each cord. With a ruler, draw a line in from, and perpendicular to, the spine–edge at each one of the dots. Measure in from the spine edge about 3/8" to 1/2" at the head. Make the same measurement at the tail. With a ruler, draw a line connecting these dots. It will be parallel to, and close to, the spine–edge. This will be your *stencil* for piercing the book block a few sheets at a time.

Separate Side–Covers

Cut the boards with an overhang at the head, tail and foredge. The boards will be flush with the book block on the spine–edge. Cover the boards and allow them to dry. *See* covering the boards, page 83.

Place the stencil on top of the *inside* of the back board with the head to the left. Center it. Place the spine–edge of the board about 1/2" to 5/8" off the edge of the table. Pierce the holes with a bradawl or bodkin.

Place the stencil on the *outside* of the front cover, head to the left. Center the stencil and pierce the board.

Sewing Fame

Ideally, any raised cord sewing is done on a sewing frame. The sewing cannot be hand held and sewn. *See* sewing on the bench, page 67. It is possible to sew without a frame. *See* making a sewing frame, page 30.

NOTE: Care must be taken each time in tightening the sewing when the loop of thread is on top of a sheet to hold the cord next to the sheet. Otherwise, tightening will pull the loop of thread up higher onto the cord. The loop must be against the sheet.

This is not a problem when the needle is under the sheet being sewn and a loop is made.

Other Information

Refer to pages 40–45 for information on swell, dimensions of the boards, hiding the stitches, sewing threads inlaid and laminating pictures to the boards.

This is the first prototype of Single Sheets Sewn Raised Cord. It opens beautifully.

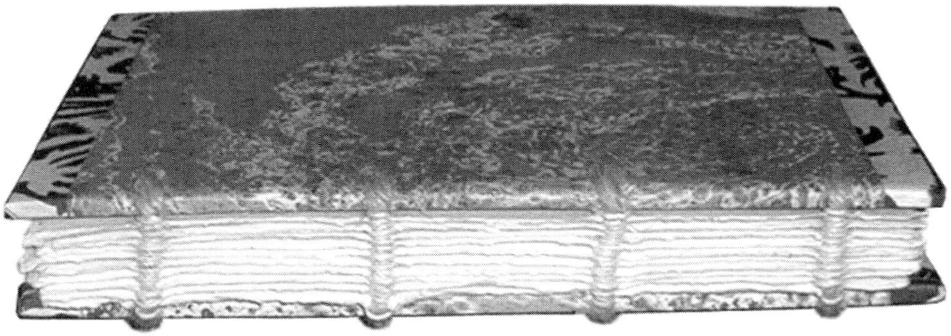

This single sheet raised cord sewing, described on page 213, places the long stitch (the thread which advances to the next station) *in on the sheet*. The long stitch proceeds from hole to hole. For a photo of the long stitch, see page 214.

On the outside, the look of the spine in this sewing resembles a traditional raised cord sewing of sections.

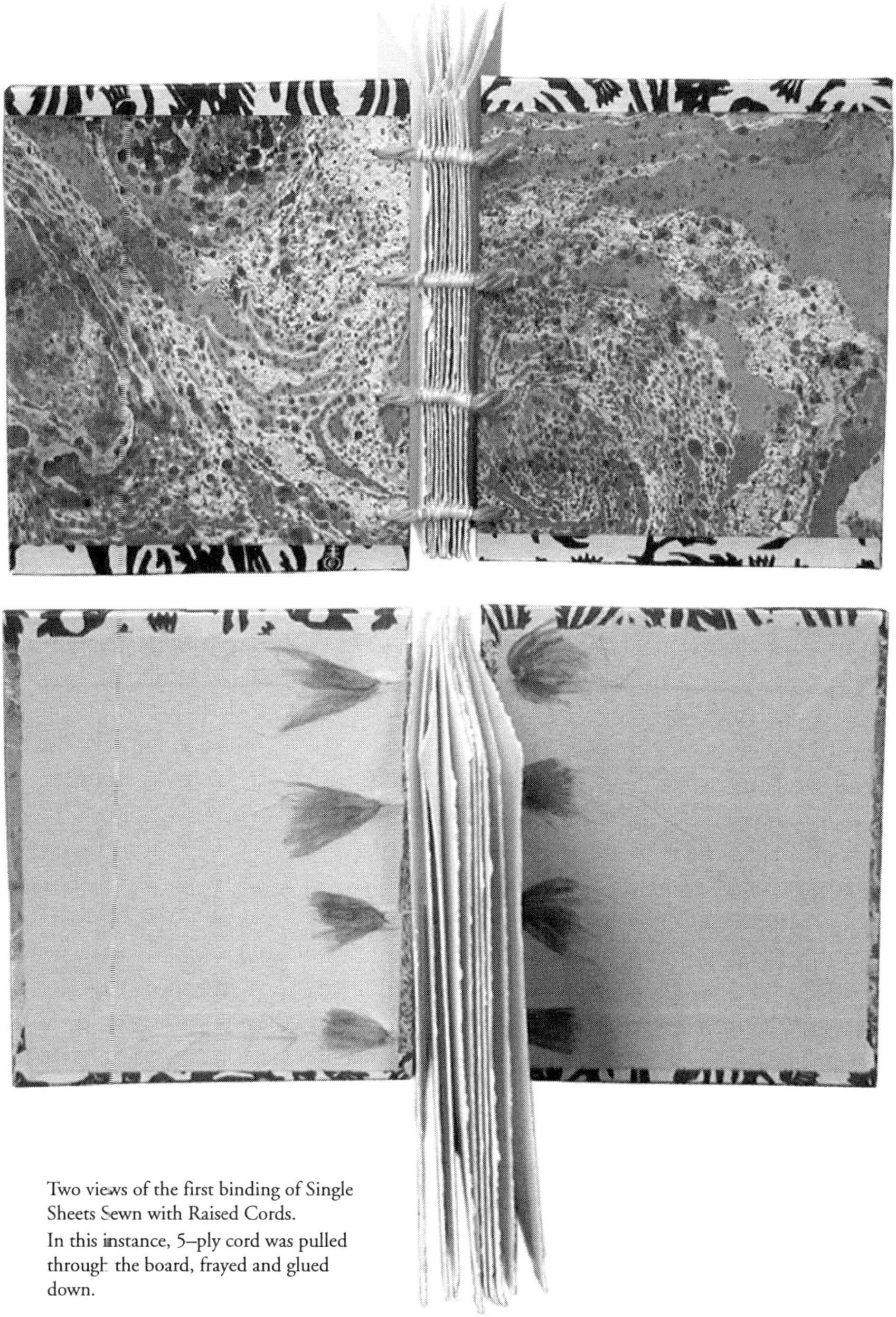

Two views of the first binding of Single Sheets Sewn with Raised Cords.
In this instance, 5–ply cord was pulled through the board, frayed and glued down.

LOOP PACK WITH CLIMBING PACK

long stitch in on the sheet

The compact layers of the book block in sewing sheets instead of sections with raised cords necessarily means the looping of thread will completely cover the cords. As stated in the *Glossary,* to *loop* is to circle around a support or sewing thread. To *lap* is to pass over a support or sewing thread.

LOOP PACK: It is hardly packing. When *sections* are sewn, the cord must be looped two or three times to have a solid pack, but a single loop will surely cover the cord in sewing single sheets. So I do not know if it is appropriate to refer to this binding as a *loop pack.*

CLIMBING PACK: At the end of a row of sewing a sheet, with the second loop the next sheet is set on. Technically it is a *climbing pack,* so I will go with this name for this binding.

If you are sewing thick book board as sheets, you will have to loop once or twice more at each station in order to have a solid pack, if that is desired.

If you are sewing a small book, three strands of heavy thread twisted will make a small diameter cord. It is easy to lace the three separate threads into the boards as shown below. The disadvantage is it will be difficult to sew the twisted thread–as–cord with a sewing frame to keep the threads twisted tightly. If the thread is not pre–waxed, you can run paste over the strands of thread with your fingers as you twist it. Allow it to dry before using.

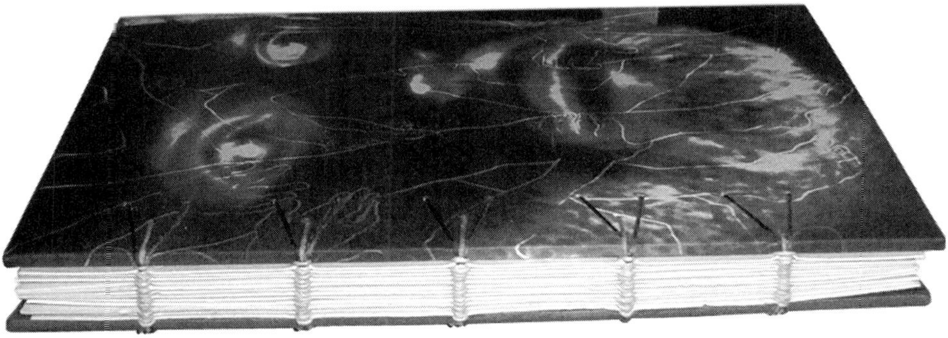

Three strands of different colors of #18 thread have been twisted together to create a 3–ply "cord". Other examples of this second attempt of sewing sheets onto cords can be seen on page 221.

Long Stitch

The thread which advances from station to station is referred to as the *long stitch.* In this sewing the long stitch is in on the sheet from hole to hole.

Change–Over

Sewing of odd numbered sheets proceeds from the head to the tail. The direction of sewing *along the spine* for even numbered sheets is from the tail to the head. The point of changing the direction of sewing is referred to as the *change–over.* As you approach the end station on each sheet, the long stitch will be either on the bottom or the top of the sheet. Depending which side of the sheet you are sewing, the long stitch is on requires a different procedure to add the next sheet to be sewn. There can be any number of stations, odd or even.

The description will use five cords, and thus five sewing stations/holes which are numbered from the head to the tail.

The pages are sewn without the cover boards. The boards are attached to the sewn book block by bringing the cords through stations in the boards.

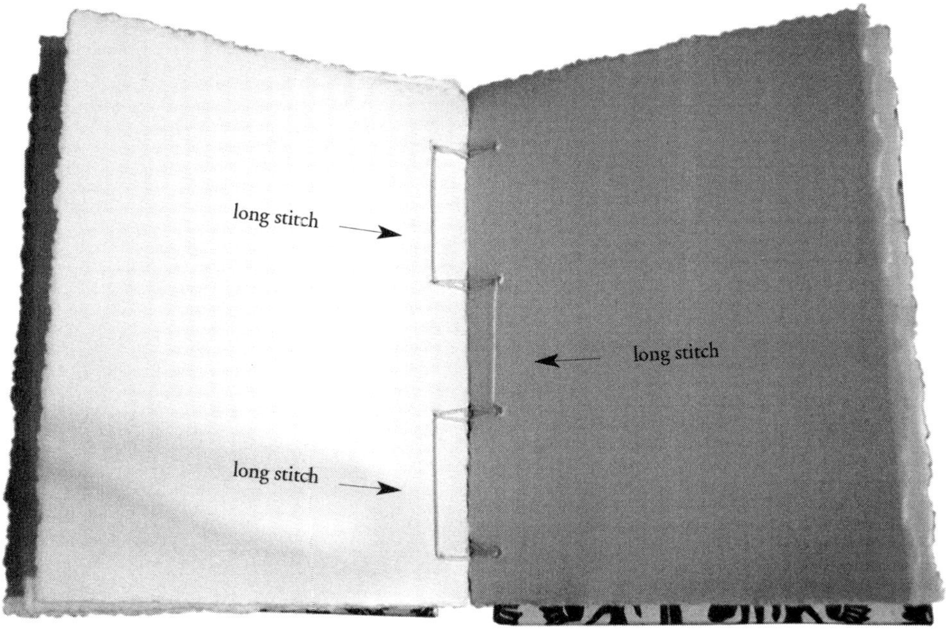

The thread that proceeds from station to station is called the *long stitch.* In this sewing it proceeds *in on the sheet* from hole to hole.

SEWING PROCEDURE

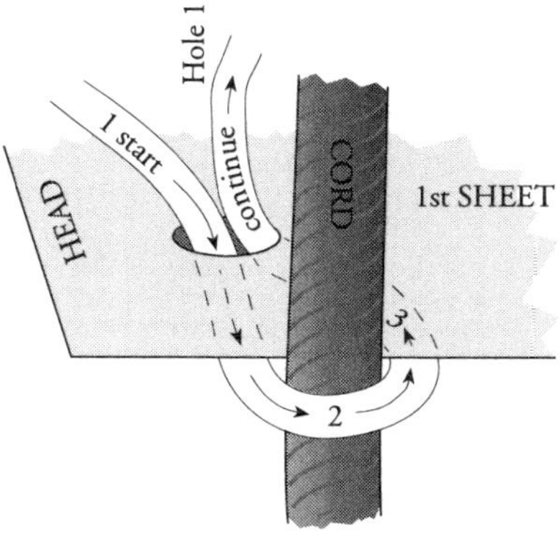

STEP 1: Go through sheet to underneath.
STEP 2: Loop the cord.
STEP 3: Proceed under sheet to the hole.

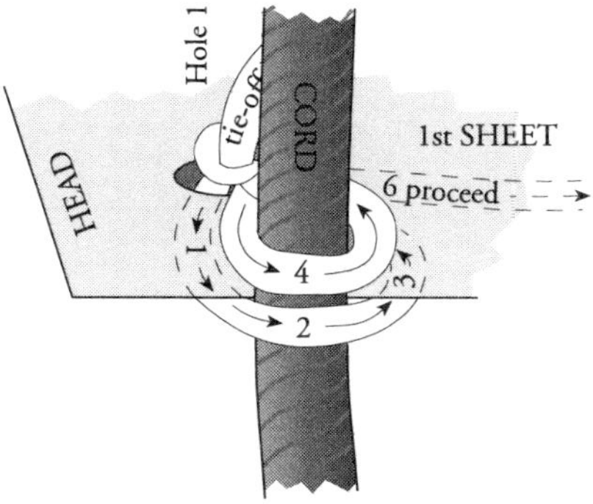

STEP 4: Proceed on the top of the sheet and loop the cord. Steps 2 and 4 are *thread loops,* seen on the spine of the closed book..
STEP 5. Tie a square knot at the hole.
STEP 6: Proceed on the bottom of the sheet to the next hole.

1. Start at the head with the first sheet to be sewn. Go down through Station 1 to the underneath side of the sheet. Leave a small amount of thread on top.
2. Proceed to the spine–edge on either side of the cord. *Loop* the cord, that is go around the support. Head back to the same station on the *same* side of the sheet.

NOTE: In *this* sewing, it does not matter if you loop from right to left or left to right, because you proceed from the hole, not from the support.

3. Go through the station from bottom to the top of the sheet.
4. Proceed to the spine–edge. Loop the cord. Proceed to the same hole on the same side of the sheet.
5. Tie a square knot at Station 1. Go through Station 1 to the bottom of the sheet.
6. Proceed on the bottom side of the sheet to the next station. The thread from the first station to the second creates the first long stitch. Go through the new station to the top of the sheet.
7. Proceed to the spine–edge. Loop the cord. Proceed to the same station on the same side of the sheet. Go through to the bottom of the sheet.

   TIGHTENING THE SEWING: Close the sheet prior to tightening or the top thread loop will ride up the cord support. To tighten the sewing pull the thread in the direction of the foredge after looping and before forming the long stitch. Tension will be on the cord. Press down all the top thread loops at each cord.

   Do not pull hard in the direction of the sewing in forming the long stitch. Tension will be on the paper at the hole. You will rip the paper.

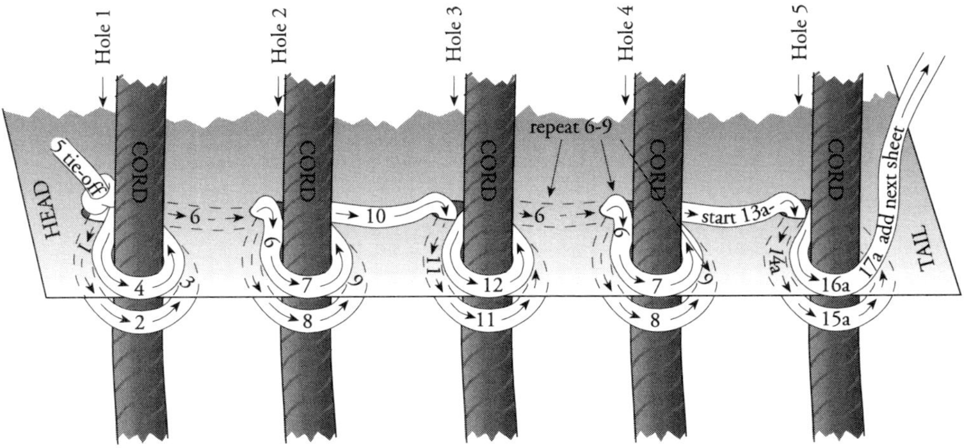

Sewing the first sheet. After sewing at the third cord, repeat steps 6–9 because you are proceeding from that station on the bottom of the sheet.

LOOPING THE CORD
FROM UNDER THE SHEET

Looping the cord is done on the same level: If you are under the sheet, exit to the spine. Go around the support and go back under the sheet. Do not climb to the top of the sheet.

LOOPING THE CORD
ON TOP OF THE SHEET

If you are on top of the sheet, go around the support and go back on the top side of the sheet to enter the station. The thread that loops the cord support will be referred to as the *thread loop.*

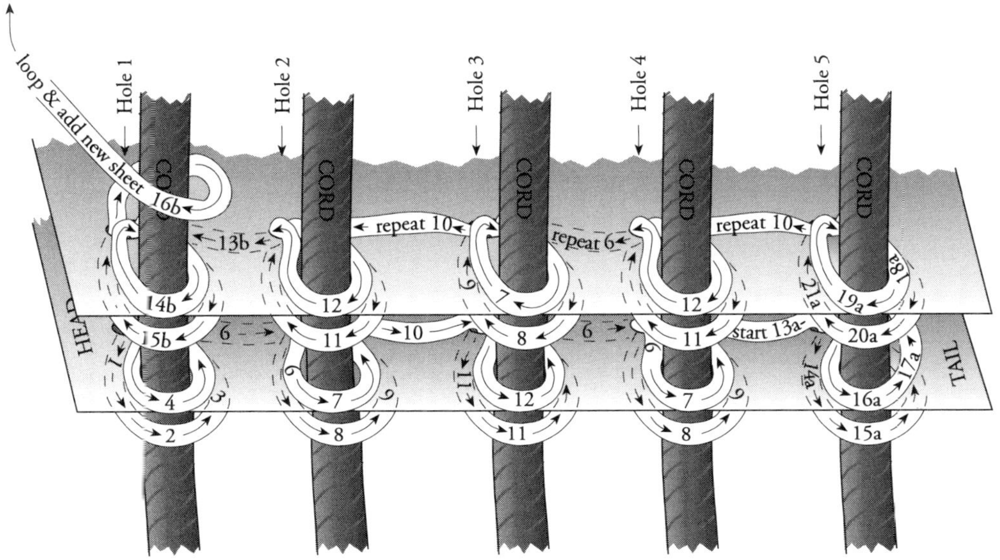

The sewing is very simple. If you are proceeding from a station with a long stitch on the bottom of the sheet, repeat Steps 6–9. If the long stitch is on top of the sheet, repeat Steps 1–12. The exceptions are sewing the stations at the head and tail.
SEWING THE END STATIONS: If the long stitch is on top, as leaving Station 4 for Station 5 on the first sheet, follow Steps 13*a*–19*a*.
If the long stitch is on bottom, as leaving Station 2 for Station 1 on the second sheet, follow Steps 13*b*–19*b*.

8. Proceed to the spine–edge. Loop the cord below the previous thread loop.
   NUMBER OF LOOPS: This makes the second thread that loops the cord at this station. For each sheet sewn, each station will have two thread loops in this description. If you were to loop the cord once or three times, the sheet would not be level, since the other stations on this sheet are looped twice.
   You could consistently loop the cord at each of the stations one time only, or three times. The former would give less swell to the spine. The latter would expand the spine permitting insertion of prints to the blank book.
9. Proceed to the same station on the same side of the sheet. Go through the station to the top.
10. Proceed on the top side of the sheet to the next hole/station. Go through the new station to the bottom of the sheet.
11. Proceed to the spine–edge. Loop the cord. Proceed to the same station. Go through to the top of the sheet.
12. Proceed to the spine–edge. Loop the cord *above* the previous thread loop. Proceed to the same station on the same side of the sheet. Go through the station to the bottom.

Sewing the Next Station on the Same Sheet

To sew at the next station when proceeding on the bottom of the sheet repeat Steps 6–9, except to sew the end station.

To sew at the next station when proceeding on the top of the sheet repeat Steps 10–12, except to sew the end station.

ON THE TOP:

Sewing the End Station and Starting the Next Sheet, Change–Over with Long Stitch on Top of the Sheet

If you complete sewing the next to last station on the sheet and the long stitch is on the *top,* follow Steps 13*a*–21*a* below. If the long stitch is on the bottom, follow Steps 13*b*–19*b* on the following page.

13*a*.Enter the end station to the underneath of the sheet.

14*a*.Proceed on the underneath side of the sheet to the spine–edge.

15*a*.Loop the end cord. Proceed under the sheet to the hole. Exit at the end station to the top.

16*a*.Loop the end cord, but *do not re–enter* this sheet.

17*a*.Set on the next sheet to be sewn. Enter the new sheet from the bottom to the top. Position the new sheet on the book block and tighten the thread. This completes second thread loop for the old sheet at this station.

18*a*.Proceed to the spine–edge on the top of the new sheet.

19*a*.Loop the end cord. This is the first thread loop on the new sheet at this station. Open the top sheet. Re–enter the new sheet from the top to underneath. Tighten the sewing.

20*a*.Loop the end cord below the previous thread loop. This is the second thread loop for the new sheet at the end station.

21*a*.Proceed under the sheet to the hole and exit to the top.

NOTE: From now on, each time the needle loops and proceeds under the sheet being sewn, be careful not to link under the long stitch on the previous sheet.

Sewing the Next Station on the Same Sheet

To sew at the next station when proceeding on the top of the sheet repeat Steps 10–12, except to sew the end station.

To sew at the next station when proceeding on the bottom of the sheet repeat Steps 6–9, except to sew the end station.

NOTE: Always pull the sewing taut with the top sheet closed, or the top looped thread will ride up on the cord support.

ON THE BOTTOM:

Sewing the End Station and Starting the Next Sheet, Change–Over with the Long Stitch on the Bottom

If you complete sewing the next to last station on the sheet and the long stitch is on the *bottom,* follow Steps 13*b*–19*b* below. If the long stitch is on the top, follow Steps 13*a*–21*a* on the facing page.

13*b*. Exit the end station to the top and close the sheet.

14*b*. Loop the cord. Proceed on the top of the sheet and enter at the end station to the bottom of this sheet.

15*b*. Open the sheet and proceed under the top sheet to the spine–edge. Loop the cord. This thread loop will be below the previous loop. Proceed on the underneath side of the sheet to the hole.

16*b*. Exit to the top of the sheet. Close the completed sheet and tighten the sewing. Loop the cord but do not re–enter the sheet.

17*b*. Set on the next sheet to be sewn. Enter the new sheet from the bottom to the top.

18*b*. Loop the cord.

19*b*. Enter new sheet from top to the bottom. You are ready to proceed to the next station with a long stitch.

Sewing the Next Station on the Same Sheet

To sew at the next station when proceeding on the bottom of the sheet repeat Steps 6–9, except to sew the end station.

To sew at the next station when proceeding on the top of the sheet repeat Steps 10–12, except to sew the end station.

Sewing the Final Station on the Last Sheet and Tying Off

To sew at the final station when proceeding on the bottom of the sheet repeat Steps 6–8.

Then proceed back to the final station on the underneath side of the sheet, but do not go through the hole. Link under the long stitch on the final sheet. Tie–off with a half hitch. See page 65.

To sew at the final station when proceeding on the top of the sheet repeat Steps 10–12. Link under the short stitch at this hole. Tie–off with a half hitch.

Adding More Thread During the Sewing

This sewing takes a lot of thread. When you are running out of thread you will want to add more with a weaver's knot. See page 61.

After you make a long stitch on the underneath side of the sheet, preferably at one of the middle stations, exit to the top. Remove the needle. Form the slip knot on the new thread and place it on the old thread close to the hole. Tighten it to become the weaver's knot. Make sure to tie right at the hole so the clipped old thread does not hang out onto the spine. Also, you do not want the knot to be part of the thread loop, showing on the spine.

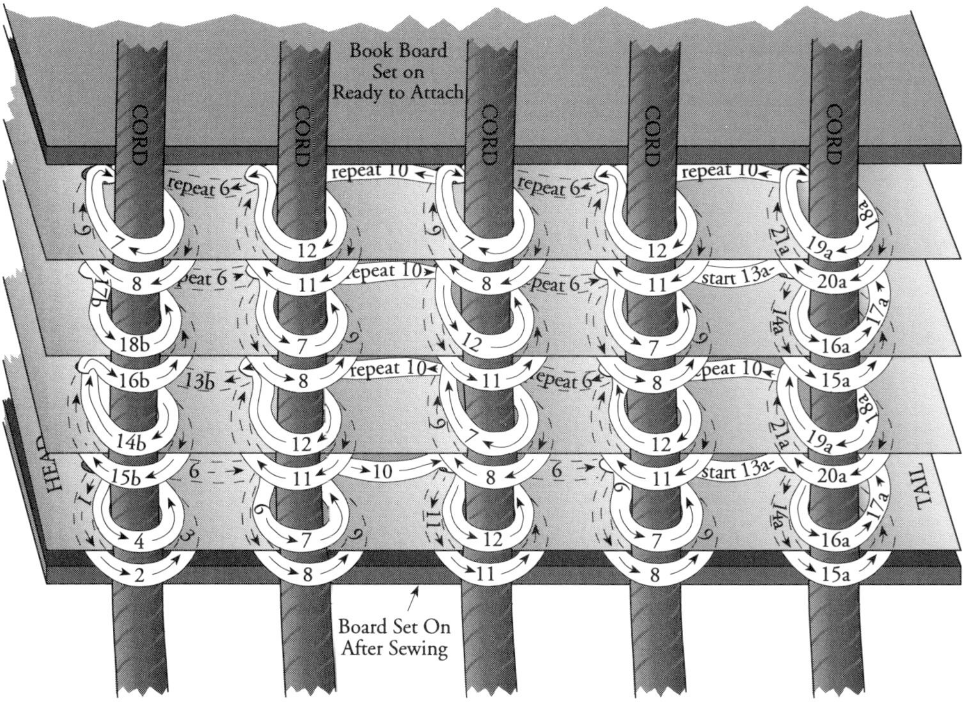

Sewing the final station on the last sheet and tying–off are described on the previous page. The sewing is completed and the boards are set on the top and bottom of the book block to be marked and pierced for attaching the supports.

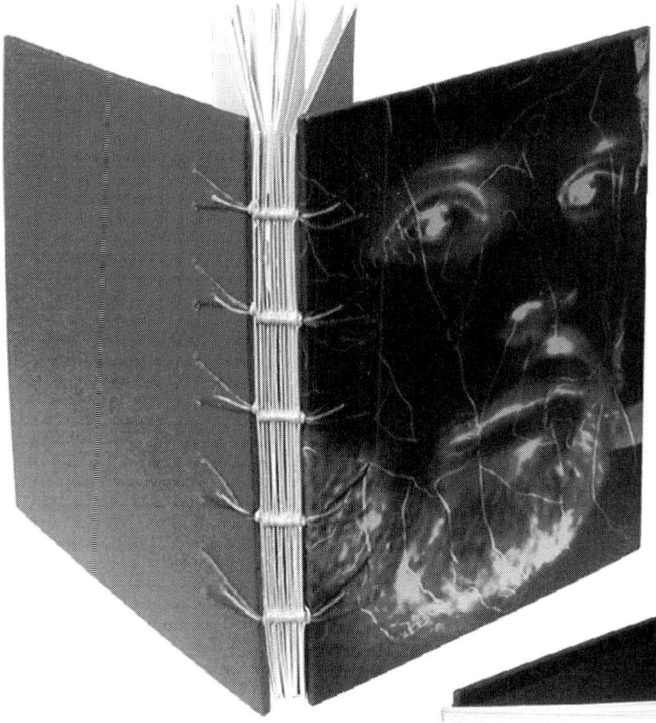

Three strands of twisted threads are the "cords". After the sewing was completed, the ends of 3–ply cords were untwisted and taken through holes in the boards individually. After tying the threads on the inside of the board, the cover was opened on a table and the knots on the inside of the boards were lightly tapped with a hammer to flatten them so the covers will close against the book block. A bone folder is safer to use than a hammer.

1–SHEET *X* SEWING RAISED CORDS

INTRODUCTION: Traditionally sections/signatures sewn on raised cords can form an *X* on the spine. Coming out of the section and dropping at a diagonal below the previously sewn section, then climbing at the reverse angle forms an *X* on the spine.

These sections are sewn raised cord in the traditional sewing called 1–Section *X*. Station1 shows the climb at the head which employs the kettle stitch, also in the illustration below.

Dropping down two sections makes a taller and rectangular *X*, referred to as the 2–Section *X* Sewing. Both are described in *Exposed Spine Sewings,* Volume III *Non–Adhesive Binding.*

This is the 2–Section *X* where the drop is down two sections to form a taller *X*.

SEWING SINGLE SHEETS WITH THE *X* SEWING

Translating the traditional 1–Section *X* pathway from sewing *sections* to sewing *sheets* on raised cords with an *X* pattern came to me without trying — it just happened. If I were to take time to think about the traditional seed pearl sewing, I expect it could be transposed to sewing single sheets, also. The seed pearl is a favorite sewing of Betsy Palmer Eldridge, and it is my very favorite raised cord sewing. At this point in time, I doubt if I add a variation of the seed pearl to this manual. It depends on how anxious I am in wanting to get this book to press.

The 1–Sheet *X* Sewing which is described on the next few pages *requires* very thick paper or better, sewing mat board as the book block. Otherwise, there will be little definition of, or height to, your *X*'s. Also, the needle goes through each hole three times. Paper would be too flimsy.

Sewing Frame

A sewing frame is not needed for this sewing, but is very helpful if you use multi–ply twisted thread as your supports. It keeps the top end of the cord from untwisting. A sewing frame is helpful when using traditional linen cord so that you do not mistakenly loop around a cord, as the ends of the cords dangle when not held in place by a sewing frame. I did not bother with a frame in sewing this prototype, but I would advise beginners to use a frame. You can build one inexpensively. *See* sewing frame, page 30.

1–Sheet *X* Sewing: This single sheet raised cord sewing climbs diagonally from one side of the sheet to the other, lapping the cord. It then re–enters the hole at the same station on the opposite side of the sheet. It repeats the diagonal climb in the opposite direction to form the other leg of the *X*.

The sewing proceeds with a long stitch in on the sheet from that hole to the next, although in the picture the thread is shown along the spine–edge prior to entering hole 1 to form the long stitch with Step 5.

Sewing Path

The two illustrations on this page show the formation of the *X* on the spine when sewing from left to right on the odd numbered sheets. For even numbered sheets, the path is a mirror image.

The illustration at the top shows how to form the *X* at the next station/cord when proceeding from the previous station with the thread on *top of the sheet.* The thread that proceeds from hole to hole will be referred to as the *long stitch.*

The illustration below is how to form the *X* at the next station when the long stitch approaches on the *bottom of the sheet.* Pattern of the long stitch will alternate top to bottom across the sheet.

NOTE: In the top illustration, the weak point appears to be where Step 2 enters the sheet and comes back toward the spine–edge as Step 3. However, pressure is not on the paper at the hole, but on the cord at the edge of the sheet.

Since in this sewing the sheet is probably 2–ply mat board, or at least very thick and stiff paper, the edge of the sheet can stand the tension of the sewing.

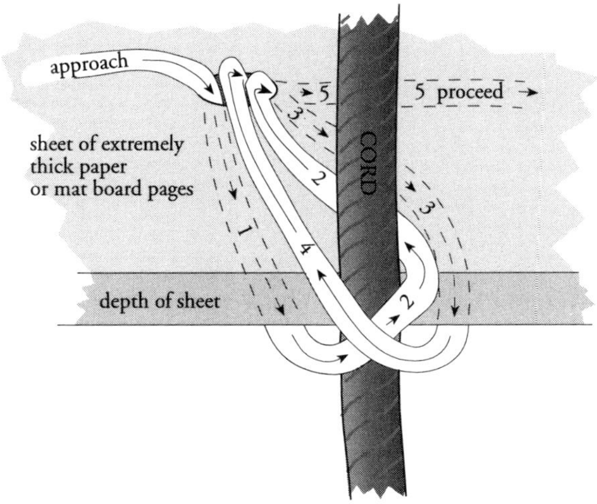

SEWING TOWARD THE TAIL: Sewing path to create the *X* on the cord when long stitch approaches on top of the sheet.

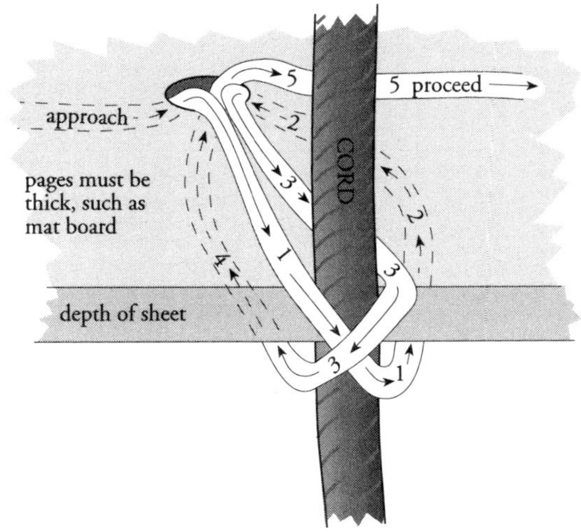

SEWING TOWARD THE TAIL: Sewing path to create the *X* on the cord when long stitch approaches on bottom of the sheet.

NOTE: Mat board or very heavy paper must be used for the book block. The needle goes through each hole three times and the pull is on the sheet. Thinner paper would not withstand the tension and would tear.

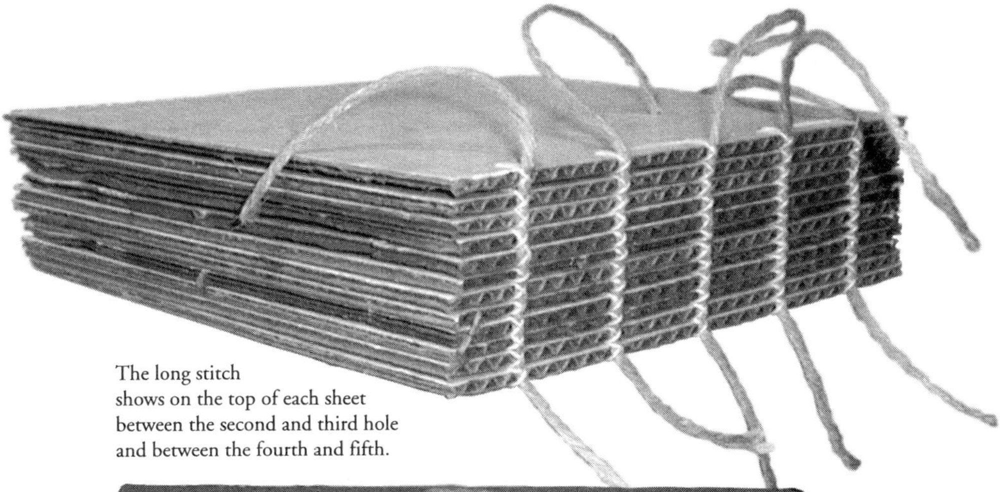

The long stitch
shows on the top of each sheet
between the second and third hole
and between the fourth and fifth.

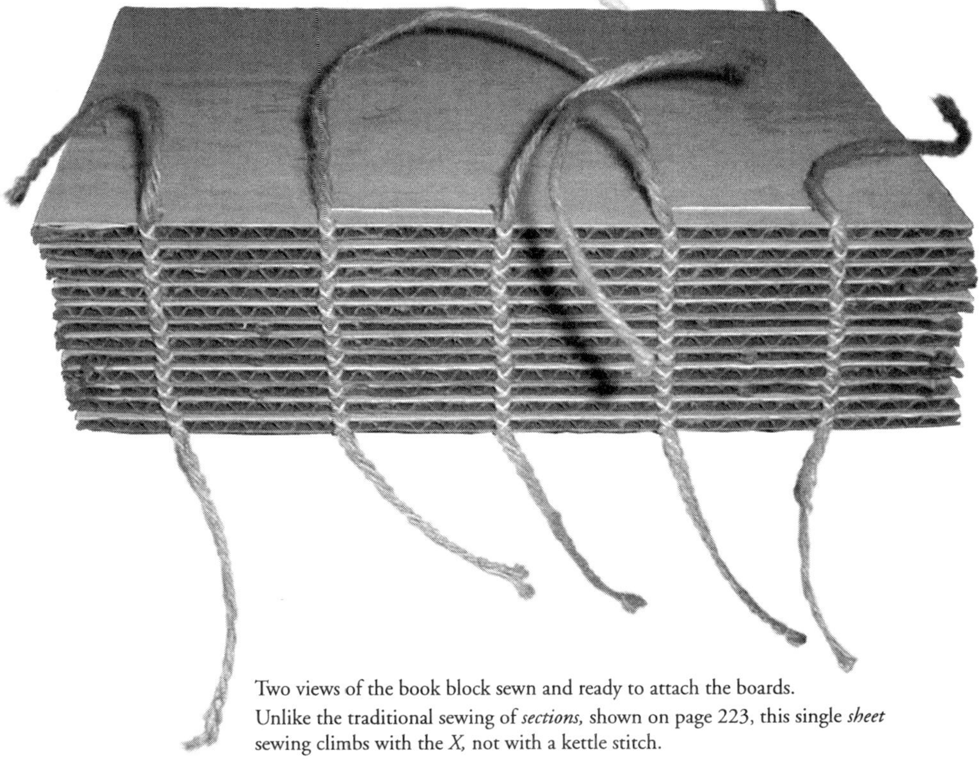

Two views of the book block sewn and ready to attach the boards.
Unlike the traditional sewing of *sections,* shown on page 223, this single *sheet* sewing climbs with the *X,* not with a kettle stitch.

STARTING THE SEWING

Sew your first attempt with five sewing stations so that the long stitch will be on the bottom as you approach the end station at the tail and on top as you approach the end station at the head. The instructions will tell you how to make the change–over to the next sheet.

Once you understand the change–over I employ, you can sew a book with an even number of stations and know how to add the next sheet by using the change–over described for the head for the tail, since you will approach the tail with the long stitch on top.

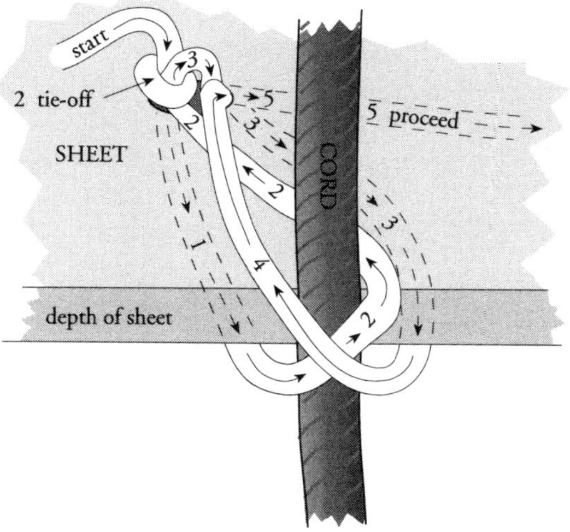

Starting the sewing forms the first *X* on the first cord and ties–off at the hole with Step 2. No sewing frame was used, but the dangling cords get in the way when forming an *X*.

1. Start with the first sheet to be sewn. Go through hole 1 from the top to the bottom. Leave a small amount of thread on top. Proceed under the sheet to the spine-edge, on either side of the first cord support.

   It does not matter which leg of the *X* is formed first. For consistency, I will always exit on the back side of the cord to form the first leg of the *X* as in Step 2.
2. *MAKING THE FIRST* X *ON THE CORD:* Lap the cord at an angle from the back of the cord to the forward side. (Since you are heading toward the tail, this is left to right.) To move diagonally is to *angle*. You will climb to the top of the sheet. Proceed to the hole on the top of the sheet. Adjust the amount of dangling thread and tie a square knot at the hole. This will be easy if the cords are strung on a sewing frame. If you are not using a frame, hold the cord and thread at the spine–edge while you determine the tension in tying the knot.
3. Enter the hole from the top to the bottom. Proceed to the spine–edge on the bottom of the sheet on the opposite side of the cord than in Step 1.
4. Angle, lapping the cord from forward to the back side of the cord, climbing to the top of the sheet. This forms the second leg of the *X* at the first station. Proceed to the hole. Enter the bottom of the sheet and adjust the tension by pulling toward the foredge.

This will place the tension against the cord, not the hole and will not rip the paper. If you have not used a frame, hold on to the cord to keep it vertical. The tightening process will show a perfectly formed *X* on the cord.

5. *MAKING THE FIRST LONG STITCH:* Proceed on the bottom of the sheet from this hole to the next. Exit the new hole to the top of the sheet.
6. Proceed on the top of the sheet to the spine–edge, on either side of this support. As before, I will take the thread to the back side of the cord to form a leg of the *X* in Step 7.
7. Angle, lapping the cord to the forward side of the cord. This time the lap drops instead of climbing. Proceed on the bottom of the sheet to the hole.
8. Exit the hole to the top. Proceed to the spine–edge on the top of the sheet with the thread on the opposite side of the cord (forward) than in Step 6.
9. Angle, lapping to the back side of the cord, dropping to the bottom of the sheet. This forms the second leg of the *X* at this station. Proceed under the sheet to the same hole. Exit to the top of the sheet. Adjust the tension by pulling toward the foredge.
10. Proceed on the top of the sheet from this hole to the next. Enter the new hole to the bottom of the sheet.
11. Proceed under the sheet past the back side of the cord support. Make sure you do not pierce the cord.
12. Angle, lapping the cord to the forward side, climbing to the top of the sheet. Proceed to the hole.
13. Enter the hole from the top to the bottom. Proceed to the spine–edge on the bottom of the sheet on the opposite (forward) side of the cord than in Step 11.
14. Angle, lapping the cord from the forward side to back of the cord, climbing to the top of the sheet. Proceed to the hole. Enter to the bottom of the sheet. Adjust the tension.

Sewing the Next Station on this Sheet

Repeat Steps 5–9 when the long stitch approaches on the bottom of the sheet, except for the end station.

Repeat Steps 10–14 when the long stitch approaches on the top of the sheet, except for the end station.

Sewing the Station at the Tail

With an odd number of stations you will approach the end station at the tail with the long stitch on the bottom of the sheet.

NOTE: On the first sheet, Station 4 ends the formation of the *X* with Step r9 (The letter *r* stands for *repeat).* Steps for sewing the end cord at the tail will start with the number 1, preceded by the letter *t* for *tail.*

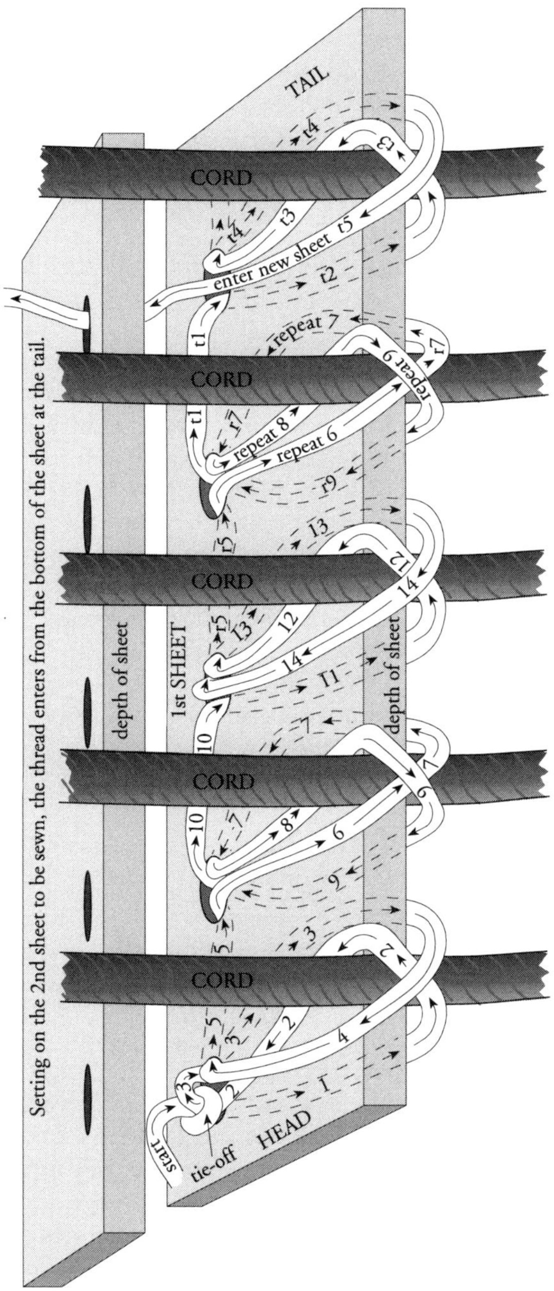

1–SHEET *X* SEWING Raised Cords: Sewing the first sheet and setting on the second.
The long stitch shows on the top of each sheet between the second and third hole and between the fourth and fifth.

These steps can only be used in sewing the stations at the tail when there are an odd number of cords.

t1. Proceed with the long stitch on top of the sheet. Enter the end hole.

t2. Proceed under the sheet to the spine–edge on the back side of the cord.

t3. Angle forward, lapping the cord. Proceed to the hole on top of the sheet to the spine–edge on the forward side of the cord.

t4. Enter to the bottom of the sheet. Proceed under the sheet to the spine–edge on the forward side of the cord. (Since you are heading toward the tail, the *forward* side is on the right.)

t5. Angle backward, lapping the cord. This completes the *X* on the end cord at the tail for this sheet. Do not re–enter this sheet.

SEWING THE SECOND SHEET

t6. Set on the new sheet. Enter the new sheet from the *bottom* to the top. Align the new sheet on the book block. Tighten tension by pulling toward the foredge. Double check to see the *X* was formed on the previous sheet and is centered on the cord.
CHANGE–OVER: Proceed to the spine–edge on the back side of the cord. (Since you are *now* heading toward the head, the *back side* side is on the right. This is why it is called the *change–over.*

t7. Angle *forward* (to the left) lapping the cord and dropping. This forms the first leg of the *X* on the new sheet. Proceed under the new sheet to the hole. Exit to the top.

t8. Proceed to the spine–edge on the forward side of the cord.

t9. Angle backward (dropping to the right.) This completes the *X* on the end cord at the tail for the new sheet. Proceed under the new sheet to the end hole. Exit the hole to the top.

NOTE: This binding cannot be sewn hand held. It is sewn *on the bench.* See page 67. The book block rests on the table with the spine–edge at the edge of the table facing you. The top sheet, only, is opened and closed to facilitate the sewing.

Sewing the Next Station on this Sheet

Repeat Steps 10–14 when the long stitch approaches on the top of the sheet, except for the end station.

Repeat Steps 5–9 when the long stitch approaches on the bottom of the sheet, except for the end station.

NOTE: In sewing the second sheet, after you lap the cord and go under the sheet to the hole, make sure you do not link under the long stitch on the first sheet. From now on you will have to be careful not to link under the long stitch on the previous sheet when you proceed in on the sheet.

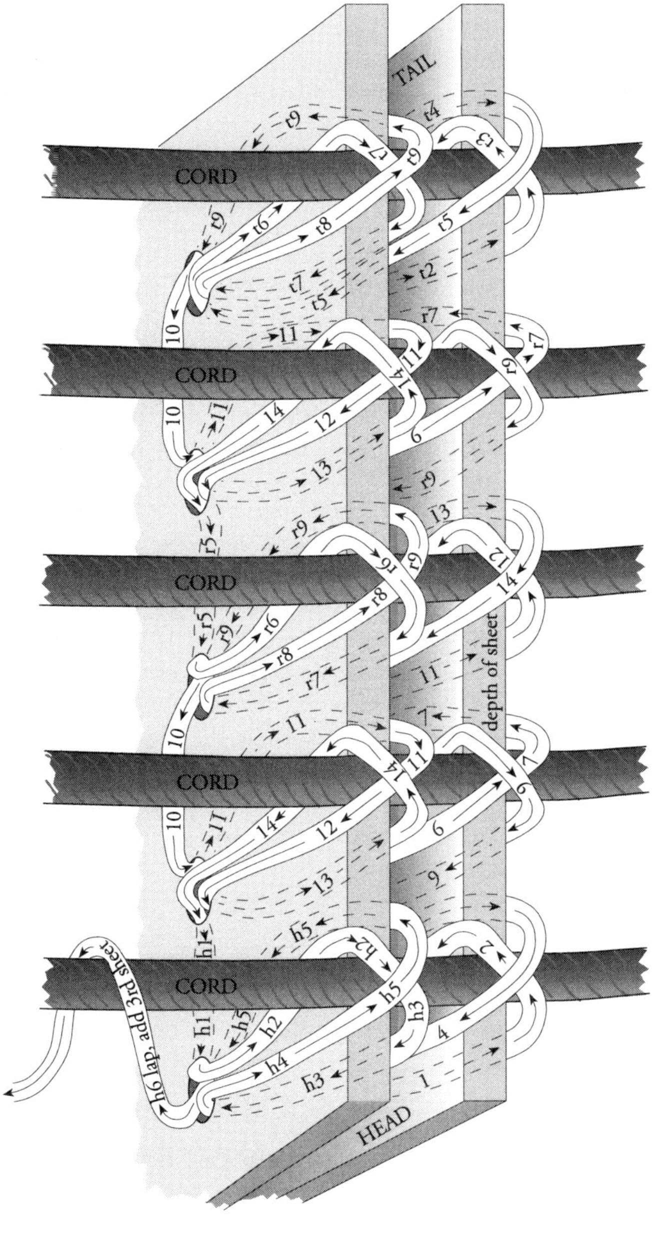

1–SHEET *X* SEWING Raised Cords: Sewing the second sheet, lapping the cord, ready to attach the third sheet. The third sheet is attached from the top to the bottom. After you add the second and third sheets, the remainder of the sewing is the same: at the tail, enter the new sheet from the bottom then lap the cord. At the head, lap, then add the new sheet entering from the top.

Sewing the Station at the Head

With an odd number of stations you will approach the end station at the head with the long stitch on the bottom of the sheet. On the second sheet, Station 2 ends the formation of the *X* with Step 14. The needle then enters the hole to form the long stitch to the hole at the head.

Steps for sewing the end cord at the head will be numbered beginning with Step h1. The *h* denotes these are the steps for sewing Station 1 on all the remaining sheets.

h1. Proceed with the long stitch on bottom of the sheet.

h2. Exit the end hole to the top of the sheet. Proceed to the spine–edge on the back side (right) of the cord.

h3. Angle forward, lapping the cord, dropping. This forms the first leg of the *X* on the old sheet. Proceed under the sheet to the end hole. Exit to the top of the sheet.

h4. Proceed to the spine–edge on the forward side of the cord.

h5. Angle backward, lapping the cord. This completes the *X* on the end cord at the head for this sheet. (Since you are heading toward the head, the *back* side is on the right.) Proceed under the sheet to the end hole .Exit to the top of the sheet.

h6. *CHANGE–OVER:* Proceed to the spine–edge on the back side of the cord. (Since you are now heading toward the tail, the *back* side is on the left. This is why it is called the *change–over.*) Steps h1–h6 are diagrammed on the previous page.

h7. Angle, lapping the cord, climbing, but do not re–enter the old sheet.

h8. Set on the new sheet and enter from the *top* to the bottom. Align the new sheet on the book block. Tighten tension by pulling toward the foredge. The first leg of the *X* has already been formed on the new sheet by Step h7. Proceed under the new sheet on the forward (right) side to the spine–edge.

h9. Angle, lapping the cord, climbing. Proceed on top of the new sheet to the hole. Enter to the bottom of the sheet.

Sewing the Next Station on this Sheet

Repeat Steps 5–9 when the long stitch approaches on the bottom of the sheet, except for the end station.

Repeat Steps 10–14 when the long stitch approaches on the top of the sheet, except for the end station.

Sewing the Station at the Tail

With an odd number of stations you will approach the end station at the tail with the long stitch on the bottom of the sheet. Sew the station at the tail the same for each sheet. Follow Steps t1–t9.

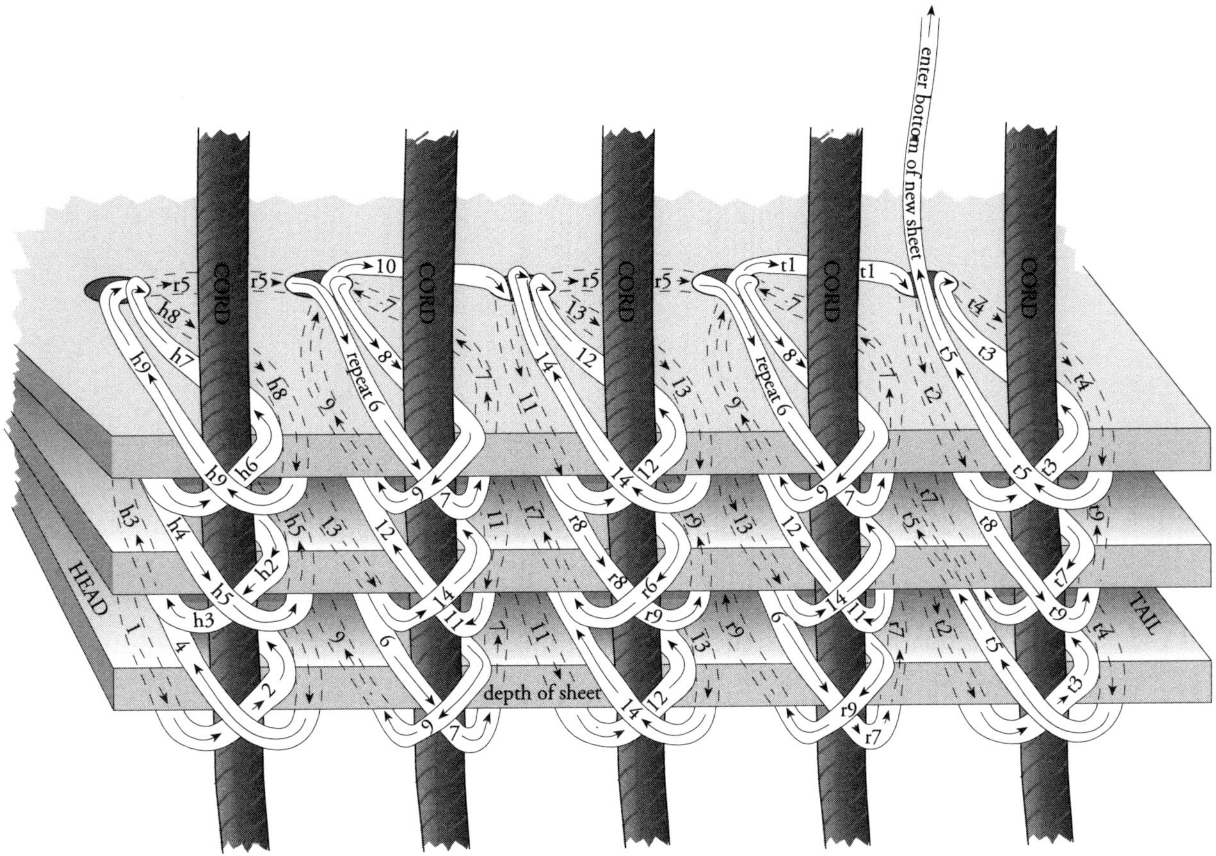

1–SHEET *X* SEWING Raised Cords: Sewing the third sheet, ready to attach the fourth in the same manner as attaching the second sheet. At the head, Step h5 is the last step on the even numbered sheet. It exits the old sheet. Step h6 laps the cord and enters the new sheet from the top. Step h6 forms the first leg of the X on the new sheet.

SEWING THE REMAINING SHEETS

Since you have an odd number of cords, each additional sheet will be sewn the same. The change–over at the tail will be same procedure as before, entering the new sheet from the bottom. The change–over at the head is the same, entering the new sheet from the top.

Sewing the Final Station on the Last Sheet

IF THE SEWING ENDS AT THE HEAD: Step h9 enters hole 1 to the underneath side of the final sheet. Link under the thread which is Step h8. Tie–off with a half hitch. *See* half hitch, page 65.

IF THE SEWING ENDS AT THE TAIL: Step t5 forms the last leg of the *X.* proceed on top of sheet to the final hole. Enter. Link under the thread which is Step t4. Tie off with a half hitch.

Adding thread with a Weaver's Knot

New thread is added any time you exit to the top of the sheet and is tied at the hole. Position the slip knot precisely at the hole so that in tightening, the weaver's knot forms at the hole. Clip the old thread short enough so that it does not hang out the spine–edge, but not so short it endangers the knot.

Add new thread at any station except at the head or the tail to insure the clipped thread does not show at the head or the tail when the book is closed.

SEWING A BOOK WITH AN EVEN NUMBER OF CORDS: After you sew the book with an odd number of cords, you will know how to sew another book with an even number. The only difference is the change–over at the head or the tail may need to enter the new sheet at the bottom, or on the top of the sheet.

MARKING THE BOARDS:
The book started on page 224 and shown on page 226 will have quarter kangaroo leather on the boards.
The cover is set in place and the cords are traced onto a paper stencil. The stencil is ruled off and used to pierce the holes into the side–covers. Pierce each board separately.

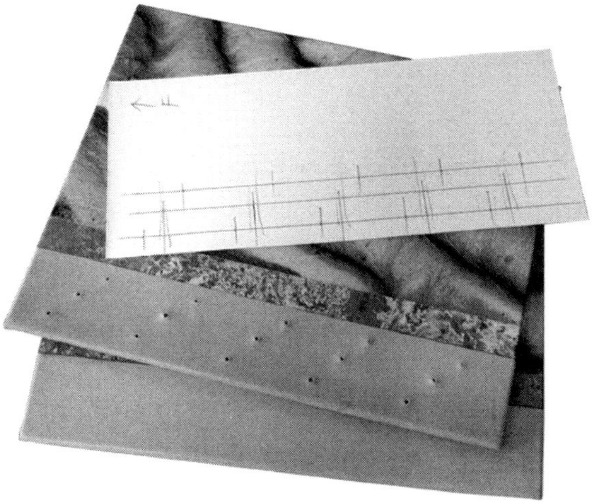

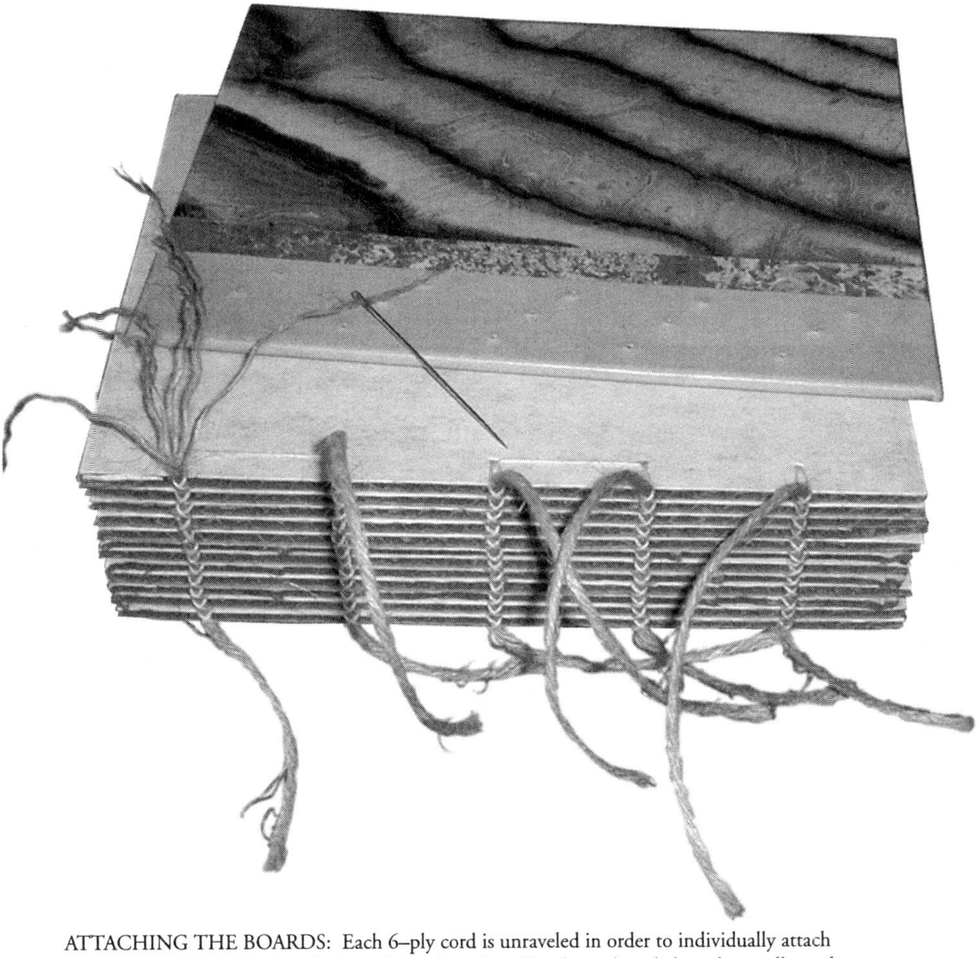

ATTACHING THE BOARDS: Each 6–ply cord is unraveled in order to individually attach each of the 6 plies to the board. One of the plies of cord has been threaded on the needle ready to attach the top side–cover. The finished book is on the following page.

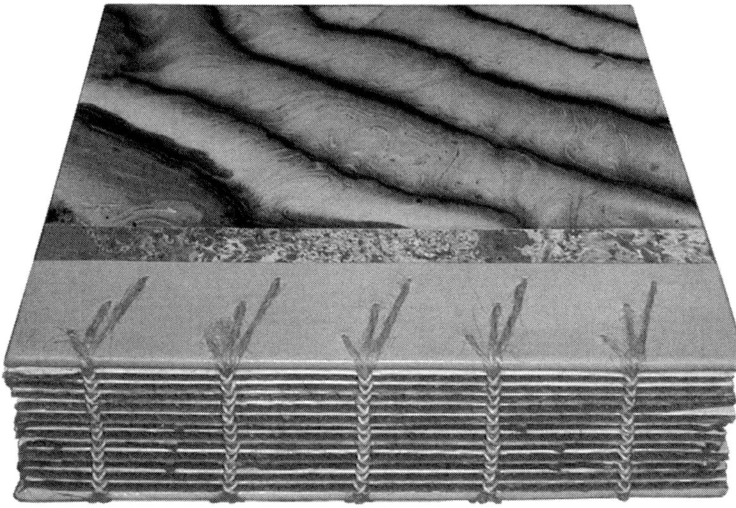

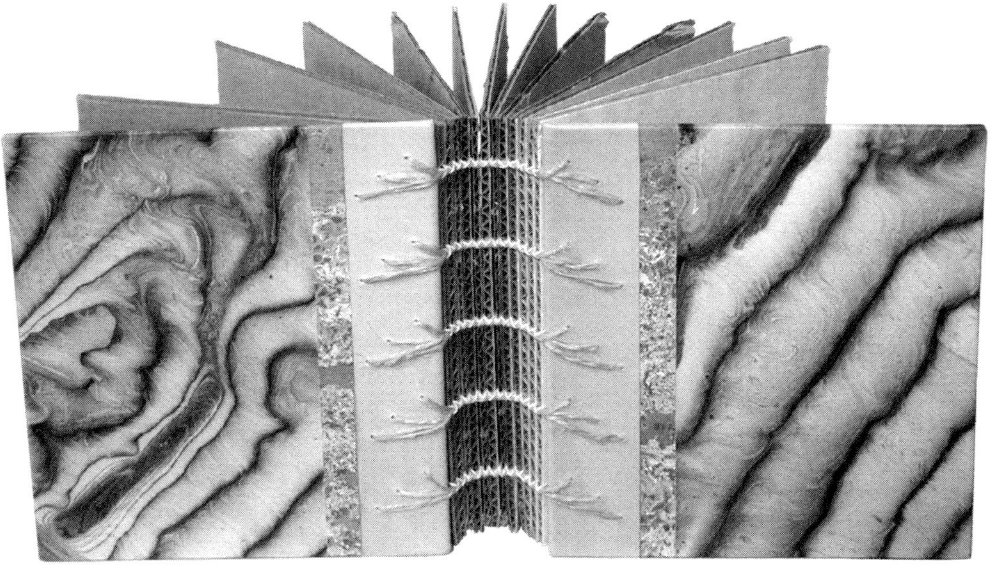

Prototype, 1–Sheet *X* Sewing Raised Cords, March 2001. A kangaroo hide was used for the quarter leather side–covers. The book block is sheets of cardboard. The book opens beautifully. Such a binding could be used on a book block of sections with only one or two or a few boards as pages. The book would open flat to any page. Illustrations of this book in–progress are on pages 224, 226, 234 and 235.

CONCLUSION

This book was a joy to write and went by rather quickly, as books go. For several years I have wanted to write a book to offer possibilities of binding unfolded sheets of paper, board, metal and/or glass in which the resulting object would open freely with the pages flat on the table. Over–sewing is a poor substitute.

Again I am writing a book where there are few existing bindings of what I am describing. In this instance, there is one major exception — the work of Adéle Outteridge.

Usually when I devise sewings, the only examples I can show are my own prototypes. Any illustrations by other book artists and binders are nice to see, but irrelevant to what I am describing. It is a pleasure, then, to show several of Adéle's pieces. Since I am doing that, I thought why not have a chapter on some favorite books and bindings I have seen recently? The following chapter, *Gallery,* features five book artists with several views of a particular book, or different pieces by the same artist.

It is a fine way to finish Volume IV of *Non–Adhesive Binding.*

PART IV

GALLERY

page

INTRODUCTION TO THE ILLUSTRATIONS

This chapter contains some books and bindings by other people. None of these are single sheet bindings, except for some of the pieces from Brisbane. Perhaps when this book goes into the Second Edition, several people will have sent slides of their sewing single sheets and I can augment theat edition of Volume IV with their examples, as well.

As the final chapter of Volume IV *Non–Adhesive Binding,* I would like to feature current work by the following people:

DENNIS Y. ICHIYAMA: The Piano Hinge Binding devised by Hedi Kyle. Dennis Y. Ichiyama has explored this structure quite extensively. Ideally I would show the bindings Dennis did in Volume I, but that book was recently revised and will not have major revisions for a few years. The Piano Hinge Variations begin on page 247.

DEBRA WEIER: Last autumn Debra Weier sent slides of a pop–up book. Page to page variations fascinate me so I wanted to show that. When I first started writing books I would show only one photo illustration of each book. Books cannot be described with a single picture. I would later show a couple pictures of a book, but tell myself I must show more. It would be grand to reproduce every page of each book, rather than a single or a couple reproductions. I am not there yet, but with Volume IV I have started showing several views of a bookwork. It is not extravagant, but reinforces that a book is not a print and requires more than one illustration to describe it. See page 259.

ADÉLE OUTTERIDGE & WIM DE VOS: Some of the most exciting binding I have seen lately was in Brisbane. Adéle and Wim share a studio. Each does fine work separately, and at times they collaborate. It is a pleasure to present some of their pieces in this book. Of course, I wanted to feature the single sheet bindings that Adéle has done. This starts on page 265.

DANIEL ESSIG: I have seen the interest in binding by Dan from almost day one. I have watched his work bud and flower. Over the years I have seen refinement in his execution and broadening of his ideas. In 1999 at Penland, Dan's books were on display. They were breathtaking. What a leap forward. He has become a binder's binder. In the past I have limited use of that term to a handful of people. One, of course, is Gary Frost. Now, in my mind, so is Daniel Essig. See page 277.

INTRODUCTION TO THE PIANO HINGE VARIATIONS

Although the *Piano Hinge Binding* is not a single sheet binding, I am going to discuss variations on this structure in this book. This chapter actually belongs in *Books without Paste or Glue,* Volume I, *Non–Adhesive Binding.* Since I recently updated and expanded that book, it will be some time before I get back to revising it. In the meantime, I would like my readers to see these variations of that elegant structure.

The *Piano Hinge Binding* was devised by Hedi Kyle. She generously gave me permission to describe it in *Books without Paste or Glue,* Volume I, *Non-Adhesive Binding.* Since then, students in my workshops have enjoyed making this non–adhesive structure. Two people even improvised on the binding. In the Revised & Expanded Edition of *Books without Paste or Glue,* I show a fine cover created by Kitty Spangler. By making the slits half the width, the rods are not exposed on the covers.

Kitty Spangler, Piano Hinge Binding with the cover she devised for this structure. The Piano Hinge Binding was devised by Hedi Kyle.

PIANO HINGE VARIATIONS

While I was teaching at Penland School in the summer of 1999, Dennis Y. Ichiyama became fascinated by Hedi's binding and spent the entire two weeks working out ideas. Ironically, he had just come from a workshop with Hedi at Haystack, in Deer Isle, Maine. Also taking Hedi's workshop was our mutual friend, Elizabeth Steiner of Auckland, so we had several conversations about the other workshop.

There are certain things one thinks of doing with this structure. In workshops I always show alternating the color of the folios to create a checkerboard effect on the spine, as in this very thick book.

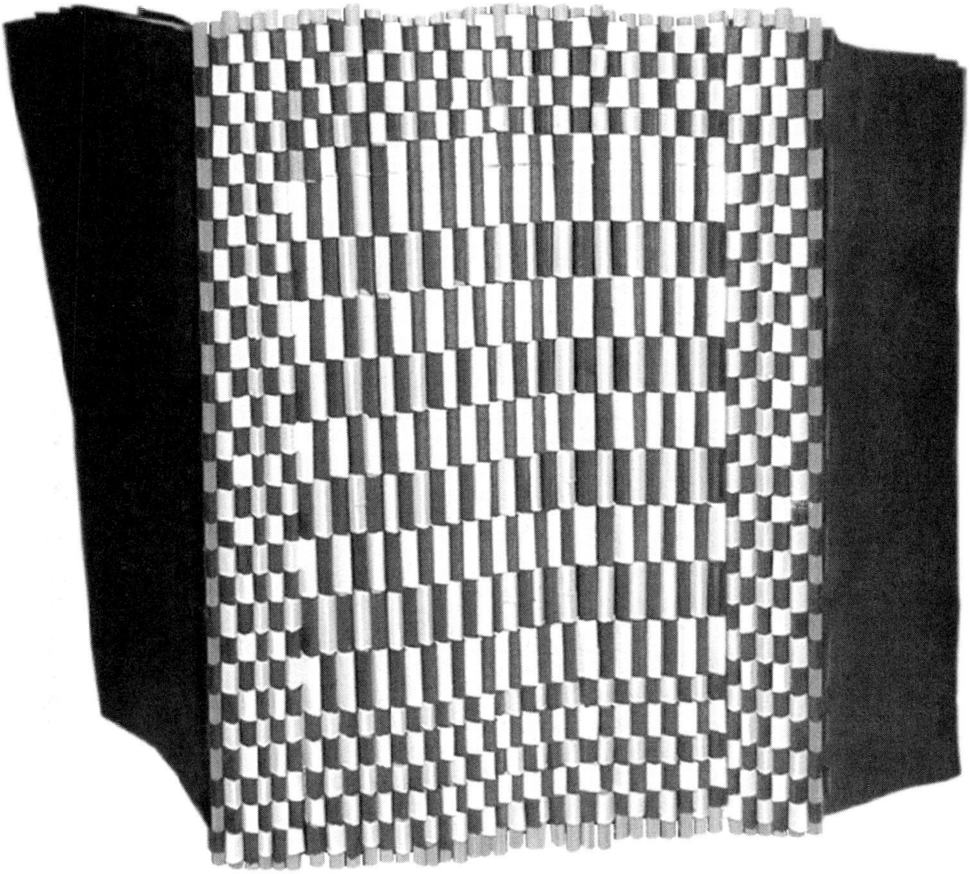

Keith Smith, sample of the Piano Hinge Binding, 1994. Alternating black and white sections creates a checkerboard on the spine. Varying the size of the slits gives a border of smaller checkerboards around the spine. The Piano Hinge Binding was devised by Hedi Kyle.

While the other students wanted to see new bindings every day, Dennis stuck with his interest in this one structure. he told the class he was "Dennis Rod Man". His concentration and explorations paid off with quite wonderful results.

Dennis wanted a one–piece cover that would attach to the first and last rod of the book shown below.

Dennis Y. Ichiyama, Piano Hinge Binding, one–of–a–kind, May 1999. Rather than alternating colors of section, a variety of colors were used.

He cut an circular opening on the spine of his white cover to allow some of the pattern there to be visible. The cover for that same book is shown below. With slits in the one piece cover, the rods on each end of the spine attach the cover to the book block. Dennis is excellent with design, but then that should be of no surprise. He teaches in the Visual Communications Design program of Purdue University.

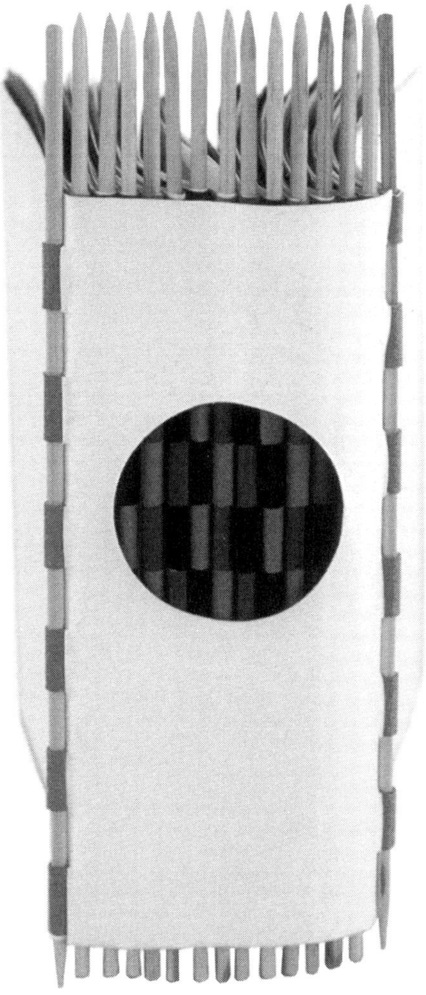

Dennis Y. Ichiyama, Piano Hinge Binding, May 1999. This is the same binding as on the previous page. Dennis designed a one piece paper cover with foredge turn–ins. The hinge–folds were slit so the rods could connect the cover to the book block. The rods on each end can be pulled out and the cover removed. The rods would be reinserted.

Recently Scott and I saw a calligraphy exhibit at the library of Rochester Institute of Technology. The pieces by Dennis were exciting and his use of color and pattern was choice. That skill is evident in the spine below.

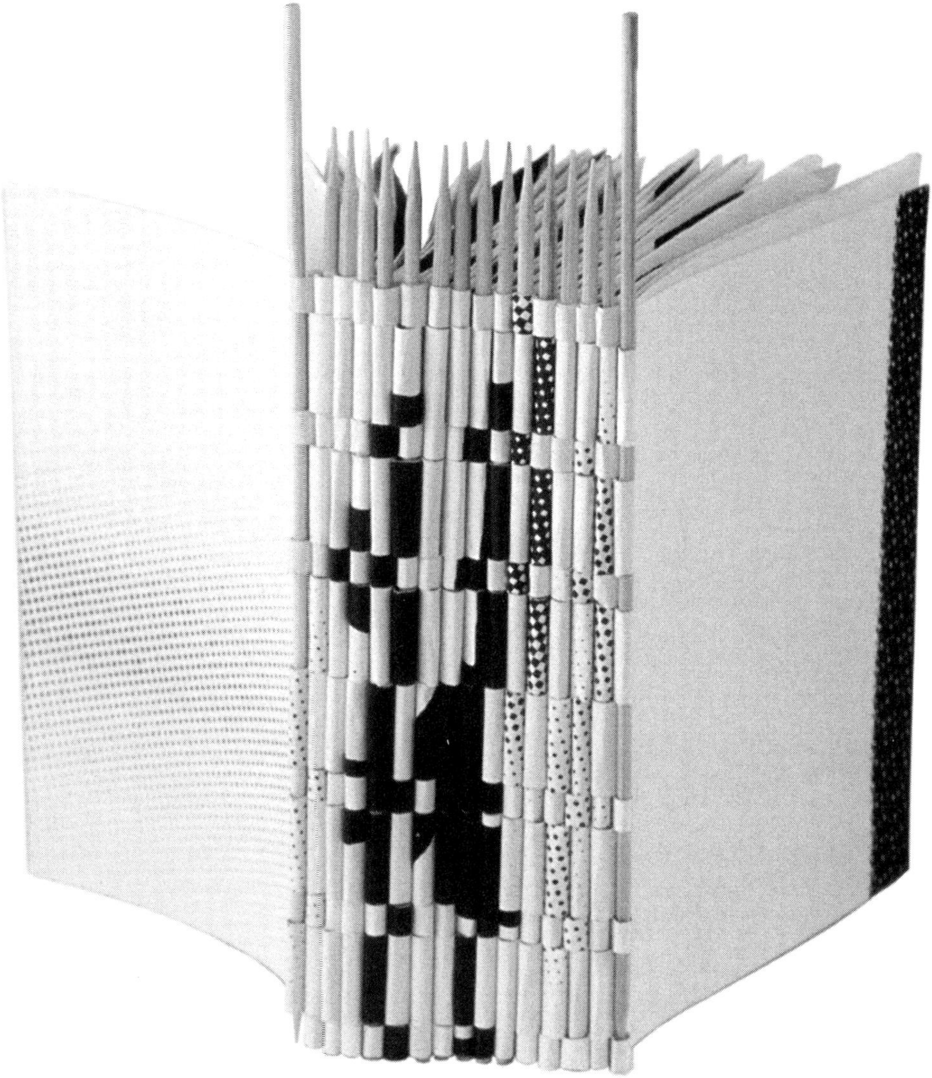

Dennis Y. Ichiyama, Piano Hinge Binding, one–of–a–kind, May 1999. Sheets in this binding are from sheets of a billboard with large color halftone dots which create texture and pattern. The rods in this book, as well on the previous page are wooden barbecue skewers. The rods on each end were probably reinserted upside down by the photographer. The points should be up.

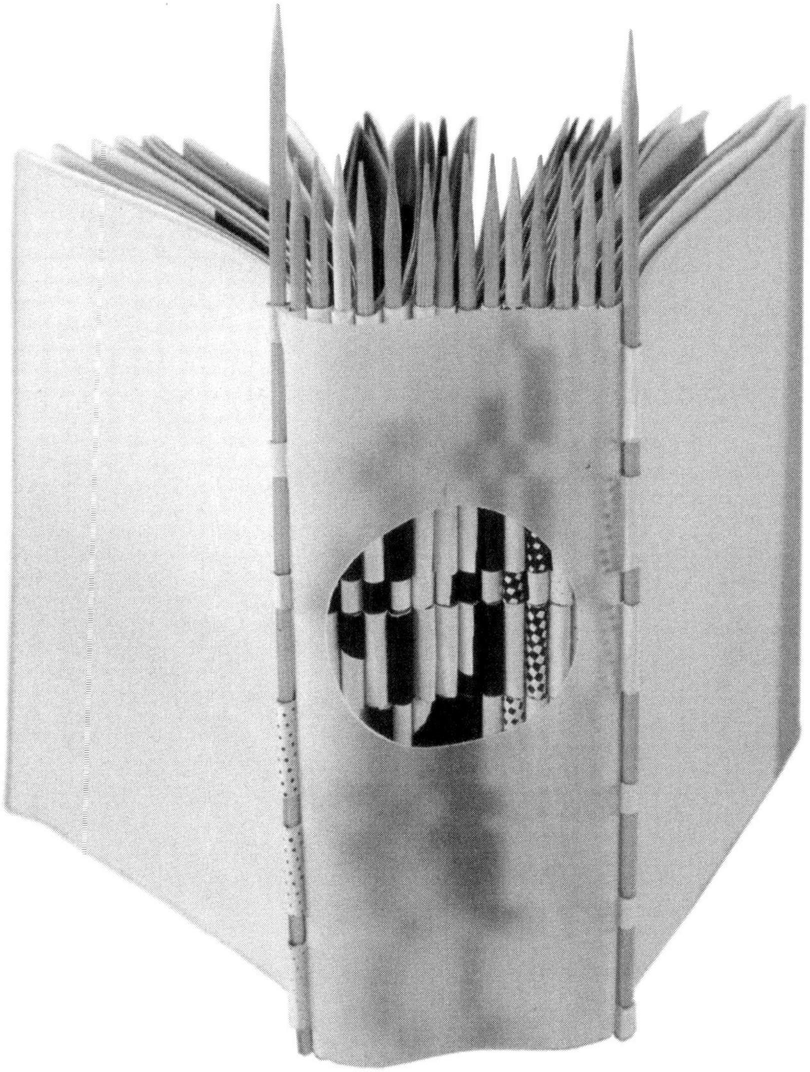

Dennis Y. Ichiyama, Piano Hinge Binding, May 1999. This is the same binding as on the previous page. A one piece paper translucent cover mutes the colors of the book within. The clean lines of paper and wood remind me of a Japanese lantern, or maybe the simple lines of blonde Scandinavian furniture. This piece has more individual flair than the previous, which is more conventional.

At Penland, Dennis asked how to alternate the diameter of the rods. I made a crude pattern and he worked out the details, resolving any problems along the way.

Dennis Y. Ichiyama, Piano Hinge Binding, one–of–a–kind, May 1999. This binding uses color glass rods. Penland Supply Store sells arm–length, various diameter glass rods used for glass blowing. Dennis scored them with a blade, then snapped them. He took them to the glass area to grind and polish the ends. This binding uses rods of two thicknesses.
The outside sheet of the sections is translucent with holes punched to allow the full saturation of the color folio beneath to be in view. This is another time when, as a publisher, I wish I could afford to reproduce books in color. The spine is reminiscent of weaving.

This binding, shown below and on the facing page has thick glass rods with thinner glass rods at the hinge–folds. The rods are hidden, except those seen intermittently on the edge of the spine.

Dennis Y. Ichiyama, Piano Hinge Binding, May 1999. This is the same binding as on the previous page with a one piece opaque black Canson paper cover.
These bindings are museum quality. They inspire me.

For one binding to use two different diameter rods requires that all sections have loops which accept both diameter rods. Half the loops are not used. On the facing page you can see the extra loops dotting the spine.

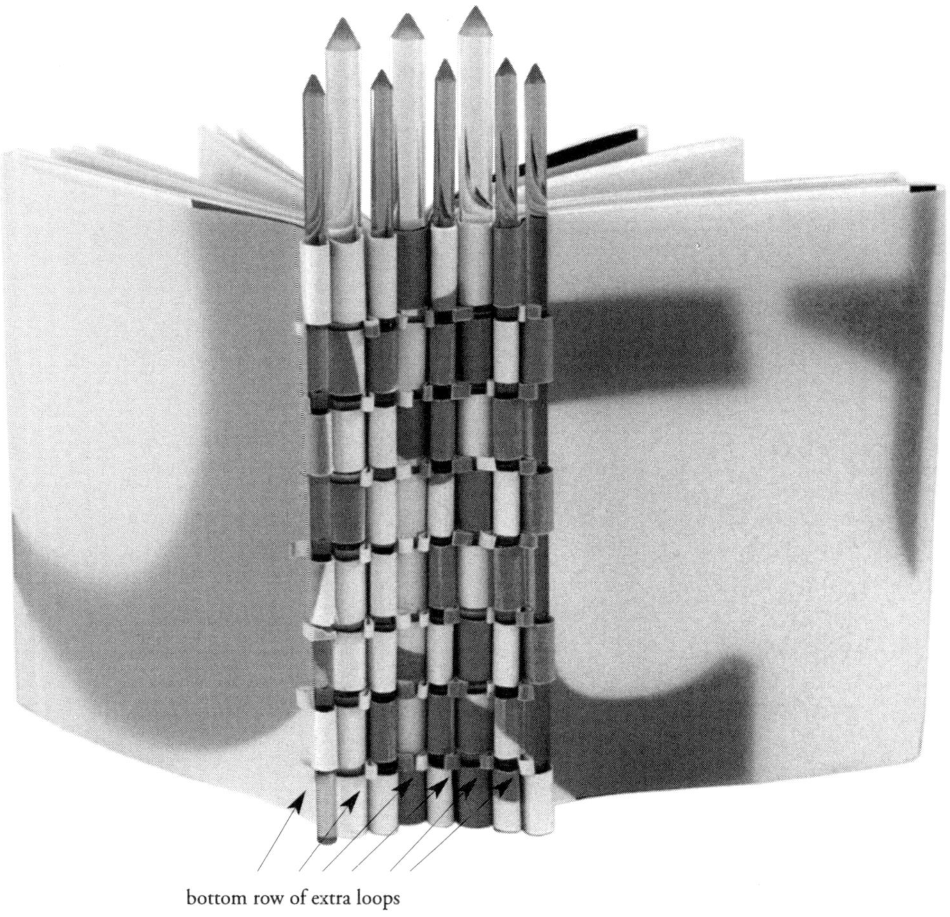

Dennis Y. Ichiyama, Piano Hinge Binding, one–of–a–kind, May 1999. Two different diameter glass rods are used. The translucent paper cover allows the large letter forms of the billboard paper pages to show through.

Note the rows of extra loops on the spine which do not have a rod through them. Areas of all the color glass rods show on the spine since the unused loops are bent to the side.

Dennis Y. Ichiyama, Piano Hinge Binding, May 1999. Detail of the binding on the facing page. To use two different diameter rods, all sections must have loops of both diameters. Only half the loops are utilized.

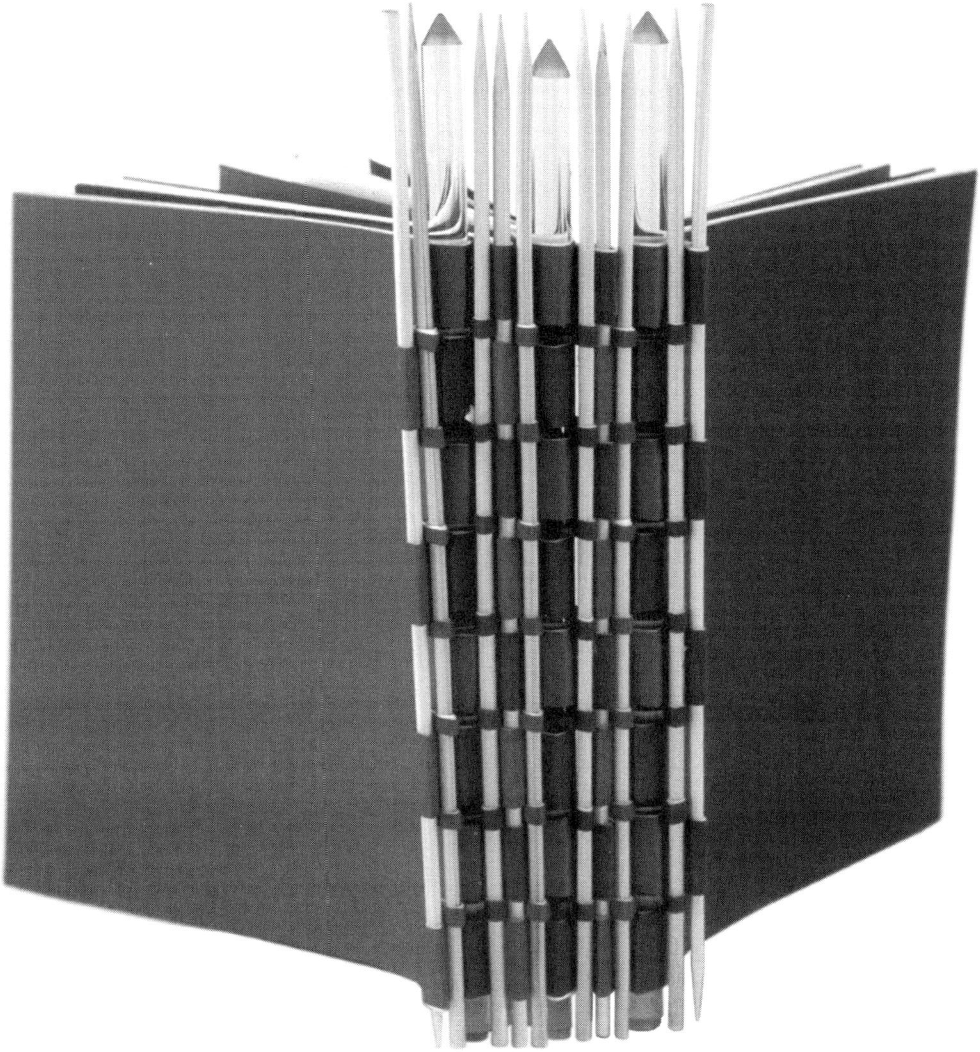

Dennis Y. Ichiyama, Piano Hinge Binding, one–of–a–kind, May 1999. Canson paper is used for the book block. The rods are wood and glass of different diameters.

Dennis Y. Ichiyama, Piano Hinge Binding, May 1999. This cover attachment is reminiscent of leather piping on the cream heated leather seats of an Aston Martin. Dream on...

A POP–UP BOOK

Debra Weier's book is a logical progression on a theme. Yet, turning the page brings surprises. The linear, rational, almost arithmetic pop–ups can become flowing, almost erratic. It is this play of opposites that intrigue me.

The linear pop–up areas become so wide at times that they are planar. There is an interesting variation on each page so the book does not become boring.

The book is in bright colors which catch the eye, but the monochromatic cast shadows dance as the page is turned in an attempt to upstage the colors. The rising objects which pop–up, however, are the main attraction.

Debra Weier, "+", one–of–kind, 1998. 49.5 x 30 cm. with varying depth of the pop–ups.

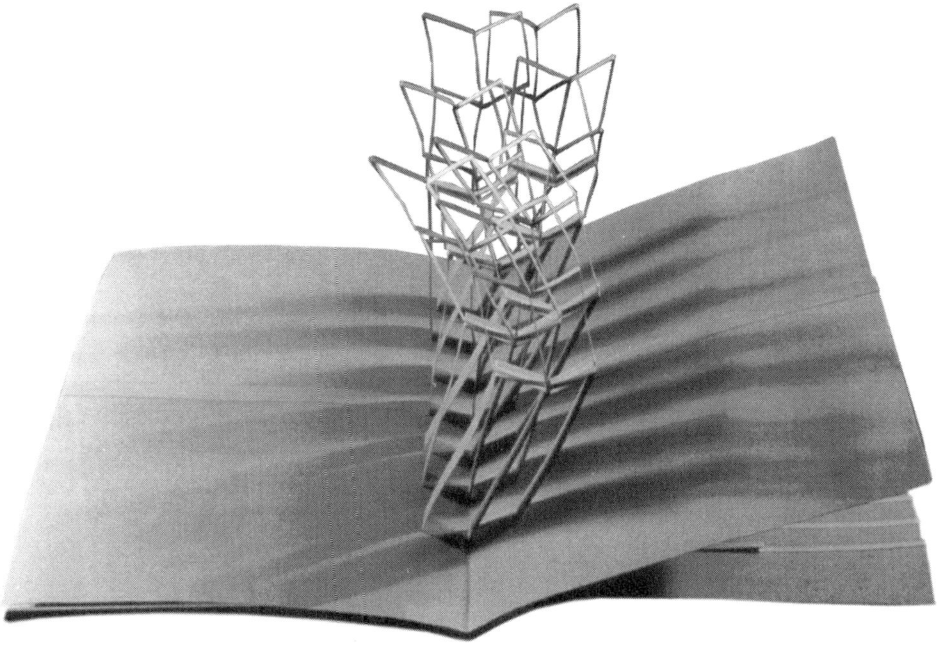

Debra Weier, "+", Various page spreads.

Debra Weier, "+", Various page spreads.

Debra Weier, "+", Various page spreads.

Debra Weier, "+", Various page spreads.

WORK FROM BRISBANE

Adéle Outteridge and Wim de Vos make their own work, as well as collaborations, in an ideal place called *The Studio, West End* on Mollison Street, West End, Brisbane. That is where they teach classes when they are not giving workshops in the Outback.

Adéle is from Australia, and was formerly a research scientist. Wim is from Holland. As a young man in Brisbane he played in support bands for Roy Orbison, the Hollies and the Beach Boys. They both make fine pieces and I wanted to show some of their work, as it is appropriate to the sewings described in this book.

The Tropic of Capricorn, latitude 23° south, runs through Queensland. Scott McCarney and I taught workshops there in May (autumn) 2000. It was hotter than a Rochester summer's day. I can't imagine what their summer's heat would be. Our previous trip to Queensland was in May, as well, further north to Townsville. Perhaps our next trip there we will try spring, but never their summertime.

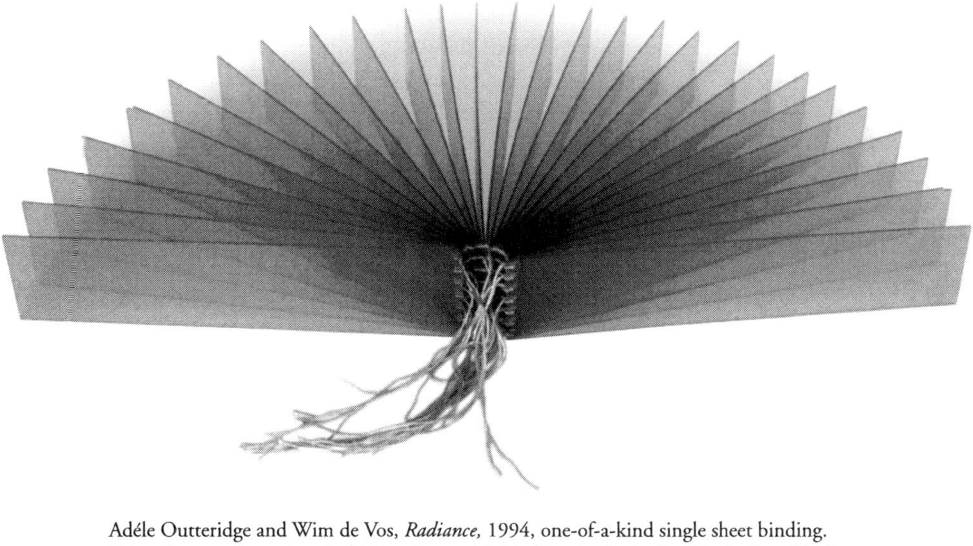

Adéle Outteridge and Wim de Vos, *Radiance,* 1994, one-of-a-kind single sheet binding. Polycarbonate, linen thread. Adéle refers to this binding she devised as *Single Sheet Binding.* By the date, you see she came up with the idea two years before I did. I don't know her sewing path, but it looks similar to a Coptic sewing. 6 x 27 x 4 cm.

Adéle Outteridge,
Awakening, 1999,
one–of–a–kind.
Perspex, thread.
Single sheet binding.
35.5 x 12 x 10 cm.
Facing page:
Detail of *Awakening.*

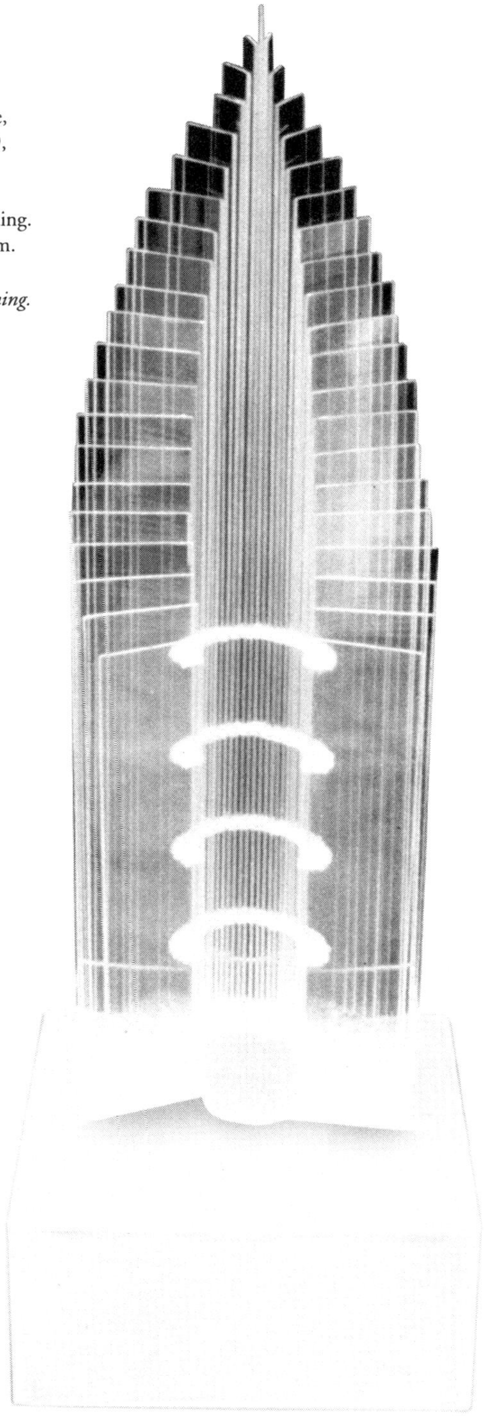

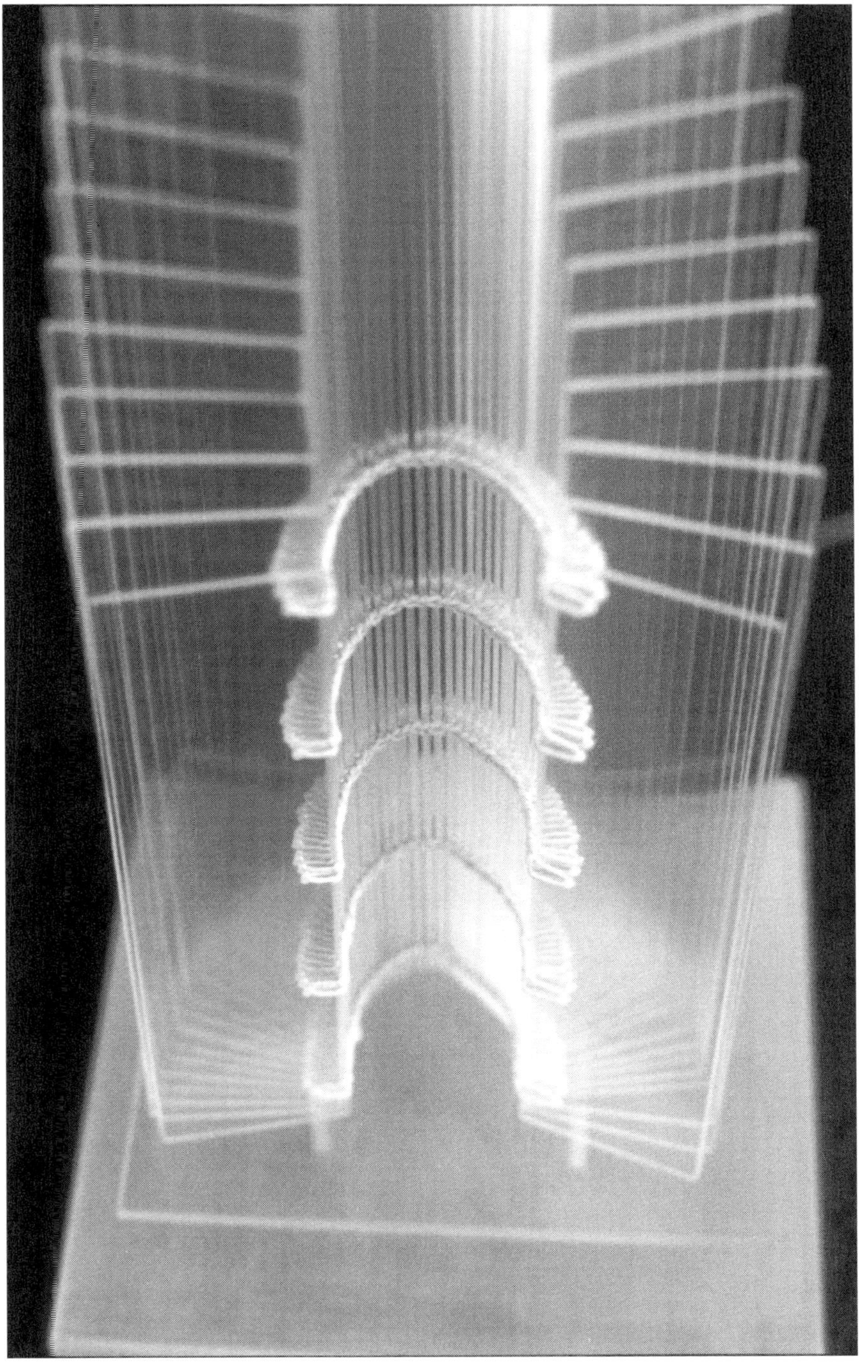

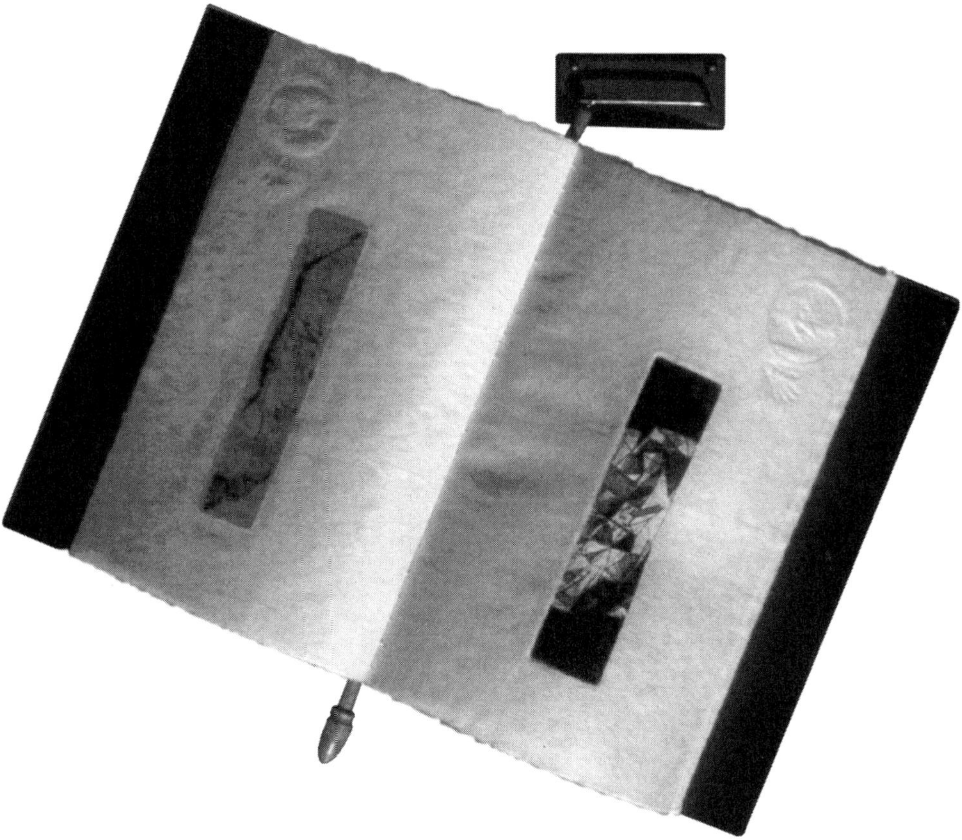

Wim de Vos, *Travel Tales,* 1987, one–of–a–kind. Book of seven pages sewn to wooden dowel, sewn to perspex covers. Wall bracket. Coloured etchings and engravings, embossing. Paper, Japanese tableau. Double binding. 170 x 227 mm. closed.

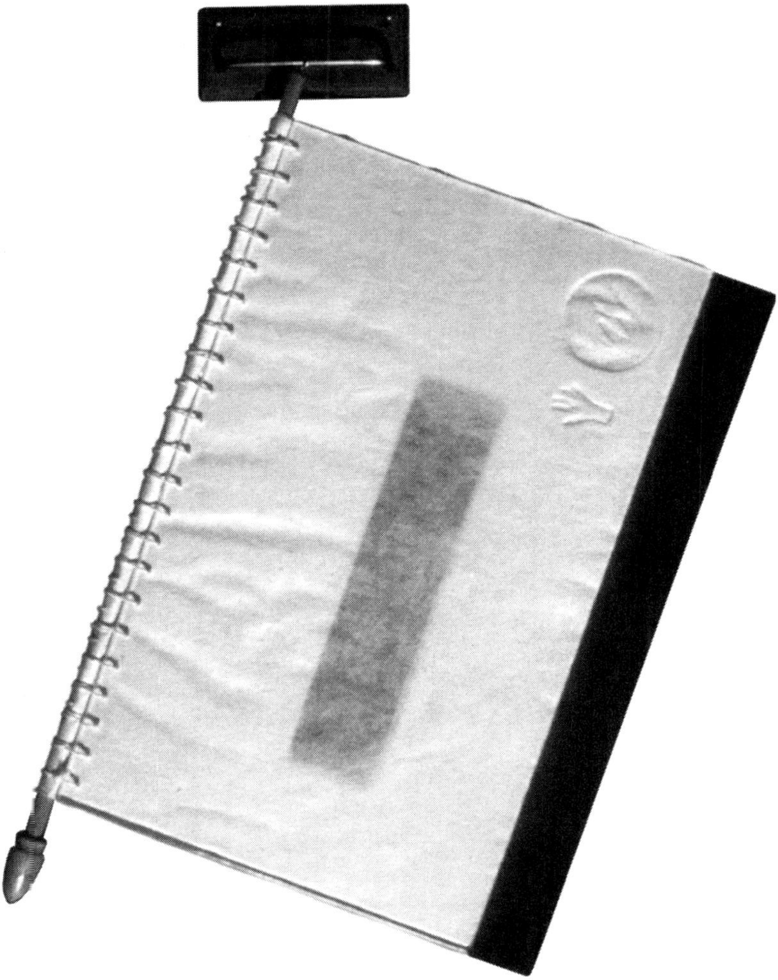

Wim de Vos, *Travel Tales,* 1987.

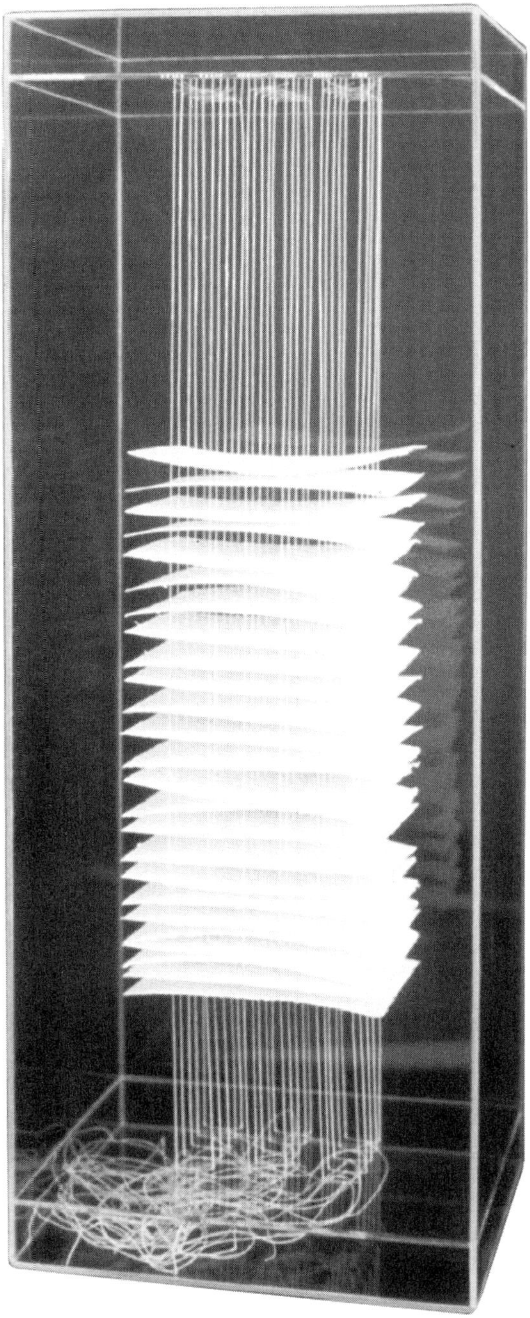

Adéle Outteridge, *Steps to Enlightenment I,* 1997, one–of–a–kind. Paper, linen thread. Box by Wim de Vos. 65 x 25 x 22 cm.

Adéle Outteridge, *Steps to Enlightenment I,* 1997. Detail.

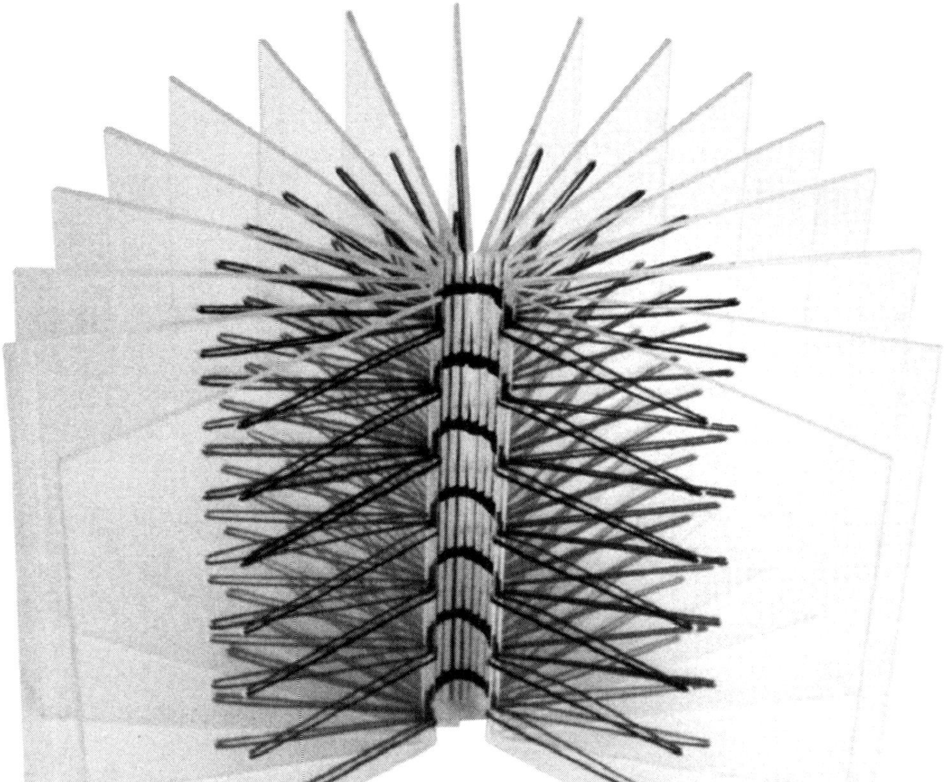

Adéle Outteridge, *Euclidis,* 1997, one–of–a–kind. Perspex, thread, single sheet binding. 14 x 8 x 4 cm. closed.

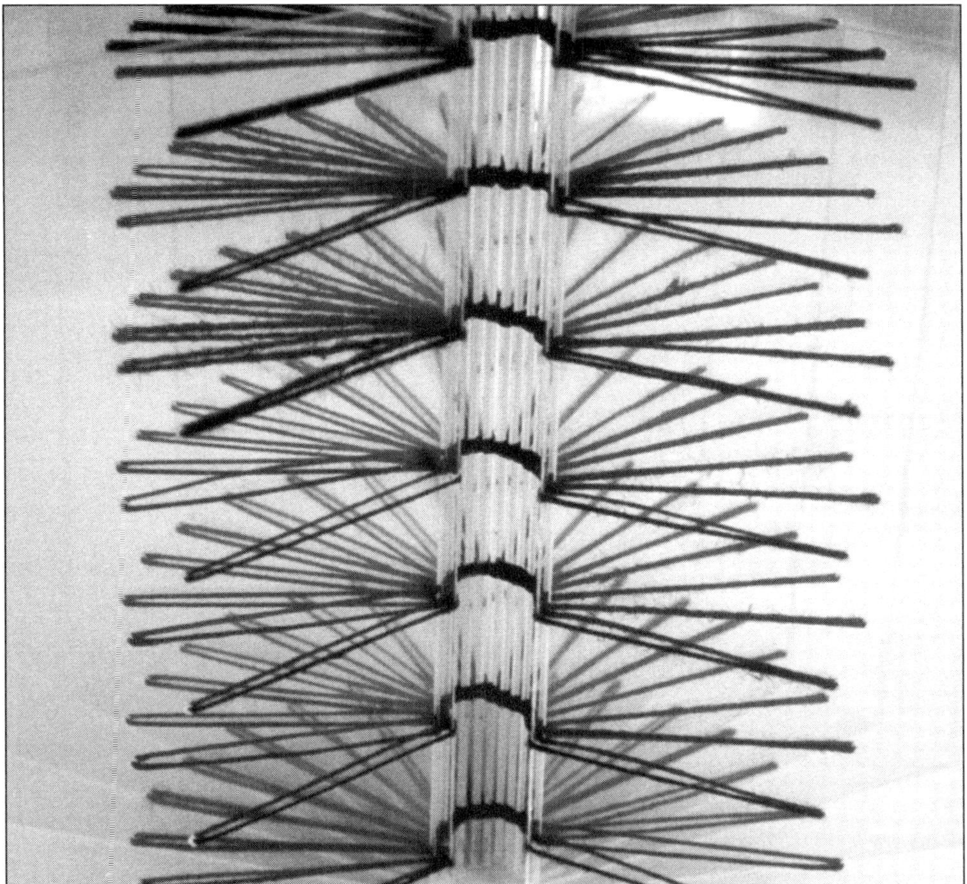

Adéle Outteridge, *Euclidis,* 1997. Detail. Rather than taking the thread in on the sheet only a centimeter to attach the sheet, Adéle uses the attachment as drawing.

Wim de Vos, *I'm Blooming on Your Warm Branch,* 2001, one–of–a–kind. Seven acrylic engraved panels, rod and paper. 114 x 140 x 196 mm.

Adéle Outteridge, *Island Postcards: The Forest at the Rabbit Fence,* 2001, one–of–a–kind. Arches Aquarelle 300gsm, thread, perspex cover. Single sheet binding. 13 x 28 x 2.5 cm.

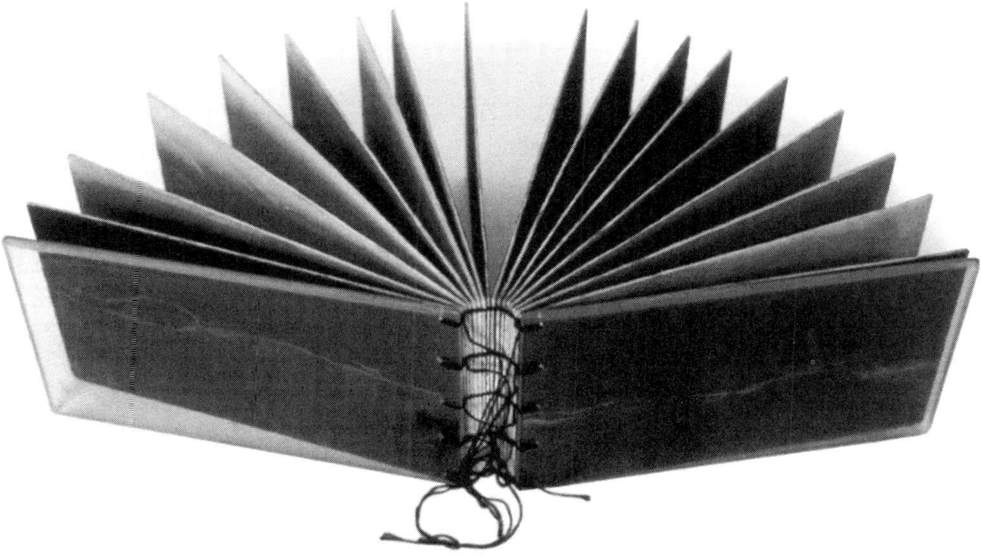

Wim de Vos, *Hot Line,* one–of–a–kind, 1995. Indian rag board, pastels, acrylic covers. Binding: Adéle Outteridge. 110 x 180 x 28 mm.

DANIEL ESSIG

Much of Dan's work is sewn boards with 2–needle Coptic sewings or a Greek binding with Coptic end bands. Almost all of the bindings have separate wooden side–covers with items set within the boards with a mica window. There are often books within books. The Caterpillar sometimes augments the sewing across the spine or a Caterpillar becomes a secondary headband. See page 287. The books dazzle the viewer, especially with his exquisite exposed spine sewings.

Chains are prevalent as thread linking the sections as well as metal holding the books closed. The chain idea may even suspend the book as illustrated below and on pages 286 and 287. Color is juggled better than about any binder I know and as fine as most painters. I have to apologize that I present the following in only black and white.

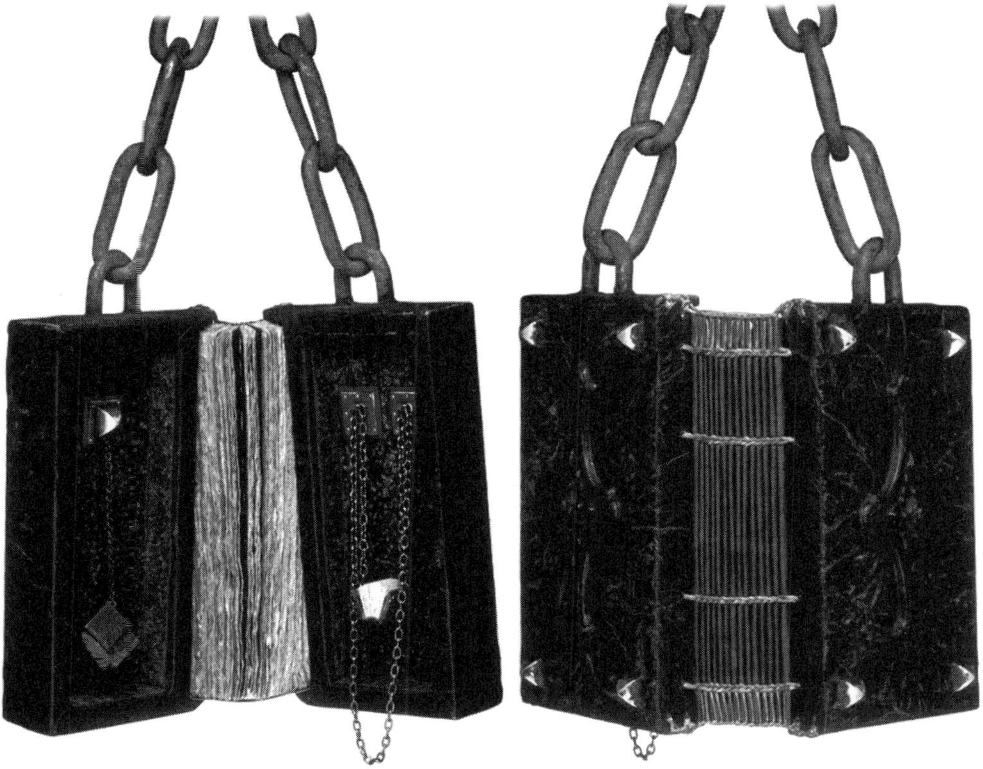

Daniel Essig, *Hanging Book,* 2000. Ethiopian and Accordion bindings. One–of–a–kind. Two views. The removable necklace has a book pendant which is an Ethiopian binding which is 20 x 15 x 7.5 mm.

Daniel Essig, *Book in a Book in a Book,* 1998. Ethiopian and Accordion bindings.

Daniel Essig, *Book in a Book in a Book,* 1998. One–of–a–kind. Ethiopian binding with Coptic end bands. The book is bound on both vertical sides. The front board spit in the middle, opening like French doors. 14.75 x 9.5 x 4.5 cm. Inside is an Accordion binding.

Daniel Essig, *Book Shelved on Book,* Ethiopian bindings. 1999. One–of–a–kind. The larger book is 15 x 10 x 5 cm. The mini book is 7.5 x 15 x 7.5 mm.

Daniel Essig, *Book Shelved on Book,* 1999. Detail of the mini book which is also an Ethiopian binding: 2–Needle Coptic, sewn board with Coptic end bands. 3/8 x 5/8 x 3/8".

Daniel Essig, *Book Shelved on Book,* opened view with mini book removed.

Daniel Essig, *Bridge Book,* Ethiopian binding. 1996–97. Closed. 50.25 x 35.25 x 15 cm.

Daniel Essig, *Bridge Book,* opened view.

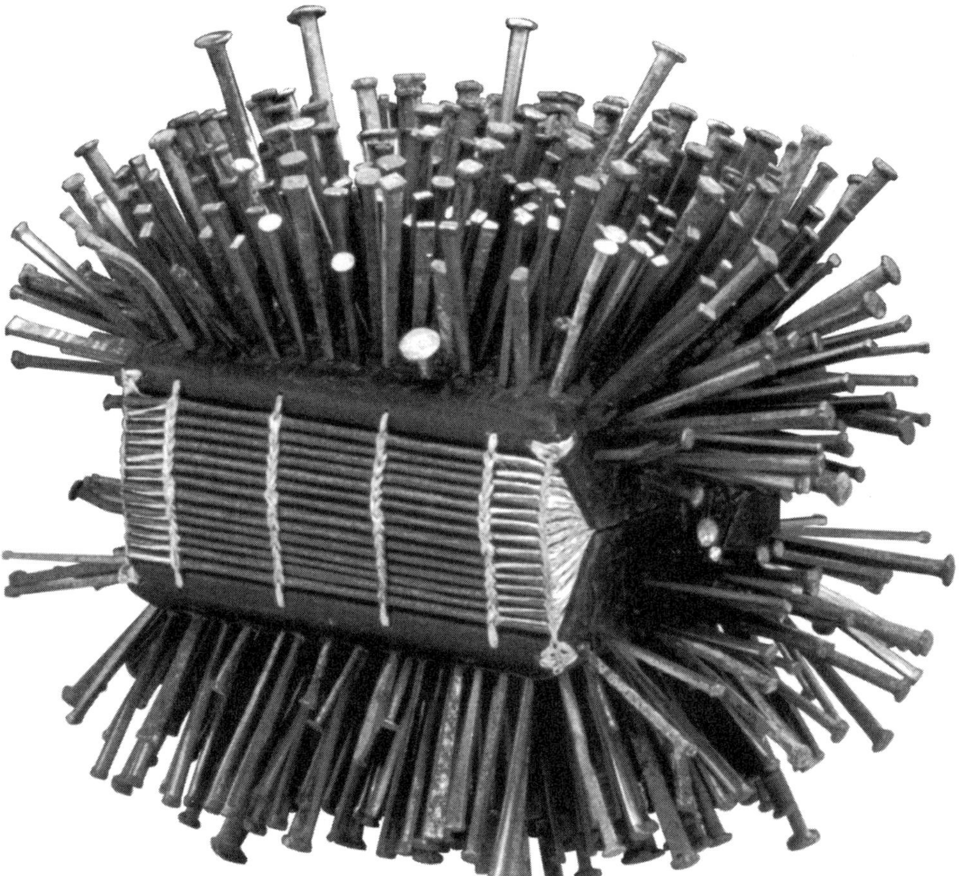

Daniel Essig, *Book of Nails,* 2000. Greek binding. Closed view. 30.5 x 19.6 x 22.2 cm.

Daniel Essig, *Book of Nails,* 2000. Two opened views.

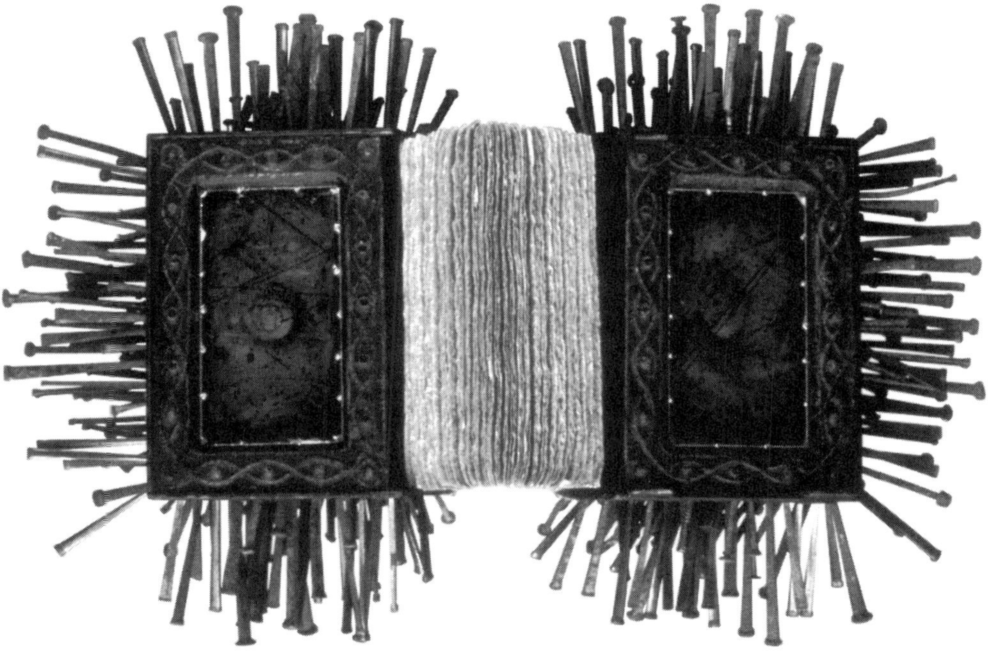

FACING PAGE TOP:
Daniel Essig, *Centipede Book,* 1998. Ethiopian and Caterpillar bindings. 12.7 x 10 x 4.8 cm.

FACING PAGE BOTTOM:
Daniel Essig, *Cicadian Rhythms,* 1999–00. Ethiopian binding. 10 x 7.5 x 4.8 cm.

ABOVE:
Daniel Essig, in collaboration with Shanna Leino. *Elk Bone Necklace,* 2000. Greek binding. The book is 3 x 1.5 x 1.2 cm.
RIGHT:
Detail of the book.

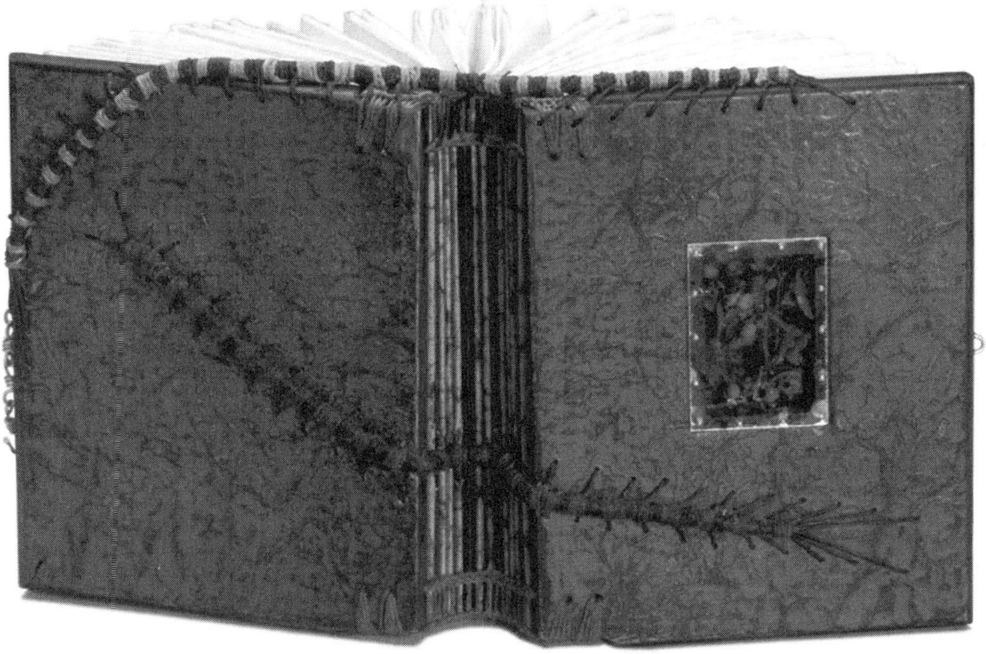

PART V

REFERENCE

NOTES

1 Page 24

SOURCES OF SUPPLIES: In my books I will no longer list suppliers of papers, tools and equipment. The lists go out of date at a rate of about 20% per year. Instead I will list organizations which provide such information. There are several source lists where you can look up suppliers. Access to these lists is generally through membership in a guild or organization. Some of these are the Guild of Book Workers, CBBAG and The Book Arts Guild. You might check their web sites and see if they offer it for non–members or better yet, join a guild. here are addresses of a few guilds:

The Association of Book Crafts, attn: John Sansom,
4 Alnack Place
Torbay, Auckland 1310 New Zealand

The Book Arts Guild, attn. Sandra Kroupa, Membership Secretary
515 North 49th
Seattle, WA 98103

The Canadian Bookbinders and Book Artists Guild
176 John Street, Suite 309
Toronto, ONT M5T 1X5 Canada
Phone: 416 581 1071
Fax: 905 851 6029
Website: http://www.cbbag.ca
Email: cbbag@web.net
They have a *Directory* of members and suppliers.

Canberra Craft Bookbinders Guild, attn: Linda Newbown
18 Turriff Street
Canberra, ACT. 2095 Australia
Email: newbown@pcug.org.au

Guild of Book Workers
521 Fifth Avenue
New York, NY 10175
They have a *Supply Directory* as well as yearly *Membership Directory.*

Papermakers of Victoria, Gail Stiffe, President
11 Keltie Street, Burwood, VIC 3125 Australia
http://home.vicnet.net.au/~papervic/
Email: Stiffe@Bluep.com

The Book Arts Web Site is a group where members ask questions and respond to related book topics. These is also a list of binding supply sources. Information about subscribing to the list can be found on their website:

http://palimpsest.stanford.edu/byform/mailing-lists/bookarts

2 Page 28

All marbled and paste papers photo–reproduced in the drawings and diagrams, as

opposed to the photographic reproductions, are from
Diane Maurer, P. O. Box 78, Water Street, Spring Mills, PA 16875
Telephone: 814 422 8651. Fax: 814 422 7858

3 Page 45
Lacing in boards is briefly described in *Bookbinding for Book Artists,* published by keith smith *BOOKS.* The First Edition, Second Printing, July 2000, ISBN 0–9637682–5–5.

4 Page 45
Gaylord Bros., P. O. Box 4901 Syracuse, NY 13221–4901. Telephone 1–800–448–6160. Fax: 1–800–272–3412. Gaylord Archival online at <http://www.gaylord.com/archival>.

5 Page 52
One of the mistakes of beginners in making artists books is not understanding pictures do not have priority, as in the single picture format or an exhibit. The book can only be orchestrated when the contents are subordinated to it. This is discussed in *Structure of the Visual Book.*

6 Page 55
The statement is not technically correct. The holes through which you sew are indeed the sewing stations, if you are sewing an unsupported sewing, such as the traditional Coptics, or, if you are sewing raised or recessed cords.

However, in supported sewings, the cords, thongs or tapes are the sewing station, not the pierced hole/s which allow access to them. This only causes a problem in the definition for sewing tapes: Each tape is the station, but each tape requires a hole on either side. The two holes per tape are not the sewing station, but merely the holes. The tape is the sewing station.

7 Page 71
"Jade [403 PVA] is one of only three brands of PVA which has been found to maintain a good *pH* level during natural aging tests, making it suitable for box–making and other book and paper uses." Cynthia Mowery, Bookmakers, Inc. 6701B Lafayette Avenue, Riverdale, MD 20737. Telephone: 301 927 7787. Fax: 301 927 7715.

8 Page 119
Gary Frost is unparalleled in this area. See pages 19 and 194 in *Books without Paste or Glue,* Volume I, *Non–Adhesive Binding* and pages 70, 71 of *Exposed Spine Sewings,* Volume III, *Non–Adhesive Binding.*

GLOSSARY

Each term is defined with its first usage in the text of this manual. In the *Index of Terms,* page numbers are listed for important uses of key terms. The definitions below are used in this manual, as well as in other books on binding by Keith Smith.

accordion pleat 1. Several parallel, alternating and closely placed folds. Pleats are usually not pages, but an additional hinging device between the backbone and the attached folios or sections. Very often the pleat is the backbone, with separate side–covers, rather than a flat back. Pleats also expand the depth of the backbone to accommodate additions to the book block. 2. Also known as the *concertina fold.*

across (also referred to as *all across)* 1. Perpendicular to the folds, cover to cover.† 2. Sewing which proceeds from section to section, generally in two or more separate sewings, using paired stations. Examples are *Blanket Stitch with Slit Strap, 2–Needle Coptic Sewing* and the *Celtic Weave.* Sewing across the spine is always more secure than sewing along the spine. If a thread breaks, only the sewing at those paired stations is affected. If the thread breaks sewing along the spine, the entire binding is compromised.

adhesive Generic for glue and paste. Glues used for binding remain pliable and are used on the backs over the sewing of most bindings. Glue on the backbone may be a heat glue, made from animals. It is archival, in that it may be easily removed, but not in the sense it attracts insects which eat it. Another pliable glue is a poly–vinyl–acetate. Plastic based, PVA does not attract animals, but is not archival, inasmuch as it is not removable and thwarts attempts at book restoration. Pastes generally are used to adhere leather to spines, paper to paper and paper to boards. Wheat or rice paste are commonly used. *See* wheat paste.

adhesive binding single leaf binding without sewing using a synthetic adhesive consolidation on the back.* Referred to as *perfect binding.*

against the grain Folding paper at right angles to the grain.

along (also referred to as *all along*) Parallel to the folds, head to tail.†

angle To move diagonally.†

Asa–No–Ha Toji Japanese name for the stab binding also known as the *Hemp–Leaf Binding.* There are four traditional Japanese stab bindings. The others are the *Yotsume Toji,* or *Japanese 4–Hole Binding;* the *Kikko Toji,* or *Tortoise–Shell;* and the

* *A VOCABULARY of TERMS for BOOK CONSERVATION PRACTICE,* by Gary Frost

† *GLOSSARY of TERMS, based on the work of Pamela Spitzmueller and Gary Frost,* a handout in a workshop by Betsy Palmer Eldridge.

Koki Toji, or *Noble.* The Noble Binding is also referred to as the *Kangxi Binding,* after its reputed originator. These stab sewings are described in *Books without Paste or Glue,* Volume I, *Non–Adhesive Binding.*

back or **backbone** 1. The binding edge of a text prior to sewing or adhesive consolidation.*

NOTE: The back differs from the spine, which is part of the cover which overlays this.

back saw Moulding saw or tenon saw used to cut the sewing stations when the book block is held in a finishing press.

backward (reverse) Counter to the direction of the sewing.†

bead 1. Top edge of the book (when viewing the book upright). 2. The little roll formed by the knot of an endband. *See* spine–bead and inside bead.

beeswax Cake of wax usually purchased in a small block from a binder's supply. It is used for waxing all unwaxed thread prior to sewing.

blind A type of book. *See* Venetian blind.

blind embossing Stamping type into leather, without gold or foil.

board or **book board** A layered stock specifically for side–covers.

bodkin A sewing tool which is a type of awl. Unlike an awl which has a shaft which graduates in thickness, a bodkin has a thin metal shaft which remains constant in diameter except for narrowing at the point. It is similar to a *bradawl,* which is a carpenter's tool. An awl is inferior for piercing sewing stations, as it is difficult to obtain proper size of the opening in the paper. Choose a bradawl or bodkin which will give a hole slightly less than the diameter of the needle which will be used in the sewing.

bone or **bone folder** A flat, polished tool, made of bone, plastic or Teflon™. Paper is folded by hand to a temporary fold. The bone is used to score the fold to a permanent position and to flatten the fold. This is done in a single stroke, as burnishing the paper will scar or make it shiny. A substitute is a dull stainless steel table knife, which will not mar the paper.

book block or **text block** Total of the collated sections (signatures), folios or sheets, constituting the body of a book.

book block pleat *See* concertina guard.

booklet 1. A one–section binding. 2. A pamphlet. 3. A magazine.

bostrophedon A Germanic term meaning *as the ox plows.* In a single word, it graphically describes moving across a field, back and forth in a continuing *S* fashion. It is as if a page of text were read, the first line from left to right, the second from right to left and continued in this alternating manner. This movement and thus his term, describes the Scott McCarney binding. He also calls this the *snake format.*

bradawl A straight shafted awl with chisel edge used to make holes for brads or screws. Like the bodkin, a bradawl is ideal for piercing sewing stations in paper in bookbinding. Either tool is superior to an awl for piercing sewing stations.

butterfly sewing An across the spine sewing which utilizes paired stations. Each needle spans, enters the next section, then crosses inside to exit the other station. The Butterfly is also known as the *Yamato Toji,* or *Japanese 4–Needle Sewing.* It is a 12th century binding. The Butterfly is described in *Exposed Spine Sewings,* Volume III of *Non–Adhesive Binding.* The Butterfly, or Japanese 4–Needle Sewing is not to be confused with the Japanese 4–Hole Stab Binding, which is described in *Books without Paste or Glue,* Volume I of *Non–Adhesive Binding.*

The Butterfly *See* butterfly sewing.

case The two side–covers connected by the spine–cloth or leather.

catch–word In early printed books, the last word on a page was positioned at the foot. The same word was repeated at the top of the next page. Perhaps this served as a bridge in reading from page to page, but its purpose was a guide in collating signatures.

chain stitch "Chain stitch" is an embroidery term; it is not a stitch in bookbinding. In binding, the chain is a result of a succession of link stitches. *Link* is a stitch; *chain* is the resulting pattern.

to change over To continue sewing in the different section.†

clamshell A box for storing a book with a lid, hinged to open like covers.

climb To move upward.†

codex (plural: codices) A book, bound along one edge. One of the four types of books, the others being the fan, blind and the fold book.

NOTE: Many binders do not agree with this definition.

compiled section A section or signature constructed by assembling two or more folios, rather than folding down a sheet.

compound binding A hybrid book structure of two of the same or differing types of books. There are 4 types of books: the fan, the blind, oriental fold book and the western codex. Creating a structure of two or more of these types of books is a compound binding. Examples: 1. Sewing sections onto an accordion pleat for a concertina binding. 2. Including a fold book as a unit, along with sewing sections into a single spine.

concertina 1. A type of binding, utilizing the concertina fold. 2. The concertina fold is also called an *accordion pleat.*

concertina guard A form of construction securing sections to folded stubs with a pamphlet sewing and, in turn, sewing the stubs together to form a text block.*

content Statement within the book of text and/or pictures. In a no–picture book, it is the cast shadows, cut shapes, holes, et cetera.

continuous support sewing Use of a single support, as opposed to sewing onto cords or tapes. The paperback sewings in *1– 2– & 3– Section Sewings,* Volume II of *Non–Adhesive Binding,* are examples. It is important to reinforce the spine on the cover. Folding or pasting a second ply of paper in this area strengthens the sewing.

to continue on To continue sewing in the same section.†

Coptic *Bookbinding and the Conservation of Books, A Dictionary of Descriptive Terminology,* by Matt T. Roberts and Don Etherington, Library of Congress,

Washington, 1982: "Coptic Binding: Binding produced by the Copts or Egyptian Christians. The Coptic style of sewing is not unlike that of present–day machine edition sewing in that it is also in the form of chain stitch linking appearing as so many braids across the spine of the book. In addition, the covers of Coptic bindings were frequently sewn or laced to the text block by a number of hinging loops. Some Coptic bindings had wooden boards (from about the 4th century to the Middle Ages), but the majority had boards built up by layers of waste papyrus. They also had lined spines with flanges, as well as headbands. They were covered in leather as early as the 4th century and were tooled in blind, or by blind blocking, although decoration with inked and painted ornaments, as well as cut–out openwork backed with pieces of painted or gilded parchment were also used. Decoration consisting of openwork with parchment backing was executed before the leather (which was already cut to size) was attached, as was blind tooling or stamping when the fragile papyrus boards were employed. The tooling was in all likelihood done with unheated tools on moistened leather. Coptic bindings make up the oldest surviving 'family' of leather bookbindings, and represent the ultimate source of all decorated leather bindings."

core A support. It might be a cord, or rolled material to form a cylindrical support, generally out of leather. The endband is formed on a core.

cover stock or **cover weight** Heavy paper used for covers as opposed to text weight used for book blocks. Commercial printing papers generally come in both cover weight and text weight.

covering Forwarding is followed by covering and finishing. If the outside of the boards are not full leather or cloth, the area of the board that is not covered with cloth or leather is covered with decorative paper. The paste–down is made on the inside of the boards.

crease A fold induced by pressure marking or die debossing, not cutting.* Some binders refer to this procedure as a *score.*

creep The successive protrusion from the outermost folio to the innermost within a section or signature.

crossbar The wooden dowel held above and parallel to the base of the sewing frame by threaded posts. The crossbar is often slotted to accept threaded hooks.

curl The distortion of a sheet due to differences in structure, coatings, or moisture from one side to the other.

deckle In papermaking, the width of the wet sheet as it comes off the wire of a paper machine.

deckled–edge The untrimmed feathery edges of paper formed where the pulp flows against the deckle.

dentille The border around a doublure. *See* doublure.

digital scan Half–tone photographic images created on a computer scanner. I do not use the term *photograph,* reserving that dear term for silver prints.

display Presentation of the object, generally through turning pages. Books with one–sided display, the fan, blind and fold book might be displayed fully extended on a table, or wall displayed. Books with unusual formatting may be presented in the round as sculpture, the pages not meant to be turned.

dos–á–dos A specific traditional format of two connected codices which have a back cover in common.

drop To move downward.†

doublure The inside of the board on a traditional binding may have a field of silk, leather or vellum inlaid. This island paste–down is called a *doublure.* If it has a border, it is referred to as a *dentille.*

duodecimo aka **12to** 1. A sheet folded down to yield a section of 12 leaves or 24 pages. 2. Four folios, each slipped inside the other, to form a unit of sewing. *See* folio, quarto, sexto, octavo, sextodecimo and Z–fold. In folding down a sheet to form a duodecimo, the first fold is against the grain, so that the final fold is with the grain.

endband Wrapping and beading decorative thread, usually of colored silk or cotton, at the head and tail of codices. Thread is wrapped around a core and periodically stitched into the book block. "Imitation" machine–made headbands are sold by the yard and pasted onto the backbone of commercial hard cover books.
NOTE: The term *headband* is often erroneously used, if the band described includes, or is specifically at the tail. Therefore, I use the term *endband,* rather than *headband,* as it includes the bands sewn at both the head and tail.

end paper In traditional binding, the sheet which is glued down on the inside of the cover board, extending across the gutter as the first page.

endsheets The first (and last) sheet or section of a book may be blank and perhaps a nice laid paper in a particular color different from the bulk of the book block. Endsheets function as a mat surrounding a drawing. It is blank space to clear the mind before the introduction of the content of the opus.

enter To pass from the spine side to the fold side.†

Ethiopian binding 2–Needle Coptic with sewn boards.

exit To pass from the fold side to the spine side.†

F&G's (Folded and Gathered) The F&G's are the assembled signatures ready for sewing.

false kettle The (true) kettle stitch is the proper sewing procedure for ending one section, changing direction of movement in adding the next. The (true) kettle drops links, slips under to lock and climbs. A false kettle would fail in one of these steps, usually failing to slip under in order to lock. True and false kettle stitches and link stitches in general are described in *Exposed Spine Sewings,* Volume III of *Non–Adhesive Binding* and in *Bookbinding for Book Artists.*

fan A book, bound at one point. One of the four types of books, the others being the blind, codex and the fold book. Fans and blinds are used by South Sea Island cultures.

finishing Finishing is decoration of the book after forwarding and covering.

first section In the sewing procedures, the term *first* does not necessarily mean the beginning of the book. On the bench, you may very well start sewing from the back, towards the front of the book. In that instance, the "first" section to be sewn is the final section of the book. *See* face up and face down, page 119, in *Bookbinding for Book Artists*.

flat back Sewing without rounding the spine.

flat back cover Paper cover with two folds which delineate the spine from the side–covers. These folds create the hinging action of the cover and are called *hinge–folds*.

flush cover 1. A cover whose front and back panels are the same dimensions as the pages. 2. In commercial binding, a cover that has been trimmed with the text block, so that cover and text block are the same size. *See* overhang cover.

fold *See* accordion, hinge–fold, fold–out, gate fold and throw–out.

fold book A book, whose binding is mechanical; the sheet is folded back and forth upon itself to create pages. One of the four types of books, the others being the fan, blind and the codex.

fold–out *See* throw–out.

folio aka **fo** A folio is a sheet folded in half to yield four pages and two leaves. The fold is with the grain. The resulting folio will have the grain parallel with the spine. Folios can be units in binding, sewing through the fold–as–hinge. A folio can be slipped inside another folio to construct a quarto, rather than folding down a sheet to form a quarto. *See* quarto, sexto, octavo, duodecimo and *Z*–fold.

foredge 1. The front edge of a book. (pronounced *forrej*). 2. The edge of the side–cover and book block opposite the spine.

format The size, style, type page, margins, page set–up, et cetera.

forward In the direction on the sewing.[†]

forwarding After the book is sewn, forwarding is gluing the back, plowing, rounding and backing, sewing the endbands and attaching the boards. Forwarding is followed by covering and finishing.

gate fold Two facing fold–outs in a codex. Each fold–out is hinged on the foredges of an opened folio. When the gate fold is opened, or thrown–out, there are four facing pages, the two at each extreme extend beyond the book block.

gathering Assembling the folded signatures into the proper order for binding. *See* F&G's.

grain The direction in which most fibers lie which corresponds with the direction the paper is made in commercial production machinery.

gutter The blank space or inner margin, from printing area to binding.

half hitch A type of knot for tying off, when there is only one loose end of thread: The needle slips under a stitch and is pulled until there is a small loop. The needle proceeds through the loop, before the thread is pulled tight. The half hitch is diagrammed on pages 64–66 in this manual.

head and **tail** The top and bottom of a book when stood upright. They are at right angles to the backbone or spine–edge and foredge.

headband and **tail band** Wrapping and beading decorative thread, usually of colored silk or cotton, at the head and tail of codices. Thread is wrapped around a core and periodically stitched into the book block. "Imitation" machine–made headbands are sold by the yard and pasted onto the backbone of commercial hard cover books.
NOTE: The term *headband* is often erroneously used, if the band described includes, or is specifically at the tail. Therefore, I use the term *endband,* rather than headband, as it includes the bands sewn at both the head and tail.

Hemp–Leaf Binding The stab binding also known as *Asa–No–Ha Toji.* There are four traditional Japanese stab bindings. The others are the Yotsume Toji, or Japanese 4–Hole Binding; the Kikko Toji, or Tortoise–Shell; and the Koki Toji, or Noble Binding, which is also referred to as the *Kangxi Binding,* after its reputed originator. Stab sewings are described in *Books without Paste or Glue,* Volume I of *Non–Adhesive Binding.*

hinge–fold The folds on either side of the spine, delineating the side–covers from the spine–cover. *See* flat back cover.

horizontal wrapper *See* wrapper.

implied compound binding A inventive folding of pages or itinerary through a book that suggests a hybrid book structure of two of the same or differing types of books.

imposition The laying out of pages on a sheet, so that they will be in numerical order after the sheet is folded down as a folio or section or signature.

inner Between paired sewing stations. The approach to a station which is towards the center of the spine, rather than to the outer, which is near the spine–hinge. Inner should not be confused with the term *inside.*

inside The position on the valley side of a section, as opposed to the mountain peak, which is called the *outside.*

to the inside Toward the head or tail.†

island paste–down *See* doublure.

inside bead In sewing endbands as change–over, the sewing procedure results in beads on both sides of the packing. The bead on the spine side is referred to as the *spine–bead.* The bead facing the foredge is called the *inside bead. See* two–sided in *Exposed Spine Sewings,* Volume III of *Non–Adhesive Binding.*
I suggest you look at *Headbands, How To Work Them,* by Jane Greenfield & Jenny Hille published by Oak Knoll Books. Email: oakknoll@oakknoll.com

jaconette A thin coated fabric used to reinforce a spine or joint in a book box.

Japanese 4–Needle Sewing *See* butterfly sewing.

Japanese 4–Hole Binding Japanese stab binding also known as *Yotsume Toji.* There are four traditional Japanese stab bindings. The others are the Asa–No–Ha Toji, or Hemp–Leaf Binding; the Kikko Toji, or Tortoise–Shell; and the Koki Toji, or Noble Binding, which is also referred to as the *Kangxi Binding,* after its reputed originator. Stab sewings are described in *Books without Paste or Glue,* Volume I, *Non–Adhesive Binding.* The Japanese 4–Hole Stab Binding is not to be confused with the sewing across the spine, called the *Japanese 4–Needle Sewing.*

jog To knock down and level to an edge, preferably at the head to keep text in registration.

Kangxi Binding Japanese name for the stab binding, named after its reputed originator. It is also known as the *Noble,* or *Koki Toji.* There are four traditional Japanese stab bindings. The others are the Yotsume Toji, or Japanese 4–Hole Binding; the Kikko Toji, or Tortoise–Shell; the Asa–No–Ha Toji, or Hemp–Leaf Binding. Stab sewings are described in *Books without Paste or Glue,* Volume I, *Non–Adhesive Binding.*

kerf or **kerf stations** Cuts made with a back saw across the section folds of an unsewn text.* *See* sewing stations.

kettle or **kettle stitch** A sewing procedure of ending one section, changing direction of movement in adding the next. The sewing drops backwards and links, slips under to lock and climbs. True and false kettle stitches and link stitches in general are described in *Exposed Spine Sewings,* Volume III of *Non–Adhesive Binding* and in *Bookbinding for Book Artists.*

key a 2–pronged metal unit, about the size of a key. A key for each cord rests under the slot in the base of a sewing frame temporarily tying the cord while the sewing proceeds.

Kikko Toji Japanese name for the stab binding known as the *Tortoise–Shell Binding.* There are four traditional Japanese stab bindings. The others are the Yotsume Toji, or Japanese 4–Hole Binding; the Asa–No–Ha Toji, or Hemp–Leaf Binding and the Koki Toji, or the Noble, or the Kangxi Binding, after its reputed originator. Stab sewings are described in *Books without Paste or Glue,* Volume I of *Non–Adhesive Binding.*

Koki Toji Japanese name for the stab binding known as the *Noble,* or the *Kangxi Binding,* after its reputed originator. There are four traditional Japanese stab bindings. The others are the Yotsume Toji, or Japanese 4–Hole Binding; the Kikko Toji, or Tortoise–Shell; the Asa–No–Ha Toji, or Hemp–Leaf Binding. Stab sewings are described in *Books without Paste or Glue,* Volume I of *Non–Adhesive Binding.*

lap To pass over a support or sewing thread.†

leaf 1. A sheet. 2. Two pages, back to back; a recto/verso.

link To pass under another thread.†

loop To circle around a support or sewing thread.†

moulding saw Backsaw or tenon saw used to cut the sewing stations when the book block is held in a finishing press.

Noble Binding Name of the Japanese stab binding known as *Koki Toji,* or the *Kangxi Binding,* after its reputed originator. There are four traditional Japanese stab bindings. The others are the Yotsume Toji, or Japanese 4–Hole Binding; the Kikko Toji, or Tortoise–Shell; and the Asa–No–Ha Toji, or Hemp–Leaf Binding. Stab sewings are described in *Books without Paste or Glue,* Volume I of *Non–Adhesive Binding.*

octavo aka **8vo** 1. A sheet folded in half three times, to yield a section of 16 pages with 8 leaves. 2. Three folios, each slipped inside the other, to form a unit of sewing. A sextodecimo, or 16mo, has 32 pages with 16 leaves. *See* folio, quarto, sexto, octavo, duodecimo, sextodecimo and *Z*–fold. In folding down a sheet to form an octavo, the first fold is with the grain; the second is against and the third is with the grain. The resulting section will have the grain parallel with the spine.

one–of–a–kind A book conceived and executed as a single copy. The word *unique,* meaning "special" should not be used to define a single copy item, as the term *unique* applies to production work as well.

NOTE: Some librarians define a book as an item which must have more than one copy by definition. Consequently, they do not recognize or purchase one–of–a–kinds. On one occasion I was dismayed at this reasoning of a librarian who could not consider purchasing a one–of–a–kind. The librarian said it was the wrong department and said take it to the museum on campus to the sculpture curator! — What would happen if this librarian should happen to run across an ancient book, of which only that single copy survived? Would she say it is no longer a "book", but now, sculpture?

1–on Sewing 1–on applies to sewing multi–section (multi–signature) sewings along the spine: In addition to using the kettle stations at the head and tail, every sewing station is used. The middle stations lap or loop the supports.

open ended Open ended stations refer to the use of the head and the tail as sewing stations. The support is not pierced. It is a passive station, that is, the thread wraps around the head or tail, marking the change–over.

opened folio The two facing pages at any point to which the codex is opened.

Oriental fold book *See* fold book.

outer Towards the outside of paired sewing stations, rather than centrally, between. Outer should not be confused with the term *outside.*

outside The position on the mountain peak of a section, as opposed to the valley, which is called the *inside.*

to the outside Away from the head or tail.†

overhand knot aka **overhand *K*** Half a square knot. For instructions how to tie, see page 59 in this manual. Knots are discussed also in *Books without Paste or Glue,* Volume I, *Non–Adhesive Binding*; and in *Bookbinding for Book Artists.*

overhang cover A cover larger in size than the pages it encloses. The amount of the side–cover that extends beyond the book block, bordering the head, foredge and tail is called the *square. See* flush cover.

pack To loop several times around.†

page 1. One side of an unfolded sheet. 2. That portion of a folio or section or signature bordered by folds and/or the edge of the sheet.

paired stations Sewing directly across the spine usually employs two sewing stations. Other paired stations along the spine are sewn independently. Each paired station uses one thread and two needles.

pamphlet 1. A one–section text. 2. A booklet. 3. Type of sewing for a booklet.

pamphlet sewing Type of sewing used to bind a booklet. See *Books without Paste or Glue,* Volume I, *Non–Adhesive Binding* and *1– 2– & 3–Section Sewings,* Volume II, *Non–Adhesive Binding.* Pamphlet sewing is also described in *Bookbinding for Book Artists.*

The term *pamphlet stitch* should be avoided, as it is a sewing, not a stitching. *Pamphlet stitch sewing* is correct, but awkward. The pamphlet sewing uses a *"B"* stitch, as opposed to a figure *8* stitch, described in *1– 2– & 3–Section Sewings,* Volume II, *Non–Adhesive Binding* and in *Bookbinding for Book Artists.*

paste *See* adhesive and wheat paste.

perfect bound 1. Adhesive binding without sewing or stitching. 2. Binding of a book which has no sewing and no folds on the backbone. The book therefore has no sections, signatures or folios, only a stack of sheets. The back is glued. Commercial paperbacks are generally (imperfectly) perfect bound. Thus, unfortunately there is a general low esteem for any book with paper covers. In the past, the main difference between trade books which were paperback and hard cover, was the latter was sewn. Now, many publishers are reducing the quality of their hard covers and are using perfect binding rather than sewing them.

pleat An Oriental fold used to attach sections, rather than as a complete book in itself. Attachment is usually with a pamphlet sewing. Pleat is also known as a *concertina, concertina guard,* or *accordion fold. See* accordion pleat.

ply In this text, the term is used as one piece of paper, rather than the process of making paper in layers. Two–ply is only used in this text to mean a sheet folded back upon itself for reinforcement, or two surfaces glued together. The term is never used to mean *duplex,* a type of commercially made paper with a different color on each side of the sheet.

production books Books made in an edition, whether by hand or published.

pull factor The characteristic of leather, some papers and fabrics to stretch when wet and to shrink or pull when they dry. In pasting these items to boards, it is not using a press, but the counter–balancing of the pull factor which prevents board warpage. See page 78 in this manual. For more information, *see* warpage, page 61, *Bookbinding for Book Artists.*

punch Metal cylindrical tool with sharpened hollow shaped end for cutting and solid head for striking with a hammer to cut through paper. Shapes are usually various diameters of circles and, rarely, squares, diamonds or oblongs.

quarto aka **4to** 1. A sheet folded in half twice, to yield a section of four leaves or eight pages. 2. Two folios, one slipped inside the other, to form a unit of sewing. *See* folio, sexto, octavo, duodecimo, sextodecimo and *Z*–fold.

In folding down a sheet to form a quarto, the first fold is against the grain; the second is with the grain. The resulting section will have the grain parallel with the spine.

ream Five hundred sheets of paper.

recto/verso Two pages, back to back; a leaf. Recto is a right hand page. Verso is the back of that leaf, not the page facing the recto in the opened folio.

NOTE: Recto does not mean *front;* verso does not mean *back.* A recto or a verso is a front side when it is viewed. Each becomes a back when the page is turned and it is not in view. Recto/verso is convenient terminology for folding and collating signatures.

saddle wire or **saddle stitch** In commercial binding, to fasten a booklet by wiring it through the fold or the side of the single section. The machine is adjusted to the thickness of the opened section and uses a spool of wire. It is looped through the section, cut and crimped, similar to stapling.

score 1. To indent with a bone folder, but not cutting. 2. A light surface cut made to facilitate folding or flexing in card or board. *See* crease.

section 1. A sheet folded down to yield eight or more pages, such as a quarto, sexto or duodecimo. 2. Two or more loose folios compiled to form a quarto, sexto or duodecimo, et cetera. A section can be blank paper, or printed. If printed, then it is specifically a *signature.*

NOTE: To avoid confusion of terms in this book, section is never used to mean a portion, or a chapter of the book.

NOTE 2: If the sheet has been printed, then folded down, it is referred to in printers' terminology as a *signature.* Any signature can be called a *section,* but only a section which has been printed is technically a signature. *See* signature.

self cover A cover of the same paper as the text block.

sew a set To sew one more than one section on at a time.†

sewing 1–on *See* 1–on.

sewing path The journey of the needle and thread, in and out of the sewing stations, in constructing a sewing.

sewing stations 1. The mark, or the pierce along the spine–fold of the cover and the backbone of the section, or folio showing the positions of the sewing. The supports are the stations, rather than the holes. Each tape requires a hole on either side. The two holes per tape are not the sewing station, but merely the holes. The tape is the sewing station. 2. Path of the needle through paper to create the sewing on the spine. If made with a saw, they are called *kerf stations. See* sewn vs stitched.

sewing 2–on *See* 2–on.

sewn vs **stitched** Sewing refers to the thread path along the valley and mountain peak, as opposed to set in from the fold. That is stabbing. Stabbing is stitching, not sewing. Path of the needle limited to the gutter is not "stitching", but sewing. Sewing is done with stitches. Therefore, "stitches" is appropriate when referring to sewing in the fold, but stitching equals stabbing.

sexto aka **6to** A sheet folded down to create a section of 6 leaves, or 12 pages. The sheet is first folded against the grain with a *Z*–fold, dividing the sheet into thirds. That is then folded in half with the grain. *See* folio, quarto, octavo, duodecimo, sextodecimo and Z–fold.

sextodecimo aka **16mo** A sheet folded down to create a section of 32 pages with 16 leaves. *See* folio, quarto, sexto, octavo, duodecimo and Z–fold.

sheet 1. An unfolded piece of paper. 2. A leaf. 3. The full size of the paper before being folded down into a folio or section. 4. In single sheet bindings, a sheet is two pages back to back; a recto/verso. A sheet is one piece of paper, consisting of two pages. It is not a section, since it has no fold as a hinge. Sheets can be folded down as folios or sections. Without being folded down, a sheet can still be a unit of sewing.

side–cover Front or back cover, as opposed to the spine.

signature A specific type of section, differing from the general term *section* in that a signature is a sheet that first has been printed, then folded down. A signature is a section, but a section is not necessarily a signature. Signature is a printer's term; section is a binder's term.

simple/compound Terms used only to differentiate basic bindings from hybrids constructed by combining two or more basic types of books.

slip (v.) To pass under itself.†

slips (n.) The ends of tapes, cords, or supporting straps attached to the covers.

slit Slit is a severing with a knife. It has length, but no width. *See* slot.

slot A slot is an opening, constructed by two slits, parallel and no more than about 1/8" apart. Slots, rather than slits, are needed to accommodate the thickness of the inserted photographs, or weaving a tape support.

Smythe sewn Commercial method of machine–stitching a book. *See* sewn vs stitched.

spacers A stub added to the mountain peak to be sewn with the folio. It expands the spine the same amount as the (photo) insert for that page. After the inserts are added, the foredge of the album will not bulge wider than the spine.

span To climb and change over to another section.†

spine or **spine–cover** 1. The depth of a bound book, connecting the two side–covers. The spine–covers the back, or backbone. 2. That part of the book that is visible when it is on the shelf. It is sometimes referred to as the *backstrip.*

spine–bead In sewing endbands as change–over, the sewing procedure results in beads on both sides of the packing. The bead on the spine side is referred to as the *spine–bead.* The bead facing the foredge is called the *inside bead. See* two–sided beading in *Exposed Spine Sewings,* Volume III of *Non–Adhesive Binding.*

spine tab A strip woven onto the spine.

square or **square of the book** 1. The projection of the side–cover beyond the book block. 2. That part of the cover that extends beyond the book block and borders the head, foredge and tail. The total surface of the cover is referred to as an *overhang cover.*

square knot or **reef knot** In this manual see page 57. For other descriptions, *see* knots in *Bookbinding for Book Artists;* or in *Books without Paste or Glue,* Volume I, *Non–Adhesive Binding,* for instructions how to tie.

station or **sewing station** 1. A place where the sewing stops to attach a section to other sections or to a common support or to both.† 2. Passive sewing stations is the use of the head and tail as change–over. This is referred to as *open ended.* In diagramming sewings with endbands as change–cover, I assign the support, usually cords, at the head and the tail a sewing station number. They are not pierced sewing stations, but passive, that is, open ended. This makes for easy reference in the drawn illustrations. *See* paired stations.

stitching *See* sewn vs stitched.

stub Cutting out a page/s from a Tight Back, close to the spine–edge, after it is bound to make space for an insert which will not bulge the spine. For a Flat Back, spacers are used.

suminagashi "The original and easiest method of marbling, inks flowing freely on water, producing meandering lines of color." –Diane Vogel Maurer with Paul Maurer, *Marbling, A Complete Guide to Creating Beautiful Patterned Papers and Fabrics.*[2]

super Super is a kind of stiffened gauze, sometimes referred to as *tarlatan, crash,* or *mull.*

supported sewings Sections sewn together around common tapes or cords, which go across the back, perpendicular to it. The supports are generally attached to side–covers.

swell Thickness added to the backbone by the accumulation of sewing threads or any guards. Swell is briefly described in this manual on page 40. For elaboration, *see* choosing the thread in *Bookbinding for Book Artists.* Also, *see* swelling the backbone in *Books without Paste or Glue,* Volume I, *Non–Adhesive Binding* and *Expanding the Spine–Pleat,* also in *Books without Paste or Glue.*

tail 1. The bottom edge of a book when standing upright. 2. The edge opposite the head and perpendicular to the spine and foredge.

tail band *See* headband and endband.

NOTE: The term *headband* is often erroneously used, if the band described includes, or is specifically at the tail. Therefore, I use the term *endband,* rather than headband, as it includes the bands sewn at both the head and tail.

tapes Woven fabric supports, usually linen, onto which the sewing occurs. They are usually 1/4" wide and always are non–adhesive.

tenon saw Moulding saw or backsaw used to cut the sewing stations when the book block is held in a finishing press.

tension Regulation of tautness. Uniform shape and tautness is desired. Betsy Palmer Eldridge says that the tension varies with each sewer. It varies even if one person stops for a break. It is best to start and sew the entire book at once. The operative word is snug. Tension should not be loose, but neither should it be tight. I find that men tend to sew too tightly. Link stitches lose their teardrop shape when pulled tightly.

text block *See* book block.

tie–off Joining two threads with a knot at the beginning or end of a sewing.

tie–downs The threads which extend from the endband, in on the spine to the next station to anchor the endband. The tie–off may enter a station on the section, or link under a support at that station.

throw–out A fold–out. The action of unfolding of a fold–out or throw–out is referred to as *thrown–out.* A throw–out might be a single fold, gate fold, or any other page which is larger than the book block and folded down for storage. Traditionally refers to a fold–out at the end of a book containing a map. The map is thrown–out, so that it remains visible while any other page in the book can be read and turned.

A throw–out has the fold at the foredge. A throw–down has the fold at the tail. A throw–up has the fold at the head.

Tortoise–Shell Binding The Japanese stab binding, also known as *Kikko Toji.* There are four traditional Japanese stab bindings. The others are the Yotsume Toji, or Japanese 4–Hole Binding; the Asa–No–Ha Toji, or Hemp–Leaf Binding and the Koki Toji, or the Noble Binding. The Noble Binding is also referred to as the *Kangxi Binding,* after its reputed originator. Stab sewings are described in *Books without Paste or Glue,* Volume I, *Non–Adhesive Binding.*

2–on Sewing 2–on applies to sewing multi–section sewings along the spine: with the exception of the first two and final two, sections the remaining sections do not use all the sewing stations, except for the kettle stations at the head and tail. The sewing alternates back and forth between two sections being sewn on at once. Therefore, not all the middle stations are used.

types of books There are four basic types of books, determined by how they are bound:

1. at one point is called a fan.
2. at two points is the Venetian blind. The fan and blind are used by South Sea Island cultures.
3. across one edge, is the western codex.
4. alternate folds back and forth upon itself is the Oriental fold book. The other three types of books are sewn. The fold book's binding is mechanical.

unsupported sewings Sections sewn directly together, without common tapes or cords.

Venetian blind or **blind** A book, bound at two points. One of the four types of books, the others being the fan, codex and the fold book.

verso *See* recto/verso.

vertical wrapper *See* wrapper.

wheat paste An adhesive, like rice paste, used to adhere leather to the spine and decorative papers to the board. For formulas of making wheat paste, see page 73 in this manual. Wheat paste is also discussed in *Bookbinding for Book Artists.*

with the grain Folding paper parallel to the grain of the paper.

wrapped stations Head and tail of the sections used as sewing stations. Passive, as opposed to a pierced or slit stations. Open ended.

wrapper Paper covering board covers without the use of adhesives. *See* flat back with boards and separately wrapped boards in *Books without Paste or Glue,* Volume I, *Non–Adhesive Binding.*

Yamato Toji Japanese name for the 4–needle sewing, across the spine. It is also referred to as the *Japanese 4–Needle Sewing,* as well as the *Butterfly Sewing.* It is sewn across the spine, utilizing paired stations. Each needle spans, enters the next section, then crosses inside to exit the other station. Yamato Toji is described in *Exposed Spine Sewings,* Volume III, *Non–Adhesive Binding.*

Yamato Toji, or Japanese 4–Needle Sewing, is not to be confused with the the Japanese 4–Hole Stab Binding, which is described in *Books without Paste or Glue,* Volume I of *Non–Adhesive Binding.*

Yotsume Toji Japanese name for the stab binding also known as the *Japanese 4–Hole Stab Binding.* There are four traditional Japanese stab bindings. The others are the Asa–No–Ha Toji, or Hemp–Leaf Binding; the Kikko Toji, or Tortoise–Shell; and the Koki Toji, or Noble Binding, which is also referred to as the *Kangxi Binding,* after its reputed originator.

Stab sewings are described in *Books without Paste or Glue,* Volume I, *Non–Adhesive Binding.*

***Z*–Fold** Procedure to create a 12 and a 24 page section. The sheet is first folded in thirds, against the grain (the *Z*–fold). Folding the *Z*–fold in half once, with the grain, gives a sexto. Folding the sexto in half with the grain gives 12 leaves, or 24 pages. It is called a *duodecimo. See* folio, quarto,sexto, octavo, duodecimo and sextodecimo.

INDEX *of* TERMS

CENTIMETERS *to* INCHES

1cm =	0.39"	35	13.78	69	27.17
2	0.79	36	14.17	70	27.56
3	1.18	37	14.57	71	27.95
4	1.57	38	14.96	72	28.35
5	1.97	39	15.35	73	28.74
6	2.36	40	15.75	74	29.13
7	2.76	41	16.14	75	29.53
8	3.15	42	16.54	76	29.92
9	3.54	43	16.93	77	30.31
10	3.94	44	17.32	78	30.71
11	4.33	45	17.72	79	31.10
12	4.72	46	18.11	80	31.50
13	5.12	47	18.50	81	31.89
14	5.51	48	18.90	82	32.28
15	5.91	49	19.29	83	32.68
16	6.30	50	19.69	84	33.07
17	6.69	51	20.08	85	33.46
18	7.09	52	20.47	86	33.86
19	7.48	53	20.87	87	34.25
20	7.87	54	21.26	88	34.65
21	8.27	55	21.65	89	35.04
22	8.66	56	22.05	90	35.43
23	9.06	57	22.44	91	35.83
24	9.45	58	22.83	92	36.22
25	9.84	59	23.23	93	36.61
26	10.24	60	23.62	94	37.01
27	10.63	61	24.02	95	37.40
28	11.02	62	24.41	96	37.80
29	11.42	63	24.80	97	38.19
30	11.81	64	25.20	98	38.58
31	12.20	65	25.59	99	38.98
32	12.60	66	25.98	100	39.37
33	12.99	67	26.38		
34	13.39	68	26.77		

INDEX *of* PHOTOGRAPHIC ILLUSTRATIONS

Digital scans and photographs are of prototypes by Keith Smith, except those photo reproductions which are credited at the end of each entry. For credits of the photographer, see page 331.

INDEX *of* DRAWN ILLUSTRATIONS

All drawings are by Keith Smith done in Macromedia FreeHand™ V5.5.

INDEX *of* NAMES

BOOKS *on* BOOKS

Concept

Structure of the Visual Book, keith smith *BOOKS,* Third Edition 1994, discusses concepts of ordering a book of pictures by means of a group, series, or sequence. Pacing is stressed by composing the pages as well as the individual pictures. Utilizing the space between pictures is part of the awareness of time in books. 240 pages with 198 photographic illustrations by 53 book artists.

paperback or in sheets: $25
ISBN 0–9637682–1–2

Concept

Text in the Book Format, keith smith *BOOKS,* Second Edition, 1995, is a concern for conceiving text as a book experience. This differs from writing a running manuscript or the single sheet format. A book experience cannot be fully revealed in a recitation but demands holding the physical object and turning pages conceived as part of the content. This approach does not treat the book format as a vessel, but allows writing to emanate from the inherent properties of the book—the opposite of sticking words into the object. 128 pages.

paperback or in sheets: $17.50
ISBN 0–9637682–3–9

All the books are printed on archival paper. Available either as Smythe sewn paperback, or, *in sheets,* folded and gathered sections, if you wish to hand bind your own copy.
Individuals or stores can order directly from keith smith *BOOKS.*
Besides store discounts, there are group discounts available for individuals ordering 6 or more assorted titles. Email for information, or check the web site.

How To Bind

Non–Adhesive Binding, Volume I: *Books without Paste or Glue,* keith smith *BOOKS,* The Revised & Expanded Edition, 1999. Introduction covers binding, paper, sewing, knots and tools. This is followed by detailed written instructions for 32 simple to complex sewings. The procedures are also presented as 320 drawings, diagrammed step by step. 116 photographic reproductions of bindings by 37 contemporary binders and artists. 352 pages.

paperback or in sheets: $30

ISBN 0–9637682–6–3

How To Bind

Non–Adhesive Binding, Volume II: *1– 2– & 3–Section Sewings,* keith smith *BOOKS,* First Edition, 1995. Written and drawn illustrations for 122 sewings which yield four, to perhaps a hundred pages imposed as one, two or three sections. Almost all of these sewings on continuous limp paper supports were devised by Smith, as the book was written. Photos of bindings by 28 contemporary binders and artists. 320 pages.

paperback or in sheets: $30

ISBN 0–9637682–2–0

To order, or for a free brochure on all titles, contact:
keith smith *BOOKS,* 1115 East Main Street, Suite 219, Box 8
Rochester, New York 14609–6152 USA
Tel/Fax: 585 482 2496 or Email: keith@keithsmithbooks.com
Web Site: www.keithsmithbooks.com

How To Bind

Non–Adhesive Binding, Volume III:

Exposed Spine Sewings, keith smith *BOOKS,* First Edition, 1995. Variations on raised support sewings with packed cords or endbands as change–over rather than using kettle stitches. Descriptions of sewings across the spine include 2–Needle Coptic, Greek Binding, Celtic Weave and Caterpillar. Most of the sewings were devised by Smith as the book was written. Nine various Coptic sewings are described. Photographic illustrations by contemporary binders are shown. 320 pages.

paperback or in sheets: $30

ISBN 0–9637682–4–7

How to Bind

Bookbinding for Book Artists, First Edition, 1998, keith smith *BOOKS.*

Bookbinding for Book Artists presents a simple approach to binding in cloth or leather. It eliminates the skill required to pare leather or to sew endbands. Household tools are substituted for traditional binding equipment.

Three bindings are described:

• Pamphlet Binding with Boards gives a substantial presentation of a book with only 4 to 32 pages. This hard cover book is presented as quarter cloth, half or full cloth. It is described both with the endsheets as paste–down, as well as exposed cloth hinges on the inside of the boards. This binding gives a substantial presentation for small projects.

• Flat Back is ideal for medium size projects. Shown as sewn onto tapes, it gives a book of 24 to 100 pages. It is the most commonly used binding for hard cover artists books.

• Tight Back and the Hollow Back variation are presented as leather bound books, rounded and backed. The arch structurally allows a book to be bound with hundreds of pages. Yet, this elegant binding can have as few as 32 pages.

Bookbinding for Book Artists has over 400 detailed drawn illustrations to augment the text. They are the most elaborate illustrations in Smith's books–on–books to date.

The book contains 60 photo reproductions of books by 19 contemporary binders and book artists. 432 pages.

paperback or in sheets: $35

ISBN 0–9637682–5–5

Autobiography

200 Books, An Annotated Bibliography, First Edition, July 2000, keith smith *BOOKS.*

200 Books is a memoir as told through all the books made by the author.

Text and pictures describe the 199 previous books by Smith with over 550 photo reproductions. The text gives background of the author and describes why each book was made with references to other artists. Sometimes there are detailed descriptions of how the imagery was technically achieved. 336 pages.

hard cover or in sheets: $35

ISBN: 0–9637682–7–1

www.keithsmithbooks.com

ACKNOWLEDGMENTS

Once again I thank my partner, Scott, for his patience and understanding.

Many thanks to Gail Ferris for proofreading and comments.

My thanks to all who permitted me to reproduce illustrations of their books and bindings, especially Adéle Outteridge who devised single sheet binding before I knew of her or her bindings. I devised my sewings independent of hers, but afterward.

PHOTO CREDITS

All books were photographed by the author, except for the following:
Adéle Outteridge, pages 16, 19, 20, 267–269, 272–275 and 277; Barbara W. Bansley, page 89; Daniel Essig, pages 278–281 and the top of page 287; John Farrow, page 81; Dennis Y. Ichiyama, pages 249–259; Walker Montgomery, pages 277, 282–286 and the bottom of page 287; Wim de Vos, pages 270, 271, 276 and 277; Debra Weier, pages 261–265.

COLOPHON

Book Number 202
was written from June 2000 through March 2001, starting on a Mac G3, and continued on a Mac Double Processor G4. Text was written in Quark XPress, formatted as it was written. Bindings were devised, photographed with a Nikon Coolpix 700™ digital camera and placed onto the page after the backgrounds were removed in Photoshop.

Smith's Sewing Single Sheets
was periodically proofed on an Hewlett Packard LaserJet 4MV. The book was sent to the printer on CD, postscript, for direct platemaking at 1270 dots per inch for the type, 200 dpi for the EPS files and 150 line screen for the drawings made in FreeHand™.

Typeface is Adobe Garamond.

Photographs of the books are by the author except for photo credits listed on page 331. Drawn and photo–digital illustrations are by the author.

Cover design is by Scott McCarney.

This first printing of the First Edition is offset in 2000 copies on Finch Vellum 80 lb. text and cover with film lamination. The book is Smythe sewn, paperback. An additional 200 copies are available unbound, folded and gathered, for anyone who might wish to hand bind their own copy of this book.

Keith A. Smith
April 2001

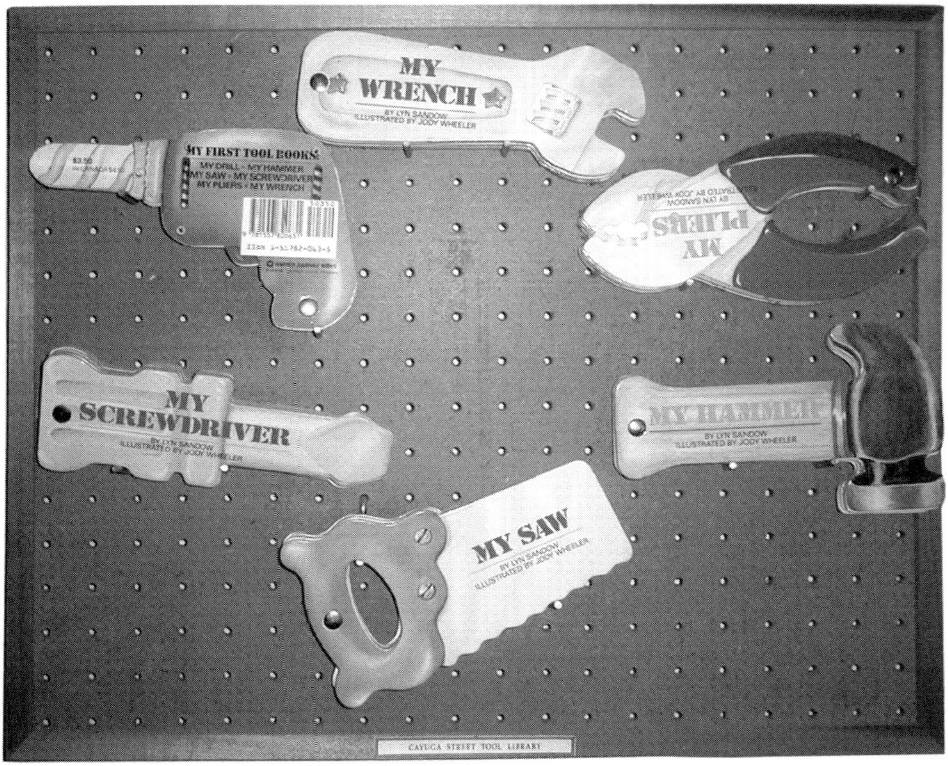

Keith Smith, *The Cayuga Street Tool Library,* one–of–a–kind, 1989.

Our home has a downstairs library which houses published books. One of the three libraries on the second floor contains one–of–a–kind books. A second is this tool "library".

Children's books were purchased and hung on a peg board which was framed. The books are a series by Lyn Sandow, Illustrated by Jody Wheeler. They were published by Warner Juvenile Books, 1988. My only contribution is the presentation and the title.